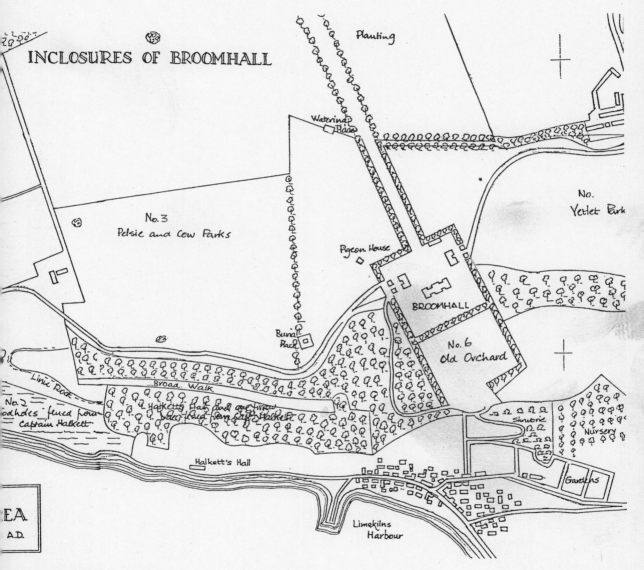

INCLOSURES OF BROOMHALL

Planting

Watering Place

No. 3
Pelsie and Cow Parks

Pigeon House

Burial Place

No. Yetlet Park

BROOMHALL

No. 6
Old Orchard

Lime Road

Broad Walk

No. 2
...odhdes feued from
Captain Halkett

Halketts Hall feued over from... ...ver Capt Halkett

Shrubrie

Nursery

Halkett's Hall

Gardens

Limekilns
Harbour

EA

A.D.

...mas, the Seventh Earl succeeded.

THE ELGINS, *1766-1917*

THE ELGINS, 1766-1917

A tale of aristocrats, proconsuls and their wives

Sydney Checkland

ABERDEEN UNIVERSITY PRESS

First published 1988
Aberdeen University Press
A member of the Pergamon Group

British Library Cataloguing in Publication Data

Checkland, S. G. (Sydney George), *1916–1986*
   The Elgins, 1766–1917: a tale of
   aristocrats, proconsuls and their wives.
   1. Scotland. (Earls of) Elgin, 1766–1917
   I. Title
   929.7′2

ISBN 0 08 036395 4

Jacket Illustrations:
Front: Broomhall, seat of the Earls of Elgin & Kincardine.
Back: Parthenon. Water colour by Lady Ruthven, after Lusieri. National Gallery of Scotland.

PRINTED IN GREAT BRITAIN
THE UNIVERSITY PRESS
ABERDEEN

Contents

List of Illustrations   vii
Preface, Olive Checkland   xi

1. Thomas the Seventh Earl and his Ambiguous Inheritance   1
2. The Young Milord Abroad   11
3. The Precocious Diplomat and the Ardent Estate
    Developer   20
4. Marriage and the Embassy to Constantinople   27
5. The Porte, the Acropolis and Victory in Egypt   37
6. Taking the Marbles   47
7. Prisoner of Bonaparte and Scandalous Divorce   58
8. Evangelical Remarriage and the Struggle for Solvency   72
9. Touting the Marbles: the Curse of Minerva   81
10. The Double Family: the Succession   95
11. James and the Jamaican Apprenticeship   108
12. Encounter with Canada: Violence and Pacification   118
13. The Broomhall Interlude: the Challenge of the East   139
14. The Indian Mutiny, the Celestial Empire and Japan   145
15. The Chastising of China: the Burning of the Summer
    Palace   164
16. The Doomed Viceroy   188
17. Victor Alexander, his Sombre Upbringing and its Curious
    Outcome   201
18. The Reluctant Viceroy   215
19. Mother India, Famine and Plague   231
20. Salmon, Boer War Logistics and the Wee Frees   239

21. The Colonial Office and the Young Winston   245
22. The Thane of Fife   260

Appendix: The Lineage of Bruce   265
Family Trees   267
Bibliography   271
Index   282

List of Black and White Illustrations

1   Lord and Lady Elgin at cards in Constantinople with the Captain Pasha.   40
2   Lord Elgin's first museum at Park Lane, London, 1807.   67
3   Benjamin West's letter to Lord Elgin thanking him for allowing some
    students from the Academy to study the Marbles.   68-9
4   Letter from J.M.W. Turner commending Lord Elgin for his collection of
    the Marbles.   84-5
5   Text of Lord Elgin's draft letter to Earl Grey accepting the Governor
    Generalship of Canada, 6 August 1846.   114-15
6   La Chine, 4 October 1847. One of Lady Elgin's watercolour sketches.   119
7   Two of the stones thrown at the Governor General, Lord Elgin, in
    Montreal, 30 April 1849.   130
8   The Eighth Earl of Elgin. (a) A daguerreotype by Doan of Nova Scotia,
    c. 1850, aetat 39. (b) A photograph by Senor Beato taken in Pekin in 1860,
    aetat 49.   135
9   Lord Elgin's visit to the water cisterns, Aden, 1860.   167
10 Colonel Crealock's ready pen makes an attractive sketch of Lord Elgin
    and his entourage, Egypt, 1860.   168
11 The Sinking of the *Malabar* presents a vivid reminder of the dangers faced
    by diplomatic personages in remote places. (a) The Earl of Elgin, for
    Britain, and Baron Gros, for France, continue to talk quietly to allay the
    alarm of others. (b) The *Malabar* having been beached at the head of Galle
    Harbour near the Kutcherrie, the women and passengers are landed, and
    the Governors Barge is sent alongside to disembark the Ambassadors. (c)
    On the Bridge of the *Malabar*. (d–g) The sinking of the S.S. *Malabar*.   170-3
12 Cartoon from *Punch*, 4 November 1860, Lord Elgin and the Emperor of
    China.   177
13 Colonel Crealock reading Sir Hope Grant's dispatch to Lord Elgin,
    describing the action with the Tartar Army under San-Ko-Lu at Shang-
    Tsia-Wan and the capture of Messers Parkes, Loch, Bowlby.   178

14   The legend beneath the picture reads 'The Fort being taken the Chinese
     send letters. Harry Parkes teaches the Chinese the meaning of a flag of
     truce'.   180
15   The Signing of the Treaty of Pekin, 1860, in the Hall of Ceremonies.   183
16   Peterhoff was a modestly proportioned unpretentious house with cor-
     rugated iron roof, similar to many other hill station houses.   196
17   (a–d) The Rohtung Pass and the Twig Bridge.   198-9
18   The bracelet presented to Lady Elgin by Queen Victoria, April 1864.   202
19   Memorial to James, the Eighth Earl of Elgin and Twelfth Earl of Kincardine. 204
20   The House Party at Haddo House, Aberdeenshire, home of the Earl and
     Countess of Aberdeen, during the shooting season, 1884.   208
21   Louisa, Dowager Countess of Elgin, on the lawn in front of Broomhall
     with members of the Bruce family, and villagers from Charlestown and
     Limekilns, on the occasion of Queen Victoria's Jubilee, 1887.   210
22   Cartoon from *Punch*, 10 March 1888. 'Cultchah!'   212
23   The arrival of the Viceroy at Government House, Calcutta, January 1894.   217
24   The Viceroy, Vicereine and Aides shortly after the arrival. The three eldest
     Bruce girls, Elizabeth, Christian and Veronica, are of the party.   219
25   The Convocation at Lahore, November 1894.   223
26   The Viceroy's State (silver) Howdah, Lahore, November 1894.   224
27   (a) The Viceregal Lodge on Observatory Hill, Simla. (b) The Retreat at
     Mashobra was rented by the Elgins and used as home whenever possible.   226
28   The Viceregal train which was so much more a feature of life for the
     Bruce family in the 1890s than it had been for Elgin's father in the early
     1860s.   228
29   The 'Xmas Tree' Viceregal Lodge, illuminated with electric lights.
     Children's Fancy Dress Ball, September 1894.   229
30   Picnic in Baghi Forest.   232
31   Lord Elgin at ease, with 'Flink' and 'Tim', May 1896.   234
32   The Ninth Earl in full Ceremonial dress.   237
33   Dunfermline High Street. The welcome received by the Elgins on their
     return to Dunfermline from India.   240
34   The family re-united.   242
35   Lord Elgin as Colonial Secretary, in Frock Coat.   246
36   *Punch* cartoon (E.T. Reed), 27 March 1907.   253
37   The Colonial Conference held in London from 15 April to 14 May 1907.   254
38   *Punch* cartoon (Bernard Patridge), 31 July 1907.   257

List of Colour Illustrations

		facing page
1	Martha, Countess of Elgin, c. 1790.	66
2	Thomas, her son, 7th Earl of Elgin and 11th Earl of Kincardine, c. 1799.	66
3	Mary Hamilton Nisbet, Countess of Elgin, later Mrs. Robert Ferguson.	67
4	The portrait painted at Biel, East Lothian, in honour of a joyful family reunion which never happened. Lord Bruce, the heir, with his sisters Mary and Matilda, and the Greek nurses.	67
5	Philoppapos.	82
6	The Marbles on display in London.	83
7	Elizabeth Elgin, Countess of Elgin, the second wife of the 7th Earl and mother of the 8th Earl.	90
8	James, 8th Earl of Elgin and 12th of Kincardine.	90
9	The first wife of the 8th Earl, Elizabeth Mary Cumming Bruce, Countess of Elgin, who died in Jamaica.	91
10	Mary Louisa Lambton, Countess of Elgin, his second wife.	91
11	Niagara Falls, 1847.	122
12	Wolfe's Cove, from Spencer's Wood, Canada 1852.	123
13	Lord Elgin and the Japanese Commissioners, signing the Treaty of Edo (now Tokyo), Japan, August 1858.	162
14	Riding on Pekin. Lord Elgin and his entourage approach Pekin.	162
15	The official processional entry into Pekin.	163
16	Burying the bodies of the murdered emissaries.	163
17	Prince Kung, the Chinese leader, with whom Lord Elgin felt some affinity as Kung struggled to bring some realism into Chinese official thinking.	178
18	Lord Elgin, the senior British diplomat, warmly wrapped against the bleak cold winds which swept across the north China plain, did not relish his bullying role and longed for home.	178
19	Victor Alexander, 9th Earl of Elgin and 13th of Kincardine, born in Montreal in July 1849, and given as a compliment to his father's stand as Governor General in Canada, the male versions of her own names by Queen Victoria herself.	179
20	Constance Carnegie, Countess of Elgin, who bore her husband eleven live children.	179

Preface

In 1922 a small boy entered his first school, in Elgin Street, Ottawa, Canada. Some sixty years later the same boy, by this time a senior professor of history long resident in Scotland, entered the home of the Elgin family at Broomhall, near Dunfermline in Scotland. Out of this meeting with Andrew, the Eleventh Earl of Elgin and Fifteenth of Kincardine, came the present book. It was both a challenge and an opportunity to a Canadian scholar to set James, the Eighth Earl of Elgin, who had first put Canada on the road to self-government, into the context of his home and of his times. But the Eighth Earl was created in part at least by the career and personality of his father, the Seventh Earl, who by his embarrassing notoriety in bringing the Elgin marbles to Britain cost the family so much. In his turn the Eighth Earl, with his distinguished career as imperial pro-consul in the days of British world supremacy, ensured that the life of his son, the Ninth Earl, should be lived in the shadow cast by his famous father. The story therefore starts in 1766 with the birth of Thomas, the Seventh Earl, and ends in 1917 with the death of Victor Alexander, the Ninth Earl. Although the outline of the book is determined by the lives and careers of the Earls, their Countesses, often remarkable women, all contributed, some in full measure, to the story of the family.

The writing of the book was made possible by the generosity of the present Earl of Elgin in making available to us, without let or hindrance, the extensive Bruce family archive which is at Broomhall. Intellectual curiosity spurs on the historian as bundle after bundle of dusty tape-tied letters is unfolded. As the research proceeds the immediacy of events long forgotten, stimulates the enquiring mind, to interpret and extrapolate. The illustrations, with two exceptions, come from the collection of the Earl of Elgin. Our thanks to his Lordship for permission to use them. The portrait of Mary Hamilton Nisbet and the Lusieri drawing come from the National Gallery of Scotland and we are grateful to the Director and Trustees for the use of them here.

The frequent letters, from Montreal, of the Eighth Earl of Elgin to Cumming Bruce, his father-in-law, during the constitutional crisis in Canada in May 1849 give an extraordinary insight into James Bruce, the man, and are in marked contrast to the cool official reports of the Governor General to the government in London. Nor can the motivation of the Seventh Earl be either readily understood or interpreted. Thomas, who by his excessive spending exacerbated the precarious position of the Bruce estate and left a heavy burden of debt to haunt his descendants, still had no qualms in memorializing Sir Robert Peel in 1830 on the expense of maintaining the pauper population of Scotland. Was he, apparently unmoved by the sufferings of the working population, responsible for the remarkable sensitivity of his sons James and Frederick? Much is made here of the way in which the response of one generation affected the attitudes and actions of the next.

The Seventh Earl was British ambassador to Turkey at a critical time when Napoleon Bonaparte was campaigning in Egypt. But his official career was always overshadowed by his activities in collecting and removing the Parthenon Marbles to London. His subsequent misfortunes haunted the second half of his life and affected his sons. The Eighth Earl, pre-eminently a pro-consular figure, was governor of Jamaica, governor-general of Canada, and ambassador plenipotentiary to China and Japan, who died in India as viceroy. The Ninth Earl was also viceroy and served in London as colonial secretary. All three were involved with Britain's overseas interests, themselves perhaps forced into uncharacteristic postures of aggression as representatives of nineteenth century British imperial power. None of the three Elgins with whom this book is concerned operated on the internal power structure of British society. Even when Victor Alexander achieved cabinet status in 1906 it was as colonial secretary destined to make decisions on a variety of far away and troublesome places, with which for commercial reasons, and sometimes almost accidentally, Britain had become involved.

These impoverished noblemen did not have the choice of staying comfortably at home and seeking careers and fulfilment in government in London. They were forced to accept one exotic challenge after another with all the discomforts and dangers of living in climatic extremes.

The genetic inheritance is also important, for although the titles and the estate pass via the male line, each succeeding generation of Bruce is challenged by the incoming wives. With this comes also a new cultural injection which is expressed most significantly in the raising of the children of the next generation. Through the pages of this book pass seven countesses. Did Martha Whyte's strict economy and evangelicalism ensure Thomas her son's financial irresponsibility? The wives of Thomas were Mary Hamilton Nisbet, whose personal tragedy was to be divorced in an age when divorce was almost unknown, and who lost all sight of and rights to her children from their infancy, and Elizabeth Oswald, who brought sound good sense and further evangelicalism to the family and who as a young girl took over Mary Nisbet's children and in addition produced a quiverful of her own. The wives of James were Elizabeth Mary (Elma) Cumming Bruce, for whom the hazards of the colonies proved too much, who died as a young wife in Jamaica, and Mary Louisa Lambton who brought a devotion almost amounting to adoration for her husband which lasted long after his death and moulded the character of the Ninth Earl. His first wife Constance Carnegie, understood much of Victor Alexander's hesitancy and self-doubt, bore him eleven live children and suffered several other miscarriages. Finally there is Gertrude Ogilvy, Elgin's bride of old age, who is only fleetingly met.

Broomhall, the house itself, the estate and the villages, formerly estate property, of Limekilns and Charlestown provide a continuum to this study. Despite its chronic indebtedness, which remained acute until the end of the nineteenth century, each generation received the estate from its predecessors together with steady increment of family memories and attitudes. The months and years of self-imposed exile suffered by the previous generations has certainly enriched the holdings of memorabilia at

Broomhall. The family home became a repository for trophies, mementos and relics as well as a resting place for parliamentary reports, collections of family letters and innumerable ephemera—for each succeeding generation—a *pietas*—and a perplexity.

The book is based on the Elgin archives which must be one of the most extensive still in private hands and we are grateful to Lord Elgin for placing his papers at our disposal. Within the collection there are not only bundles and boxes of personal letters but also considerable holdings of state papers, often bound, which accrued to the various Earls in the course of their official duties. As a scholarly team we were fortunate in having the services of Lord Elgin as research assistant. He not only collected our lists of 'desiderata' but later emerged, laden with dusty volumes and boxes.

We worked in the 'school-room' directly below the replica of the memorial to James, the Eighth Earl, dominated by a benign but ghostly white head in bas-relief and bearing the plaques illustrating his time in Jamaica, Canada, China and India. The enormous cantilevered table was piled high with boxes and papers of all kinds. Here, seeking to understand, we would also discuss with Lord Elgin at length the intricacies of the family history. Despite Lord Elgin's continued interest, the responsibility for the writing and the opinions and judgments made are the author's alone.

The research was encouraged by a grant from the Nuffield Foundation for whose assistance we are grateful. In the autumn of 1983 while Visiting Professors in the Department of History at the University of Alberta, work was done on James Bruce, as Governor General of Canada. We appreciated the help received including that from the historians including David Moss and Ged Martin. In the autumn of 1984 as Visiting Professors at Keio University in Tokyo we continued to pursue the Eighth Earl of Elgin in the Japanese Diplomatic Archives. We benefited much from the support and advice of Norio and Setsuko Tamaki. During September–October 1985 we were visiting scholars at the Rockefeller Foundation's Study Centre at Bellagio and there in the *Veduta* found an atmosphere congenial for steady work. We appreciated the opportunity of enjoying golden days on the shores of Lake Como although the presentation on *The Elgins* which my husband gave to the scholarly community there was to be his last.

When Sydney Checkland died on 22 March 1986 the manuscript of *The Elgins* was complete. It has been edited and prepared for publication by Sarah Jane and Olive Checkland. Our other children John, Stephen, Deborah and Clare have all given comfort and support encouraging us to bring Sydney Checkland's last book to public attention.

A number of works by earlier scholars have proved invaluable. These include William St. Clair's *Lord Elgin and the Marbles*, W.C.Costin's *Great Britain and China* and Ronald Hyam's *Elgin and Churchill at the Colonial Office*.

In the course of our work we have incurred many debts. Through Sir David Ogilvie, we made contact with Mr. and Mrs.Julian Brooke who made it possible to see Mary Nisbet's original letter diary and other Hamilton Nisbet documents. At the Scottish Record Office we found the Commissary Court reports of the Seventh Earl's divorce. Duncan McNaughton, the Earl's archivist, kindly gave us a sight of his interesting paper on the Elgin railway. Constance Babington Smith guided us over Hahnemann and Homeopathy. Henry Scrope helped us to understand the misfortunes of Lord Thurlow. Ian Millar, the secretary at Broomhall, has always responded to our requests with kindly efficiency. Ian Hutchison of the University of Stirling generously shared with us his expertise on Liberal politics in late nineteenth century Scotland. Jean Robertson in the University Library, Glasgow, and Margaret Pamplin in the University Library, Cambridge, responded with care and good humour to our many queries. We wish to record our thanks to them all.

The Earl and Countess of Elgin have followed the progress of the book with great interest and perhaps some curiosity. Their unfailing courtesy and hospitality have been much appreciated especially during the last months of final preparation. Both Sydney Checkland and the Earl had been tank commanders in Normandy, in 1944, in the Canadian and British armies respectively, both received permanent leg injuries with which they subsequently had to live. However fleetingly the five Bruce children have also welcomed us to Broomhall, Georgiana, Charles, Antonia, Adam and Alexander have always been courteous hosts. We have been glad to draw on the skilled services of Adam Bruce who has prepared the Family Trees.

Margaret Lamb in Glasgow generously took responsibility for preparing the Bibliography, while Aileen Forbes Ballantyne in Paris made the Index. The project would hardly have been feasible without the back-up services of Isabel, Bill and Craig Burnside in Glasgow and Neil Payne in Cambridge. Whatever challenges were offered to the word-processing team they have responded with prompt efficiency. In Cambridge Neil has quietly fielded and diffused various crises. Our indebtedness to them is great.

It is inevitably a sad task for the remaining member of a partnership, which sustained us for forty-four years, to complete a project such as this. As my husband wrote just before his death, 'Jointly with Olive, in a very real sense our works have been a collaboration for a good many years.' It is therefore jointly that we present this family biography to a wider public.

Olive Checkland,
Cellardyke,
Fife,
Scotland.

CHAPTER 1

Thomas, the Seventh Earl and his Ambiguous Inheritance

Robert the Bruce, sixth generation from a Norman Knight, King of Scots from 1306 to 1329, led his army to a great victory over the English King Edward II at Bannockburn in 1314. By so doing he restored an independent Scotland, governed by its own laws and institutions. He made the name of Bruce one of the two most resounding in Scottish history, rivalled only by that of the Wallace. The lineage and the name have been carried by a collateral branch, that of the Earls of Elgin and Kincardine, with their seat at Broomhall in Fife, some two miles south of Dunfermline. The sword of the Bruce is kept at Broomhall.

The history of the family between the great Bruce and the seventeenth century is a complex affair, but with no real high points. The Bruces were not among those Scottish families that excelled in the game of land acquisition or which became prominent in the tortuous public affairs of Scotland through royal favour or otherwise. But the seventeenth century did produce Bruces of note. There was Edward who had profitably anglicised by accompanying King James VI and I to England in 1603, founding a noble line there, though retaining Scottish connections, culminating in the earldom of Ailesbury. It was his line that was awarded the title of Earls of Elgin in the peerage of Scotland in 1633. By contrast, his son George made himself a proto-industrialist with his celebrated salt works and coal mines under the Forth at Culross, for which he was knighted by James VI; his son became first Earl of Kincardine in 1647.

Alexander (grandson of Sir George the industrialist) became a Lord of Session, and one of King Charles II's Commissioners for the government of Scotland. Thomas (third Earl of Elgin and second of Ailesbury), was so deeply attached to the Catholic cause of James II that he refused to take the oath after the Glorious revolution of 1688 and was imprisoned in the Tower in 1696, but was later allowed to live in Brussels, which he did, in considerable state, having acquired by marriage the large estates of Tottenham and Savernake Forest. His granddaughter became the wife of Bonnie Prince Charlie. Thereafter until the later eighteenth century, though there were still Jacobite sympathies in the family, its members once more played a minor part. The fortunes of the Bruces are dealt with in greater detail in the appendix.

It was in Charles Bruce, born in 1732, that in 1740 the family titles were first combined, making him at the age of eight fifth Earl of Elgin and ninth of Kincardine. It was with him that the Bruces entered upon the modern age, seeking a development policy for the Broomhall estate through the exploitation of its rich limestone deposits. Broomhall was an estate made up of land purchased largely from monastic holdings. The age of high farming came early in Fife and the Lothians with their superlative soil and large farms: it was the agricultural market for lime that Charles hoped to exploit. Broomhall was strategically placed in one of the most fertile and agriculturally progressive parts of Scotland, with lime in much demand for lightening heavy soils.

His mother, Janet, Countess of Kincardine, was one of those doughty dowagers who punctuate the Bruce family story. Her husband having died young in 1740, she was to have thirty-one years of widowhood. She became custodian of the estate until Charles reached his majority. At the same time she became intensely devout in the Calvinistic manner, searching the Bible for those passages 'which give the distinguishing marks of those who are blessed from those who are cursed.' She found her infant son's inheritance encumbered with debts and strove by economies to reduce them. By the time Charles reached manhood the estate was viable. Meanwhile Janet had watched anxiously over his upbringing and education. She sent him to St. Andrews University in 1751 to St. Salvator's College under Master Henry Rymer. In spite of financial pressures he did the grand tour, spending 1754 and 1755 in France and Italy. Janet, like other mothers of aristocratic sons, warned him against the two great tour temptations, gambling and women. 'For God's sake', wrote Janet to her twenty-three year old son, 'keep clear of mistresses ... they always turn out to be the most expensive petts in the world.' At the same time Janet warned Charles of over-ambitious plans to develop the limeworks and quarry at Broomhall. In July 1759 he was commissioned a Cornet in the Royal Regiment of Dragoons. In 1761 the young Elgin attended the coronation of George III, perhaps this was intended as a signal that the family's Jacobite connections were at an end. In the same year he became Grand Master in the Masonic Order. The house at Broomhall had been built in 1702 in the old Scottish style with small rooms and poor natural light, with perhaps a largish hall. It was scantily furnished, making it an austere and somewhat comfortless place: indeed its bareness made it difficult for Janet to let it. But it was pleasantly set, with a splendid view south to the Firth of Forth.

Charles seems to have been a thoroughly amiable person, of whom all spoke well. There was a family tradition that the last Earl of Ailesbury in his search in 1747 for an heir would have chosen Charles Bruce had the youth been prepared to settle in England, but that Charles declined to leave Scotland. Certainly Thomas, Lord Bruce of Tottenham, Ailesbury's heir, for all his great wealth, regarded Charles as the head of the Bruce clan, for Charles was the bearer of the oldest of the Bruce family titles, that of Elgin. The modesty of his estate did not impair his status as a nobleman or as the head of the Bruce clan. Nor did his industrial and trading activities lower the esteem in which he was held, for it was accepted that a Scottish nobleman and landowner should seek to develop his estate by such means. It is possible that because of a degree of Jacobite taint still surviving, his energies were canalised into the estate, politics or diplomacy being precluded.

Charles went about the business with such energy as to attract approving attention. A good deal of borrowed money was sunk in limestone quarries and in limekilns and estate roads. A new labour force of some hundreds was attracted to the estate. There was already the village of Limekilns near by, evidence that lime burning had long been done, though on a modest scale. It was from its tiny harbour, as Stevenson described it, that David Balfour in *Kidnapped* was helped across the Forth by the innkeeper's daughter. But Charles thought and acted on a new scale. From the outset the perspective of a conscientious landowner was present: he was a true paternalist, unwilling that his labour force should struggle to find lodgings. Instead he planned and built a model village, calling it Charlestown. Adjacent he built a new harbour so that there was ready access to the Firth of Forth. His limeworks thus seemed to have excellent prospects, with the great kilns, probably the largest in Britain, on the very edge of his port, with coal available nearby. He designed its layout with care, providing a village green playground as its centre, big enough for all recreations. Good stone houses were built, with generous gardens. So began the tradition of estate paternalism, bringing to the family the affection and respect of its employees. Meanwhile Charles and his family lived in simplicity and economy in the old house. The connection with the Earl of Ailesbury continued to be a strong one.

In 1759 when he was twenty-seven Charles married eighteen year old Martha Whyte. Her father was termed 'banker in London', and was a contemporary of the Coutts family; her mother had died a few days after her birth, followed by her father five years later. She was raised by her father's brother Robert Whyte, a merchant of Kirkcaldy, and his wife. Charles conducted a spirited wooing, defeating his rival, the Earl of Galloway. Martha bore Charles eight children in twelve years of marriage (five sons and three daughters), of whom four reached adulthood (three boys and a girl).

When Martha was within a fortnight of her eighth child, in 1771, Charles, aged thirty-nine, suddenly died. He was laid among his ancestors in the family vault of Dunfermline Abbey to universal sorrow. His industrial enterprises were only half completed: they were still far from the point of producing a profitable return on the debt incurred by building the works, the little new town and its harbour. In particular the housing and the harbour tied up money that could not generate a return for decades. A few months later the young widow, barely thirty, lost her eldest son, when the six-year-old sixth Earl of Elgin died from what she called 'stifling', perhaps asthma or croup. Her beloved husband and son had disappeared almost together. She was left with three infant boys and the baby Charlotte. Martha thus took her place in the succession of Elgin dowagers at an early age. Like them she had control of her life and of those of her children quite suddenly thrust upon her. She ruled the family until Thomas, born on 20 July 1766, came of age in 1787, and indeed in some senses thereafter. Thomas at the age of five became the seventh Earl of Elgin and eleventh of Kincardine and master of Broomhall. The estate, in the interest of the creditors, was placed in trusteeship. Little Thomas was provided with a set of guardians, the chief of whom was his English kinsman Lord Bruce of Tottenham, Ailesbury's heir. But it was Martha who determined Thomas' formative years.

With the Broomhall estate in such financial difficulty the widowed Martha had only her jointure of £500 per year on which to maintain herself and her young family. She found herself in the same position as Janet before her. She responded in the same brave fashion. She embarked at once on a regime of the most strict economy. Perhaps her deep sense of religion, with its powerful puritan element, responded to this necessity. Outlying properties were sold to relieve the debt; it was not long before Janet's jointure was extinguished by her death in 1772. Over time the prospects of the lime works slowly improved, though still far from the extent that was required to lift the debt burden.

More immediately there was the question of the schooling of Martha's three sons, especially Thomas the new Earl, now approaching his sixth birthday. It was essential that he be educated as befitted his station as head of the Bruce clan in both Scotland and England. Here the kinship net sustained Martha. The Scottish and English branches of the family had maintained unbroken contact, as exchanges of letters show. The young Elgin's cousinhood included in England, in addition to Lord Bruce of Tottenham, the Duke of Chandos and the Duke of Montagu. It was Bruce of Tottenham, who had held Thomas' father in great affection, and who regarded the boy as the head of the Bruce clan, who took the initiative. He and Montagu brought influence to bear on King George III, explaining the circumstance of the juvenile head of their family, brought low by the confusion of the affairs of the late fifth Earl of Elgin. They obtained a pension of £300 per year for Thomas. Support for this purpose was mustered from the great men of Fife who provided Tottenham with documentation which he showed to the prime minister. Lord North pointed out the high esteem in which the Bruces were held by all ranks in that part of the country, where they were indeed the leading family, and where the dead Charles had been popular both as landowner and as a provider of quarrying and limeburning employment.

Tottenham's help went further. He offered to become responsible for Thomas' education in an English school, paying his fees and any other expenses, taking him into his own home for holidays; in short becoming almost a foster father, treating Thomas as one of his own sons. More than this, Lord Bruce offered to take similar responsibility for the education of Martha's other two boys. She, in spite of the pangs of separation, accepted the offer on behalf of Thomas, but declined it as affecting the younger two. Bruce of Tottenham and the wealthy ambience he provided thus became a powerful formative influence on the small boy entrusted to him.

Martha had become almost morbidly pre-occupied with little Thomas, especially in terms of his health. She had already lost two sons (the first had died within a few months of birth; the second, the short lived sixth Earl of Elgin, had not reached his seventh birthday). Thomas, like his dead elder brother, suffered from 'stifling', though he had survived small pox and measles. Martha was convinced of his delicacy, and so had drawn up a stringent set of health rules. They were also intended to induce hardihood: Thomas was allowed one blanket in summer and two in winter, with his room 'well aired'. This was a spartan provision of warmth, especially in winter when the cold and dampness of the Forth was so penetrating. Salted meats, mince pies and fish were denied him. The 'phisicians' had been carefully consulted, laying it down that he might have 'a little beer to drink at dinner if he gets no wine'. Nor must he overstrain himself, but should be 'allowed to take as much moderate Exercise as he can but as Violent Exercise throws him into profuse Sweats he must be stopt and made cooll himself deliberately as a sudden Check to the Perspiration is very apt to bring on the stifling.' So began the intense, almost neurotic concern with health that was to make Thomas a hypochondriac through most of his adult life.

In his reading the young Elgin was not so advanced as he might have been because his mother had rather kept him back for fear that he might acquire too strong a Scottish accent, 'The English one being much prettier'; in short she wished Thomas to sound like a cultured Englishman. She wished Thomas to 'behave prettily at the Table', and in general that he should be imbued with gentlemanly standards. Fundamental to her whole scheme of upbringing was her deep religious sense, with much emphasis on prayer, Bible reading and self-scrutiny. But there was a certain robustness about Thomas: indeed the child of a Scottish nobleman would have much closer contacts with people outside his class or among the family's servants than would be the case with a young English aristocrat. Thomas remembered his birthday (20 July) because it came on the first day of the Leith Races. He knew how to entertain his elders with his drollery and archness, in short he could perform as a precocious extrovert when required.

It was agreed that little Elgin should be despatched to Tottenham Park to spend the summer holidays of 1772 there, acclimatising himself to English ways before facing the challenge of school. The great dwelling and its setting soon enchanted the little boy. He was to refer to it in his letters as 'Happiness House'. It was indeed a splendid place. It was built in the early eighteenth century, of brick: its long line of portraits told the story of the English Bruces from the time of James VI and I, and included works by Lely and Van Dyke. Some of the portraits reflected alliances with other aristocratic families including the Dukes of Rutland and the Earls of Burlington. From the windows of the house could be seen the great avenue that ran into Savernake Forest and thence to Marlborough, five and a half miles away, where Lord Bruce, arriving in his stately family coach, presided over local affairs. Marlborough, indeed, was his pocket borough. This grandeur was a far cry from the simplicity and austerity of Broomhall: so too was the status of an English grandee from that of a Scottish earl in straitened circumstances. In addition there was the London house on Clapham Common, Tottenham Park and the London house, and their way of life, were to have a profound effect on the young Elgin, such that his mother's insistence on frugality, reinforced by her increasingly stern Presbyterian austerity, were to conflict with the urge to spend and to live gracefully.

Not that Lord Bruce was any kind of easy liver: had he been such Martha would never have entrusted Thomas to him. Bruce, like her, was deeply religious, a highly exceptional characteristic at a time when it was commonly said that Lord Dartmouth was the only peer who said his prayers. Indeed Ailesbury and Martha were part of the clean-living, family-based element of society in late eighteenth century Britain, which though headed by George III and his QueenCharlotte, was a minority element among the landed aristocracy and gentry, or at least of those who frequented London.

Daily from the opulence of Tottenham Park family prayers ascended, interspersed with Bible readings, just as at Broomhall. With this went Bruce's enforcement of discipline on his own boys, though it was of a much more cheerful kind than Martha's. Living in the world as he did, and seeing so much of the Court, he was aware that Thomas could not be kept away from the theatre, a place disapproved of by Martha, for to do so would be to isolate the boy from his peers, making him conspicuous and unacceptable. Indeed Lord Bruce in his experienced courtier's way sought to steer

Thomas between unbending rectitude and a certain acceptance of the world, carrying Martha's permission step by step with him, and so lifting what might have been resented restraints. Lord Bruce (with the title of Earl of Ailesbury revived for him in 1776), enjoyed high status at Court, being close to King George III and the Queen. He was to make it his business to introduce Elgin to the people he should know, including of course their Majesties. Ailesbury had a warm affection and a deep respect for the King: the young Elgin watched the construction at Tottenham Park of a monument in the royal honour.

The British aristocracy at this time was a pretty tight affair, very few hereditary peerages having been created for a hundred years since 1688. The apex of British society was thus some two hundred aristocratic families. The young Elgin was one of the two hundred, by status, but not by wealth. Much of the aristocracy was self-indulgent, with lavish entertainment and expensive hobbies including eating and drinking, gambling, mistresses, quarrels and duels. All this, of course, Martha knew, and it frightened her. She clung to the puritan tradition, reinforced as it was by the rise of evangelicalism from the later eighteenth century.

The son and heir of Ailesbury had been for two years at a school in Wandsworth kept by Mr. and Mrs. Cormick: Elgin was to join him there as one of thirty-eight pupils. The boys shared the same room with two Ailesbury nephews, 'where a maid servant always lyes.' At school Elgin, like his cousins, was plunged back into austerity. The Cormicks, as Ailesbury well knew, would not follow the painfully detailed regimen set out for Elgin by Martha. Elgin settled well and was soon at the head of his class, applying himself as his mother urged: he had begun Latin almost at once. An outbreak of mumps was treated with sow's milk and bleeding, the usual 'remedies'; chicken pox meant a dose of 'physic'. Waistcoats, embroidered by Lady Elgin, arrived for Thomas and young Bruce. By the time Elgin was seven he was learning Latin and French grammar and reading the history of England together with the *Moral Miscellany* and the Bible. Because of the shortage of washing facilities and lack of supervision at ablutions, together with long hair, skin infections were endemic in boarding schools, and those taking the sons of noblemen were no exception. In the winter of 1774-5 ringworm found the Wandsworth school a congenial culture. It began with Elgin himself, appearing on his face and spreading mostly among the small boys: ink was applied by the school to the red spots as a treatment. The doctor regarded this outbreak of ringworm as one of the most infectious and difficult to cure that he knew of, and was at a loss.

It was decided that Elgin must be removed from Wandsworth. Ailesbury charac-teristically conducted the search for an alternative. Harrow was chosen as being 'more out of the way of temptation to vice than either Westminster or Eton'. Elgin was whisked off to Harrow in February 1775.

He entered the house of the Headmaster, Benjamin Heath. This was the man whose election in 1771 to the headship had caused the Great School Rebellion that had almost wrecked Harrow. Elgin was soon grappling with Ovid, his first contact with Greek culture that was to dominate so much of his life. The rigours of Harrow were relieved when his pocket money was increased from three pence to six pence per week. Harrow, however, was no more immune from filth and personal slovenliness than Wandsworth had been: Ailesbury sadly referred to its 'extreme dirtiness'. Elgin on arriving at Tottenham Park for his holidays brought with him a scruffy and uncared for wardrobe. Worse still, his eyes were giving him trouble and he twice brought a head of lice to the Park.

It was while Elgin was at Harrow that the thirteen American colonies revolted. Colonel Thomas Bruce, Elgin's uncle, after whom Thomas had been named, was stationed at Halifax, Nova Scotia. Ailesbury had helped to promote his career: General Conway, the Commander-in-Chief, was the husband of the dowager Lady Ailesbury. There was some fear that the Americans might attack Halifax, but Ailesbury, very much in the know, informed Martha that there was no such danger. On his return from North America Colonel Bruce became General and was sent to India.

Meanwhile Lady Elgin had been rethinking the education of her boys. The two younger, Charles Andrew and James, had been placed in a school in Kensington. She now resolved to supervise directly the education of all three of them, assuming full-time motherhood. She moved with her three sons and daughter to Dean's Yard, London not far from Westminster School where were entered the three boys. Elgin, now twelve, had been some three years at Harrow, a place for which, in spite of its unsanitary nature, he kept an affection throughout his life. Lady Elgin had been able to let Broomhall for a good rental, the tenant taking it unfurnished, which had indeed been in effect its condition. The house in Dean's Yard was small and confining for the five of them, but it was all she could afford. But what she called her 'self denial system' was bringing its rewards, for the financial position of the Broomhall estate was steadily improving, demonstrating its recuperative power if not subjected to extravagance. So much so that Martha now felt that she could ease her own condition and that of her boys a little. Whereas she had paid for her son's schooling from her jointure, passing the pension to the relief of the Broomhall debts, she now felt justified in applying the pension to Thomas' education.

Ailesbury now stood very much as Elgin's male mentor. Indeed it was his wish, as he put it, 'to be rather his friend than his monitor', though, he said, 'if necessary, I shall act in both characters'. He was Lady Elgin's ideal of a gentleman on whom her sons should model themselves. 'Note first of all his piety', she urged on Elgin, 'That is exemplary, his diligence in employing his time. His temperance, his neatness without affectation of foppery and nonsense, his activity in rising in the morning ...' Elgin did indeed respond: 'Lord Ailesbury', he wrote to his mother, 'is always inventing something kind'. In 1775 Ailesbury was offered the role of Governor to the Prince of Wales and his brothers, but on consideration, and perhaps wisely, he declined. Had he accepted there is at least some prospect that there would have been a less serious problem with royal reprobates later. In 1781 he accepted the office of Chamberlain to the Queen. Lady Ailesbury was an invalid; her sister thought her a self-indulgent hypochondriac, but Martha believed her to be genuinely ill. With his wife in such a condition Ailesbury seems to have been susceptible to the charms of young widows, and was chaffed by the ladies for being so.

Though Lady Elgin had an austere side, she was far from being inhuman. She could make mild jokes; she enjoyed the London world and the company of her aristocratic friends, especially Lady Glenorchy, Lady Linlithgow and Lady Lothian. She knew how to carry herself, making a good impression when presented at Court. Public affairs interested her and she would occasionally take part in local Fife politics: the inside information and court gossip that Ailesbury could give her she much appreciated. In particular, no doubt because of her sons, she became interested in education. When she recommended certain reading on the subject to Ailesbury he replied, 'I should rather wish your good ladyship to be writing such a book as you recommend to me as I know scarce anybody more capable of treating the interesting subject of the education of youth as it deserves.' Martha did not seek another husband: she idealised the dead Charles, reminding her children of his virtues, keeping alive for them the sacred flame of his memory. No less than twenty-one epitaphs were drafted for her husband's memorial in Dunfermline Abbey before she was satisfied. At perhaps another but unrecognised level, having born eight children in twelve years, she had no wish to resume.

That Britain was at war was brought home to the Elgins in 1779 when the American fleet (under John Paul Jones, father of the American navy) appeared off the coast of Fife. Lady Elgin's close friends the Oswalds of Dunnikier near Kirkcaldy had the enemy's ships before their windows for three days, throwing everybody into horror and confusion. There was only a twenty-gun frigate to defend them. Mr. Oswald had had all his valuables packed and his wife and children ready to fly to the Highlands at an hour's warning. The Presbytery of Kirkcaldy called the people onto the beach to pray for a change in the wind. Happily this occurred, blowing John Paul Jones and his fleet back out to sea and the danger passed. But though she took comfort in an over-ruling Providence, 'who can change in a moment our adversity into prosperity', Martha was greatly alarmed.

Elgin was four years at Westminster School from the age of twelve. Ailesbury continued his interest in the family, though his most intimate and intense period of influence was drawing to a close. Always Martha and Ailesbury were concerned that Elgin should not fall into the company of boys of bad influence. At cricket they were 'Without supervision', cricket was an occasion on which there was a good deal of drinking. On the other hand, when he heard a sermon that he liked Elgin would sometimes do a précis of it for his mother.

The shape of Elgin's career had yet to be determined. But that of Charles Andrew his youngest brother could not be left open. By the usual judicious working of the patronage system a place was secured for him as a cadet in the East India Company. Charles was a devout young man, always carrying his pocket Bible with him.

In the late summer of 1782 Lady Elgin and Thomas, now aged sixteen, returned to Scotland. It was time to resume his connection with his native country. Attending a Scottish University was an excellent way of doing so, and so Elgin was enrolled in the University of St. Andrews, as his father had been, where he was to spend two years. Charles was in Amsterdam preparing for India, presumably studying eastern languages, and James was still at Westminster School as a boarder. James was the most lively of the boys, the most likely to get into scrapes and the most irked by the closeness of his mother's control. His interests lay in horses, phaetons and shooting. Ailesbury had to report that one of James' eyes was bandaged as the result of an escapade in the dark when a son of the Archbishop of York had thrown a piece of cheese at him.

Ailesbury did his best to watch over James, whose vigorous mischief was now in contrast to the failing health of his own heir, whose lungs were being destroyed by consumption. The therapies tried were pathetic in their futility, including 'the Bark' and 'a Pectoral of Water Parsnip'. The invalid Lady Ailesbury died early in March, followed soon by her eldest son. 'It is the Pride of my Life', wrote Ailesbury, 'to have contributed to bringing up in innocence and virtue a valuable and dear youth in this degenerate age.' Elgin had become deeply attached to his distant cousin and was greatly distressed.

Lady Elgin set up her little household in St. Andrews. Broomhall was in rather poor repair, but the lime works was now doing well. At the university between 1782 and 1784, Thomas acquitted himself with credit. He was placed under the charge of George Hill, the youthful Professor of Greek, aged 32. Hill had been among the St. Andrews professors who had entertained Dr. Johnson and James Boswell in 1773, and was seen by the moderate party in the Church of Scotland as a man of great promise. Like Martha and Ailesbury, Hill was a man of high moral tone: this was no doubt one reason why he was chosen. 'Sound principles of religion and morality', he abjured the young Elgin, 'are at any time the only sure foundation of that steady good conduct which brings true reputation.' This was especially true for a young aristocrat for whom heavy responsibilities accompanied his position. Hill, like Martha and Ailesbury, believed that they lived in a frivolous age. It brought 'forward into public stations persons totally unfurnished with knowledge, devoid of public spirit, and so dissipated and embarrassed that they cannot make use of their natural talents.' But Hill believed that this general decadence was in a sense an advantage for Elgin, sound principles being 'so rare as to give any person in your rank who has them a most decided superiority, and the fairest chance of rising to eminence.'

Elgin's basic mental diet at St. Andrews was of course Greek and Latin and the classical authors. He won a University Prize for an essay on 'Tragedy'. There can be no doubt that the classical world as a source of wisdom and aesthetics entered deeply into the young man's mind. He developed an interest in civil law, of which Hill warmly approved. The Professor, fully in the spirit of the Scottish Enlightenment, as befitted a protégé of Principal Robertson, emphasised to the young lord that 'The Civil Law is the law of nature as applied by an enlightened people to their situation.' Moreover to understand something of how a particular people did this was a practical preparation for studying the behaviour of other societies. In short an understanding of the civil law was an essential training for the politician, and perhaps especially the diplomat. Hill outlined a reading programme for the young Elgin in which featured Fergusson's *Institutes*, Puffendorf and Grotius. Such a programme naturally turned Elgin's interests away from the English Universities towards the continent, where lay the roots of Scottish jurisprudence. After two years at St. Andrews he decided to go abroad to study civil law. In the European educational system of the day such a course was perhaps the best available preparation for a diplomatic career.

But the question of Elgin's longer term future was becoming pressing. It involved operating within the patronage system which permeated the life of Britain, governing the grandest appointments down to the level of an overseer of the poor. What he needed was a patron, as high on the scale as possible: this Elgin had in Ailesbury.

George III also operated his own system of patronage which he could still use effectively, for example in dishing the Whigs in 1784, bringing in the twenty-four year old Pitt as Prime Minister.

Entering the army had always been a possibility. Ailesbury was against this, feeling that Elgin, in his straitened circumstances, should either devote himself to the development of the Broomhall estate, or seek a career that was more lucrative. There was also a second objection that weighed heavily with both Ailesbury and Martha – that the Guards were notorious for debauching young men, leading them into lounging, extravagance and vice. To escape such snares required exceptional strength of character. But as Elgin persisted in a strong desire for a commission, Martha concurred and Ailesbury loyally set about working the patronage system. But he urged Elgin to delay committing himself until he had completed his foreign studies. He pointed out that the army would yield little income for many years until Elgin achieved senior rank.

Pressure was put on Ailesbury's relation General Conway. An application was made to the King and a memorandum sent to the new Minister of War. In addition Ailesbury continued to interest himself in the career of General Bruce, Elgin's uncle. His account of affairs in India was eagerly awaited by Ministers. The General, though somewhat dull in company, was, in the Bruce family tradition, a man of integrity, returning from India without the usual fortune, having retained, as Ailesbury put it, 'a thorough good conscience which is far beyond wealth got in the Nabob way.' On the subject of Elgin's commission, the General dismissed compromise, insisting that Elgin should wait for his turn in the Guards, rejecting any lesser regiment and refusing to accelerate the process by purchase. The General's opinion carried weight, for he had shown himself a capable military man. This was indeed the course followed.

Immediately demanding resolution was the question of where Elgin should study on the continent. His guardians met in September 1784 to discuss the matter. Ailesbury, as usual, was the moving spirit. He preferred Germany, in particular Gottingen 'which is the King's University as Elector of Hanover'. But just as Elgin persisted in his pursuit of a commission, so too he made up his own mind about his place of study. He rejected Germany in favour of France. At the age of eighteen he had shown a certain stubbornness.

CHAPTER 2

The Young Milord Abroad

It was to Paris in February 1785 that Elgin went, in spite of the anxieties and advice of his mother and Ailesbury. He was eighteen, a handsome, highly presentable young nobleman, with an entrée to the highest circles. It is not clear why he was so insistent upon France, rejecting the preference for Germany held by his mother, Ailesbury and his guardians and indeed the King who believed German society a more sober and safe place for a young man. He was accompanied by a family servant, one Lavaux, his late father's butler, who valeted him, made his bed, cleaned his room and served him at table. His health-conscious mother provided him with a large quantity of tincture of rhubarb to keep his bowels open. Many young men sent abroad were accompanied by tutors or male relatives but Martha could not afford this virtual doubling of costs, so that Thomas was on his own.

Elgin's first impressions of France reflected a good deal of culture shock. He was repelled by outdoor shrines and crucifixes with the 'figure of our Saviour, as large as life'. He dismissed the altars and images in the cathedrals as absurdities and idolatories. He was shocked at the constant use of the name of God by the French in conversation, a casualness that was terrible to him. Most of all he was struck by the profanation of the Sabbath, with shops and theatres open on the sacred day. His first impression of French life and Frenchmen was, indeed, one of disgust. He was inhibited too by his inability to speak the language, though he could understand a good deal. But his attitude to his surroundings began to change as he became accustomed to them. His earnestness in pursuit of self improvement, however, did not.

His devotion to his mother was intense. He had been five years under her direct influence from the ages of thirteen to eighteen. The penury under which she lived had depressed him for years. He missed her goodnight kiss and their intimate conversations. Martha, though keeping such close surveillance on him, had conditioned herself to accepting him as the head of the family in the place of her dead husband. She now encouraged him to take an almost paternal attitude toward his two brothers and his sister. This he did. He gave advice to Andrew on his career in India, urging him to study Persian and arithmetic on the voyage out; he requested his mother to buy a selection of books for James which he himself had chosen.

Elgin was to study under Monsieur Bouchaud, one of the Professors of the Ecole de Droit and a member of the Académie des Inscriptions et Belles Lettres. He and his wife lived in an apartment in a large building in the Place St. Genevieve, then recently erected for the accommodation of the Professors of the Faculty of Law: Elgin was to join their ménage. The Professor, he wrote, as a result of being sixty-six, was 'rather whimsical'. While instructing Elgin he wore a kind of night-gown, with a waistcoat and a nightcap. In spite of this Elgin found him a good teacher. At first, communication was difficult because of the weakness of Elgin's spoken French, compounded by his adenoids which made some of the sounds hard to encompass. The Professor could read and write English tolerably, but could bring neither ear nor tongue to bear.

Elgin attended Bouchaud's lectures on Civil and Public Law. Somewhat later he went three times per week to hear the Professor lecture on ambassadors. There were also tutorials, or *conferences*. the Professor would read a paragraph of Justinian's *Institutes*, for example, then explain it partly in Latin and partly in French. Elgin would later write down these disquisitions on a text, together with relevant material from other writers such as Blackstone and Erskine. Elgin and Bouchaud got on together excellently, especially after Elgin had carefully explained why a conscientious member of the Church of England, taking a serious view of the Fourth Commandment, could not participate in classes on a Sunday. Elgin's prejudices against things French rapidly dissolved, partly by learning from Bouchaud and partly by living contact.

In addition Elgin had a French master, a dancing master, a mathematics master and a fencing master. This meant a very demanding programme. He fought off invitations to dine and other social occasions, rather ruffling the British Ambassador, the Duke of Dorset, by appearing too seldom at his table. Protestant church-going was difficult in Paris, but Elgin continued his reading of the Bible and the Prayer Book, especially on Sundays in the privacy of his room.

He wrote long and frequent letters to his mother; these she cherished. She searched anxiously for signs of danger, just as Janet had done before her. There had been profound misgivings about Paris, a place where most young Englishmen spent their time in idleness and dissipation. Martha, for all her puritanism, was no innocent: she was well aware, largely through the gossip among noble lady friends, of the snares that could be laid by designing females. From the outset she was suspicious of Mme Bouchaud. Elgin described his hostess as too young for her husband, much more gay and 'only a little painted'. She was very sociable and had a public day every Tuesday. 'She is fond of cards' wrote Elgin, 'but not so bad as you suppose, and her conversation is very good.' The Bouchauds prevailed upon the young man to join them at the Longchamp races. Mme Bouchaud warned him against the dangerous ladies who might invite him to parties, especially a certain young Countess of some notoriety who would, as Mme Bouchaud tartly remarked, '*imprinteront sans ceremonie ma bourse et ma personne.*' All of this Elgin reported to his mother, leaving her with the disturbing picture of the aged Professor and his young and attractive wife sharing their home with her virginal son. Martha was not reassured, especially when she learned that an exchange of gifts had taken place with Madame: Elgin giving a pair of opera glasses (better made in England) for a watch. Elgin's relations with the Bouchauds were briefly upset when Lavaux got drunk and started to abuse the Professor, refusing to serve at table when Elgin his master was not present. The incident ended when Lavaux dissolved in tears and all was made up.

One way in which Martha, like Janet, could tell how her son was spending his time was the number of his requests for money. As long as these were modest there could not be much gambling, drinking or womanising. Elgin in his early months in Paris was very economy conscious, making frequent calculations of his expenses. He feared they would come 'very high, not less then £450 per year', of which £300 went on board at the Bouchauds. But the overall figure crept upward and his first year in Paris cost £600. This was ominous. As Elgin's expenditures thus rose, Martha proposed to give up her carriage as an economy measure, an oblique rebuke: Elgin begged her to keep it. She sent him Gibbon's *Decline and fall of the Roman Empire*, lately published but warned him not to let it be generally known that he was reading such a Godless book.

Martha was reassured when in addition to his religious observances, Elgin sought out and enjoyed the company of older men of learning and achievement. Among these was Dr. William Robertson, of the University of Edinburgh, a historian and one of the illuminati of the Scottish Enlightenment, who reported warmly of Elgin to Martha. Robertson became a valued friend: Elgin read his *Charles V* with much interest. He also visited Benjamin Franklin shortly before the celebrated American returned home.

On 6 April came the news that Ailesbury had succeeded in getting Elgin's commission: he had been made an Ensign in the third Regiment of Guards. This meant that luckily he was officially on leave. The Duke of Argyll, colonel-in-chief of Elgin's regiment, was in Paris, and the new Ensign was able to drop a hint about extended leave so as to complete his continental studies. The Duke promised to facilitate the matter; Elgin for his part now added to his studies, fortifications and the drawing of military plans. Ailesbury continued his good offices by putting a word in the ear of the King himself, thus helping to ensure that there was no difficulty concerning Elgin's leave from his regiment. At the same time, however, the idea of a diplomatic career was still in the air. By learning, the *'forts et foibles'* of France, Britain's greatest rival, Elgin was laying the basis for a possible career abroad.

In the midst of his Parisian preoccupations Elgin was giving some thought to the estate at Broomhall. He was gratified by its general finances, with the lime works and the family port of Charlestown doing well and hoped that this prosperity would not make him extravagant. It did, however, have the effect of making him want to acquire more land. He was aware that the estate he had inherited was by no means homogenous. There were many gaps, of land lying in other ownerships, each of which could, and did, produce problems, access and drainage being the most pressing.

But he was determined for the time being to make his studies his main concern, partly for career reasons and to please his mother, and partly to try to sublimate his sexual tension. His classes and reading became heavily demanding as he sought to cover more and more ground. Gradually however his social life extended, partially because such contacts were necessary as part of his learning. But he was a poor card player and an indifferent dancer. He was presented to the King of France at Versailles, describing to his mother in glowing terms the Palace, its gardens and the Grand Trianon, but reporting that the apartments were full of a great crowd of blackguards.

The French Catholic way of life continued both to fascinate and repel him. The Grande Fête Dieu brought three days of magnificent processions to Paris. The Host, hung with the richest tapestries, passed through the streets while the houses were decorated and the devout placed altars at their doors, while the Curé or Abbé gave the benediction to the people. Elgin thought the spectacle impressive, but noted that householders were fined if they did not decorate their homes, and like many a Protestant before and after him, Elgin wondered how all this related to the simplicity of our Saviour. On the other hand Elgin was amazed and pleased by the gay, happy spirit of the peasantry when he saw them *en fete* at a wedding; this he contrasted with the English view that they were deeply oppressed.

Searching for guidance on the subject of his relations with women he read a novel by Francis Brooke, called *Lady Julia Mandeville*. In its hero he saw someone very like himself, 'an inexperienced youth, with lively passions.' Lady Julia's young man found his solution in a mature woman of perception and sympathy who introduced him into society and gave him advice and warnings concerning its pitfalls. Elgin felt a need for such a woman but in French society did not know where to look. He sensed the delicacy of consulting his mother on such a matter, but still did so. He felt embattled by his own feelings and by what he saw happening around him in Paris where, the object of most young men was to become the gallant of some married woman. He asked her whether Lady Holderness might help him in his search. Martha's suspicions that Mme Bouchaud might have made advances were revived, but Elgin denied this absolutely. Martha's letters contained exactly the admonitions of Janet's, a generation earlier. Martha conceded that a patroness would be helpful and suggested the Duchesse d'Orleans, but Elgin felt his French, his dancing and his card playing to be inadequate.

Over Christmas 1785 he was desperately homesick. With the Bouchauds in bed, he made his way alone to Notre Dame where the Archbishop of Paris was to say Midnight Mass. The ceremonial surrounding the Archbishop still shocked his puritan soul a little, but he comforted himself with the thought that God would see good intentions behind the display. He was missing having raisins and almonds under his pillow on Christmas morning, going to kiss his mother and accompanying her to communion. Fighting against his sense of pending sin he attended communion in the Ambassador's chapel, finding himself the only male among twenty ladies.

Poor Martha was by now in a state of terrible anxiety for her son, both for his morals and his health, fearing the asthma would return. Though she was gratified with the accounts reaching her from the Duchess of Buccleuch and others, of her handsome and charming son and his social success, these too contributed to her anxieties. His letters had become fewer and shorter. She deeply distrusted Lord Dorset, the Ambassador and his mistress, 'la Baccelli', warning her son against them. Professor Hill at St. Andrews, who had maintained a correspondence with Elgin, and who now had his younger brother James in charge, was, she said, being neglected. Martha urged Elgin to remove himself to a German Court which would be 'a better place for your mind and your morals.' His kinsmen, the Duke of Roxburgh, Lord Dartmouth and Lord Ailesbury, urged that he would get better instruction both on law and on military matters in Germany, believing the Germans to be more manly and upright than the French. When Elgin suggested that he should leave the Bouchauds and live in an hotel Martha was further alarmed. On the other hand she enjoyed receiving the Paris gossip.

Elgin was caught in a lonely struggle with the sexual flame, made the more searing by the seductive gestures of attractive women clearly willing to yield to so pleasing a young man, or even to seize the initiative and carry him off. Most young Englishmen abroad released all this tension casually, but in Elgin it built up to a terrible pressure. The ever watchful admonitory vision of his mother and confidante was always in his mind and prayers, together with that of Ailesbury on whose good opinion his career prospects and those of his brother depended.

The crisis came in September 1786 when, at the age of twenty, Elgin had an affair. Later he fled to Dijon, from whence he wrote to his mother explaining the whole business. She was filled with anguish and horror. 'Many young Creatures like you', she wrote 'have been duped by an Artfull Woman, and raised to that Paroxism of Delirium, that they would gladly sacrifice every prospect in time and Eternity for what they fancy mutual happiness.' Although the woman is not named, we know that she was a great beauty, one who had been an adulteress and kept mistress before her marriage. Elgin had written her letters and made her presents. His letters she declined to return. Mercifully Elgin had refused her invitation to run off with her, but Martha feared that Major Boyd, Elgin's friend in the matter, might not be able to retrieve the letters. If the woman persists, wrote Martha, 'You have nothing for it, my Dear Child, but flight—if the memory of your Dear Father is dear to you, or the Life of your Miserable Mother, who would gladly give up hers to save you from ruin.' At all costs, she said, Elgin's guardians and sponsors, and especially Lord Ailesbury, being of such high moral strain, must not know. Martha reminded her errant son that his fortune was small, and that he would have to rely in life in large measure on the interest of powerful friends, which would depend entirely on his character: if he lost that he lost everything. And would greatly damage the future of his brothers. Major Boyd seems to have been successful over the letters, perhaps, as Martha suggested, by threatening to approach the woman's husband. Nevertheless the young Elgin did flee, first to Dijon, then Geneva and finally to Dresden.

Elgin's sponsors, headed by Ailesbury, were of the strait-laced party around the King and Queen. In particular if Elgin were to aim at a diplomatic career, where postings were very much a question of royal approval, the young man had to be exemplary in the eyes of their Majesties. It was Martha's great fear that Elgin, whose best future probably lay in diplomacy, might destroy his chances by involvement in scandal. She worried too that Ailesbury, whose support had been so valuable, and who was the direct route to royal favour, might feel betrayed and drop Elgin. After a period of listening anxiously for signs that news of the affair had reached England, Martha was able gradually to relax, with the matter successfully hushed up. Engrossed in her four children she described herself as 'like a sentry on a watch-tower', with 'four points I am continually studying.'

Martha was anxious too that Elgin should finally make up his mind about his career. There was correspondence with Ailesbury about whether Thomas should seek to enter politics through the House of Lords. As a Scottish peer the only way he could gain a seat in the Upper House would be as one of the sixteen Scottish representative peers provided for in the Act of Union of 1707, chosen from among the body of the Scottish peers at the time of each general election. Ailesbury advised on how this might be managed. He assured Elgin that his youth (he was nearly twenty-one) would be no bar. He urged Elgin to stay above the virulent party politics then prevailing, and to present himself as a man not involved in faction, though of course he would have to seek support within the prevailing system of alliances.

Dresden now became Elgin's continental base; he spent something like a year there, on and off. He found learning German heavy going, but bent himself to the task. He fraternised with notable personages, including ministers. Various trips were made to Switzerland, to Saxony (where he dined with the Elector), to Berlin, to the Prussian Camp at Breslau, to Hanover and to Brunswick. On 20 July 1787 he came of age. To mark his manhood he had a full-length portrait of himself painted in oils. The artist, Anton Graff of Dresden depicted him as an Ensign in the Guards, in scarlet tunic wearing his single epaulette. An English artist later made a drawing of this original in which Elgin is shown leaning on his sword in a most unmilitary pose of studied nonchalance, his legs gracefully crossed. The drawing shows a handsome young milord, between whom and the ladies there could certainly be strong mutual attraction. The almost cavorting posture shows an engaging degree of self-parody which could hardly have reassured his mother. He made friends with intellectuals and pseudo-intellectuals, including Johann Lavater the celebrated authority on physiognomy: Martha hoped Lavater would give a reading of Elgin's face.

Even in Germany the female danger was present, and the presentable young Elgin was a good deal pursued. He told his mother that he had taken to heart the lesson of Paris, and in order to reassure her recounted at length another attempt to ensnare him. 'It is my ill fortune rather than my fault', he told his mother in jest, 'that I have only to show myself to excite tender passions. *Veni, vidi, vici.*'

On 19 October 1787 Elgin returned to England. He had dug far more deeply into European learning, especially concerning the nature and law of states, that was common among milords. He had met scholars of high achievement, as well as being brought into the company of ministers and princes. He was fluent in French and well acquainted with the life of Britain's greatest rival: he knew the Germanic states and had acquired something of their language. He had learned a good deal about the world, its snares and its devices.

But his mother and Ailesbury were worried how he would behave in the next year or so, a period critical for his career. As a junior officer in the Guards, and as a young man about town, he would be exposed to the evils of the clubs and the dangers of the card table, as well as to the fruit shops in St.James Street which were notorious places of *rendez-vous* with whores. Both places had earlier been bitingly caricatured by Hogarth. Ailesbury expressed concerned over 'the trials he must experience during the coming winter ... his character (reputation) will be decided for ever in the course of it by his conduct.' The mentor believed that Elgin's fellow Guards officers would try to bring him down to their level, sharing with his King a deep contempt for the *Ton*. Elgin was inept enough to write to Ailesbury from a fruit shop, which as Ailesbury remarked somewhat tartly, 'is the very centre or headquarters of the *Ton*.'

It was no time for Martha to relax her vigilance. She took a house in Downing Street and Elgin moved in with her. He continued his studies, making elaborate notes on the Prussian and Russian armies and reading a good deal. Ailesbury, after inquiry, advised on the officers of Elgin's regiment, suggesting those he should be friendly with and those he should avoid. He held out the debauching of Lady Erroll's son in the Guards as an awful warning.

Professor Hill continued to write from St. Andrews. He urged Elgin to study the constitution of Great Britain and to acquire practical knowledge of it so that in the future he might use such knowledge 'to your own credit, and for the benefit of your country.' Hill, like Ailesbury, was anxious that Elgin should become one of the representative Scottish peers and so involve himself in public affairs.

Under such conditions Elgin was able to keep Ailesbury's approbation. Ailesbury was now deeply concerned for the Royal family, for the monarch had been overtaken by the first bout of what appeared to be madness. Martha received accounts from Ailesbury of the course of the King's illness and the delicate question of a Regency. He recounted how, the King, fearing that the Queen might be shocked by his emaciated condition, tried to button his coat over a pillow.

Ailesbury had his own troubles. He wrote freely of these to Martha, like Elgin himself he turned to her over every circumstance of his family life—she even chose his senior servants and his son's tutors. Current problems included one of his daughters becoming stiff and censorious, the other a woman of the world; neither got on with her stepmother. More seriously, Ailesbury's heir had become withdrawn, solitary and hypochondriacal. The reason for this was that the boy had been raised by elderly tutors in absolute solitude. Ailesbury, fearing the corrupting effect of schools and colleges and of servants, adopted this course after the death of his eldest son.

Late in 1788 Elgin, much to Ailesbury's approval, went north to Broomhall to involve himself directly with the affairs of his estate for the first time. The agent of the Fifth Earl and his trustees, John Grant, a great character, had died, making it necessary to find a successor. Soon this sanguine young man began to think of a programme of development, just as his father had done before him. There were some eighty proprietors of the land of the parish of Dunfermline of which Elgin was by far the largest. Though the estate had become profitable once more, especially through the limeworks and the port of Charlestown, there was much that could still be done. The estate roads were in poor condition, the improving practices of high farming had not been adopted. Was there the possibility of acquiring coal-bearing lands to supply the limeworks? The house at Broomhall was inconvenient and still in bad order (although Martha had recently had water piped to the kitchen).

Elgin, on leave from his military duties, brought home with him a recruiting party from the regiment, consisting of a sergeant and a corporal. The former was highly literate, writing letters that would have done credit to an officer. The lower limit of stature was five foot six inches, with very few recruits approaching six feet. First three men claiming to be tailors enlisted but they turned out to be colliers in the employ of a local mine owner, Sir Archibald Hope. The old Scottish system of collier serfdom was still so strong he could reclaim them after they had served one month in prison for their deception. Then in another case a collier proved himself to be a free man and so joined the regiment. As the weather was bad, and there was much unemployment, the recruiting went well.

The question of Elgin's seeking election as a representative Scottish peer now came to a head. Ailesbury continued to approve of this plan, recognising that as a member of the House of Lords Elgin's claim to promotion as an army officer, and of an appointments in the diplomatic service would thereby be strengthened. It could also have the effect of opening the prospect of a career in politics. But Elgin's streak of wilfulness again showed itself here, as it had done earlier when he insisted on living in Paris. He was attracted to the group, led by Lord Selkirk and Lord Kinnaird, who wished the Scottish peerage to be independent of the system of political control run by Henry Dundas since 1784. This was Elgin's only brush with the radicalism of the day in which a good many young contemporaries including Lord Selkirk were caught up. Professor Hill held the view that 'the independence of the Peerage is a most interesting object to all who have the honour of belonging to that body', and so may have helped to inspire such thoughts in Elgin. Ailesbury, as a loyal King's man, anxious that the King should continue to out-manoeuvre the Rockingham Whigs, was aghast at Elgin's independent attitude. He told Elgin that he must either disassociate himself from the Selkirk/Kinnaird group or resign his Commission in the Guards, for he would have no future there if he persisted in his support of the 'independents'. The matter remained unresolved until the General Election of 1790 when, as was customary, all sixteen representative posts were to be voted upon.

Elgin, now aged twenty-four, entered the contest with zest. He enjoyed the personal politicking among his fellow peers, savouring the passionate approach of some and the cool calculation of others. The negotiations, alliances, groupings and awarding of proxies had begun as early as April; the matter was not settled until late July. The Dundas interest was marshalled with skill, especially by the Duke of Buccleuch with whom Elgin and his family were friendly. Elgin was still loath to align himself totally with the Dundas party, being anxious to be able 'to act in some degree independently', deciding 'with steadiness and on my own grounds.' The machinations were so elaborate that at times Elgin, a new hand at the game, became confused in the welter of tacit agreements and secret bargainings. A somewhat tenuous distinction between ministerial *influence* and ministerial *direction* was made in the attempt to relieve the tension. In order to end this backstage intriguing, Pitt had been willing to accept between four and six 'independent' peers out of the sixteen. In the midst of this dangerous ground Elgin seems to have shown considerable skill of manoeuvre. The election meeting was held under austere conditions in the Palace of Holyrood House, the peers seated on wooden benches, with much pushing and shoving among the spectators. There were 33 peers present, of whom 30 were candidates. It was a considerable triumph for Elgin to be elected. He was to survive successive General Elections until 1807. Martha thought that he had involved himself too deeply, but he had clearly enjoyed himself. Also he felt that, though in the end elected as part of the Dundas group, he had displayed 'the true principles of honour and Independence', not tying himself hand and foot to the ministry. Thus ended Elgin's brief aberration from Toryism. As a member of the House of Lords he now had a voice in Parliament, together with an opportunity to make his presence felt in national affairs.

Perhaps exhilarated by the peerage election, Elgin now began to take a more expansive view of his estate at Broomhall. On impulse on hearing that the property of Mr. Wellwood of Pitliver (adjacent to his own) was coming up for sale he immediately sent for his lawyer, and instructed him to make an offer. In so doing

Elgin wished to remove an obnoxious family, the source of endless disputes over the years. 'But chiefly', he wrote to his mother, 'the command of the water would enable me to make Charlestown a second Birmingham'. Here was the beginning of Elgin's forward policy for Broomhall that was planned to outdo that of his father. He took this step without consultation with Martha, informing her of it after it had been settled, though with profound apologies.

Elgin and his brother Andrew had in their respective ways escaped the more oppressive side of their mother's surveillance. But poor James was now in deep depression over his failure to live up to maternal expectations, to which were added invocations of his father's memory. He had fallen into extravagance and perhaps worse ('vice' is mentioned) at Oxford and was now going through agonies of conscience. 'My mother frequently talks of the profligacy of the present age', he wrote to Elgin. 'But how', he continued, 'can My Mother be a judge of this? The Education of a very few young Women permit them to know anything of young men. She found in My Father everything her heart could desire; She saw in him every perfection that Love, Humility, Modesty and Manliness brought forth and she fondly conceived that she would see the same perfection and the same Virtues blazon forth in his children ... His reason had got the better of all Youthful Passions and he appeared to her (as indeed to everybody) a nearly perfect work of God.' Elgin did his best to reassure James of the love and dedication of their mother.

For his own part, he was now an officer in the Guards and a member of the House of Lords. It was time to make progress with his diplomatic ambitions.

CHAPTER 3

The Precocious Diplomat and the Ardent State Developer

Elgin's performance in the 1790 election of Scottish peers had brought him to the favourable attention of Dundas, always on the look-out for promising young men who might become part of his system of political management. Dundas, having formed 'a very respectable opinion' of Elgin, was prepared to try him out in diplomacy.

Already, in the same year, Elgin had gained his first experience of this strange world. He had been attached briefly to the embassy of Alleyne Fitzherbert (Lord St. Helens) at the Hague. Elgin busied himself gathering information on the trade of Holland and the adjacent Austrian Netherlands. He developed something of a system of contacts to keep him informed, for his government was greatly concerned about the terms of access for British trade to Holland and the continent. There were a great many conflicting claims of maritime right and commercial interest between Britain and Holland. It was important to resolve or at least to ease these in the interests of the Anglo-Dutch alliance. France had long been the traditional enemy, and though since the outbreak of the revolution in 1789 that country had been temporarily unable to indulge in foreign adventures, there was always the danger that she would do so, especially in the direction of the Low Countries.

But there was a more immediate threat to the peace of Europe. It arose from the chronic rapacity of eighteenth century monarchs, stimulated by the decline that was clearly overtaking Turkey. Catherine II of Russia and Joseph II of Austria, sensing the weakness of the Ottoman Empire, had conspired to seize her European territories and divide them between themselves: they had taken several Turkish provinces in campaigns of 1788-9. But Frederick William of Prussia, being no less greedy, and seeing an opportunity, in his turn, demanded a share. He prepared for war, entering into alliances with Poland and with Turkey herself against Russia and Austria. At the height of the crisis in 1790 Joseph II had died, to be succeeded by his brother. The new Emperor of Austria, Leopold II, accepted the mediation of Britain and the Dutch. He did so because he was faced with revolt in the Austrian Netherlands. Britain and the Dutch guaranteed Leopold's continued dominion over the Netherlands on condition that he restored their constitution; in return Leopold agreed to abandon his aggressive alliance with Catherine.

This was the setting in which the young Elgin found himself at the Hague in 1790. His earnest studies of the civil law under Professors Hill and Bouchaud as 'the law of nature as applied by an enlightened people to their situation', now encountered the *realpolitik* of Europe. He soon learned that Britain had two objectives on the continent, namely access and equipoise. Britain needed trading opportunity, and she needed a Europe in which the many and variegated components were so balanced that war was minimised by each power being held in check by the manipulation of the others. Political events, on the surface at least, seemed always to spring from the arbitrary will of rulers, especially as they concerned the acquisition of territories. And yet the royal will could be influenced by courtiers' advice: hence the need to understand a court in terms of its changing personalities. Partly for this reason monarchs habitually used noblemen like Elgin himself in their relations with one another.

Later, in 1791, when Elgin was twenty-five, Dundas and Pitt needed someone to go quickly to Vienna to the court of Leopold II, where Sir Robert Keith the Minister had been taken ill. Elgin, having gained further credit with Dundas by his first speech in the House of Lords, was offered the Vienna job which he accepted with enthusiasm. He attended a tête-a-tête dinner with Pitt after which the prime minister wrote out Elgin's instructions. But the Turkish situation had taken a new turn. The Empress Catherine, though under the duress of the Triple Alliance of Britain, Holland and Prussia, was ready to make peace with the Sultan, but insisted on retaining certain relatively minor territories. This the King of Prussia rejected. George III and his government, depending heavily on its alliance with Prussia for its general European policy, was now in a very difficult position. There loomed the prospect of a war against Russia, conducted in alliance with Prussia and Turkey. Such a war, especially with the Turks as allies, would be desperately unpopular in Britain. What was to be done? Could Catherine be made more amenable by persuading Leopold to join the Triple Alliance?

It was to help bring Leopold round that Elgin was sent to Vienna as Envoy Extraordinary. The Emperor had gone to Italy to pacify his provinces and there Elgin followed him. The King of Prussia sent his ruling favourite, Colonel Bischoffswerder to support Elgin's representations to Leopold. But the Colonel exhibited only temerity, vanity and absurdity. Leopold played for time. He thought he had much to gain by sticking with Catherine, for his armies were still on Turkish territory and the Empress of Russia had resumed war against that country. By July Sir Robert Keith returned to his post and Elgin, having found himself in a situation with no hope of success in his primary objective, was able to emerge with credit. Lord Grenville the new Foreign Secretary, declared himself impressed with Elgin's knowledge of 'the Emperor's manner of conversing', congratulated him on the talents he had shown in his months at the Austrian court, in making contacts and acquiring intelligence, and hinted at further diplomatic appointments.

Elgin's second assignment came quickly. The King had spoken to Grenville about the advisability of an Envoy Extraordinary at Brussels in the Austrian Netherlands, that buffer territory against France, now torn by revolution, and still dangerous. In September 1791 Dundas sounded Elgin about his availability. Elgin welcomed the proposal, for Brussels was a convenient posting making it possible for him to make fairly frequent attendances at the House of Lords, to keep in touch with the course of events at the British nerve centre, and to visit Broomhall. Dundas described him as 'although not very rich, ... easy in his circumstances' and so was motivated 'not by the desire for emolument, but to assist in the public service.' All this was set out in a letter from Dundas to Grenville, read aloud to Elgin and approved by him.

By 1792 the Austrian Netherlands had become an area to be closely watched. There was the fear that revolutionary France would make a thrust (north and eastward) to the mouths of the Rhine and further, thus setting western Europe in a turmoil and threatening Britain. While the French initiative was anxiously awaited, the monarchy was overthrown in August with a massacre of noble families in the Tuileries. Elgin from Brussels wrote to Grenville with a scheme for 'putting into your Lordship's hand what means may present themselves of saving the Royal Family of France, and securing that most essential merit to England', offering to go to Paris himself for the purpose. Nothing came of this gallant proposal.

It was in Brussels as part of this Austrian bulwark against the French revolution that Elgin really discovered the nature of an envoy's job. It was a varied one, consisting of gathering intelligence through discreet conversations and paid agents, generating favourable attitudes toward Britain and her interests at the Court to which he was accredited, and doing a range of odd jobs like dealing with Royalist Frenchmen seeking asylum and offering their services. Information gathering could be a seedy and uncertain business, made the more difficult by George III's eager following of events. Interpreting events at the Austrian Court could be no less invidious, involving a knowledge of the delicate play of personalities.

In November the Duke of Brunswick retreated in the face of Dumouriez's revolutionary army. Elgin was in a quandary whether to leave Brussels with the Court as the Austrians suggested. He did so. He discovered he was trusted by the formidable Austrian General Mack who favoured Anglo-Austrian co-operation. In dealing with the British, the General said he wished Elgin to be 'the organ of my ideas, of my sentiments, of my griefs and of my hopes', entrusting him with highly secret papers. Elgin, having had discussions with two British envoys, Lord Malmesbury and Sir Morton Eden, discovered they had widely differing views: and informed Grenville. Elgin's last communication to the Foreign Minister from Brussels (to which he had returned when the counter-offensive of the allies against the French was pressed), was dated 1 July 1794. In it he stated his 'clear conviction that, on the one hand, France, in men and resources, was infinitely more formidable than the generality of intelligence received'. This was a highly perceptive view. On the other hand, Elgin believed, the Court of Vienna should not to be trusted, and dependence on Austria was highly dangerous. This was due to the sort of political and military intrigue that had now discredited General Mack. Moreover the Austrian army was held in contempt by the British: this view Elgin, having spent a month with the Austrians in the field, shared. He had been Envoy to Brussels for almost three years.

When first appointed to Vienna, Elgin had begun a developmental programme for Broomhall: this he pushed forward with great vigour during the Brussels years. The same urge that had driven his father now seized hold of him, namely to raise the productivity of the estate by participating fully in the age of high farming, while at the same time playing the part of the paternal aristocrat with his tenants and workers. By this time, due to the good stewardship of the late factor, Grant, and the estate managers, as well as the economies of the Dowager Martha, the burden of the debt incurred by Charles had been lifted. Indeed, Charles' projects had in the longer run succeeded beyond expectation. The lime had proved to be of very high quality, lying in a thirty feet ridge high along the foreshore, so that 80 to 90,000 tons of stone were quarried annually by more than 200 men. Some 1,300 separate cargoes of lime left Charlestown each year, with thirty to forty vessels lying in the port during the peak summer months. The principal markets were along the Firths of Forth and Tay and up the North-East coast where Scotland's high farming regions were located. The Broomhall venture had, indeed, greatly stimulated the economy of the parish.

Thomas proposed to go much further. Aware that his limeworks consumed large quantities of coal, he decided the time had come to secure his own supply on his own terms and with regular deliveries. He bought up more than 900 acres of coal bearing land at West and Midbalbridge, Clune, Liscar and Rosebank and opened new workings. A good deal of land had been acquired earlier on ambiguous terms from the Wellwood family, with whom the Elgins had long feuded: much of the purchase price was in the form of debt to the Wellwood family and later their trustees. Elgin built a wagon way four miles long to connect his collieries with his limeworks—a very ambitious programme which involved large borrowing and a heavy burden of interest. Martha was distraught at the thought of another long period during which debt would bear down upon the family.

But Elgin's imagination was inflamed. He had plans to build a new harbour a little to the west of Charlestown for the export of his coal: and a canal from the new harbour to Dunfermline. By such a scheme Elgin believed he could command the sea carriage and much of the land carriage of Dunfermline burgh and parish. In the end this grand scheme fell, difficulties of borrowing and carrying such an additional burden of debt proved insurmountable.

Even so the Elgin enterprises had a profound economic and social effect on the Bruce family's corner of Scotland. The two ministers of Dunfermline parish, though applauding 'the extensive circulation of money' thus brought about, objected to the character of the incomers. 'The profligate' they wrote, 'repair to these works, where they are under no restraint.' They corrupted the young of the parish, damaging 'the morals of unguarded youth.' Moreover these newcomers were themselves damaged by 'their unseasonable labour ... hurtful to their constitutions.' The Ministers thus, like others of their kind, found themselves in a dilemma, approving of the jobs and wealth created, but deeply concerned about the effect on the Godliness, coherence and morality of their parish as it became subjected by Elgin to the forces of development.

To these fears Elgin responded in the only constructive way open to him, namely through education. The Ministers had said: 'Education is too often neglected. Many cannot read. Proprietors are not sufficiently attentive to the instruction of youth ...' so Elgin built his own school at Broomhall. In this he was creating a new role for himself as paternal aristocrat.

For Elgin's improvements on the land the parish Ministers had only praise. He gave new leases to most of his tenant farmers, building good farm houses and offices for them. The fields were neatly subdivided with wellmade stone walls or hedgerows and ditches. Trees had already been planted by John Grant between 1780 and 1790 in belts and clumps to act as windbreaks and ornaments. The cost of all this was, of course, reflected in raised rentals, but such landlord leadership had a positive effect on tenant husbandry.

But as with the quarries and mines, there was another side to such landed improvement. The farms rented were relatively small, economically capable of growing oats and barley, though not wheat. Leases could be for up to fifteen years, but often did not run for more than five. The high rent policy of the estate led to a speedy turnover of tenants as many failed. The danger was that the chancier kind of tenant who would take the heart out of the land would be attracted by the Elgin policy. At this time it does appear that the rental revenue from the Broomhall lands exceeded that from the industrial developments.

Such energetic developments of the estate could not fail to impress those with whom Elgin's career chances lay, for the improvement of one's inheritance was a highly approved activity. It meant also that he was a man of business in the private as well as the public sense. The fact that his most extravagant plans had been shelved because of their cost saved Elgin from the serious difficulties involved in servicing such a debt, which would have put the family back into the kind of stringency with which it had long been familiar. These almost incredibly ambitious intentions may well have been the first serious sign that Elgin was not strong on financial judgment.

Elgin had found time to interest himself in aspects of Scottish public affairs. In 1792 he became involved in the design of a new bridewell (prison) proposed for Edinburgh, and corresponded with Jeremy and Samuel Bentham on the panopticon principle.

After the Brussels appointment Elgin's diplomatic career stalled for some two years, between 1794 and 1796. He spent the time partly in London, where he attended the House of Lords, and partly in Scotland. But now a new candidate for heavy expenditure arose. The old house, originally built in 1702, had been inadequate for some time to Elgin's needs and view of his station: he began to think that his development of the estate should be accompanied by a rebuilding of Broomhall. His mother took exception to the plan, stating flatly that 'a prodigious house would be a monstrous burden.' However, in 1796 construction began on the new house: it was to incorporate some part of the old. Elgin's architect was Thomas Harrison (1749-1829), a shy, reserved and abrupt Yorkshireman of humble origins, whose design of Chester Castle had become the basis of his reputation. He worked in the Greek style, having studied classical models at Rome. The choice of Harrison reflected Elgin's predilection, made strong by his education, for Greek culture. His decision to rebuild Broomhall, on top of his already heavy borrowings marked the beginning of the financial pressures that were to affect the rest of his life, as well as those of his son and grandson.

Even more expense was undertaken, this time connected with Elgin's military ambitions. In September 1794 Henry Dundas wrote to leading landowners, including Elgin, suggesting that, because of the invasion threat from the French, they might raise Fencible Regiments for home service in Britain and Ireland. Elgin responded promptly and in November he was authorised to form a regiment. Lady Rachel Drummond, Elgin's aunt, had already planned to raise the Drummond Fencibles, but finding the expense too great suggested that Elgin take the Regiment over. This he did, becoming its sponsor and commander. His men were kitted out in Highland dress and soon with Elgin as Lieutenant Colonel became known as the Elgin Fencibles. The regiment was raised in Perth where Elgin briefly got involved with the Provost's wife. It was supplied with a band and presented with standards. The men were largely organised by pensioned Warrant Officers from the regular army and officers from the local gentry. Andrew Carnegie's uncle was a member of the regiment. Elgin marched it to Liverpool and by June it was at Armagh, ready to contain the restless Irish and to repel any French attack. By November 1795 Elgin was back at Broomhall having shown himself responsive to the wishes of the government. To meet the debt he borrowed £6,000 from Greenwood and Cox, military bankers in London on a bond. It was in a sense an investment in his future career.

His diplomacy was resumed in December 1795. This time he was sent to Berlin as British Minister Plenipotentiary to the Court of Prussia. His mission was to strengthen the will of the Prussian Court against revolutionary France. Prussia could be a useful military ally, and was indeed a crucial element in British continental strategy. But she was unstable in her allegiances and enthusiasms. The Court was a debauched place, where the play of favourites and mistresses around King Frederick William II was notorious. Elgin had to acquaint himself with such matters and report them to Grenville, mixing personalia with military and political intelligence. He had to gather his information under constant police surveillance: 'Nothing can be more active,' wrote Elgin, 'than the police against foreign Ministers. Everything we do and everyone we see is known.' So complex did matters become that Grenville, secretly sent a certain M.de Luc to enter into negotiations with the Duke of Brunswick, commander of the Prussian army. When Elgin heard of this, he was highly indignant, both because he had been bypassed and because his position in Berlin would be undermined when Prussian trouble-makers put it about that he had been humiliated by his own government.

Elgin had other trials at Berlin. He was still unmarried, though it would seem that he sought consolation with a Madame Ferchenbeck, a frequent visitor to his house. His querulous health, described as rheumatism, laid him low from time to time, prompting visits to German spas, especially the baths at Poplitz, though he could use his health as a means of forestalling unwanted visitors. The hydropathic movement with its water-cure for rheumatism, was popular in Germany at the time. Elgin's pains occurred variously in his chest and in his arms.

In July 1798 he learned from a foreign *Gazette* that his brother James had drowned while crossing the River Don in Yorkshire. His floating hat had served as identification. Thomas had long been close to James, constantly mediating between him and their mother. No longer did Jamie need to fret himself over the extent to which he had failed his father's memory. Martha was prostrate by James' death, and her fears for Thomas' health rose almost to panic level. She now had only two of her sons living, one of them in India and the eldest in Berlin, unmarried and unsettled.

Mercifully, however, she had found a new responsibility, though in some ways a difficult one. Matters had become deeply strained in the royal household, with the Prince of Wales and his wife, Princess Caroline on bad terms. In spite of this, however, Caroline on 7 January 1796 bore a daughter, Charlotte Augusta, who was heiress presumptive to the throne. Later in the year her parents separated. The question arose as to how the child was to be raised. She was in effect taken out of the hands of her warring parents by the King and Queen and Martha, Dowager Countess of Elgin, high in the esteem of Ailesbury the Queen's Chamberlain, was made Governess to the child. An establishment was provided at Blackheath near Montague House where Princess Caroline was settled. Martha thus entered upon a kind of proxy motherhood, caring for the only legitimate child produced by any of the royal brothers. It was a highly delicate situation, with Queen Charlotte in effect virtually adopting her namesake and placing her in Martha's care as foster mother. Hannah More, that famous old maid, full of evangelical zeal, became a friend and correspondent of Martha's, generously offering advice on the raising of the Princess.

Elgin lived in some state in Berlin, providing through his generous entertainment a centre for British visitors. He was greatly interested in wine, having by 1810 laid down 7,800 bottles in the cellars at Broomhall. Years later some of the claret and burgundy was taken by his son James to Jamaica and Canada. Though the petty aspects of his job sometimes bored and frustrated him, and his military career having scarcely begun, he could feel that he was steadily advancing in the diplomatic service. He returned from Berlin in July 1798, once more greatly concerned about his health.

His forward policy at Broomhall had not flagged. Most of the old house had been pulled down and the new one was rising in its place under Thomas Harrison and his son. It was intended to be a fit abode for a member of the House of Lords, a diplomat of increasing standing, the head of an ancient line and the proprietor of a progressive estate. Though not comparable to the greatest houses of either England or Scotland, it was impressive. But it added a good deal to the debt incurred over the limeworks, the coal mines, the wagon way and the Fencibles. Financial pressure was beginning to converge with emotional needs and the necessity for an heir, pointing to marriage to a young woman of generous prospects.

CHAPTER 4

Marriage and the Embassy to Constantinople

The King, with his beloved only grandchild and heir presumptive to the throne in the care of Martha, dowager Countess of Elgin, was well aware of Elgin's career. When lucid he concerned himself continuously with the diplomacy of Europe, thus gravely complicating the lives of his Ministers. Though the American Revolution had contributed to the weakening of his personalised monarchy he was still powerful in the diplomatic field.

Suddenly the eastern Mediterranean became a focus of attention. In July 1798, the young Bonaparte, with the approval of the Directory, had invaded Egypt. In so doing he affronted and challenged Turkey, an ally for many generations. Indeed at that time the French were in the process of trying to modernise the Turkish army and navy. Egypt was part of the Ottoman Empire, and though ruled for centuries in an almost independent manner by the Mameluke Beys it was considered a proud possession. But even more sinister was the fear that France under its revolutionary leaders would seek to make much larger inroads into the Turkish Empire, if not to dismember it. On 1 August Nelson attacked the French fleet which was totally destroyed at the Battle of the Nile thus cancelling out Bonaparte's earlier victory at the Battle of the Pyramids. The French ambassador in Constantinople and his staff were escorted to the notorious Prison of the Seven Towers and war was declared on France. Bonaparte simply abandoned his stranded force, returned himself to France, his dream of Eastern splendour, of becoming the heir of the pharaohs, replaced by the problem of extricating his imprisoned army.

In western Europe the Turk was regarded as beyond the pale of civilisation: his was a barbarous country where gorgeous splendour rested upon the grossest subjugation of peoples. In the Turkish code there seemed no place for the attempts to limit the all-consuming fury of war by a degree of chivalry among an officer class, and by tactics aimed at limiting the blood-letting. Turkey was a vast reservoir of fearful diseases, including smallpox and the plague, from which Europeans sought to insulate themselves by a strict system of quarantine. Turkey was also the most powerful representative of a pagan faith which Christians had fought since the Crusades. The British Foreign Office and the Chancelleries of Europe regarded the Asiatic nations, in spite of their vast armies, as militarily negligible: Bonaparte had thought, quite correctly, that in occupying Egypt and the Levant there would be only feeble resistance from the rabble armies of the Porte. Indeed Turkey hardly counted—the reality of Bonaparte's action, apart from the lure of Empire, lay in an oblique attack on Britain and her access to

India. For Britain, on the other hand, with enormously extended supply lines to Egypt (almost twice as long as those of the French) and with no bases or facilities, an alliance with the Sultan could be invaluable.

So it was that the Ottoman Empire, once the great aggressive threat against Europe, had by Elgin's time become a danger to Europe in a quite different sense as a potential source of plunder, with whole provinces exposed to seizure by adjacent powers, Prussia, Austria and Russia.

These considerations caused George III to think that Britain should send a full ambassador to Constantinople to make the most of a favourable opportunity in Turkey. In November 1798 Elgin, at the suggestion of the King, wrote to Grenville proposing himself for the post. After discussion between Grenville and the King, Elgin, now thirty-two, was within a few days appointed Ambassador Extraordinary and Minister Plenipotentiary to the Sublime Porte of Selim III, Sultan of Turkey. To Elgin's great satisfaction he found himself closeted with what was in effect the inner cabinet, consisting of Pitt, Lords Grenville and Dundas, discussing Bonaparte's invasion of Egypt, and Britain's interests as related to Turkey and to access to India now threatened by the French. Because of the amplitude of these discussions it was thought unnecessary to draw up formal instructions for Elgin.

Elgin did not set out at once. Indeed it was not until nine months after his appointment that he and his party at last left for Constantinople. During this interval three things had happened. Elgin had at long last married, the British government had so acted as greatly to complicate his embassy, and Elgin had been inspired by Harrison his architect with a sense of mission concerning Greek sculpture and architecture.

Elgin's wedding, following a courtship of some four months, was on the 11th of March 1799: it was to be a cardinal event in his life. It was to last for nine years, during which time his career as a diplomat reached its peak, his collection of the Parthenon Marbles was largely made and his crushing misfortunes began.

His bride was Mary Hamilton Nisbet, daughter of a Scottish landowning family with wide aristocratic connections. An only child, she was an heiress with very large expectations whose favourite home, among several, was in East Lothian at Archerfield, once owned by the Benedictines. There was also the impressive estate of Biel near by, and that of Belhaven, together with town houses in Edinburgh and London. In addition Mary could expect to inherit Bloxholm Hall in Lincolnshire from a maiden aunt. Even though there were entails on much of these estates, Mary's expectations could hardly have failed to appeal to Elgin whose own estate was so seriously encumbered and whose taste for expenditure had risen steadily since his escape from his mother's economising control.

As a person Mary was no less attractive. She was twenty-one years old, twelve years younger than Elgin, with dark hair and eyes, a longish nose inherited from her mother and an attractive mouth. Her lively face was matched by a shapely figure, both of which had appealed to the young men of Edinburgh, where her social life had been based. She was skilled at the pianoforte, enjoyed concerts, was adept at whist, and loved Scottish reels. She was no great reader, but enjoyed entertaining novels. She liked to be the centre of attention, which position she could hold by her vivacity; she had an eye for a handsome man, very often reciprocated. Perhaps as an unconscious hint of her store of affection she lavished much attention on her five dogs. An addiction for nicknames caused her to scatter them about her family and friends. She called herself Poll and Elgin became Eggy. These often reflected her inner estimates of people, which was frequently acute and could be acerbic. She was on warm joking terms with her father, knowing his male strengths and weaknesses, and made her mother a close confidante.

There was another side to all this. Like Elgin she suffered from asthmatic 'choakings' from time to time, as well as being attacked by what she, again like Elgin, called rheumatism. Though wealthy and a big spender, she had a good eye for a household bargain, and was conscious of the comparative prices of things, a trait learned from her mother. But like other young ladies of her day she had had no real education. This meant that though she could show sound judgment, she could not really enter into Elgin's view of public affairs or of his place in them. Though far from being a child-wife, she could not penetrate to the level of *gravitas* in Elgin that gave rise to his reputation in some circles of being cold and reserved. This meant that though there was a love between them, and though she was to enter upon almost continuous pregnancy, she does not seem to have been able to lose herself in her feeling for Elgin.

Her father, in his early fifties, was an archetypal landed laird of the improving kind. Having served in the Third Dragoon Guards as a young man, in maturity he had remade the estate of Archerfield according to the best ideas and practice. As Member of Parliament for Haddington, a family seat, he maintained a London house in Portman Square. He was an excellent shot and was interested in wines and blue stories. Women of good flesh and blood he admired, referring to one so endowed as a 'Whapper'. A bluff man, he was impatient of formality and a perpetrator of puns. Mary encapsulated her father in the nickname 'Sir Phillip O'Kettle'. She joked about his eye for the ladies, partly as a tease of her strict mother. Elgin, it would seem, was somewhat frightened of his robust father-in-law, though in private he would amuse Poll by mimicking his dancing. Hamilton Nisbet provided Mary with a dowry of £10,000; Elgin received this however, not in the form of cash, but as a non-negotiable bond of the Earl of Selkirk which would provide him with annual interest only.

Mary's mother, daughter of Lord Robert Manners and granddaughter of the Duke of Rutland, was a patient and sympathetic person of cultured mind. She was a strict disciplinarian who had retained the deep affection of her only child. Mary used to remind her mother, of 'a certain birch rod, that used to live at the top of your bed!' Indeed Mrs. Hamilton Nisbet, with her sense of total rectitude and strict sabbatarianism, shared the same value system as the Dowager Countess of Elgin. Both also believed in economy and efficiency in the management of family affairs. Mary as bride, took her mother round the new Broomhall, seeking her advice in the decorating of the principal rooms, a challenge to which they jointly responded. Within four months of marriage Mary was pregnant, sealing the bond between mother and daughter. There was now the promise of a joint heir for the Hamilton Nisbet families and the Elgins.

Mary had enjoyed a good many suitors, but Elgin was probably the most eligible. He was a nobleman, handsome and polished in his manner, with the bearing of a man who had negotiated with emperors, kings and princes while representing his sovereign in Europe's centres of power, as well as sitting for Scotland in the House of Lords. He was a leading landowner of Fife with an impressively extended house. Though Mary's father might well have wondered how sound were Elgin's finances, Hamilton Nisbet seems to have been attracted by the prospect of both his daughter and his estates passing to a noble family.

The wedding was interrupted by a dramatic incident, the meaning of which left the guests mystified. During the ceremony Mary became intensely agitated, so much so that Bishop Sandford stopped the proceedings and insisted upon withdrawing to another room with the bride to ask what was wrong. All persuasion and entreaty that she should confide in him failed. She declared she had nothing to tell him, and so the marriage proceeded. Oblivious to this setback, eight or nine hundred lime and coal workers converged on Broomhall to mark the marriage, enjoying porter, whisky and reels.

Mary's confusion was hardly surprising, for in accepting Elgin she had also agreed to undertake a difficult and dangerous journey to Constantinople, with the risks of pirates, French warships and terrible diseases, together with several years of absence from home, as well as being expected to bear children in a distant and alien land. Mary had however read the *Turkish Embassy Letters* of her namesake Lady Mary Wortley Montague and was a good deal intrigued thereby.

Elgin, in pursuit of Mary, had offered to resign his ambassadorship. But Mary accepted him, embassy and all. She and her family hoped, as did Elgin himself, that this could prove a splendid career opportunity, leading perhaps to the Moscow embassy or when the war was settled, to the greatest prize of all, that of Paris. Were that to happen Elgin could expect to become a full member of the House of Lords and indeed reach the cabinet. They did not yet know that, trying to stabilise British relations with Turkey in the face of French deviousness, was to write in the sand.

As an imaginative young woman Mary could respond to the excitement and splendours of so exotic a mission, so far beyond the experience of most of her East Lothian and Edinburgh friends. But she knew she would be homesick for her parents, and made them promise to visit her in Constantinople. Elgin asked Grenville to delay the departure of the embassy so that he and Mary could learn each other's ways: to this Grenville assented. There was another reason for delay. In May and June, Mary became very ill, this being diagnosed by Sir Lucas Pepys as 'spasmodic asthma'. Elgin too was sick. He frightened Mary with the medicines with which he dosed himself.

Martha, given Mary's personality, person and prospects, together with Elgin's need, could hardly have disapproved of the marriage: Mary for her part saw her mother-in-law as a warm-hearted person, to whom she promised to report fully and frankly on Elgin's health. Martha presented Mary with a wreath of diamonds. She was pleased that Elgin had taken a wife who could provide him with an heir, as well as the prospect of a rich inheritance.

The interval of so many months before Elgin's arrival at Constantinople was to cost him a good deal. There was already some ambiguity about Britain's representation in Constantinople. Successive British governments, having chartered the Levant Company, giving it a monopoly of British trade in the Eastern Mediterranean, had, when it needed a diplomatic representative in Turkey, accepted a Levant Company nominee: indeed Elgin's own appointment had been approved by the Company. One of its employees, Spencer Smith, had represented both the Company and the British government in such minor diplomatic matters as had arisen. When Bonaparte attacked Egypt in the summer of 1798 Smith was told by the British government to seek a treaty of alliance with Turkey. Having lived long in the East Smith was in an excellent position to do this. He was a master of intrigue in the oriental fashion, and by matching the Turks at their own game earned their respect. He was backed up by a British military mission under General Koehler intended to modernise the Turkish army, and by a similar mission to reorganise the Turkish navy, tasks taken over from the French. He also shared the prestige of his brother, Sir Sidney Smith whose laurels, as a naval commander in defending Acre against Bonaparte rivalled those of Nelson himself. Spencer Smith had gained much approval both in London and in Constantinople. The two Smiths, indeed, had been awarded diplomatic status by the British government as joint Envoys Extraordinary to Turkey. So it was that Elgin missed the opportunity of negotiating the Treaty, and was left with the mundane role of ratifying it. Spencer Smith so well established at the Sultan's Court in Constantinople, had developed a strong disposition to make trouble for Elgin whom he deeply resented.

While renovating Broomhall, Elgin had found Harrison the architect a stimulating presence. With his interest in the classics, Elgin responded to Harrison's enthusiasm for the Greek achievement. The Enlightenment, with its cool rationality and its demand that the world be seen in terms of observation and reasoning, had been especially strong in Scotland: it had an affinity with the spirit of Greece as expressed in philosophy and the arts. The almost accidental opening to Britain of the ancient Greek lands by Bonaparte's action in Egypt, and Elgin's own appointment as ambassador, offered a dazzling opportunity. Whereas much that had been acquired by collectors and antiquarians from the classical world had come from Italy and so was Roman or Romano-Greek, here was a chance to go to the very source, namely to Periclean Athens and its Parthenon to make drawings and measurements, and, even more exciting, to produce replicas by making casts. It might even be possible to acquire some fragments and bear these back to Britain to embellish Broomhall. There were also architectural, commercial and industrial aspects. Elgin hoped, with Harrison, that the architecture and design of Britain and even of Europe might be re-energised by the sight of the Greek achievement.

There was perhaps a third motivation. With the Treaty with Turkey concluded, it was not clear to Elgin how he could make his name in this his first full Embassy: to his roles as diplomat, soldier and politician he proposed to add that of collector and patron of the arts, and on a grand scale. But the cost would be considerable. Elgin asked Grenville for money, but received the reply that the Foreign Office had no funds for such a purpose and that, in any case, so much had already been done by the Society of Antiquaries, the Dilettanti Society and private persons, that the kind of initiative proposed by Elgin was unnecessary. Though rebuffed, Elgin was by no means chastened. He would pay for the work himself. He knew that what had been done so far was arbitrary and unsystematic, made so partly by the wilfulness of the Turks: he, on the other hand, would be able to exploit Britain's new standing as an ally of Turkey to do something on a planned and sustained basis. Characteristically, he was immensely optimistic, minimising the convolutions of Turkish actions and the bitter personal resentments that were endemic among the antiquarians. Elgin had a deep streak of stubbornness that made him persist in the face of heavy obstacles. After all, Bonaparte had taken to Egypt as many as 175 engineers and scholars.

One of Elgin's first problems was to find artists who would work for him on reasonable terms. This proved impossible in Britain. Elgin made a number of approaches, but found that the wages demanded were far too steep. Moreover some of Elgin's conditions were too binding. The President of the Royal Academy, Sir Benjamin West, recommended J.W.M. Turner, then twenty-four. Turner asked for £400 per year and Elgin on his side required Turner to give drawing lessons to Mary as well as to surrender every product of his skill to his employer. The breakdown of talks betwen these two proud men was inevitable. Had Turner headed Elgin's team of artists, Turner's art would probably have developed otherwise and Elgin might well not have had an artist willing to assist in the stripping of the Parthenon, acting as his Clerk of Works. In a rare burst of economising Elgin decided to hire his artists en route, in Italy.

But though Elgin could not raise support for his architectural and sculptural initiative, he did have a set of enthusiasts for another project. There had long been in Britain the belief or hope that libraries in the monasteries and *seraglios* of the Middle East had copies of lost works by the great Greek authors, dispersed by the Turks after the fall of Constantinople in 1453. To two influential bishops, those of Lincoln and Durham, Elgin's embassy seemed to offer a splendid chance to make a search of these otherwise inaccessible places. Surprisingly, perhaps, a man was ready to hand, the Reverend Joseph Dacre Carlyle, aged forty, Professor of Oriental Languages at Cambridge since 1795. Carlyle was a deeply serious celibate, a published expert on Arabic and a minor poet. He was ardent to Christianise the Arab speaking peoples of Africa and Asia by distributing the scriptures to them in their own tongues. He hoped to promote this scheme by joining Elgin's embassy and making direct personal contacts in the East. Mary liked him and enjoyed his company. Though so mild a man, Carlyle was to prove himself able to hold his own when abused during the subsequent rivalries between antiquarians and archaeologists.

Finally, Elgin's mission acquired a scientific and practical side. Since the Crusades Western Europe had been vulnerable to epidemics of the plague and smallpox which had swept out of the East. Doctor Hector McLean, scholar and physician, was attached to Elgin's party as a medical man with a special interest in investigating these diseases.

The final strain on Elgin's finances was the buying of gifts to serve as an essential part of his Turkish diplomacy. He laid out no less than £2,000 on lustres, chandeliers and other cut glass. Other sweeteners included telescopes, watches, and firearms.

The finances of the Broomhall estate were by now in grave difficulty. James Dundas, Elgin's Edinburgh lawyer and agent, warned about expenses and urged him to give considered instructions for the management of his affairs in his absence. Dundas had been greatly concerned over Elgin's expenditure on the house. In addition work on the Pitferrane coal workings had proceeded against Dundas' advice and without the means of payment. Dundas warned him that the marriage settlement of £10,000 was not a liquid asset. Indeed it had been part of Mary's mother's marriage settlement a generation earlier. No more money could be raised in Edinburgh, Dundas pointed out; London was the only hope, probably on ruinous terms. Elgin nominated a commission to run his affairs in his absence; it consisted of his mother, Hamilton Nisbet his father-in-law, Oswald of Dunnikier and his uncle, Erskine of Cardross.

Central to Elgin's embassy was his personal secretariat. This, in the manner of the day, consisted not of professional diplomats, but of men of the ambassador's own choice. Elgin's entourage consisted of two private secretaries and a chaplain who also, under pressure of work, was to undertake secretarial and even quasi-diplomatic duties. The secretaries, both aged twenty-two, were at the beginning of their careers. The first William Richard Hamilton, one of the Hamiltons of Wishaw, having been lamed for life by an accident at Harrow, had just finished his studies at Oxford and Cambridge. His father, vicar of St. Martin-in-the-Fields, had a fond hope of getting him into parliament. Colonel Anstruther, a Fife neighbour of Elgins, recommended him warmly to Elgin. Hamilton was to justify this confidence, serving Elgin well and loyally supporting him in after years as Elgin's fortunes faded and his own career in the Foreign Office flourished. When Napoleon was finally disposed of in 1815 it was Hamilton who was largely instrumental in returning the fallen Emperor's cultural loot to its proper places in Europe. He was to become, too, the Secretary of the Dilettanti Society, the arbiter of antiquarianism, archaeology and artistic taste in England.

Secondly there was John Philip Morier. Born in Smyrna where his father had been Consul, he too was a man of promise. He was to undertake difficult commissions with the Turkish armies for Elgin with credit. At 28, the chaplain, the Reverend Philip Hunt, was under the patronage of the Earl of Upper Ossory, but, released by the Earl, saw the Constantinople mission as a great opportunity. A small man, he had great drive and energy as events relating to the Marbles of the Parthenon were to prove. He was a good preacher, performing without notes, was fluent in French and Greek and could act usefully as a mediator when Elgin's temper frayed. Elgin and his suite were very regular in their religious observances, over which Hunt presided. He became a kind of tutor to Mary, helping to fire her with an enthusiasm for the names of Cimon, Pericles, Phidias and others. Elgin's supporting suite was tiny for the tasks it was to assume, but he had chosen it well. Elgin had picked strong-minded men with youthful energy who became bound to him by loyalty and by their own hopes of laying the basis for their own careers.

All of this, of course, cost a great deal. Elgin was expected to run his establishment out of his salary: this was fixed at £6,600 per year. Before leaving, he asked Grenville for a more generous provision, but the Foreign Secretary would go no further. Subsequent appeals were no more successful. Moreover it was the custom of the day at the Foreign Office that an ambassador was not reimbursed until his mission was completed. Thus Elgin and his staff had to finance themselves. Nor was Elgin fortunate in terms of honours. He was made a Privy Councillor in September 1799, but what he really wanted was an Order of Chivalry, with ribbon and star to embellish his person in the presence of the Sultan and his court. The Duke of Hamilton had just died, leaving a vacancy among the Knights of the Thistle, Scotland's own Order, but it had already been promised elsewhere.

On 3 September Elgin's party sailed from Portsmouth in the *Phaeton*, a small, single-deck frigate of thirty-eight guns, with very limited accommodation. As well as the

Elgins there were the two secretaries, the chaplain, the physician and the professor, Duff a family servant, three personal maids for Mary with a number of other female servants, together with Mary's dogs crowded into the stateroom which was divided by green baize curtains. Hunt described the scene with some humour to his father: some days out he preached a sermon on Noah and the Ark. The new Broomhall, the lime and coal developments and the farms in Fife were left in the care of the commissioners. Elgin was not to see home again for six years and nine months.

Poor Mary had a dreadful time of it on board the *Phaeton* being two months pregnant and chronically seasick. Elgin was full of self reproach for imposing such suffering upon her. Twice the decks were cleared for combat as the officers and crew of the *Phaeton*, hot for action and prize money, took off after what were thought to be enemy ships, but turned out to be an American and a Dane. But Mary enjoyed the visits ashore, at Lisbon and Gibraltar where she revelled for the first time in the deference and pomp that went with her husband's office, discovering too that her own charms added to the warmth of their reception. Elgin himself was now a serious man, made the more so by rheumatic pains, thus exaggerating the difference in age between himself and Mary. He found Carlyle the most interesting companion of his entourage, with whom he could discuss the Greek, Arabic and Turkish worlds, a little to the chagrin of the rest of his suite. The younger men were the more put out when Elgin told them that they could expect no payment until the mission was over. But the excitement and prospects sustained them, for with luck they might play important parts in great events and so earn reputations that would in the longer-run prove more remunerative.

It was at Palermo in Sicily that the party had a brief encounter with both greatness and notoriety. For Nelson was there, together with Emma, Lady Hamilton and Sir William her complaisant husband. The King and Queen of Naples and their Court were making the best of it, exiled by war from their capital. Mary was delighted to find herself for a fortnight in the company of celebrities who were the subject of such eager gossip in Edinburgh as elsewhere. She was fascinated by Emma's control over Nelson, apparently reducing the hero of Britain to total thralldom and humble dependence. Elgin saw a different man. He contrasted Nelson's decrepit external appearance with his unimpaired powers of decision and action. 'He looks very old' (he was 41), he wrote to his mother, 'has lost his upper teeth, sees ill of one eye, and has a film coming over both of them. He has pains pretty constantly from his late wound in the head. His figure is mean, and, in general, his countenance is without animation.' But despite decrepitude and infatuation the vigour of the great commander was still present, 'Lord Nelson, when on business,—particularly in private—shows infinite fire,' wrote Elgin. This Elgin knew from lengthy talks with the Rear Admiral about the situation in the Mediterranean and the East. Nelson's indignation about the granting to Sir Sidney Smith of diplomatic as well as naval rank certainly commended him to Elgin.

There were long talks, too, with Sir William Hamilton. Now aged 69, he had lost, due to the costs involved, the great consolation of his life, namely the opportunity to collect more classical antiquities. His first collection of vases and medals had been sold to the British Museum, but not before he had published a splendid catalogue of it. A second collection also had to be sold, reflecting the enormous expense of such activity. Sir William's book had helped to inspire the pottery designs of Josiah Wedgwood, guiding him in recovering some of the ancient techniques, resulting in the enormous success of Wedgwood's Etruria works. Sir William responded with delight to Elgin's plans for drawing and making casts of the antiquities of Athens, and gave him warm encouragement. It was through Hamilton that Elgin found the artist Giovanni Batista Lusieri who was to play so large a part in his great scheme.

Lusieri was a Neapolitan, 48 years old, with a considerable reputation for his landscape painting, then working for the King of Naples. The King was prepared to release him; Elgin was to pay him £200 per year, clear of his keep and expenses, in return for which Elgin was to become the sole owner of all that he produced. Elgin was much relieved to find a man around whom he could build his artistic staff. Lusieri was not to know how much was to be demanded of him; he was to play a crucial role in Elgin's relations with the Parthenon. Once employed, Lusieri was sent to Naples and Rome with Elgin's secretary, William Hamilton (no relation to Sir William) to recruit supporting artists and moulders (*formatori*). It was a difficult task, for the Italian art world was in confusion because of the depredations of Bonaparte. Hamilton informed Elgin that Bonaparte had stripped Rome of its best sculptures. The most celebrated antique works of art, including the Laocoon, the Apollo Belvidere and the Venus de Medici, together with much else, had been seized and sent to the Louvre. Many of the Italian artists had succumbed to revolutionary visions, so that Hamilton had to make sure he had checked their political as well as their professional credentials. Young Hamilton had a further cultural mission, namely to select musicians for the chamber orchestra that Elgin planned at Constantinople. This he did.

In his earnest way, between Nelson and Sir William, Elgin enjoyed himself at Palermo. So too did Mary, glad to be free of her frightful seasickness and much intrigued to be favoured by the King and Queen of Naples and to observe and record in her letter-journal to her mother the extraordinary *ménage a trois*, of which Emma was the centre. When Nelson sailed for Minorca, Eggy and Poll debated whether he would be back; Eggy's view was that Nelson now saw how absurd he looked in his subjection, but Poll thought that Emma's hold was so tight that he would be back. She was right. But Poll did not take a romantic view of Nelson's behaviour, believing, 'If he returns he is undone, for Lady Hamilton makes him do such exceedingly ridiculous things.' Elgin at dinner at Sir William's table proposed the toast 'Lord Nelson', at which Emma burst into tears. More than a fortnight passed before it became necessary for the *Phaeton* to resume its journey. By this time Mary had added homesickness to seasickness.

At the Dardenellas the tiny *Phaeton* was welcomed by the *Sultan Selim*, the flagship of the Turkish fleet, a tremendous man-of-war, carrying 132 guns, with 1,200 men on board (built at Constantinople under the Frenchman Le Brun), bearing the Turkish First Lord of the Admiralty, the Captain Pasha. After reciprocal gun salutes, Elgin was escorted by Prince Isaac Bey to the Turkish ship. Mary, however, was not to be left behind. From the outset, indeed, she had determined, though apparently without consulting Elgin, not to be treated like a docile wife of the harem, or indeed like the douce wife of the usual western diplomat. She had told the Prince that she too wished to go aboard the *Selim*: in half an hour he, no doubt having consulted the Pasha, returned for her in a gilt boat with cushions of golden cloth. The Turks had decided at once that the ambassador's wife should be indulged, treating her rather like a nubile child. On deck she found the soldiers drawn up, a superb riot of colour. They presented arms while their band played English airs on the fifes and drums.

The Turks were of course quite unaccustomed to having a barefaced woman in their midst, especially one so vivacious and vigorous: Mary at once learned that her charms carried a certain power. The Pasha and Elgin greeted her at the door of the admiral's cabin. It was a cave of oriental magnificence, set in the stern of one of the most modern men-of-war. The yellow damask sofa was richly worked in gold, the walls hung with jewelled weapons, guns, pistols and swords and other arms. There were two Japanese cabinets, two large bowls of goldfish and elegant candlesticks. Elgin was deeply impressed with the keenness of the swords. Mary was in her element, delighting the Pasha by her temerity in asking to be shown over the ship. The guns were exercised for the benefit of the visitors, eliciting real though somewhat grudging praise from Captain Morris of the *Phaeton*. Back in the cabin coffee was served in the finest Dresden china. Then began the flow of gifts in which Mary was to take so great a delight, and the reciprocals of which were to add so much to Elgin's expenses. There was a sumptuous Indian shawl (valued by Mary at 70 guineas), perfumes and a model of the *Sultan Selim* with guns and flags picked out with rubies and emeralds. More practically the Turks reprovisioned the *Phaeton* on an embarrassingly sumptuous scale.

It took a further week to reach Constantinople. At the Dardenelles, by the gift of the Captain Pasha, Elgin received the celebrated ancient Boustrophedon inscription from the promontory of Sigaeum, a monument which even Louis XIV of France had failed to acquire. It stood at the door of a Greek chapel, where for generations the peasantry had rubbed against it for the relief of their ague, thus obliterating more than half of the inscription. It became Elgin's first acquisition, a real appetiser.

On 6 November the Elgins were conveyed from the *Phaeton* in gilded chairs to the British Palace (formerly the French Palace). An immense place, Mary began at once 'routing all over' it, arranging the apartments, planning the repapering and furnishings. A full fortnight was to be taken up with the welcoming ceremonies. First came a high Turkish officer with ninety servants, who inundated the Elgins with flowers, fruits and sweets, which were arrayed in two rows on each side of the hall from end to end, with eight trays of fine Berlin china. A few days later a second officer brought further gifts. Elgin, of course, had to respond in kind, dispensing a gold watch, splendid English pistols and a diamond ring. Largess extended down to the lowest servant. In the absence of the Grand Vizier who was with the army in Syria preparing to attack the French, Elgin was presented to the Caimacan Pasha, the Vizier's deputy. The Caimacan was virtually the Vizier's equal in status, as well as being younger. The climax to all this was being brought into the presence of the Sultan himself.

CHAPTER 5

The Porte, the Acropolis and Victory in Egypt

Elgin was impatient to begin real business, but as an experienced diplomat, he knew that due ceremony was required by every court and had to be tolerated. He was dismayed to find that the English Brigadier General Koehler, with his plan for the modernisation of the Turkish army, together with a strategy against the French, had been treated with all honours but relegated with his military mission to the repairing of the Dardanelles forts. In spite of his humiliation, or perhaps because of it, Koehler had assumed a certain grandeur that had gravely annoyed the Turks who resented being taken into military tutelage. The hostility and deviousness of Spencer Smith, officially Secretary to the Embassy, was even more exasperating.

Mary was divided by two emotions. She had periods of deep homesickness. She urged her parents to come without delay to Constantinople, setting aside rooms for them in the Palace. But she also revelled in the high ceremony of the Turkish court and the lavish giving and receiving of gifts. There was too, the society provided by the other foreign embassies, including the Russian, the Austrian and the Prussian. Mary was soon as well informed on the amorous intrigues of the Europeans as Elgin was to become on the politics of the eastern Mediterranean. Whist was the staple time filler at the embassies; the Elgins were alone in banning card playing and dancing on Sundays. Mary urged her mother to bring samples of the silks intended for the Elgin London drawing room, for she said silks in Constantinople were 'as cheap as dirt'; she also asked her mother to bring all 'the pretty little new tunes you can find', to be played on her pianoforte, safely arrived by merchant ship. Her mother was also to bring some fine coloured muslins, now at a premium in Turkey as the war had stopped caravans from India, remarking that 'when we go they will sell wonderfully.'

At the presentations to the Caimacan Pasha and the Sultan Mary scored a personal triumph. The Pasha had agreed that she could attend these intensely masculine affairs provided she appeared as a man. Accordingly she adopted the character of Lord Bruce (the potential Lord Bruce being some four months in her womb), dressing herself in her riding habit, her epauletted greatcoat and a cockaded beaver hat. Standing behind Elgin's chair she listened with quaking heart while Eggy read out his complimentary speech of which only she and Smith understood a word. Elgin was then enveloped in a magnificent pelisse, followed by Smith and 'Lord Bruce'. Mary was delighted with her sable robe, though almost dropping with its heat and weight. Elgin received also a beautiful horse with gold embroidered caparison. That evening the Elgins gave a dance and supper for the other embassies, with Mary teaching her guests Scotch reels.

As a preliminary to the visit to the Sultan Elgin presented a gorgeous cut glass chandelier, sending his servants to the palace to install it. The servants came away with money gifts exceeding a year's wages. In the meantime the Elgins dined with the Grand Vizier now returned from Syria, with Mary once more in the character of Lord Bruce. There was a long preliminary while the Elgins watched the aged Vizier sitting in state adjudicating causes, with the Grand Seigneur himself peeping at them through a lattice. After dinner, when pelisses were again distributed, there was a dreadful skirmish among the Greeks grasping for the presentation of Kaftans. Mary was placed on a stand behind Elgin's chain, from whence she saw her countrymen, including the *Phaeton's* officers, hitting out, their pelisses flowing about them, while the Turkish officials knocked the disturbers down and dragged them out with their heads on the ground.

Then came the great moment of being escorted to the Sultan's apartment. Each member of Elgin's party processed with a man in gold embroidery on each side with a hand on each shoulder. The room was small and dark, but as her eyes adjusted to the gloom, Mary became aware that she was in one of the most gold and gem encrusted rooms in the world. The Monster as she called him sat on a bed-like throne covered with immense pearls, with on one side his sword studded with brilliants and on the other an inkstand gleaming with diamonds. In his turban was the famous aigrette, with two further diamond-laden turbans displayed nearby. This was the inner heart of a vast empire into which the gold and gems of outrageous exploitation of Turks and subject peoples alike had been accumulated. But in a sense the scene was a sham, for the man squatting on the throne was no originator, like Bonaparte, but the tool of the personalities and factions who had incarcerated him there among his silks and baubles. Elgin delivered his speech creditably, and was responded to by some aged Great Man whom the Grand Seigneur good humouredly prompted three times. Elgin gave both of his pelisses to Mary, one of which she sent to Martha in London to have it valued, remarking that in Constantinople it was worth £500.

All this receiving of gifts had to be balanced by giving. Elgin knew that he must equal his Turkish hosts, and though there was some scope for matching gold, brilliants, fabrics, and horses with ingenious European manufactures like clocks and watches, music boxes, telescopes, pistols and the like, most of what he gave had to be in the Turkish idiom of guns and encrusted boxes and rings, not to speak of coin for the servants. The expense was very great. Within the first fortnight in Constantinople gifts had cost him more than £7,000, the claim for which he could not be certain would be fully met by the Foreign Office.

Amid all this ritual splendour Elgin was beginning to come to grips with his real task. Spencer Smith and General Koehler, especially the former, continued to be difficult, each cherishing his frustration and resentment. There were repeated rows with Smith, who went far beyond his allocated responsibility, namely that for trade and promoting the interests of the Levant Company. His meddlings in diplomacy and his claim that Elgin had no right to interfere in the matter of tariffs and trade strained Elgin severely, causing him to stand over Smith several times, reading aloud the terms of his ambassadorial appointment. Elgin suffered great pain from 'rheumatism in the head', no doubt partly at least psychosomatic, leeches were applied, Turkish leeches being very violent.

But it was Sir Sidney, Spencer Smith's naval brother, who caused the most trouble, placing Elgin in a difficult position with both the British and Turkish governments. Based in his ship the *Tigre*, then standing off the coast of Egypt, Sir Sidney had begun negotiations with the French commander, General Kléber. The gallant and skilful Kléber, who did not conceal his detestation of Bonaparte, believing that his Egyptian ambitions were insane, accepted Sir Sidney as empowered to act for both British and Turkish governments as he wished to end the affair before disaster did so.

Meanwhile the Grand Vizier having returned to Syria, was advancing with his vast army to deal the death blow to the French. Both Smith and Kléber believed that reason would prevail: Smith made every effort to persuade the Vizier to halt his army. But the ancient Vizier was deaf to all entreaties and continued his march, sending to Elgin a fierce protest at Smith's interference. Elgin dispatched Morier post-haste to act as a pacifier, to liaise with the Vizier and his army, and to rebuke Sir Sidney for exceeding his powers. Although Elgin did not directly order Smith to desist in his French negotiations, he wrote to Grenville urging that Spencer Smith be sacked and Sir Sidney reprimanded. Grenville, under the pressures of European war, set complaints and counter-complaints aside allowing the mounting file of correspondence from Elgin, the two Smiths and Koehler to remain unanswered. The Middle Eastern bungle was left to work itself out. Poor Elgin, frustrated by this neglect, consoled himself with his correspondence. Nelson wrote to Elgin that he would have preferred to see the wretched French perish in Egypt to a man.

Late in January 1800 Sir Sidney achieved success in his unauthorised negotiations in the form of the Convention of El Arish. Under it Kléber agreed to evacuate Egypt. His men were to retain their arms and their troopships, and be given safe conduct to France, provided they guaranteed that they would take no further part in the war. Smith wrote to Elgin, asking for safe conducts for the French troops that were to be evacuated, urging that 'the great national object is attained if we get the French army *out of the country*, even if they took the Pyramids with them'. Smith's success was not to be gainsaid: Elgin wrote on 16 February to Grenville informing him in approving terms of the French capitulation. Eight days later an official despatch from Grenville arrived, having been on its way since 13 December. In it Grenville gave unequivocal instructions that only a full surrender by the French as prisoners of war would do. He had formed the impression, quite mistakenly, from an intercepted letter of Kléber's to the Directory, that the French were on the point of collapse, and believed that they could not be trusted to honour the parole system. Thus was El Arish repudiated without ever becoming public knowledge. Ironically the Turks had by this time come to accept the Convention, for after all it restored Egypt to them at no cost.

Elgin had now the intense embarrassment of reporting the volte-face to the Turks. But the feast of *Bairan* had begun, making business impossible for a further fortnight. When it came, the audience with the Caimacan Pasha was very difficult, with Elgin having the humiliation of confessing that Sir Sidney had been beyond his power to control. The Turks then proposed a strategem that horrified Elgin, namely that the French army should be embarked as under the Convention, and when safely at sea, be made prisoners. With this Elgin would have nothing to do. But disorted news of this dastardly proposal reached the French, with dire effects as Elgin was to discover later.

Morier, it would appear, had lost in Egypt a notebook that seemed to suggest such a scheme of betrayal: the French published the ostensible document. Not only so, they stored this incident too in their mental dossier against Elgin.

But by now the British government had reversed its position, accepting Smith's *fait accompli*. On 28 March Grenville wrote to Elgin accepting the Convention. For it was indeed a sensible solution, putting an end to hostilities in Egypt and the Eastern Mediterranean at minimal cost to Britain. But Lord Keith the British Commander-in-Chief had already on the receipt of the previous instruction brusquely told General Kléber that the Convention was nullified and that the only terms were those of unconditional surrender. General Kléber responded with vigour. Much of the Turkish army that confronted him was little more than an armed rabble, colourfully described by Elgin's envoy, Morier. Its camp resembled a vast fair, with all manner of tradesmen, horsedealers, coffee house operators, with the troops firing their muskets at whim. The Grand Vizier, an old man who knew nothing of military command or war, had a retinue of some 10,000, while his army contained some 40,000. On 20 March Kléber in a brilliant manoeuvre destroyed this ramshackled host near the ruins of Heliopolis, with perhaps 10,000 Turkish dead and many more lost in the attempt to reach home across the desert. The victorious carnage only saddened Kléber further. There was to be another fifteen months of war in Egypt, involving a British army, with further

1   Lord and Lady Elgin at cards in Constantinople with the Captain Pasha. Pencil drawing by G.B. Lusieri.

thousands of casualties. Bonaparte came to believe that Elgin had contrived the whole El Arish business.

It might well have been expected that Elgin would now stand disgraced both with his own government and the Turkish court. But somehow this did not happen. Grenville and the British cabinet, perhaps mindful of their own contribution to the mess through the equivocal position in which they had placed Elgin, did not blame him for the confusion. The Turks, for their part, were in greater need than ever of British support, confronted as they now were by the once more victorious French in Egypt. Elgin received a further flood of presents.

Elgin, deeply preoccupied with his diplomacy, was finding it increasingly hard to tolerate the interminable ceremony that surrounded his dealings with the Turkish court. Harrassed by Spencer Smith's annoyances at the Embassy, he was under great strain, placing his health at risk. His rheumatic pains continued to be severe, causing him against medical advice to consume large quantities of mercury. He had little energy for Mary who at the time of the Heliopolis massacre was within a month of giving birth.

She too had her health problems, suffering from attacks of 'suffocation' or 'choakings', alarming Dr. McLean and making Eggy 'take sad fright'. She spent much of her evenings at whist, being a consistent winner; there was, too, a billiard table to liven the company at her parties. But she began to worry about the enormous expense of her ménage, for in addition to her own table to supply, she had sixty servants to feed.

The Captain Pasha enjoyed the company of this beautiful European woman inviting her to visit his sister Hanum at his home. Hanum, who kept house for the Captain invited Mary to spend two days with her. On the first evening Hanum presented Mary with two Turkish costumes. Dressed in one of these she greeted Elgin who did not at first know her. All the women insisted that Mary was very like the Sultan's favourite. She showed her hostess Eggy's picture, causing Hanum to comment that she must love him very much to carry it about with her. Mary sent for her pianoforte and taught the ladies of the harem to dance a Scottish reel. While she played, the Captain Pasha sat beside her, enjoying his first acquaintance with a vivacious European woman. He astonished her by picking out with one finger several of her tunes on this his first acquaintance with the pianoforte. There was the usual profusion of gifts. A local poet, Aboo Talibkhan, wrote a Persian Ode to Mary, revealing the general Islamic male appreciation of her charms:

> 'Her sugar lips are breeding smiles divine
> and overspread the world with heaven's shine'.

All of this, when the word spread, created intense jealously among the women of the other embassies, a reaction that greatly pleased Mary.

On 5 April 1800 she gave birth to a son. She was very, very ill during the delivery, but the sight of the infant made her the happiest of creatures. The Elgins now had an heir, George Charles Constantine, Lord Bruce. Mary's spirits were further raised by the imminent arrival of her parents, the Porte sending a high official to escort them over the last stage of their journey.

There was a yet additional excitement. William Hamilton, after many difficulties, arrived on 15 May with his band of artists and musicians. There were six artists and craftsmen, headed by Lusieri and including two *formatori* for the making of plaster casts. Mary was enthralled by Elgin's chamber orchestra which consisted of six Italians, led by one Belloti. There was one violin, one viola, two cornets, one 'clarionette' and one 'violoncello'. She had her reservations, however, about the *formatori*, thinking that Elgin should not go beyond the making of drawings because of the expense. The artists were a curious crew, headed by the tiny Lusieri. They included Theodor Ivanovitch, a Tartar who had once been a slave. An accomplished painter of figures, whose extreme ugliness was proportionate to the purity of his Calmuck descent he was to become known as 'Lord Elgin's Calmuck'. The principal architectural draftsman was Balestra, a tortuously deformed hunchback, whose assistant was a young student called Ittar. In a sense Hamilton had exceeded his remit, for his instruction had been for three men only, rather than six. But Elgin accepted Hamilton's explanations and dispatched the team to Athens at once.

They arrived in August ready to begin making their measurements, drawings and casts of the buildings and sculptures of the age of Pericles. The greatest embodiment of these was of course the Parthenon, standing high above the city, still magnificent in its wrecked and neglected condition. It had been built between 447 and 432 BC, the culminating achievement of Pericles' magnificent programme of public works intended to celebrate Athens as an imperial metropolis, the head of a confederacy of Greek city-states. Athens was now a slum city of some 1,200 houses, primitive, provincial and half Turkish and Levantine, ruled by the Turks since 1458. The Parthenon, now semi-ruinous, crowned the Acropolis, rising into the sky in noble homage to the greatness of the goddess Pallas Athena, or Minerva, the goddess of Wisdom, and once the presiding deity of the city. It had been built of the finest marble from Mount Pentelicus ten miles away, with Ictinus as its principal architect and Phidias the superintendent of its building and sculptures. In the opinion of many then and now, this magnificent Doric temple represents the highest achievement of mankind in its siting, design, construction and embellishment. In addition there was at the approaches to the Acropolis the great porched ceromonial gateway, the Propylaea, combining both Doric and Ionic orders. Below the Acropolis was the Erechtheion, a small Ionic temple setting off the austere grandeur of the Parthenon. Female figures or caryatids supported the roof of one of its porches on their heads, under which the olive tree sacred to Athena was supposed to have been preserved.

To these splendours of a vanquished and vanished race the Turks were largely indifferent. The Parthenon had been made into a mosque in the fifteenth century, and after serving as a gunpowder magazine the Propylaea had been wrecked by lightning exploding its contents. The tiny temple of Athena Nike, (with its sculptures commemorating the victory of the Greeks over the Persians), had been cleared away to make a gun site in preparation for Venetian attack. The Propylaea used for the storage of gunpowder had exploded and the Parthenon itself had sustained a direct hit from the guns of the Venetian General Morosini in 1687, which blew off the roof and tore great gaps in the colonnading on each side. Morosini had tried to remove the sculptures from the western pediment in order to carry them to Venice where they would join other expropriated treasures, including the four horses of Byzantium which pranced over the porch of the cathedral of St. Marco. But the sculptures, depicting the contest between Athena and Poseidon for the land of Attica had crashed to the ground when the tackle broke and were shattered, their components buried by detritus. To all this destruction by man, nature had added her toll; there had been over the 2,300 years much natural decay. Nor had the Greek Orthodox Church shown any affection for the Acropolis with its pagan monuments. Indeed, centuries before Morosini, the east pediment of the Parthenon had lost more than half its sculptures when the building had been converted to a Christian church. At this time the iconoclasts had seized the opportunity to deface the figures in their attempt to break with the pagan past.

But a good deal of the Parthenon remained. The exterior still had its metopes, (panels in high relief each about four feet square) depicting scenes from the mythical wars between gods and giants and lapiths and centaurs as well as the triglyphs, the vertically grooved stones, which separated them. Almost as breathtaking was the frieze which ran round the entire temple inside the colonnading showing in low relief the religious procession of the Great Panathenaea. To make casts of both the metopes and the frieze was the great objective of Elgin's *formatori*.

Already the Turks had responded in two ways to these glories of ancient Greece. Having discovered that the marble made excellent lime on easy terms they had used it for the making of mortar. In this way many splendid works of art and architecture were smashed, pulverised and burned. The second form of vandalism was their response to Western European travellers, who, excluded from Italy by Napoleon, had reached Greece, avid for mementos, especially those which echoed their classical education. So with formerly valueless bits of marble now carrying a price, Turkish entrepreneurs had started to break pieces from buildings and sculptures, including the Parthenon. Some puzzled that such bits of stone should prove so valuable, concluded that gold must be hidden therein and so by their own destruction added to the vandalism. On the other hand the Turkish authorities seem dimly to have realised that the Parthenon, or Temple of the Idols, though incomprehensible to them, might represent something unique in human achievement. There was therefore an official regulation, absolute prohibition against the removal of the surviving sculptures from the Acropolis. This the Voivode (Governor of Athens) and the Disdar (military governor of the Acropolis) were both to enforce.

In the 1780s, the French Comte de Choiseul-Gouffier had already made the most sustained attempt to circumvent this prohibition, using Louis Francois Sebastian Fauvel as his agent. The Comte had been appointed French ambassador to the Porte in 1783: thus anticipating Elgin by nearly twenty years in the making of drawings and casts, exploiting the favourable relationship of the French with the Turks. Instructing Fauvel to collect Greek sculptures, he had used all the arts of bribery, persuasion and threat, to ship them to France while Elgin's predecessor the British ambassador had indignantly protested against this vandalism. But the Turks had refused the Comte permission to remove sculptures from the Parthenon itself so he had to content himself with a piece of the frieze and a metope that had fallen from the building. As Choiseul-Gouffier was a royalist, he was branded as a traitor by the revolutionary government and fled to

Russia. Fauvel stayed on in Athens, achieving for himself something of a monopoly in Greek antiquities. With Bonaparte's invasion of Egypt, Fauvel found himself in the Prison of the Seven Towers along with other Frenchmen, leaving an open field to Elgin.

From the beginning the Disdar proved very troublesome to Elgin's agents. He summarily banned Lusieri and his men from the Acropolis, insinuating that they would spend their time peering down at the Turkish women in their homes and courtyards. Thus frustrated, Elgin's team set to work on the two notable monuments outside the Acropolis, the Theseum and the Monument of Lysicrates. For their work the *formatori* needed lifting tackle and a cart: the Turks obliged by making available Fauvel's gear, the only such equipment in all Athens. In February 1801 the party finally managed to enter the Acropolis, buying their way in paying the Disdar at the exhorbitant rate of £5 per day. Though Elgin had failed to achieve the necessary firman (or official written permission) from the Porte, through his servants he was willing to pay bribes.

Back in Constantinople, Mary, with the arrival of her parents in May 1800, her joy in 'Bab' her baby, and her social triumphs, achieved a kind of happiness. Things also eased somewhat for Elgin. At long last in January 1801 he managed to persuade Grenville to remove Spencer Smith, that source of discord at the heart of his Embassy: in this Dundas gave useful support. Smith did not return directly home, but toured the Levant denigrating Elgin, visiting his brother Sir Sidney's naval squadron, and biding his time to even scores. The winter of 1801 was a terrible one in Constantinople, being cold and damp, with temperatures varying by as much as 16 degrees in an hour. In consequence Elgin suffered severely from 'inflammation about the head.'

Back in England Spencer Smith was shortly to enter parliament, from whence he could continue his campaign of enmity against Elgin. He carried with him ammunition, the value of which he was not then aware. It concerned John Tweddell, a brilliant young scholar, observer and writer. One of the most accomplished travellers of his time, Tweddell had compiled journals, inscriptions and the like that could have become the basis of one of the most splendid of travel books, embellished by the work of Preaux, a painter who had accompanied him. But Tweddell had died of a fever in Athens in 1799, leaving a legend of gifted youth perishing at the moment of fulfilment. Subsequently part of Tweddell's papers had been destroyed by fire and part was lost at sea on its way to Spencer Smith (as British envoy at Constantinople). Some of the material had been recovered from the wrecked ship and forwarded to Constantinople where it had arrived shortly before Elgin. Hunt and Carlyle, at Elgin's request, spread the material out to dry in the cellar of the British Palace. After sorting and packing, the papers were then despatched, at Elgin's expense, to England to Tweddell's family. Out of this episode Smith and Tweddell's brother, the Reverend Robert, were to construct a scandal in which Elgin was portrayed as a thief, doing immense damage to the name of an honourable man and to his career prospects.

In the meantime Elgin warmly welcomed Alexander Stratton as his new secretary, whom he had known and liked at Vienna. On his arrival in Constantinople Mr. Hamilton Nisbet had presented Elgin with a gloomy account of the Broomhall finances, having inspected the coal works and informed himself, as one of Elgin's commissioners, of the affairs of the estate.

In January 1801 the French forces in Egypt were still largely intact. The British were assembling an army of 17,000 men at Malta (captured by the British in September 1800), under Elgin's Scottish neighbour, General Sir Ralph Abercromby. Sir Ralph was one of those extraordinary Britishers who did great things on land and sea, but whose fame was to be eclipsed by the twin suns of Nelson and Wellington. He and Sir John Moore (another Scot) had been largely responsible for rebuilding the morale and discipline of the British army after its grave demoralisation during and after the American Revolutionary War. He had gained many battle honours when, in 1799 at the age of 65, he had two horses killed under him while commanding the retreat from the Duke of York's disastrous campaign in Flanders. Always in the forefront of the fighting, he was so shortsighted that he had to rely on his officers to tell him what was going on.

While Abercromby made his preparations, Bonaparte, as First Consul, was setting up a new expedition at Toulon to rescue his army abandoned in Egypt. It was clear that the fight for the control of the Eastern Mediterranean, was approaching its climax. There could be no peace between Britain and France until Britain had cleared Egypt and the Levant of her ancient enemy, now threatening British access to India and the far east. Bonaparte had persuaded the eccentric Tzar Paul to move against Britain in India: the Russian army was preparing to do this when the Tzar was assassinated. Elgin was determined to play a full part in these dramatic developments. He was in a key position to act as a logistic co-ordinator and facilitator.

Abercromby and his army moved to Marmoris in south-western Asia Minor, almost directly north of Egypt. There, without any funds or any knowledge of the country, he was having great difficulties in raising supplies for his army. Elgin, as Britain's principal diplomatic representative in the area, came to Abercromby's relief, organising large sums of money and assisting in the search for horses, fodder, food and other necessaries, as well as in the construction of boats. This aid to Abercromby was eventually to lead to enormous complications in Elgin's personal financial relations with the Foreign Office in London. At least Elgin had the satisfaction of being indispensable to the British forces. Abercromby's successor General Hutchinson, wrote to thank Elgin from his camp, before Alexandria in Egypt, saying,

> 'I do not know how we should have been able to have existed at all in this country had it not been for the great exertions which you have used to procure us money, and to administer to our other various wants .... I shall ever bear testimony to the zeal and ability with which you have exercised the most important public functions.'

Abercromby organised his expeditionary force well. He had carefully trained his men in amphibious landing at Marmoris. On 8 March they fought their way ashore at Aboukir Bay to the east of Alexandria. By this time Kléber had been assassinated, to be replaced by Menou, a contemptible toady of Bonaparte and a fumbling general. The gallant Abercromby was mortally wounded, dying on the 28 March. Under General Hutchison, the British were victorious at the Battle of Alexandria on 21 March.

Also among the dead at Aboukir was Elgin's one-legged cousin General Erskine, affectionately known as 'Peg Leg'. He had worn a silver gorgette around his neck: this made it possible to identify his body more than a century and a half later so that his regiment, the Seaforth Highlanders could bring him home and bury him a second time with full military honours, briefly reviving a long forgotten victory.

Hutchison now prepared to attack Cairo. The Grand Vizier was there with a new Turkish army, including the remnants of Koehler's military mission, together with 1,500 Mamelukes. Menou, after pledging resistance to the last man, suddenly decided the game was up and offered to surrender on the El Arish terms, under which the French would evacuate Egypt, but would keep their arms and be given safe conduct to France. This was accepted and the British entered Cairo in July. The remaining 10,000 French troops beseiged in Alexandria capitulated on the same terms on 2 September. Sir Sidney Smith had been right all along. Elgin was now violently against the El Arish terms, writing to the new Foreign Secretary Lord Hawkesbury to say so. He was apprehensive that the British would be indignant that after so costly a campaign the French had been let off so lightly, retaining their honour and their arms. Sure enough the officers in Hutchison's army inundated him with letters of protest. But Elgin was to change his mind when he learned that the British army had been in danger of decimation from sickness in the intense heat. Ophthalmia and dysentery had already taken a heavy toll.

Elgin had sent Hamilton as his representative to the British army in Egypt: there Hamilton assisted in the capitulation negotiations. He also secured for Britain the multi–lingual Rosetta stone, now in the British Museum, that when deciphered was to make possible the translation of Egyptian hieroglyphics: the French had tried to retain it by hiding it under some mats in a warehouse.

The Turks intoxicated by the victory had no misgivings over the terms of surrender. From this Elgin was to benefit enormously, being showered with gifts and made once more the centre of high ceremonial.

CHAPTER 6

Taking the Marbles

In May 1801, after a twelve month stay, Mr. and Mrs. Hamilton Nisbet, left Constantinople on their return journey. Carlyle and Hunt travelled with them as far as Athens. Mary watched forlornly as their ship disappeared around the Seraglio Point. Choakings and fever followed. She was somewhat consoled by the move for the summer to a pleasant house at Bouyouk Dere. This village about twelve miles from Constantinople was favoured by the Sultan with his mountebanks and rope dancers. On 4 June Hunt arrived back from Athens bearing letters from Mary's parents and Carlyle.

Elgin had had little time to indulge his enthusiasm for Greek antiquities. But the Hamilton Nisbets' letters from Athens, and Hunt's eager presence there, fired him with a new enthusiasm. His parents-in-law had indeed themselves become keen collectors of antiquities, revelling in what they saw on the Acropolis. Mr. Nisbet had first caught the acquisition fever, when the Archbishop of Athens presented him and his wife with the marble seat on which the Gymnasiarch (the Director of Public Amusements) used to sit at the Athenian games. It was decorated with bas reliefs of the sacred olive, the owl of Minerva and other symbols. Mr. Nisbet declared himself and his wife the first members of the 'Athenian Club' by having their names carved high on a pillar of the Parthenon, leaving space for those of Elgin and Mary. As a result Mary herself caught the vision. Like her father she had formerly been against the expense of the *formatori*, but now, like him, she changed her mind.

But the greatest enthusiast of all was Hunt. His deep involvement with the classical world had come about through his association with Carlyle, when they had travelled together in search of lost manuscripts from classical times, sponsored by the bishops of Lincoln and Durham. Carlyle was the senior scholar, but Hunt proved a good companion and an eager learner. On arrival at Constantinople in December 1799 Carlyle had been frustrated in his attempt to gain entry to the Seraglio Library, but with Hunt was allowed into the mosque of St. Sophia. The long-locked chamber in which they had hoped to find ancient books and manuscripts proved empty. Quiet and retiring as he was, Carlyle was soon to rise to another adventure. In January 1800 he and General Koehler, both disguised as Turks, were on a dangerous journey through Asia Minor, to join the Vizier's army. The expedition was heroic, but it weakened Carlyle's health. Returning to Constantinople, Carlyle continued his manuscript searches locally, with Hunt's aid. In November, through Elgin's good offices, he succeeded in gaining access to the Seraglio Library. But it too proved a bitter disappointment: none of the ancient texts were found. But there still remained the twenty-four monasteries on Mount Athos to search: Carlyle and Hunt set out to visit these, Hunt picking up a few statues and inscriptions for Elgin.

The plain of Troy had a powerful fascination for the British intelligentsia and Elgin was no exception. In January 1800 he tried to pursuade officers of the Royal Engineers with General Koehler's force to survey the ground, but without success. When Carlyle and Hunt arrived at Troy they met a rival party, that of Reverend Edward Clarke (another Cambridge don) and his pupil, J.M. Cripps. It was not long before a bitter argument broke out over the location of the site of the city. This quarrel was to fester, turning Clarke into another ally of Spencer Smith ready to slander Elgin. Carlyle and Hunt carefully catalogued the monastery libraries, but again the results were disappointing. By now Carlyle was near exhaustion. He never recovered his health. He returned home from Athens accompanying the Hamilton Nisbets, to die within a few years.

Hunt returned to Constantinople a considerable traveller and scholar. He told Elgin that 'the Athens of Pericles seemed to rise before me in all its pristine beauty', with its ancient buildings in their 'solid masculine style', a 'union of simplicity and beauty'. Treasure seeking had become more difficult than ever at Athens. Elgin himself was inadvertently the cause. He had informed the Turks on the basis of intelligence he had received that it was highly likely that the French were about to invade Greece. This was to be the first step in dismembering the Balkan part of the Turkish empire. As a result the Disdar banned Lusieri and the rest of his team from the Acropolis, which was, after all, nominally at least, a fortress.

Perhaps it was the failure of his searches for manuscripts that fuelled Hunt's enthusiasm for a real coup on the Acropolis. What was needed, he insisted to Elgin, was a firman from the highest authority, which would force the Voivode, the Disdar and the Cadi (the chief justice of Athens) to give full access. On 14 June 1801, three months after the British victory at Alexandria, and with Cairo under siege, Elgin began negotiations with the Captain Pasha to obtain the essential firman.

It was a uniquely propitious time, a brief interlude in which the Turks were prepared to give Elgin almost anything. He was fortunate in enjoying the support of the Sultan's mother, the Valida Sultana, for the town of Athens was part of her jointure. Hunt provided the draft of the firman for submission to the Porte and on 9 July Mary recorded Hunt's rapture at its being obtained. Signed by the Caimacan, second only to the Grand Vizier, it included the right to erect scaffolds all round the Parthenon, to dig and discover any marbles 'that may be deemed curious by their having inscriptions on them.' But the most important provision, on which so much was to hang, was ambiguous. Elgin's servants, 'when they wished to take away any pieces of stone with old inscriptions or sculptures thereon, no hindrance or opposition be made thereto.' Hunt was to exploit this sentence to the limit and perhaps beyond, relying heavily on 'the friendship, sincerity, alliance and good will' described in the firman as subsisting between England and the Porte, and 'which is manifestly increasing.'

Hunt set out at once for Athens to fulfil a double mission in Greece. He was to press as hard as possible on the Athens authorities to expedite the antiquarian work of Lusieri and his men, using the firman. But his official task was to visit the pashas in the Morea (the Peloponnesos) to dispose them against the French, should any beguiling overtures come from that quarter. To achieve this was to warn them of the very real possibility that the French might renew their imperial ambitions in Greece. Alternately, they might use Greece as a diversion, encouraging the peasantry there to rise, thus drawing off Turkish military power, leaving Egypt exposed. These fears had to be conveyed by Hunt to those Greeks who held office under the Turks. He was also to gather military intelligence, estimating the strength and state of the Turkish armies and the availability of food, as well as to prepare the pashas to receive British garrisons if necessary. In particular Elgin was in search of grain to feed the British troops, trying to do so without being too grossly exploited by the local pashas and other official and unoffical monopolists.

For these purposes the Reverend Hunt was made a temporary private secretary and diplomat, jokingly regretting he had not time to read Machiavelli. The military and diplomatic aspects of his mission meant that he was provided with all kinds of documentation as a friend of the Sultan, together with a high official of the Porte called Raschid Aga whose authority exceeded that of any local governor or pasha. Hunt described him as 'a kind of *ad hoc* man'. Elgin supplied Hunt with a treasury of gifts—crystal lustres, pistols, jewellery, telescopes, lengths of fabric all to be used either for diplomacy or to pay for antiquities.

Despite his many preoccupations, Elgin's mind ran a good deal on the completion and embellishment of Broomhall. He had brought the plans with him and frequently pored over them, his mind exercised by the problem of completing the portico and the supporting wings. He began to imagine that Broomhall might become the repository for the Greek artefacts: its main hall adorned with columns—he had already had the cellars vaulted to provide the necessary support. The columns were to be of fine marble, each different from the others as in the great church he had seen at Palermo. Lusieri was to seek such columns.

Meanwhile Broomhall featured in a more immediate way. When the Sultan added to the gifts showered on Elgin, the provision of land and money for the building of a worthy English Palace at Constantinople, to replace the French Palace in which the Elgins were living, Elgin proposed that a replica of his Fife seat should be built in the Turkish capital. His idea was accepted. Elgin's Broomhall look alike British embassy was to become the first such building to be owned by the British government. Until 1814, with the exception of Constantinople, British ambassadors lived in rented houses so that when the lease ran out it might be necessary to remove the archives in a cart. The embassy was completed in 1805 but was destroyed by fire in 1831.

The capitulation of Alexandria on 2 September 1801 spelt the end of Bonaparte's Egyptian adventure. The Sultan sent the Dragoman of the Porte, a very high official, in state to Elgin; the congratulations and consultations went on for two and a half hours. Cannon were fired day and night for a whole week, the city and the Bosphorous glittered in its illuminations while music was played and masquerades enacted. 'The Turks', wrote Mary, 'were as merry as Christians!' The Sultan eager to find a new mode of expressing approbation accepted Elgin's suggestion that he should set up an Order of Chivalry on the European model. The Order of the Crescent was instituted, with two grades, with diamonds and without. Elgin chose a designer and the insignia were made by Rundel and Bridges, court jewellers of London. The Sultan at once awarded the Order with diamonds to Elgin, Admiral Lord Keith, the British Commander-in-chief and General Hutchison the taker of Alexandria. Nelson too was a recipient: the Crescent was there among the four stars that glittered on his flag officer's coat when he was shot by a French sniper at Trafalgar. It was the only Order Elgin was ever to receive.

Amid the celebrations however there came news of an unpleasant incident concerning the Mameluke Beys, whose power in Egypt, though nominally subject to the Turks, was much resented at the Porte. The Captain Pasha who had so charmed Mary at the pianoforte had gone to Egypt with the intention of inviting seven of the Beys to a conference where they would be assassinated. General Hutchison was horrified by the idea, but managed by his intervention only to save four of them. This kind of behaviour tormented Elgin who was appalled at such murderous disposal: the Pasha, whom Mary noted 'is very cunning', was meanwhile writing deceiving letters to the Sultan about the General's attitude.

Hunt had meanwhile arrived back at Athens in the suffocating July heat, still determined to make the best of any advantage. He descended upon the Voivode. He began by complaining about the way the Disdar and the Disdar's son had so shamelessly extorted money from Lusieri and allowed Elgin's men to be subject to harassment and insult. Such treatment, he said of the servants of the ambassador of the Porte's great ally was intolerable. As the Disdar was dying, his son and successor was sent for. He was threatened with the fate of being put to the oar as a galley slave. Hunt also hinted to the Disdar the possibility of condign punishment for him. The Voivode's misgivings weakened and were finally overcome. All servants of Lord Elgin were to have access to the Acropolis from sunrise to sunset and were to be provided with all necessary facilities.

The Reverend Hunt now demonstrated further his powers of organisation and command. His status and confidence as an English gentleman and a direct representative of the ambassador meant that he had greater influence than the harassed Neapolitan Lusieri. He was now clearly bent on acquisition on a major scale rather than simply drawing, measuring and making casts. He mustered a large force of Greek labour, varying from two to three hundred. The fragments of inscriptions and statuary lying on the ground were gathered up. Elaborate excavations were begun to find others and sure enough, these things yielded a marvellous return. From below the west pediment there came massive fragments that had been blown off by the explosion of 1687, including the torsos of Poseidon and Athena as well as that of Hermes. Hunt proposed to Lord Elgin that he should send a large man-of-war to the Piraeus so that the porch of the Erechtheium with its splendid caryatids might be transported whole to England. Moreover there were the treasures that Choiseul had hidden in the French Capuchin convent: Hunt hinted that Elgin should contrive means of obtaining these.

The marvellous metopes on the south side of the Parthenon were even more tempting to Hunt so he approached the Voivode for permission to remove the best surviving of these. The Voivode knew in his heart of hearts that to do so would be to strain the firman too far, and would breach the long-standing protection that the fabric of the Parthenon had received from the Greek-hating Porte. He was in a terrible dilemma, knowing that whichever way he acted, he might be exposing himself to fearful punishment if circumstances changed or if the Porte in its arbitrary way took against him. The Disdarship had now passed to the son on the death of the father so that no resistance came from that submissive quarter. The Caimacan sent a second communication to the Voivode. When Hunt had obtained a translation he acted with added confidence believing that the new instruction gave him added powers. The Voivode finally succumbed. He knew very well that the terms of the firman and its follow-up did not provide unequivocal permission literally to strip sculptures from the building, but perhaps he believed that in the circumstances he was acting within his implied powers, and that on balance it was the best course open to him. To affront the agent of the British Ambassador could surely not be the intention of the Porte, engaged as it was in celebrating its victorious alliance with the British. Certainly there was no *specific* prohibition in the firman against removing component members. It could be argued, in not stopping the operation, the Voivode was consenting to it.

Neither Hunt nor Elgin troubled themselves with legal or moral justification. Once the dazzling prospect of the metopes and the frieze had materialised, all they wanted was to remove and ship them with the minimum interference or stoppage by the Turkish officials. They were in tune with the morality of the day. The question of Elgin's entitlement to remove components of the Parthenon arose only later when a sale to the British government was in contemplation.

Hunt lost no time. He brought the carpenter from the British warship that had carried him back to Greece. With five of the crew and twenty Greeks this ingenious man detached the choicest of the metopes from the fabric of the Parthenon and on 31 July 1801 lowered it safely to the ground. Using Fauvel's indispensable cart it was conveyed the four miles to the Piraeus.

Hunt proceeded at once to remove the second metope. On the following day, on its being safely lowered he, in jubilation, wrote to Elgin congratulating him on these two 'works of Phidias' which 'will immortalise your name'. The operations had been tense: 'When I saw the beautiful statues hanging in the air depending on Ragustan cordage', wrote Hunt, 'I was seized with a trembling and palpitation.' Thereafter, he was set to take fourteen metopes in all.

Thus it was that the greatest act that stands in the name of the seventh Earl of Elgin was undertaken in his absence, by his agent, a young man in holy orders, capable of exercising an indominable and independent secular will, able to seize the brief opportunity of favourable coincidences. Of course Elgin had chosen and sent him. At this time Elgin became as excited, indeed euphoric, by the prospect now opened up as was Hunt. The original intention of drawing and casting only was abandoned. The fever of Hellenism and the rage of possession had seized him. Here was the opportunity to carry out one of the greatest artistic adventures of all time, rescuing for western civilisation the finest expression of its dawning. Were they not bearing to Britain the artistic apogee of the classical world, in the face of fierce and resentful competition from the French, and also saving it from the deterioration and destruction which could have resulted from the careless custody of the Turks? Hunt was authorised to spend all that was necessary in order to consolidate the great acquisition. No question of restraint, financial or otherwise, seems to have entered Elgin's mind.

Under Hunt's direction, Lusieri and his men worked ruthlessly. Some of the blocks of marble had to be sawn away from their lodgements and others levered free with crowbars. The Parthenon, though still a noble ruin, was to be left considerably despoiled. But as Hunt noted, this systematic stripping had been proceeding over the years by far-reaching piecemeal casual damage. Indeed Hunt regarded these depradations as justification for what he himself was doing. The Janissaries, the Acropolis garrison, the latest vandals, had wantonly broken apart sculptures and bas-reliefs in their search for the lead clamps that held them in place. In 1749 there had been twelve figures on the west pediment but by 1800 only four remained. Slabs of the frieze too had disappeared in this time. So much had been destroyed or removed by 'Mohamedan bigotry seconded by French intrigue', Hunt convinced himself, that there was a positive duty for Lord Elgin to salvage what remained. Moreover there was a special need for haste: the French, including Bonaparte, lusted after the sculptures, and no one could tell when the unpredictable Turks might be blandished into a new alliance with France, their old ally, once peace had been agreed. The acquisition of the Parthenon sculptures became an extension of the war against Bonaparte's France.

Within three weeks Hunt and Lusieri had completed the first critical phase on the Acropolis. They had achieved prodigies of levering, lowering, excavating, crating and conveying Fauvel's cart along the road to the Piraeus. Any difficulties raised by the Turks had been smoothed over. Hunt had left Athens on 2 August, on his mission to the Pashas and Greek officials, scarcely hours after the lowering of the second metope. He was also to undertake a widened search on behalf of Elgin for busts, vases, inscriptions, coins and medals.

On 22 August Lusieri was relieved from his trials and allowed to accompany Hunt on a second tour of the Greek lands. In his brief travels the Neapolitan, like Hunt, now found himself in yet another rôle, that of military intelligence, reporting back to Elgin the state of Turkish preparedness at Corinth and elsewhere. In the Morea they discovered that the troops were five years in arrears in pay. While travelling Lusieri thought about the next phase of the Parthenon programme. One of the great difficulties was the weight of the slabs, making them very cumbersome to handle and transport. To lessen this he decided that they should be sawn lengthwise and so rendered thinner by the removal of their backs. On their return they borrowed the only available saw from the convent. Lusieri hurriedly asked Elgin for a dozen marble saws of different sizes which he said would be essential for further work on the metopes and on the frieze. Being over fourteen feet long, the great central slab of the East frieze would require twenty-foot saws. Crowbars were needed to loosen and lever the elements of the frieze. Elgin quickly managed to find and send the necessary tools. The attitude of Lusieri, no less than that of Hunt, was critical to the success of Elgin's plans, being another fortuitous circumstance suggesting that Athena actually approved of his taking into safe custody the remains of her shrine. In October Lusieri removed one of the finest of the caryatids from the Erechtheum porch as well as sawing off a fragment of the cornice, replacing the statue with an unsightly brick pier; it was actions like these which were to inflame Elgin's critics the most.

On 31 August Mary gave birth to her second child, a daughter, named Mary for her mother. Things were a good deal easier for her this time although there was the very real fear of smallpox in Constantinople at the time. On their way out the Hamilton Nisbets had met in Vienna the celebrated Dr. de Carro famous for his smallpox vaccinations. Discovering that he was a Swiss who had studied medicine at Edinburgh under William Cullen, the Nisbets were impressed. They persuaded Elgin to send to de Carro for vaccine. It arrived in a quill enclosed in a bottle. Elgin already knew the name of Jenner, the English vaccinator, for his father the Reverend Henry Jenner, had been Elgin's mother's chaplain. Little George Constantine, Lord Bruce, was accordingly vaccinated and within a week the new baby was also inoculated in both arms. By this time Mary, along with Dr. Scott, had become an enthusiast for inoculation, and some seventy people in their household were treated. Letters reached Elgin daily from Smyrna, where hundreds of children were dying, asking for such help. Mary had been taken by missionary zeal, 'I think', she wrote to her mother, 'that we shall compleatly establish the vaccine in this country.' But Bruce it seems needed to be done a second time. Dr. Scott 'brought a fine healthy child to the house, and took the vaxine from its arm to Bruce's.'

Serious though Mary was in promoting smallpox inoculation, it, together with her entertaining, was not enough to occupy her. She was much concerned with the runaway house and kitchen expenses of the Embassy. In 1800 no less than £8,472 had been spent: during 1801, partly on her mother's urging, she reduced this to £4,847. Among other duties she dealt with drunkenness among the English servants. But there was still plenty of time for the gossip of the *corps diplomatique*. All manner of liaisons flourished, the details of which Mary duly reported to her mother, together with the petty jealousies and mutual aggravations. One of Mary's economies was to dispense with Elgin's chamber orchestra although Belloti its leader was allowed to stay on without pay but with food. He was languishing for love of a Madamoiselle Leiger. In his dejection he had sought consolation, so that Mlle.Leiger had discovered him sitting on a tombstone 'earwigging a Grecian beauty.'

One of the honours bestowed on Elgin was for Mary to be received by the mother of the Sultan, the Valida Sultana. On 3 October 1801, dressed in her English Court gown, Mary was received by the black eunuchs. As soon as the Great Door was closed, a vast number of women magnificently dressed gathered round her in excited welcome. 'Two led me by the arms, whilst one great lady walked before me with perfumes smoking in a beautiful gold thing; in this State I was led upstairs; upon the top stood Hanum (the Captain Pasha's sister) screaming with joy at seeing me... the Valida was sitting upon a very small sofa, I made her three bows ... she said she received me publickly that all the world might know it, for that both she and her Son were under such obligation to the English that they could not sufficiently express their thanks; that they hoped Elgin was to remain here, for that his superior sense, prudence and abilities, added to his friendship for them, had been of the greatest utility to her Son.' There was the usual exchange of gifts, with Mary's servants doing very well and Mary herself receiving an encrusted gold watch. Mary seized the opportunity of telling two of the Valida's favourites of the powers of the vaccine. It appeared that one of these women had born eleven children of whom only one had survived, most of the others had died of smallpox. Three days later it was Elgin's turn to be honoured. He was received by the Sultan in a special audience, the highest recognition available.

Meanwhile it became apparent from her letters that Martha, Elgin's mother in England, was subjecting the Heiress Presumptive, the Princess Charlotte, aged 5, to the same evangelical fervour as had been exerted on Elgin. 'This day she said to me', wrote Martha, 'on reading the Catechism of Watts for seven-year olds, "The question is, how do you know you have a soul?"' The next day the Princess made faces and said bad words. 'Punish me, Eggy,' she sobbed, so that Martha tied her hands with a handkerchief and with her sash tied her to the post of the bed.

Elgin knew perfectly well the precariousness of his position at Constantinople. The fact that the British had ejected the French from Egypt and Syria thus generating the current Turkish effusiveness, did not detract from the fact that, the Turks could, incline back to the French, once the British had foiled Bonaparte's ambitions in the eastern Mediterranean and the Balkans. Even the offer to provide the British with a new palace, so that the French one could be vacated, could well be seen as a preparation for the French return. Elgin suspected that the French if allowed back into Constantinople, would at once set about turning the Porte against him, hoping to impound his gains from the Acropolis. For as yet none of the Parthenon trophies were safely in British hands: the Marbles lay about in Athens and the Piraeus. Indeed on 2 December Mary reported to her mother that 'a smart French beau' had arrived to sign a treaty with the Turks, thus putting the Elgins, in spite of all Mary's panache, in danger of being eclipsed by this new novelty. Nor did Elgin wish to be at odds with the French. Both he and Mary would dearly have loved, when the war was over, to preside over the British Embassy in Paris, a career plum in a capital he knew and liked, comfortably close to London.

Hunt and Lusieri's prodigious acquisitions had to be accompanied by no less a transportation achievement. Elgin hoped that English men of war could be directed to Athens to pick up the prizes, but it was difficult to persuade captains still vigilant for French ships and eager for action, to encumber their decks. Nor had Lusieri's zeal flagged: by late September 1801 the attack had begun on the frieze. Though he did succeed in placing some pieces in warships, such arrangements proved much more difficult than Elgin had hoped. In near-desperation he bought the brig *Mentor*.

Late in December the old French Palace which the British had been using, was pulled to the ground. For its replacement, wrote Mary, 'Elgin has made a very handsome plan in the stile of Broomhall.' This pleased her, but she wished it had happened two years ago so that she could have used her architectural and decorative talents. The hunchback Balestra was the professional architect, carrying out Elgin's instructions. At Broomhall the facade and porch were still incomplete and would remain so for many years: at Constantinople a porch was provided, complete with triglyphs and metopes.

Before her departure, Mrs. Nisbet had made Mary promise that she would work on Elgin to bring about the freedom of some 136 Maltese slaves held by the Turks. In 1800 Malta had become a British possession. This Mary did and Elgin prevailed upon the Captain Pasha to release them. This action was in reality a gift to Elgin, worth perhaps some £40,000 for the slaves could no longer be sold. The chains of these miserable men were struck off and they were sent to the bath. Mary was deeply moved by their pathetic gratitude: 'They will pray for us while they live', she wrote to her mother. Elgin also obtained the release of French prisoners held under barbarous conditions, issuing some 2,000 of them with safe-conducts.

Dr. de Carro in Vienna proposed that Elgin's Turkish embassy might be used as a vaccine station on the route to India; to this Elgin assented. De Carro saturated a piece of lint with the vaccine and sealed it between two plates of glass, one of them concave, having the whole covered by a candlemaker with layer upon layer of wax. The package arrived safely in Constantinople and Elgin immediately forwarded it to Baghdad where it arrived on 31 March 1802. From there it proceeded to the Persian Gulf and on to Bombay, vaccinations being performed on the way. From there it was disseminated to various parts of India where vaccination Boards were set up.

Over a period from early February 1802 to late March Elgin himself became frighteningly ill, being much affected by what Hunt called 'the plagues, both moral and physical', of Constantinople. Matters were complicated by his insistence on dosing himself heavily with mercury. As a result a corruption had set in that was eating away his nose, a hard fate for a once-handsome man. Mary too was very low with anxiety over Elgin's health, as well as being pregnant for the third time. Elgin was near exhaustion. His health had never been good and he had already been exposed to the insanitary conditions of Constantinople for some two years.

On 28 March 1802 the Elgin family left Constantinople for Greece and the Aegean historical sites. On the way they inspected the work at Athens and furthered the diplomacy done by Hunt with the pashas, picking up artefacts as they went. They reached Athens early in April and were based there until late June, some two and a half months. Elgin, of course, had never previously visited the Athenian scene where so much was being done in his name. On leaving Constantinople his health had improved at once by the time he reached Athens he had become full of energy, an enthusiastic traveller once more. Mary too, though pregnant, recovered her spirits, showing her old zest for exotic scenes and high hospitality, enjoying the lavish receptions by pashas *en route*.

But Elgin's great concern was with the further increase of his collection. To this end he undertook two extensive tours in Greece, taking Mary and the children on the first of these, but leaving them in Athens on the second. On both journeys he eagerly seized upon new ancient artefacts.

There was also the need to still the mounting alarm of the Disdar at Elgin's seemingly endless depredations. The Disdar pleaded with Elgin to obtain a further firman, justifying what had been done and giving renewed instructions. Elgin promised to do this on his return to Constantinople. The Disdar's fears at the extent of the operation on the Acropolis did not cause Elgin to desist, but rather to quicken the pace. He felt no guilt at expropriating the Greek heritage, for in his eyes the present occupants of the country were a polyglot lot, with little claim to be the descendants of the men of the age of Pericles. He planned to acquire 'a complete representation of Athens', so that it might be preserved in perpetuity in England as part of the successor civilisation to Greece. Nor was he greatly disturbed at the damage being done to the Parthenon, (though to be fair the worst was to take place after he had left). Some seven metopes and portions of the frieze had been removed by the time he departed, without major damage to the fabric.

The problem of transport was as pressing as ever, so while Elgin was absent on the second of his tours Mary exerted her charms, her 'female eloquence' on one Captain Hoste, who, after initial refusal, took away eight cases. Mary was greatly pleased by her success, asking her husband in a letter, 'Do you love me better for it, Elgin?' To complicate matters the French were making things difficult in Athens: the Calmuck, one of Elgin's employees, was suspected of aiding them.

The journey back to Turkey was slow. The Elgins did not reach Constantinople again until 8 September by which time Mary's pregnancy was far advanced. Matilda was born about a fortnight after their return. Meanwhile Elgin's brig, the *Mentor*, loaded with seventeen crates had sunk on its way to Malta while trying to make harbour in a violent storm. The Marbles lay some 12 fathoms deep off Cerigo, at the tip of the Peloponnese, only the tops of *The Mentor's* masts marked the place. The great central slab of the east frieze sawn down the middle to reduce its bulk, was part of the shipwrecked cargo. Elgin did not learn of the calamity until late in October.

Meanwhile at the request of the Voivode he had gone to the trouble of obtaining another firman, from the Grand Vizier. After dispatch to Athens, Lusieri surrendered it up to the Disdar, and as no copy having been taken, no direct evidence of it survived. From all reports it seems to have been a blanket endorsement of all that had been done so far, with permission to continue. Were this document available it might have been possible to determine the legitimacy of what was done in Elgin's name. Mary had become very uneasy about Elgin's zeal remarking 'We might have seen the Seven Towers (prison) after all.' By this time Lusieri was becoming increasingly anxious about the damage he was doing to the Parthenon in Elgin's name. The ninth metope and much of the frieze had now been removed, leaving a dismal sight. He wrote to Elgin of 'barbarisms that I have been obliged to commit in your service.' As atonement he pledged himself to 'execute here the best work of my life.' But this he could not yet do, 'when the work of collecting is going on so furiously.'

As soon as Elgin heard of the fate of the *Mentor* he began frantic attempts at her salvage. The faithful Hamilton had been purchasing Arab horses for the stud Elgin proposed to set up at Broomhall. He was now sent to rescue the sunken Marbles, a thankless task on a barren shore threatened by pirates with almost no facilities. Elgin's best hope was probably to persuade a ship's captain to try to raise her, or to appeal to Nelson for aid. Moreover twelve or fifteen further cases still waited at the Piraeus for shipment. At last their party had a stroke of luck. By December Hunt was back in Athens, and when Captain Clarke, commander of the troopship *Brackel*, ineptly ran her ashore nearby Hunt was able to muster local aid to rescue him thus earning Clarke's gratitude. And so against the protests of his officers Clarke consented to uplift a cargo of forty-four of Elgin's cases, including the chief statues from the East pediment. Hamilton struggled on at Cerigo with his local divers becoming ever more difficult. At Constantinople the plague had again attacked, with one hundred and fifty deaths in one day. When Elgin returned from the city to Pera he changed his clothes and washed himself in vinegar.

Elgin had hoped his embassy would end shortly after his return to Constantinople.

But it was not until 17 January 1803 that he and Mary and the children finally left. Elgin's health had once more deteriorated. They took with them their two Greek *paramanas*, or wet nurses to care for the toddlers and the baby. On the journey home Elgin was to make a tragic mistake which was to change his life. As a consequence he lost the eclat of an ambassador returning home laden with laurels, his career prospects withered, his finances sank into chaos and Mary disgraced and deserted him.

CHAPTER 7

Prisoner of Bonaparte and Scandalous Divorce

The journey home was leisurely. The party travelled the first in the *Diana*, reaching Athens on 25 January 1803 where Elgin spent a week instructing and exhorting Lusieri. Moving on, they called in at Cerigo to view the melancholy remains of the sunken *Mentor*, still with its cargo of Marbles in its hold. On 3 February they were held up in Malta for the quarantine, one of the real divides between western Europe and the east. While at Malta Elgin made the fateful decision to proceed from Marseilles overland through France. By 16 March they had reached Naples; Holy Week was spent in Rome. There Elgin sought out Canova, the most celebrated sculptor of the day, to discuss with him the idea of 'restoring' his Parthenon treasures. Canova to his great credit said that it would be sacrilege to touch them with a chisel. Meanwhile Lusieri had been left alone in Athens, the other artists having been sent home.

In Rome, Mary, for her part, made confidential approaches to Lady Beverley, a family friend. For though the recipient of Mary's long and loving letters, her mother, Mrs.Nisbet, was far away, and in any case, with her strict view of marriage, could not be expected to hear the sort of problems which troubled Mary most. They had to do with her feelings toward Elgin which had become very confused. Mary had suffered much during her three years of married life, what with the travel, the heat, the disease and the childbearing. Perhaps Elgin had been unfaithful although no such charges were ever made public. In any event Mary unburdened herself to Lady Beverley, seeking understanding and advice and trying to clarify her own thoughts and feelings.

Elgin's decision to travel overland meant that the three children were sent on by sea in the *Diana* with their *paramanas*. For Mary this was a great wrench, though it simplified the travelling arrangements. It may be that the couple wanted to avoid Mary's seasickness, so terrible in the Bay of Biscay on the way out. There was also the prospect of spending time in Paris.

For weeks there had been talk of renewed war between Britain and France. But Elgin had received assurances that under any circumstances he could safely pass through France. However Bonaparte was to break with the European tradition here, as with so much of aristocratic Europe to which Elgin was accustomed. While at Lyons the Elgins learned that the Peace of Amiens was at an end, but by then it was too late to turn back. When they arrived in Paris they discovered that the British Ambassador, Lord Whitworth, had left. On the night of 23 May 1803 the First Consul ordered that all British citizens between the ages of nine and sixty be seized. Of these Elgin was among the most important. He was astonished to find himself in this position, thinking that his ambassadorial status would have assured him of inviolability. Among those held, and as it turned out much in the Elgin's company, was Robert Ferguson of Raith the younger, heir to an estate in Fife not far from Broomhall and a personable young man. Mary was greatly upset by the arbitrary action of Bonaparte, which separated her from her children and her parents, so near the home she had not seen for so long. 'It is extremely hard', she wrote to her mother, 'after having escaped the Seven Towers to be laid up here'. A depressed Elgin refused to stir out and by mid-June she was pregnant again. She was also greatly worried about Elgin's finances and the endless difficulty of controlling them. She had the consolation that the three children were safely in the custody of her parents in Portman Square. Meanwhile Elgin himself was well aware that the momentum of his diplomatic career was in grave danger. Then too there were the Marbles, the first of which were due to arrive in England, and others of which had yet to be safely embarked, with yet others lying at the bottom of Cerigo Bay. Elgin's health began to deteriorate once more. He was advised to go south to Barèges in the Pyrenees to take the waters: the necessary permission was obtained for this and the move to Barèges made.

There now began great exertions to persuade Bonaparte to let Elgin go. Count Sebastiani, Bonaparte's cousin, whom the Elgins had known and entertained at Constantinople, undertook to mediate. He said that Bonaparte had decided to release Elgin, but that Talleyrand had persuaded him not to. And so the handsome Sebastiani failed. The international banker and great friend of Elgin, M.Perigeaux, whose daughters were married to Napoleon's marshalls, brought his influence to bear but without success. Martha the dowager Countess of Elgin wrote frantically to all her contacts in Europe but without avail. She had her own troubles, for as governess of Princess Charlotte she was caught up in the conflict between the Prince of Wales and George III over the Princess' upbringing and education, with poor Queen Charlotte, Lady Elgin's friend, torn between them. But she managed to retain the goodwill of the royal couple, as evidenced by the presentation to her by the King of portraits of himself and the Queen by Benjamin West.

Barèges turned out to be an excruciatingly boring setting for Mary, with few interesting walks or rides although there were some excellent whist players. It was much cheaper than Paris offering no temptations to Elgin's extravagance, so that Mary began to hope they would save a little cash. Also the waters seemed to have a good effect on Elgin, with him spending two hours a day in the bath. Indeed Mary believed Barèges had saved Elgin's life. He was cheered to hear of the safe arrival in England of his Arab horses, though Mr. Nisbet, gravely concerned with the Broomhall estate, was urging him to sell them.

By coincidence, Elgin's great rival for the Marbles, Le Comte de Choiseul-Gouffier turned up. He, like Elgin, was now overtaken by tribulations having lost his fortune and having just heard that the French frigate carrying his antique treasures, once kept safe from Hunt in the Capuchin Convent in Athens, had been taken by an English ship. He wept as he told Mary of his misfortunes, entreating Elgin to write to Nelson so that he might help recover his antiquities. Elgin did all he could to have Gouffier's Marbles returned to him, behaving altogether honourably throughout. Nevertheless, the Gouffier Marbles became part of the Elgin collection.

Barèges not being congenial, the Elgins moved in late October to Pau where they rented a modest house and Mary set about making it a home. She was captivated by the setting. But there was one snag. Although Elgin had assisted some 2,000 French prisoners after the Egyptian campaign and given them safe conducts it was believed in France that he had abused them: 'Ah, c'est ce Milord Elgin', was the local remark, 'qui a si maltraite nos compatriotes à Constantinople!' At the level of the local governor and Commander, however, the Elgins were accorded the honours of their rank, in the old chivalric hostage style, dining with their captors and enjoying their company.

Mary yearned for her children. Late in November it was decided that she would go to Paris to work for Elgin's release, and to seek a temporary passport to allow her to visit England. On reaching Paris however all her papers were seized. They included the undertakings of Elgin's safe passage through France, including that of Talleyrand. She was immediately caught up in bureaucratic confusion, a passport for her having been issued but lost in transit. She was, moreover, kept under close surveillance.

On 24 November Elgin was informed that the French were prepared to exchange him as a prisoner of war with General Boyer, who had been captured in the West Indies, and that he was to be treated as equivalent in rank to a General of Brigade. It would seem that this was the result of Mary's approaches to Talleyrand. He sent to inform Mary of this, urging her to use all possible influence in England to obtain agreement. But now the rumour was rife in France that Boyer was being abused in England. For retaliation Elgin was suddenly arrested and conveyed to the fortress— prison of Lourdes, high on its rock, a truly forbidding place, where he was held a true prisoner, in a dreary and intensely cold room. A distraught Elgin destroyed all his papers and made his will. The loss of Mary's letters was particularly bitter.

Mary was horrified when she heard of this development, knowing that confinement in winter under such conditions could kill him. She sent Elgin a loving letter and a lock of her hair: it was strong and dark, but with a golden tinge. She saw at once that it was imperative to bring about the exchange of Elgin for Boyer, now dependent on the agreement of Britain. She urged Elgin's mother to speak to the King and she wrote immediately to Lord Hawkesbury (later Lord Liverpool) sending her letter to London with Molvitz her servant as a courier. She saw Talleyrand for a second time, and was assured that because of her intervention, Bonaparte stood by the exchange. Moreover via Talleyrand she prevailed upon Bonaparte to release Elgin from Lourdes so that he might return to the villa they had rented at Pau. He had spent about a fortnight under dreadful conditions. Negotiations went well; Mary arranged for a tambourine to be sent from England for Madame Talleyrand. Although Mary never met Bonaparte, she created quite a stir in Paris. 'I am just now in great vogue at Paris', she wrote in her old ebullient style, 'since the First Consul was so amazingly captivated with my letter'.

In the end Mary's main initiative failed. Lord Hawkesbury wrote to say that the King could not see his way to 'sanction the principle of exchanging Persons made prisoners according to the Laws of War, against any of his own Subjects, who have been detained in France in violation of the Law of Nations'. And so in spite of the favour enjoyed by his mother with the King, Elgin thus found himself the victim of high principle. Nor did the fact that his mother had presented his children and their *paramanas* to the King do anything to ease Elgin's and Mary's detention. So ended all hope of Elgin's early release.

1 Martha, Countess of Elgin, *c.* 1790. Miniature by Cosway. 2 Thomas, her son, 7th Earl of Elgin and 11th Earl of Kincardine, *c.* 1799. Miniature by Cosway.

3 Mary Hamilton Nisbet, Countess of Elgin, later Mrs. Robert Ferguson. Courtesy of the National Gallery of Scotland.

4 The portrait painted at Biel, East Lothian, in honour of a joyful family reunion which never happened. Lord Bruce, the heir, with his sisters Mary and Matilda, and the Greek nurses. Lord Bruce holds up a miniature of his parents Thomas and Mary.

2 Lord Elgin's first museum at Park Lane, London, 1807. Drawing by C.B. Cockerell.

My Lord

London Newman Street Sep.t 16. 1812

Agreeable to your Lordships request, I this day sent a Draft I am undertaking a few one in which the drawing of the Temple of Theseus are compiled with much truth. When the one in present shape meets round them. Your Lordship will find that I have done agreeable to your Lordships wish to find the situation there made to your instructions in the situation there made by the vicinity with the hill. They have been favoured to Edinburgh, and I shall be proud of still times to be removed with your commands.

I cannot close this letter without noticing to your Lordship how happy you have made some of our ingenious students of the Royal Academy, in giving one the permission for views, and drawing from your Matchless of Burlington for Service. That this may Your Lordship might have with Drawsom. I have permitted anyone who have gained Medals at the academy to draw after them; this permission has created a spirit of Emulation in this means of Studying, of the greatest importance, and will be produce have I more real use in improvement, than has ever been attain stage to the arts improvement.

This (country) (beyond) for which the country, and the arts indebted to your Lordship.

Mr Benj.n Wyatt the architect of Drury Lane Theatre, has desired to me her permission to sketch some of the figures from the Marbles for finishing to embellish some conspicuous parts in the Theatre, but wish your Lordships consent for that purpose, I am not empty with his request on this subject, but will be happy to know your pleasure.

I desire I send the picture from the councle Affair.

I am with profoundest respects
My Lord
Your Lordships
Much obliged
Benj.n West

Since in council much for the
for I in my right hand nearly Drum
one is stay

The Earl of Elgin

London Newman Street Sepr 15, 1812

My Lord,

... ...

... ...

I cannot close this letter without noticing to your Lordship, how happy you have made some of our ingenious students of the Royal Academy, in giving me the permission for them seeing, and drawing from your Marbles at Burlington House. That this indulgence might be done with decorum—I have permitted only those who have gained Medals at the academy to draw after them: this permission has created a point of elevation in their means of studying, of the greatest importance, and will be productive of more real advantage to the arts improvement than has ever been attained in this country, and for which the country and the arts are indebted to your Lordship.

... ...

Inclosed I send the paper from the coach office and I am with profound respects.

My Lord,

    Your Lordships,

        Much Obliged,

            Benj[ami]n West.

P.S. Excuse incorrections for the gout in my right hand nearly deprives me of writing.

The Earl of Elgin.

3 Benjamin West's letter to Lord Elgin, with transcript of part of letter below, thanking him for allowing some students from the Academy to study the Marbles. West explains that he has 'permitted only those who have gained Medals at the Academy to draw after them'.

were our own'. 'What a horrible desperate idea', she continued, 'that nothing but death can make me free ... I feel I cannot live without you'.

Elgin had to make his decision with his wife in this state of confusion and near hysteria. It was asking a great deal that he should accept a future of marital celibacy. No less important was the precariousness of the succession of the Elgin family. He had only one surviving son, the least robust of his children. As a younger son himself, he had succeeded on the deaths of two older brothers, and so was well aware of how much hung on George, Lord Bruce. There was also the real possibility that the gossips would get hold of the story of his cuckolding: for it to be known that he had taken no action would be a sorry humiliation. He chose to divorce, with all the painful and lasting consequences for them all and the end of the hope that the rich Hamilton Nisbet estates would be joined to his own.

Ferguson did his best to head off a public trial, instructing his lawyer to try to persuade Elgin through his solicitor not to press matters. Ferguson had however written very damaging things about Elgin, including the suggestion that the condition of his nose was due to syphilis. He offered to make any necessary apology on this and other matters, such as would be 'consistent with the honour and feelings of a gentleman.' If Elgin were willing to allow a discreet veil to be drawn over the whole matter, Ferguson would offer no defence, accepting the judgment of the court.

There was, however, a complicated set of legal problems. Under English law it was necessary to obtain an Act of Parliament to end the marriage and as a preliminary to this, the ground for dissolution had to be laid in the civil courts. This involved an action against Ferguson for 'criminal conversation with the Plaintiff's wife'. It took place before the Court of King's Bench in London on 22 December 1807 when Elgin demanded £20,000 damages. The proceedings were relayed to the public in two lurid documents, 'The Trial' of Ferguson, and one 'authentic account' of an 'Enquiry of Damages'. Such publications would mostly find their way into gentlemen's libraries. Ferguson admitted without argument that he and Lady Elgin had been lovers; moreover he instructed his four counsel not to say anything attacking Elgin's character or behaviour. The job of Elgin's counsel was to suggest that the marriage had been faultless until Ferguson's appearance, that Mary was a gem of a wife to lose, and that Ferguson was the seducer of a highly vulnerable woman in a lonely and bewildering situation. There was thus a good deal of advocacy of the Sergeant Buzzfuzz kind. Ferguson's counsel argued that, Lady Elgin was a woman of great charm who might well induce uncontrollable passion in a man: indeed the more purple passages of Ferguson's letters, it was suggested, were not so much signs of a lascivious seducer but of a man caught up in a wild infatuation who had temporarily lost control. A second theme was that in so personal and impalpable a matter as the loss of a wife, financial considerations were out of place: Ferguson had given Elgin 'justice' by confessing his role. Instead of the £20,000 demanded, £10,000 was awarded. On this basis the necessary Act of Parliament was passed, a further very expensive proceeding. Ferguson at this time ceased to be a Member of Parliament, probably by resignation: he was not to resume his political career until 1831.

Meanwhile Elgin took a further step under Scots law, raising an action in the Commissary Court of Edinburgh in March 1808. This was necessary because both

and begin a new family, and that Elizabeth should be its mother. Accordingly he paid suit, to the great interest of his sister Charlotte, her husband and others of the family and friends, as well as Mrs. Oswald. But in her innocence Elizabeth did not read the signals. On Elgin's return visit to Dunnikier, between breakfast and church he suggested they should take a walk. They strolled through the groves and woodlands where she had spent so much time combining her search for knowledge and her literary and personal fantasies. Choosing his moment carefully, Elgin proposed to Elizabeth. Astonishment overwhelmed her, she was speechless and deadly pale. She stammered that she must consult her father and mother. There was silence as they walked back to the house. Elizabeth ran up to her mother's room, dropped into a chair and breathed out 'Lord Elgin has proposed to me!' Her father, on being told, burst out: 'It will be ruination for us all!' Mrs. Oswald, however, perhaps with the title Countess of Elgin ringing in her ears, took a more lenient view of Elgin's behaviour. In the past, when her husband had returned from Broomhall after trying to deal with its financial chaos, she had taken Elgin's part making excuses for him. She now insisted that Elgin's proposal was most gratifying. So, finding the two women to be of one mind, Oswald finally assented. Elizabeth returned to the grand walk in front of the house where she had left Elgin and told him of her parents' consent and her acceptance. They had walked a little way in silence when he said, 'I may now venture to offer you my arm.' It was their first physical contact.

Elizabeth became deeply in love with her 'bright being', with 'his beautiful dark blue eyes shaded by those dark eyelashes ... so full of spirit and life.' The affliction of his nose seems to have had no adverse effect on her. In his courtship Elgin became vastly energised, to the point perhaps of euphoria, full of fun and vivacity. He took his watch, a repeater by Brequet, from round his neck and put it round hers. He regaled her and the company with tales of his embassy, the Marbles and his imprisonment, teasing them that Oswald's steward at Dunnikier resembled Fouché, Napoleon's Minister of Police. Such anecdotes entertained Elizabeth and confirmed her unusual love which combined the filial confidence of a child with devoted and passionate love. But there was also the urge to make amends to him for what he had suffered in his first marriage. She thanked God for the gift of such a man.

Her mother, though pleased, took a more considered line. She took Elgin to one side and said, 'Now my dear son, you will remember that you are going to marry a very young girl who may be very ignorant of her new duties. You must be careful of her and also you must be very prudent.' The marriage date was set for 21 September 1810.

Then came the question of the marriage settlement. In his grand fashion Elgin insisted that £1,500 per year be settled on Elizabeth, as it had been on Mary Nisbet. When Oswald protested that this created too heavy a burden on Broomhall, Elgin announced that the provision for Mr. Oswald's daughter must not be inferior to that for Mr. Nisbet's. Moreover he had seen his mother suffering as a widow from smallness of income. And so this settlement became yet another encumbrance on Broomhall.

They decided on two wedding services—Episcopalian followed by the Scotch Presbyterian form. The first family service was in the drawing room of Dunnikier, the second in the library, with all the indoor and outdoor servants present. Elgin's four motherless children attended the ceremonies, a reminder of the task Elizabeth was undertaking. The carriage which left for Broomhall after the wedding was drawn by four greys, with two servants separately mounted with holsters and pistols in the old style of travelling in state. As the party slowly passed the gates of the Raith estate, Elizabeth could not help thinking of Mary, who 'by her error had been the cause of my bliss.' At Broomhall the windows were filled with the servants to see the arrival. At dinner Elgin was resplendent in a white cashmere waistcoat and knee breeches with white silk stockings, causing Elizabeth to admire 'his beautifully formed limbs and feet.' On Sunday he read prayers to Elizabeth alone, without convening the servants.

The days of her courtship, wedding and initiation as mistress of Broomhall were always to remain in Elizabeth's mind in the difficult years that were to follow, to be recalled as a time of bliss, redolent of memories of Elgin that were never to fade. But a shadow fell over the honeymoon. Within a fortnight came the news that her father had suffered a stroke and was paralysed down one side. Back at Dunnikier Elgin showed tender care for her stricken father. Elizabeth sensed that for her home at Dunnikier a generation was passing.

A little later, when Elgin was the President or the Preses of the Hunt Ball at Cupar, she became fully aware of the curiosity they aroused. His gallant appearance and their age discrepancy would have been enough to make them the centre of attention, but to that was added the notoriety that surrounded him over his previous marriage. Elizabeth became aware that the tongues that had wagged so vigorously over the divorce were now active discussing her youth and innocence.

So it was that within weeks Elizabeth abandoned her self-engrossed reading and her plan to embark on the study of mathematics. In their place she had acquired Elgin, his four small children, and the frightening keys and domestic account books of Broomhall. With all this there was the title of Countess, and the ranking of first lady of much of Fife.

Elgin was hoping for a second family, though he knew that this would increase the financial pressure on him, and soon Elizabeth was pregnant. He had given the Oswalds serious undertakings to economise, as he appreciated that Mrs. Oswald had overruled her husband's misgivings over Elgin's extravagance. The sale of the lease of the London house was to be accelerated and he had taken the first steps towards the preparation of a sales prospectus for his antiquities.

Early in March 1811 the couple set out for London. Negotiations over the sale of the Marbles to the government appeared to be reaching a critical stage. Still deeply concerned with the Marbles, Hamilton was an almost daily visitor. They spent much time discussing their craftsmanship and cultural meaning. Elizabeth, now well advanced in pregnancy, tried hard to follow: to help her Elgin asked Hamilton to find her a Greek master which he did, choosing Peploe the translator of Herodotus. There was much business to attend to, for example the sale of the lease of the Piccadilly house to the Duke of Gloucester (although this raised again the problem of where to keep the Marbles). The Duke of Devonshire temporarily came to the rescue, generously offering to store the Marbles in the courtyard behind Burlington House. At the Foreign Office Elgin's agent, Charles Broughton, was beset by his Lordship's impatient creditors. Elgin showed Elizabeth the sights of the city and took her to see his Arabian horses at

Cowens farm beyond Chelsea where Ferguson had placed them. She was in rhapsodies over his appearance as he set out for the Prince of Wales' fete, resplendent in a purple velvet coat with a deep border of embroidered silver flowers, with sword and the ribbon and star of the Order of the Crescent. She seems, however, to have known little or nothing of his business affairs, being treated as something of a child wife.

Early in May came the government's offer for the Marbles. At £30,000 it was in Elgin's eyes derisory. Profoundly shocked, he appealed to the Speaker of the House of Commons and to the Prime Minister, but to no avail. For the time being he was left with them still on his hands.

On 20 July 1811 in London came a great consolation: James Bruce was born. He came into the world just as Elgin was supervising the carting of the Marbles to their fourth London repository. While the operation was going on the Duke of Devonshire suddenly died, calling the whole operation into question: but fortunately the new Duke accepted the Marbles. To Elizabeth's delight James Bruce's birthday was also that of his father. Elgin now had a second son. He was to become the eighth Earl of Elgin and the most distinguished of his line. In the same month Elgin made repeated attempts to see Byron, having heard that Byron proposed a verbal attack on him on the subject of the Marbles. Byron however fended Elgin off. They never did meet.

On returning to Broomhall following the failure of the attempt to sell the Marbles to the government Elgin retired with his family old and new to the west wing of the house. He had set himself an annual expenditure limit of £1,500 so almost all his servants, horses and dogs had to go. Even the famous Arabian horses, Elgin's pride and joy costing some £450 per year to maintain, were disposed of. Closing up much of the house of course reduced general expense, although his hope that by so doing he would escape the window tax was frustrated. It was under these conditions that Elizabeth had to begin to meet the realities of life and to care for both Mary Nisbet's children and her own. In 1813 Robert was born, followed by Frederick in 1814. In this way Elgin acquired three healthy sons, together with the cost of raising and educating them. It was just as well: in 1813 George, Lord Bruce, at the age of thirteen produced unmistakable signs of epilepsy.

It was indeed high time to take money matters seriously. Yet Elgin's continuing passion to complete and embellish Broomhall had caused him to spend £13,410 on the house from 1807 to 1809, mostly on the interior under the architect William Porden. He had also hired William Stark and James Smirke to work on designing a worthy north front, left incomplete from Harrison's time. Stark was asked to design a fountain in the manner of the monument to Sir John Moore, the hero of Corunna. The harbour at Charlestown also needed to be improved: so Rennie the great engineer had been commissioned and produced a report in 1807. But because of cost nothing was done.

Still the urge to acquire more land had proven too strong to be resisted. The Wellwood family of Pitliver had long possessed lands that Elgin coveted: and now it seems that the Wellwood entail had reached a critical moment at which sale was possible. But the Elgins and the Wellwoods were mutually antagonistic; the elder Wellwood having publicly declared that he would never sell to Elgin. Their long enmity had arisen because the Wellwoods' lands carried a right of passage through those of Elgin, an endless cause of friction. It was necessary therefore for Elgin to act through secret proxy and in April 1807 he was successful in acquiring the lands. Wellwood was enraged, neighbouring landowners sympathised for they resented this kind of tactic. He took Elgin to court in 1809 and the case, at great cost, went to the House of Lords. Like so many landed transactions, this was a highly complicated matter, for Elgin had not bought the land outright for cash (almost nobody ever did), but acquired a 999 year lease, a very unusual arrangement. In addition Elgin 'paid' key money of £15,000 (or more probably did not pay, but treated this sum as a mortgage loan, paying only the annual interest). Finally Elgin paid annually a 'meal' rent, namely the money equivalent of so many bolls of oatmeal at feuars' prices (eg. the going price in local markets). This was an idea of his father, Charles and was a form of indexation of annual value. It was this kind of transaction that helped to make it so difficult for accountants or anyone else to discover the true state of affairs of a landowner like Elgin. The upshot was that Wellwood obtained an injunction against Elgin which, while it stood, prevented him from new borrowings.

There was a second land purchase, also with an intriguing aspect regarding the lands of Grange which Elgin also coveted. They belonged to Ferguson the Elder of Raith who had bought them for £12,000. It seems possible that the £10,000 damages Elgin received from the younger Ferguson in effect went into this purchase of the lands of Grange, completed in 1812, a curious outcome.

By 1812 the Broomhall estate was itself in urgent need of a new infusion of capital. The re-equipment of the limeworks could no longer be posponed because of the corrosive nature of the operation. The horse drawn railway system also needed to be modernised. Some £15,000 was thus spent. The purchase of the Wellwood lands was justified by the fact that they made it possible for Elgin to improve the transport system—linking his coal and lime works.

A landowner like Elgin was functioning in a setting which was traditionally illiquid. Such men entered into borrowing and lending operations with one another in which little ready money passed. For example Elgin's wedding settlement from Mr. Hamilton Nisbet for £10,000 in 1799 had taken the form of a claim on the Earl of Selkirk, on which Elgin received interest, but on which he could not raise money. This meant that whereas the big spenders, like Elgin, contracted their personal debts in cash, they had little means of meeting them except out of current revenue.

Three of Elgin's most pressing creditors were Charles Broughton, his former agent at the Foreign Office and the two banking houses of Greenwood and Cox, and Coutts. Broughton was himself being dunned by Elgin's creditors, most of whose claims presumably dated from the embassy: they included a coachmaker, a jeweller and a bookseller. By 1812 Elgin owed Broughton £18,000. The debt of some £4,000 to Greenwood and Cox was over the outfitting of the Fencible Regiment in 1795 which had been disbanded in 1806. Elgin himself, still nominally a military man, was raised to the rank of major general in 1809. After much wrangling Elgin's half-pay as a general was to be set against this sum finally, extinguishing it in 1838. Coutts received the lion's share of the proceeds when the lease of the London house was sold, though the price was disappointingly low and the Duke of Gloucester was slow in paying.

There were a good many additional financial calls on Elgin. In 1811 there was a plan to restore or rebuild Dunfermline Abbey, the Elgin's 'family' church, containing their burial vault. The tower had collapsed and covered the place where tradition said that King Robert the Bruce was buried. As principal Heritor of the Abbey Church Elgin was required to contribute £2,000. The rubble was cleared to reveal a skeleton which seemed indeed to be that of the Bruce, as the sternum of its chest had been pierced. According to tradition his heart had been thus removed and carried to the Holy Land. In the same year Elgin gifted to the people of Limekilns a burial ground along the Forth shore. The poor law, and his liability under it, had begun to attract his attention.

It would seem that Elgin's debts, in 1812, reached the immense sum of £103,440, excluding the London debts, perhaps another £20,000. The legal limit to the rate of interest was 5%, but there were many ways of evading this. One of them was to borrow on annuities. But this was ruinous, costing from 10% to 14% per year. Annuities indeed were a desperate measure, causing Hay Donaldson, Elgin's solicitor, to urge more vigorously than ever that he should reduce his debt. He pointed out to Elgin that if he could get £40,000 for the Marbles now (1813) would be better for him than £60,000 in five years time. Indeed Elgin's advisors were almost desperate to sell the Marbles before the compounding debt and frustrated creditors made it necessary to dismember the Broomhall estate. It was under this pressure that Elgin finally instructed Lusieri to stop the search for antiquities. But he had not the heart to throw Lusieri adrift after so many years service: the ageing Neapolitan became Elgin's pensioner, living out his life in Athens. He died aged 70 in 1821, hated by many Athenians as a despoiler of their inheritance. He had been Elgin's man for more than twenty years.

By 1814 Elgin's debt to Broughton at the Foreign Office was £18,000 and the Crown prepared to proceed against him. The following year the Marbles were impounded by the government. They were placed under security and so could not be shown to the public. The architect Stark's widow pressed pathetically for payment (which she received fairly promptly). The British Linen Bank at Dunfermline demanded new security. Great pressure was placed on Elgin's tenants, when his agents raised their rents to muster every sixpence they could.

There was, however, some financial relief for Elgin beginning in 1813. The rule in the Foreign Office was that an ambassador who had completed a minimum of three years' service was entitled to no less than £2,000 a year pension for life, payment to begin ten years after the ending of his service. Elgin had now met this requirement in minimal terms, and so was to receive this generous provision for nearly thirty years. In addition his military pension was £300 per year although he had served only a few months with his Fencibles in Ireland. In addition the Broomhall annual income was indeed considerable, being in 1816 thus:

Rental of land	£6,627
Limeworks	3,263
Coal	2,850
	———
	12,740

So there was still hope, but only if a most vigorous programme of economies was to be followed. It required that the compounding of the debt be stopped, with the sale of the Marbles the best hope of doing this, at least in part. Finally a means had to be found to fund the more pressing parts of the debt for a time. The Oswalds believed that an additional step was required, namely that Elgin's affairs be passed to trustees, taking the working of the Broomhall estate out of his hands. This was done in 1815.

CHAPTER 9

Touting the Marbles: the Curse of Minerva

The disastrous effect of the Marbles, together with other expenditures, on the family finances was to haunt Elgin and Elizabeth for the rest of their lives. It was to continue into the next generation, imposing a constant regime of economy upon the two sets of children throughout their formative years. With this went a deep sense of grievance against the government for they believed that their father had been badly treated.

When Elgin had written from France in 1804 asking Martha to present his collection to the nation, he had no doubt hoped that such a gesture would invoke a response of an *ex gratia* payment. Had this happened it would have stopped the accrual of compound interest on the debts incurred and ended the heavy handling and storage charges. The financial desperation arising from the Marbles might then have been avoided. For at that time Elgin had only laid out some £28,000 (an immense sum in itself, but not if compared to the final charges). This expenditure, representing some two or three years income from Broomhall, and would have been less had government paid up. Today, it is merely conjecture that had Elgin not been trapped in France he could have disposed of the larger part of his collection before its costs had escalated two and half times, and before he was obliged to expose his collecting activities to critical scrutiny.

When he returned to England in 1806 Elgin could not, of course, have predicted the problems in store during the ten long years before they finally became the property of the nation at the British Museum. Throughout all his bitter buffetings, indeed to the end of his life he regarded himself as a great benefactor of the nation. But he was obliged, in the midst of all his trials, to learn how complex were the responses of the British public to the treasures he was offering it, involving as they did artists, antiquarians, curators, romantic poets, travellers and various meddlers, along with the politicians. Together these men were to debate his title to the Marbles, their historical and artistic validity, his justification for removing them, and, finally, their appropriate money price. One undercurrent beneath all this was the newly dawning feeling in Britain about Greek freedom, deeply stirred by Byron and his *Childe Harold*. Indeed the ten year inquest on the Marbles provides a telling vignette of the world of English culture. In the course of it a gallery of enemies stepped forward, anxious not only to discredit the Marbles, but to play upon Elgin's misfortunes, including his financial embarrassment, his cuckolding and his ravaged nose. A second bout of notoriety, though not so painful as that of the divorce, was thus imposed upon him. Had he foreseen such a travail he might well had offered his collection to the nation without conditions in 1806, as intended in 1804, or accepted the offer of 1811.

The first hint of hostility came from Richard Payne Knight, the arrogant and dominant figure of the Society of Dilettanti. Knight was an extraordinary character who by the mysterious processes of the critic and collector's osmosis had risen to dominate the world of British artistic opinion. He combined a kind of anthropological interpretation of art with views on the ultimate nature of beauty. Surviving the publication of his first work, which dealt with phallic worship, he had in 1805 established his reputation with *An Analytical Inquiry into the Principles of Taste*. When in July 1806 Elgin had returned to London after his release from imprisonment in France, an encounter occurred between the two men which soon became an eager item of gossip. Knight had not seen the Marbles (they being still in their cases), but, at dinner at Lord Stafford's, announced to the company that some at least of the Marbles, in particular those from the pediments, were not of the Periclean age, but dated from the time of Hadrian, the Emperor having decided to restore and embellish the Parthenon. 'You have lost your labours, My Lord Elgin', he boomed. Though some eighteenth century commentators had held this view Knight's statement was entirely without real foundation being an outrageous piece of self-display. But it was the pronouncement of the man whose views dominated the archaeological establishment of the day, to whom wealthy aristocratic patrons and lesser men, unsure of their judgment, looked for guidance. Payne Knight continued to denigrate Elgin's Marbles, showing an almost irrational vindictiveness in so doing. It was to be little consolation to Elgin that in the end Knight wrecked his own reputation over the Marbles affair, for by then profound damage had been done. In 1809 in the text of the Society of Dilettanti's latest folio *Specimens of Antient Sculpture* Knight reiterated his dismissive view of the Marbles. The young Lord Byron added the voice of satire, pillorying Elgin and his collecting activities in *English Bards and Scotch Reviewers*, with reference to '... Phidian freaks, Misshapen monuments and maim'd antiques,' and in a footnote Byron referred to the damaged noses of many of the figures, a scurrilous reference to Elgin's face, hinting at syphilis.

Against all this there was enthusiasm from the rest of the artistic community. From the first opportunity to view in June 1807 there was an eager host of sculptors and artists anxious to study and to draw. Most of these men became Elgin's allies, proclaiming the extraordinary merit of his acquisitions. Indeed the Park Lane shed became a place of artistic pilgrimage. Hamilton acted in effect as curator. The sculptor, John Flaxman—in spite of his large output of statuary in the smooth Roman manner, resting on a notion of 'Ideal Beauty'—announced that Elgin's pieces far outshone the Italian works that Napoleon had expropriated for the Louvre. The aged American, Benjamin West, President of the Royal Academy, acclaimed the sublimity of the Marbles, regretting that he could not have his youth again so that he could fully assimilate them. Inspired by the Marbles, he hoped London might become 'a new Athens.' The youthful Benjamin Robert Haydon, soon to make his mark as a historical painter, was lyrical to the point of near-hysteria, proclaiming the Marbles as 'the most heroic style of art combined with all the essential detail of actual life.' His friend Henry Fuseli was no less enthusiastic, pronouncing in his Swiss-English, 'De Greeks were godes!' Sir Thomas Lawrence the portrait painter also frequently braved the chill of Elgin's Park Lane shed.

5   Philoppapos. Watercolour by G.B. Lusieri.

6   The Marbles on display in London. Watercolour by Benjamin Haydon.

8 James, 8th Earl of Elgin and 12th of Kincardine.

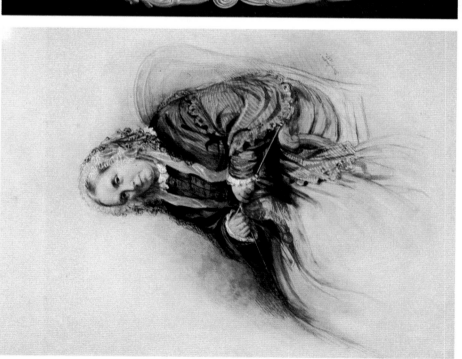

7 Elizabeth Oswald, Countess of Elgin, the second wife of the 7th Earl and mother of the 8th Earl, as an old lady, knitting, in Paris.

9   The first wife of the 8th Earl, Elizabeth Mary Cumming Bruce, Countess of Elgin, who died in Jamaica.

10   Mary Louisa Lambton, Countess of Elgin, his second wife.

Elgin was the rightful owner of the Marbles, as distinct from the British government on whose business he had been employed, and whose navy he had used to transport them. Here too Elgin was vindicated. Thirdly there was the question of the artistic merit of the Marbles and the appropriateness of making them public property 'for the purpose of promoting the study of the Fine Arts in Great Britain'. Once again Elgin's point of view was approved. Thus far things were going Elgin's way.

Then came the critical matter, that of price. No figure had come to the Committee from Elgin. At this point the Committee found itself involved in a classic aspect of economics, namely the theory of price. How were objects unique in themselves, with in effect a single buyer, to be priced? The criterion of cost of production (namely Elgin's expenses) was an inadequate guide, for in such a business much might be spent, achieving a result of no value. Nor could accidents such as the loss of the *Mentor* be taken to add to the value of the collection. Nor was there much help in arguing by analogy from other collections such as that of Charles Townley which the government had purchased. In the end, price theory proving barren, the Committee turned to a common sense solution, namely what would be politically acceptable in prevailing conditions. Alternative uses for public money in difficult times had to be borne in mind. Cruickshank in his cartoon had already shown John Bull and his starving family objecting to the purchase of stones, and broken ones at that, when what they needed was bread. So the Committee in effect adopted the political judgment of 1811 of £30,000, adding £5,000 to take account of additions to the collection and the further accrual of expenses. Perhaps it was significant that the collection had been seen only under very bad conditions, huddled in cold, dim and unwelcoming circumstances, with no proper display and lighting.

Elgin and Hamilton had reached the end of the road: they had tried every device and solicitation they could think of. Nothing could shift the £35,000 ceiling. This figure, was engrained in the mind of Charles Long and in that of most of the British Museum's trustees. For nearly six years Elgin had been struggling to raise the price of his only large vendible asset, and had woefully failed. Indeed in net real terms he ended up with less in 1816 than had been available in 1811. The repeated appeal for a British peerage could only detract further from Elgin's name. He had hoped that the government, unable for political reasons to award the true value of his Marbles, might make an additional payment in this non-pecuniary sense, but this was wholly unrealistic. Elgin sadly accepted the £35,000, voted by Act of Parliament and the promise that he and his heirs were to be trustees of the British Museum in perpetuity. The Marbles could now undertake the last of their journeys to the only place in Britain worthy of them.

More than half the money went at once to pay off Charles Broughton who had a year or so earlier obtained a lein on the Marbles. Throughout the story the loyalty of Hamilton had shone through, to be placed, almost alone, in the British controversy, against the bitter cohort of Elgin's enemies. There was also poor Lusieri whose great promise as an artist had been absorbed into Elgin's service as he acted as agent excavator, collector and clerk of works, doing so under conditions of Turkish and French hostility, often isolated without instructions or money.

It had all begun with modest enough intentions, proposing no more than to draw, measure and make casts. No doubt Elgin had had the idea of publishing a volume or two of engravings that would set out the architectural and sculptural achievement of the age of Pericles and Phidias, as embodied in the Parthenon, and establishing his place among the cognoscenti. Others had published such volumes of antiquities with great success, sometimes by subscription. Elgin was not a scholar or antiquarian, but, like so many of his generation, he, as all cultured gentlemen, was deeply conscious of the classical world. He had responded eagerly to the suggestion of his architect, Harrison, that it was time to shift the emphasis from Roman to Greek models, a movement in which Elgin could claim himself the leader. There was, moreover, a considerable tradition of European diplomats enlivening their missions by such cultural activity, especially in Mediterranean countries; Bonaparte's emissaries and generals were certainly expected to acquire the relics of Greece and Egypt. The elision to collecting was inevitable as so many loose pieces were lying about, to be picked up casually or to be acquired through the time-honoured method of the giving of gifts to Turkish officials. Indeed by Elgin's time the picking up of fragments from the classical world as part of the foreign tour had become almost an extension of the British aristocratic character, like high farming and mansion building. Many of those who were to criticise Elgin had themselves made such acquisitions. Indeed, through their offers of money, they had contributed a great deal to the damage done to classical sites by the Turks. Yet Elgin, engrossed in the complexities of his misson to the Porte, might well have gone no further than a few accessible pieces. It was the enthusiasm of Mr. and Mrs. Hamilton Nisbet, who had acquired some substantial prizes, especially the Gymnasiarch's chair, together with the driving energy of Hunt, that carried Elgin beyond the point of no return, making him an enthusiast for acquisition on the grandest scale. No less fortuitous was the character of Lusieri who became infused with a great zeal for vicarious acquisition, showing great energy on Elgin's behalf, not least in his bitter struggle with his opposite number, the Frenchman Fauvel.

There were two major underestimations that made it possible for the whole business to go forward. One was the ease with which the Marbles were removed, starting when Hunt had extricated the first and second metopes. Had more damage been done to the building then or had the cordage snapped, bringing down windlasses and metope, it is probable that the plunder would have ended there. The permission of the Voivode at such dismantling of the building itself would have been withdrawn, or at the very least the matter referred to the Porte with the full implications of what was being done in Elgin's name made clear. As it was, Hunt's success with the first two metopes set a precedent that was to lead much further. It opened in Elgin's mind a dazzling vision, namely the bringing together of a collection that would provide by direct authentic exemplification 'a full and accurate knowledge of the school of Phidias'. To this was added the intention of compiling examples of inscriptions such as would illuminate the evolution of the Greek language. And so in this way Elgin developed, step by step, and to some degree retrospectively, a rationale of what he was doing. At the same time he fell into the clutches of collector's fever. Everything that had any interest was to be acquired, as Hunt and Lusieri were instructed. Elgin himself on his visit to Athens and Asia Minor joined enthusiastically in this rummaging of Greece and the Aegean.

There had to be great haste, for no one could tell when the capriciousness of the Turk or a breakdown of the alliance would suddenly close the brief and fortuitous access to the glory that was Greece. Moreover the cultural rapacity of France must be forestalled. Bonaparte, having seized the treasures of Italy and placed them in the Louvre, lusted for those of Greece. Thus it was that the two great expansionist powers of the day shared an obsession with the relics of fallen empires and vanished cultures: this was part of their rivalry and was no less real for being unreal. These elements of compulsion were reinforced by a streak of stubbornness in Elgin, combined with a lack of a sense of proportion. It was one of the stresses that Mary had to bear that he could not be brought to make a cool calculation of the long-run effects on his estate and family of the expenses which he was incurring. But Elgin's financial fecklessness was a necessary condition to bring his collection into being: few if any, of much greater wealth, would have laid out so much.

At a certain level of consciousness, too, there is the possibility that Elgin was seeking to create his own monument; something that would remain and bear his name long after the memory of his embassy had faded. He knew better than most how fluid was the relation between Britain and France in their long war, and how ephemeral were triumphs, except those of a major kind.

The second great underestimation made by Elgin had to do with transport. He was not to appreciate the immense accumulating bulk and weight of his acquisitions. He seems to have been over-sanguine about moving his enormous trophies, both locally in Athens, to the Piraeus and overseas. He was almost presumptuously optimistic about his influence as ambassador in securing the aid of admirals and naval captains in using the British navy as his carrier. They, engaged in a major war, were not over-anxious to burden the Mediterranean fleet with tons of antiquities in awkward cases. Just as Elgin was drawn into commitment stage by stage over his acquisitions, so he generated for himself and Lusieri a transport problem which, if appreciated earlier, might have moderated his zeal. By 1815, when the last Elgin pieces reached England, at least twenty-two ships had been used. The comedy of Fauvel's cart (it changed hands no less than four times between the Frenchman and Lusieri), represented the all-too-serious problem of how to move great masses of marble where land transport facilities scarcely existed. There was, however, a curious irony that it was the transport problem which saved Elgin's second collection from removal by the French.

And so Elgin was caught up in the momentum of what became, in psychological terms, an absolute goal. But at the same time the Marbles literally exacted a great price from him and his family being a major financial disaster. In this respect they contributed to the destruction of Elgin's first marriage. They also damaged his career prospects, for in his attempts to extract a British peerage as part of his price he adopted the role of importuner. The Marbles episode no doubt contributed to the inveterate hostility of Napoleon that cost Elgin three prime and critical years of his life. Perhaps most damaging of all psychologically, there was Byron's curse on him and his sons. The Marbles were the central element in Elgin's life; they were his great preoccupation for some fifteen years. They gave him fame, linking his name with one of the greatest collections of all time, but it was an equivocal and uneviable fame.

Its dubiety had two aspects, those of cultural theft and cultural barbarism. As to entitlement to the Marbles, for Elgin the Greeks he saw around him in Athens had no claim to be the descendants of the age of Pericles, their blood having been so diluted by that of the Turks and various Levantines. To him the locals, the sycophantic Greek minor officials and the Orthodox priests, together with the debased labourers he hired, gave no sign of caring for the relics of 2,400 years ago. For the Greek Church indeed the Parthenon was as pagan as it was to the Islamic Turks.

As to the charge of vandalism, there can be no doubt that real damage was done, once the phase of rapid acquisition had been entered upon. The worst aspect was the throwing down of the cornices of the Parthenon to release the metopes, leaving the naked triglyphs pointing forlornly skyward, though it should be remembered that the most devastating description of this operation came from Edward Clarke, another of Elgin's inveterate enemies. There was also the taking of one of the caryatids and replacing it with a crude brick column, perhaps one of the most insensitive acts of all, which inflamed the minds of Elgin's critics. British travellers were appalled as they gazed at this bleak piece of brickwork standing wretched among the remaining caryatids. The degree of damage in removing the frieze is difficult to assess; it must be remembered that a number of slabs had already fallen though others had required heavy work with crowbars. But Elgin's men left most of the west frieze because the damage involved in its removal would not have been acceptable. It is worth noting that the casts they made of it are all that remain today, for the originals have been almost totally obliterated. The carving of the names of Lord and Lady Elgin on one of the Parthenon columns (together with those of Mr. and Mrs. Hamilton Nisbet, and other members of the 'Athenian Club'), though minor in itself, was taken by sympathisers with Greece as being particularly offensive. One person who was assailed with guilt over the 'barbarities' he had committed in Elgin's name was Lusieri who after the Marbles had set off to England, pledged to redeem himself by dedication to his art.

However, there is little doubt that Elgin, as against all his critics, saw himself as a great benefactor to British and European culture, one who had completed a stupendous rescue. Elgin could indeed regard himself as a latter-day secular crusader, saving the relics of high culture from indifferent or even hostile barbarians, and bearing them to a place where they would be appreciated for what they truly were. There is really nothing comparable in the history of collecting for scale, unity, beauty and evocativeness. Although the appreciation of the Elgin Marbles was certainly not reflected in the price they finally raised from the British government.

CHAPTER 10

The Double Family: the Succession

In 1816 Elgin was fifty. His career was permanently stalled. He was too old to make anything of soldiering; in any case Britain was now awash with unemployed half-pay officers. As to diplomacy or politics, his name had suffered too much damage for him to be employed, though he could never really accept that this was so. And so the Broomhall estate, the education of his sons, and his own health, became his chief preoccupations. But he continued to be lively-minded, greatly interested in, albeit distrustful of the marvels of the new age like the coming of the steam railway. On his visits to London he still had the entrée into great houses. He became an ever-higher Tory, an attitude that expressed itself most dramatically in his abhorrence of the first Reform Bill of 1832.

Broomhall had Elgin in its grip just as the Marbles had done. It was to occupy much of his thought and affect much of his life for his remaining years. There were two possible policies. One was to call a halt, and sell up the estate or a large part of it while the capital value still exceeded the debt by a considerable margin. The other was to pursue a forward policy, borrowing and sinking yet more money in an effort to bring the complex of railway, coal, lime, brickworks and the harbour to a new plateau of productivity which could then through its profits, melt the debt. Temperamentally there was no argument in Elgin's mind—he must stick with Broomhall. He knew that his creditors would foreclose only as the last resort and he hoped also that if he incurred further obligations to contractors and others these would be met out of increased profits. Since his early manhood Broomhall and its mansion had been the centre of his world: to lose them as he had lost the Marbles would be unbearable. Accordingly between 1817 and 1819 there was considerable further expenditure on the railway and by 1821 it at last linked Dunfermline and Charlestown. It was more accurately a waggon-way, horse drawn, using two inclined planes. About this time an accountant from Edinburgh called John McKean entered Elgin's service, becoming his principal financial and business adviser. Like so many of his predecessors he urged caution on Elgin, trying to restrain his more wilful schemes, though with no great success.

As an economy measure, however, Elgin and Eliza lived mostly in France where prices were cheaper and his creditors could not reach him. By visiting them for longish periods the children became fluent French speakers. By 1820 Eliza had borne four babies and had become increasingly engrossed in religion, infusing her children with a strong evangelicalism. But the Elgin ménage was an unsettled place, being a kind of itinerant affair.

In April 1821 George, Lord Bruce, came of age, and prepared to set off on a journey to Paris. As part of his personal declaration of independence, he proposed to visit his mother, Mary Hamilton Nisbet Ferguson. Elgin had refused to allow any contact between his first family and their mother who had borne Ferguson no children. Elgin had determined from the time of the divorce that for the daughters to be known to visit their mother would prejudice their marriage chances. But Elgin could no longer control Bruce, who insisted, on meeting his mother in spite of his own nervousness. Elgin himself delivered Bruce to his delighted mother in London. After the reunion Bruce continued to Paris, keeping a diary and writing mature letters. His father had used the occasion of Bruce's coming of age to make a further appeal to Lord Grenville for a British peerage, arguing that Lord Bruce, being heir to both the Elgin and Hamilton Nisbet estates was entitled to inherit a place, as of right, in the House of Lords when he succeeded his father. Grenville patiently pointed out that the proposal was unacceptable.

That year James, the eldest of Elizabeth's children, now ten, composed for himself a prayer to be shown to his mother: it was a mixture of precocity and heavy evangelical conditioning, reminiscent of that which his grandmother Martha had brought to bear on his father. James asked of God to 'Be with me this week, in my studies, my amusements, in everything. When at my lessons, may I think only of them; praying when I play: when dressing may I be quick, and never put off time, and never amuse myself but in play hours. Oh! may I set a good example to my brothers. Let me not teach them anything that is bad, and may they not learn wickedness from seeing me. May I command my temper and passions, and give me a better heart for their good.' Here is encapsulated the evangelical view of personal responsibility, including economy of time, a sense of its allocation between work and play, the control of the passions, the setting of an example, though at least there was a concept of playtime. It shows the extent to which at an early age a deep, almost morbid, sense of responsibility was inculcated. James and his brothers had a resident tutor at Broomhall, Fergus Jardine, who, with Scots care, taught them the rudiments of Latin and Greek.

In March 1821 news came of Lusieri's death in Athens—an old and lonely exile. He died amid a welter of unfinished drawings and paintings, most of which were lost by shipwreck in the Mediterranean on their way to Elgin by sea. The only surviving completed work from over twenty-one years that reached his master was Lusieri's painting of the monument of Philopappos. He was buried in the grounds of the Capuchin Convent.

Amidst his frustrations Elgin was a restless man, travelling about a good deal, visiting London to keep abreast of politics. There was some consolation in being elected as a representative Scottish peer in 1820, a seat he was to hold for the rest of his life. He visited Merthyr Tydvil to inspect the great ironworks there. At the Military Asylum in London he encountered Mr. Chase with his course of gymnastics, and having eagerly taken lessons he recommended them to his sons. The state of the poor law continued to interest him: his ideas on the subject being similar to those of Dr. Thomas Chalmers with whom he had become friendly. When in the 1820s there was a proposal to erect a Scottish national monument on the Calton hill in Edinburgh, to be a pantheon of great Scotsmen, taking the form of a replica of the Parthenon, Elgin was active in support. The scheme however foundered for lack of money, producing only a fragment of a colonnade. This, however, so dramatically poised above the city, helped to gain for Edinburgh the title of the Athens of the north.

Bruce had shown signs since the age of thirteen of being an epileptic. When in Paris in 1824 he suffered a serious attack which marked the beginning of a long and painful decline. From now on he required continuous attention, his attacks becoming increasingly painful and violent. Elgin, always zealous in matters of health and medicine, began an intensive search for a suitable doctor. All of this imposed an immense strain on the whole family. Eliza had by now taken a revulsion to her stepson. Poor Matilda, too, found that she could not tolerate her brother; his presence sent her into a state of agitation. Matty had indeed herself begun to show general signs of tension deriving, as Elgin sensed, from stress which arose from her parents' separation and Elgin's refusal to allow her and her sisters to see Mary their mother. She turned her affections toward her half-brother James, and a close bond developed between them. In childhood she used to call herself James' wife. James reciprocated her feelings, cherishing her letters when they were apart. Matty, like her step-mother, had become deeply involved in evangelicalism, reinforcing its impact on the young James. Elgin had to get used to the idea of having an invalid heir who was very unlikely to marry. If Mary, Bruce's mother, outlived her son, the Elgin claim to inherit Mary's fortune would lapse.

The Elgin family was usually based in Paris Eliza's own three daughters, Charlotte, Augusta and Frances were largely brought up there. Her middle step-daughter, Matilda, became Eliza's great support and confidante. Eliza liked Paris because it was free of the preoccupations of Broomhall, and living was cheap. In the course of time Eliza began to develop a salon, with her daughters enjoying the social duties involved. Despite the unusual circumstances in which Elgin's second family was formed and lived, its solidarity and intimacy was remarkable.

Eliza's sons were shaping up well. In 1825, James, now 14 and known variously as Jim, Jam or 'the Jos', went to Eton, where he showed great promise. His teachers spoke warmly of his talent and assiduity. He kept his expenses to a minimum, keeping a careful account of all he spent. Elgin on visiting his room found the Bible and religious books laid on his table. He was working so hard at his studies that he had little time for other reading except that of a religious nature. In the Fifth he was required to learn three hundred lines of Greek by heart each week. Elgin congratulated Eliza on her raising of her boys: 'May God bless them', he wrote, 'to give you all the comfort your anxiety and services to them so well deserve.' Somewhat later James completed a Greek play. He paid visits to Bruce as a kind of duty. Frederick followed James to Eton, partially overlapping with him. In spite of the straightened family circumstances Elgin saw to it that his eldest sons went to Eton and later to Oxford where the best connections were to be made.

At Eton James met William Ewart Gladstone, another deeply earnest young man, with whom a friendship developed, the two walking a good deal together. James had already learned to express himself well: Gladstone regarded him as the most eloquent boy of his generation. His inward searchings, as intense as ever, did not turn him into an introvert, as might have been expected, but contributed to his powers of self expression. Holidays were often spent at Torquay, where Lord Bruce lived for his health, or sometimes at Broomhall. On these occasions James would help his brothers Robert and Frederick with their classical studies.

By the end of James's Eton period the three oldest brothers had consolidated a fraternal compact that was to bind them together as long as they lived. It combined mutual affection and trust with a great feeling of public conscience. They seem to have sensed early that they needed mutual support in order to meet the challenges of the future, conditioned as it was by their inheritance. Though Frederick was Eliza's favourite, this did not impair the tripartite bond. Frederick's cheerfulness was a bonus, for the Elgin household could be a sombre place, what with Eliza's religious emphasis, the continuous strain as Bruce's health deteriorated, together with Elgin's own periods of bad health, usually taking the form of his facial tic and rheumatism of the jaws, making speaking and eating difficult. In 1827 Robert obtained a commission in the Guards, as his father had done, purchased for him by the faithful McKean. Edward, the fourth son, became a midshipman in the Royal Navy: Elgin saw the boy to his ship at Portsmouth.

By 1827 the finances of Broomhall were more precarious than ever. Elgin still hoped to complete the north front and main entrance to the mansion and had commissioned yet two more architects for this purpose. The pressure from his creditors reached a climax. It was the usual story of Elgin taking action to extend his property regardless of his indebtedness. However, the Elgin collieries were described as one of the most valuable coal properties in Scotland. There it was possible for a collier family to earn £12 to £14 per fortnight while Sunday and weekday schools were provided with libraries and medical attendance, all on reasonable terms. In spite of this however, there had been fears of militancy on the part of the colliers in 1825. They had submitted a list of their grievances, but without signatures, fearing victimisation. It is worth noting that the quarrymen and limeburners, from estate families, unlike the colliers, acccepted the paternalism of the estate.

Trustees were appointed yet again to try to sort things out. They calculated that the total value of the Broomhall Estate (excluding the mansion) was just over £300,000. This figure was arrived at by capitalising the average of three years profits on the three main functions of the estate: the rental had yielded £6,272, coal £5,155 and lime £2,890. The coal earnings had indeed doubled since 1816, but they, along with the railway, because of the capital invested in them, were responsible for more than their share of the debt increase. Against the capital value it is probable that the debt of the estate was about £100,000, involving a heavy interest bill. After the receipt of what remained of the Marbles money from the government in 1816 the debt had been about £70,000: Elgin's forward policy of further investment had gravely aggravated the debt problem. It was a heavy blow to him thus to lose control of the estate in which he was so emotionally involved. Eliza was worried that he would try to instruct the new trustees as to what they should do. But he confined himself to suggesting that there should be a comprehensive and competent examination by independent and qualified men of business, a step which he himself might well have undertaken long since.

Elgin continued to seek involvement in public affairs, perhaps a little wistfully. He was pleased to have access to the Duke of Wellington who several times dined him.

He continued to travel about the country, riding in 1830 in the recently-opened Liverpool to Manchester Railway which had brought powered rail passenger transport to the world. He was appointed along with Wellington to a House of Lords Committee on the Coal Trade, which revealed his rampant Toryism. If the price of coal was lowered it would cause an increase among manufacturers and 'the dangerous classes'. He seems not to have appreciated his own role in bringing such classes together on his estates in Fife. He had periods of remission from pain which gave him an opportunity of having a last fling in a steeplechase with his old friend Sir Robert Preston, Elgin's colours being black and white for coal and lime and Sir Robert's *couleur de rose*: Preston won, but could not stop his horse, as he disappeared hauling on the reins with his whip between his teeth.

In 1829 James went up to Christ Church, Oxford where his Eton promise was well fulfilled. He worked with great conscientiousness at his studies so that the hard reading involved became a dominant memory. He had intended, like Gladstone, to read for double honours but the strain proved too great, so that in the end he confined himself to classics. In them his spirit thrived. His interest in the ancient world burgeoned; and in his mind he related the Greek and Roman period to his own times. Their languages, Ancient History and Philosophy he made his own. He had the same studious earnestness as his father had shown, but his education was wholly English, without Scottish or continental injection. About half-way through his Oxford career he was awarded a studentship. One of the electors, a Canon of Christ Church commented, 'There is no young man, of whatever rank, who could be more acceptable to the society, and none whose appointment as the reward of excellent deportment, diligence, and rightmindedness, would do more good among the young men'. James was fulfilling the spirit of his childhood prayer. But he was also paying a price for his hard work. Disabling illness had overtaken him manifesting itself through headaches and constipation. By this time his father had encountered the celebrated Dr. Jephson who had built up a thriving fashionable practice at Leamington Spa. With Bruce already in his care, Jephson expressed quite unwarranted optimism. James, however, pulled himself round. At the Michaelmas Examination of 1832 he achieved a First, believed by common report to be the best of his year. Shortly thereafter he was elected a Fellow of Merton College.

Just as with Gladstone, the classics for James had a rival, or rather a complement, in the form of the Bible. James wrote a memorandum intended to guide his course of study. Ancient History, together with Aristotle's *Politics* and the classical orators were to be read in conjunction with Bible history, with a view of seeing 'how all hang upon each other, and develop the leading schemes of Providence.' In this way he expressed the urge for synthesis between the two great elements working in his mind.

Meanwhile he had formed a remarkable coterie of friends, to some extent an extension of his Eton circle. We find him a member of an Essay Club formed by Gladstone. There was, in addition to W. E. Gladstone, Charles Canning (later Lord Canning), James Ramsay (later Lord Dalhousie), Lord Lincoln (the Duke of Newcastle), and Sidney Herbert. Among these men who were to make their mark on mid-Victorian Britain and her empire, James Bruce stood high. He was inclined to keep his feelings and hopes to himself, standing apart from trivia and gossip, but his friends, confident in his soundness of judgment and steadiness, often sought his advice. It was from James that Gladstone learned that Milton had written prose. Indeed James had his heroes of ideas, among whom Milton came to feature as the advocate of free speech, and Coleridge as the believer in an ordered and organic society. With his brother Frederick, James was especially close. They corresponded in serious vein over the classics, philosophy and politics, sharing the family's evangelical values. But whereas James was rather short in stature, Frederick was tall and impressive. James and his brothers could hardly have been unaware of the curse pronounced upon them by Minerva in Byron's poem. It must have been chilling for them to read what the goddess of wisdom had pronounced upon them, that they be 'Without one spark of intellectual fire' and senseless. It seems likely that Byron contributed something at least to the brothers' urge to succeed in things of the mind, and to the deep solidarity between them.

During the 1830s Oxford and the nation were being swept by two great controversies. The first beginning in 1833 was theological centering on Keble, Pusey, Newman and the Oxford Movement. In this James took a deep interest; he did not involve himself in the violence of its differences. The second, even more disturbing, was the debate and the political action over the Reform Bill during 1831 and 1832, a profound challenge to the thinking of any young man concerned with public affairs at the level of fundamental principle. But here too James remained intellectually on the sidelines. He and Fred contented themselves by reporting the great campaign for reform with great animation during their visits to their mother and their sisters in Paris—these joyous occasions were gladdened by the bright, happy confident faces of the young men. Their father was a vigorous enemy of the Reform Bill, attaching himself to Wellington's campaign against it.

The stringency of the family finances was always in James' mind. At Oxford as at Eton he struggled to keep his expenses to a minimum, on one occasion burning a cheque which his father had sent. This care with money confirmed in him an evangelical hatred of waste and ostentatious spending. He was in strong reaction to the lavish outlays of his father which had so greatly reduced the family estate and so constrained the family life.

Elgin himself had not finished his outlay on the Broomhall estate. In the teeth of the opposition of both his trustees and legal advisers in 1830 he launched one further scheme. The linen spinning and weaving industry of Dunfermline had been expanding: his plan was to adapt his railway to provide an outlet for it via Charlestown harbour. In addition he bought a horse-drawn passenger coach for his railway with seating for fifty passengers. The necessary new linkages were complete by early 1834. The trustees had no choice but to go along with this *fait accompli* in the hope that Elgin's optimism could be justified. In 1836 they joined Elgin in the issue of a puffing prospectus, in effect offering the railway for sale, together with the option to industrial or house-building speculators to purchase feus, leases of ground adjacent to the railway. The hoped-for response did not materialise: no sale proved possible. At this point John McKean, in effect the nominee of the principal creditor, Royal Bank, stepped in, offering to take over the operation of the railway. The passenger railway had some success. In 1848 the Carnegie parents, with Andrew and his younger brother, left

Dunfermline for America by this means. Andrew, who was to become the boss of the United States steel industry, liked to claim that the Earl of Elgin was their clan chief.

Shortly after James left Oxford his friend William Ewart Gladstone paid a visit to Broomhall. He took warmly to the family, especially to Elizabeth, Lady Elgin, conversing with her at length on the atonement, predestination and the fall of man. While at Broomhall Gladstone found and read a paper on public affairs written by Sir Robert Preston of Kirkfarther, a neighbouring landowner and friend of the Elgins who much admired James's ability.

After so brilliant an Oxford career it might have been thought that James Bruce would be ushered at once into Parliament, as was Gladstone. But the Elgins, in their straitened circumstances, could not afford this. James considered the law, entering his name at Lincoln's Inn, but went no further. In effect he became the manager of the Broomhall estate, struggling in filial duty with the killing debt and seeking to make the farms, coal mines, railway and lime kilns efficient. As deputy to his father and elder brother, Lord Bruce, he took the chair at tenants' dinners, for at least one of which he wrote an appropriate song. Among other causes he supported the church extension movement in the Church of Scotland under the influence of Dr. Chalmers. A military career had no attraction for him: he did not seek an army commission as his father and brother Robert had done. Apart from commanding a troop of the local yeomanry at its amateur drill there was to be no playing at soldiers for him who, paradoxically, in middle age was to wield a vast British force in China. James spent some seven years at this stewardship at Broomhall, lasting from his Oxford days until 1841 when he was thirty. Meanwhile Gladstone and his other friends were advancing politically.

James suffered increasing frustration with the estate. By about 1839 he had come to the conclusion that the only answer was to wind it up. He deeply envied what he called 'a steady-doing landed estate', untrammelled by industrial ventures. His father still saw the estate as his creation and gift to his family; for James it was a trap, a labour of Sisyphus. But there could be no question of breaking it up while his father lived. James pondered much on why the estate of 'my poor father' was incapable of redemption. The profits on land, coal and lime were calculated without taking account of the proportion of debt, and hence of interest payments, pertaining to each, so that there was no way of working out whether profitability was possible. There was confusion between the various functions of landed management, coal, railway, lime and harbour, making responsible policies very difficult to enforce (for example the horses used to draw the railway trucks were charged to the home farm where they were kept); there were no separate accounts for the railway and the harbour. There was a growing recalcitrance among the colliers. The estate was encumbered by the over-generous provision the Earl had made in 1810 for Elizabeth and the children of his second marriage. Perhaps most serious of all, in its non-agricultural functions the estate was now seriously sub-optimal, and so not able to reduce the debt, with its heavy interest charges, significantly. The trust had made no progress against the debt since it took over in 1827. Frederick shared James' feeling towards the estate, referring to 'these cursed affairs'.

Instead of winding up, however, a forward policy was adopted. A new pit known as the *Wallsend*, was sunk in 1839 becoming one of the largest and the deepest in Scotland, The entire output of coal seemed to come from this source and new offices, workshops and dwelling houses for the colliers were built. The upshot was that the Elgins now had a consolidated mining community, with strong rules restricting each man's output. A boy of ten was reckoned a quarter man, at twelve or fourteen a half man and a eighteen year old a full man. The output was 60,000 tons per year, 40,000 of it exported. There were now 620 employees, 450 men and boys and 170 women and girls. In all some 1,500 persons were dependent directly or indirectly on the mine and the new development meant a large increase in the debt. The old Earl revelled in this new achievement, being borne about his new tunnels and galleries in a special chair.

Through such estate experience James learnt a good deal about the world of business. Curiously W.E. Gladstone had a similar experience, trying to redeem his wife's family estate from the quagmire of the Oak Farm Iron Works. James lifelong interest in railways, began at Broomhall. He also learned how to deal with men of business and with local politicians. The Dunfermline weavers in the depression of 1837 suffered great distress: James proposed to create temporary jobs for some of them, principally on the Broomhall railway, but the radical Provost of the town raised objection, causing the weavers to rise in protest.

The colliers sought to organise a union and to bargain. On this James remarked that 'It is of no use in my opinion to bind your men down not to combine'. Moreover, 'I never saw any good come of combinations among masters. They sound oppressive and are never effectual'. Instead he calculated the correct tactic was, when a strike threatened, to raise the price of coal. If this brought more revenue, the colliers could be propitiated. If it caused less demand, then the effect of a strike would be reduced and the labour force slimmed. At the same time note should be taken of the names of the ringleaders, so that, later on, when stocks were full or trade dull, these men could be among those dropped. It was in relation to the colliers that James' sense of paternalism was put under greatest strain, for it was the coal workings and the related railway that were the most serious drains on the estate in terms of debt. James had learned that in the industrial sector the ideal of a social bond could not stand up to the new conditions and that a relationship of confrontation was becoming inevitable. 'My own view,' he said, 'is that colliers will always strike whenever the time is favourable and the men at other works choose to combine. I believe that our colliers are better off than most, but colliers are very gregarious while they are acting in bodies and when their blood is up they are not accessible to reason.' The realisation of an indefinite confrontation with the colliers could only add to his frustration over the estate. Nevertheless he tried to keep a good stock of 10,000 tons available from Wallsend which allowed him a chance to manoeuvre.

During these years that were in career terms so lean James was searching, as his upbringing and inclination demanded, after truth and light in public affairs. This was at a philosophical level, seeking from his classical and biblical studies the principles that should guide men in their public actions. Here again Gladstone provides an intriguing comparison. William Ewart too had his period of travail; indeed it never ceased. But central for him was religion: it was from the church and what he felt it stood for, or should stand for, that he approached civil society. James's perspective, in spite of his evangelicalism, was more direct and more secular, more classical than biblical.

And yet James too had a deep interest in religious matters as witnessed by his relationship with Thomas Chalmers. This great Scottish church figure of the day, leader of the dominant evangelical element in the General Assembly of the Church of Scotland, was a family friend who exerted a profound influence on the searching young man. All his life James Bruce was to venerate Chalmers, remembering his sermons, and able on his deathbed to quote at length from one of the most famous of them, 'On the Expulsive Power of a New Affection.'

For the young James Bruce two views of society and its governance were in conflict. First he had inherited from his father's Toryism a belief in a structured, organic society of the Burkean kind, held together by a vertical moral bond, with beneficent guidance reaching down from the aristocratic and gentry landowning element. Jurisdiction and trusteeship properly belonged to a class of men whose position and property made them capable of thinking and acting in the interests of the whole society. They were answerable both to their own consciences and to God, and not directly to the *demos*. Secondly, with the vastly increased productivity which sprang from the industrial revolution, there was a new demand that government should be more widely shared, admitting to the franchise and to parliament a broader band of men. By the same token there was the controversy over Free Trade. For the Corn Law which protected the rent incomes of the landed class to which James belonged, did so at the expense of cheaper food for the urban masses. Free Trade would, of course, mean removing one of the great constraints on the working of free market forces, exposing the structure of British society to blind change. The 1832 extension of the franchise had taken place while James was at Oxford, but the Corn Law was still a dominant focus of contention. The realist in James inclined him toward accepting both the democratic and the free trade trends. But he was painfully aware of the conflict they posed for the Burkean view, and with that of his aged father. As a young man, he wished to adapt to the times, but he was unwilling to abandon as sheet-anchor the values of a responsible order of men who could serve as arbiters and administrators along the lines of Plato's guardians, and whose chief concern should be the underdogs, the least fortunate in society.

Ultimately it was the conservative strain that became dominant with him believing that 'our admirable Constitution' rested 'on principles more exalted and holy than those which Owenism or Socialism can boast', proclaiming 'between men of all classes and degrees in the body politic a sacred bond of brotherhood in the recognition of a common welfare here, and a common hope thereafter'. But a conservative government must act rightly, protecting the rights of the working classes against 'the capitalists and the landlords', remembering always that 'the only capital of the labourer was his skill in his own particular work.'

This earnest young man struggled long and hard in his double search, both for a personality and for a public philosophy. He disappeared on long solitary rides over the Fife countryside, communing with himself, with the classical and other authors, and with nature. Perhaps the riding was a means of fighting off his frustrations, together with the vexations of the Broomhall estate. He continued to correspond with his brother Frederick on matters of philosophy, morality and politics as well as the affairs of the estate. Frederick indeed, beginning to make his way as a lawyer, provided a kind of safety valve. To his sisters James would sometimes shyly show a sonnet. Indeed there was quite a romantic strain in James, reflected in a considerable poetic output. In the immediate politics of the day he was, as he put it, 'riding at a single anchor', that is, he was not 'held bow and stern by allegiance to a party', but could veer about as his reading and thinking dictated. There is here an echo of his father's attempt at an independent stance in the election of the Scottish representative peers in 1790. In his search for clarification he sat down and wrote out his thoughts, filling a number of manuscript books. These he was to cast into the Red Sea a quarter of a century later.

Though James could not resolve his intellectual difficulties in the tidy way he wished, this long period of mental gestation served to clarify his mind as to the thought-frames within which he could approach society. Out of it all came a deep sense of justice, especially toward the weaker members of society, together with the realisation that the reconciliation of the aristocratic and the democratic principles is not to be seen in a single, absolute formula, but was a matter of particular times and places. He remained throughout his life deeply distrustful of 'that kind of superficial information' which makes it possible 'to draw sufficiently plausible conclusions, upon very slight grounds'.

The great obstacle to a public career, was of course lack of money. More locally, in his own county of Fife, as in Scotland generally, the Scottish Reform Act of 1832 had created a new set of voters, the 'Ten pounders', proprietors of horses, gardens and workshops, worth £10 per year or more, who were in Scotland strongly Whig. The result had been that the Conservative gentlemen like James Bruce were at an electoral disadvantage. In 1834 at the age of twenty-three he had published a pamphlet, 'A Letter to the Electors of Great Britain', justifying the actions of the Tory leaders, especially the Duke of Wellington. It fell upon stony ground. In 1837 he stood as a Tory candidate for Fife, wishing to demonstrate that a Tory with a strong sense of social and political continuity was not necessarily, (as the caricatures of the radicals suggested), a self-seeking bigot. But, announcing his candidature at a late hour on an uncharacteristic impulse, and being without financial resources and unwilling to use them even if he had had them, he was heavily defeated, Captain Erskine-Wemyss attracted 1,086 votes and James Bruce 567.

Elgin read James' election speeches with great satisfaction, commenting on how much his son had learned and matured during the contest, noting with approval that James had 'kept clear of party tactics and party delusions'. But his frustrations continued. The hated Ferguson, having lost his seat in Parliament in 1807 over the divorce, had been returned for Kirkcaldy Burghs in 1831, 1832 and 1837: in the latter year he was made Lord Lieutenant of Fife, a post Elgin coveted and had only briefly held. Poor Elgin's health was now very bad. His facial neuralgia was such that he was often unable to speak, each motion of his lips bringing a paroxysm of pain. On occasion he was reduced to writing instead of speaking. He also suffered from a *tic douloureux*. By 1837 he had become totally disillusioned with Jephson, as he had been with so many medical men in the past. But he had found a new figure on which to base his hopes for himself,

Bruce, Matty and indeed any other ailing member of the family. This was Samuel Christian Frederick Hahnemann, the founder of homeopathy. It was while translating the *Materia Medica* of the Scotsman William Cullen, that Hahnemann had conceived what he called the 'law of similars'; in 1810 he had published his *Organon* setting forth his medical philosophy, to be known as homeopathy. By using very small quantities of drugs, and thus slightly aggravating the symptoms, a cure was induced. Hahnemann had suffered much from the hostility of orthodox doctors and apothecaries who saw in his treatment a serious threat. In 1837 Hahnemann was eighty-three but had just married the fair-haired, blue-eyed Mademoiselle Marie Melanie d'Hervilly, barely thirty years of age. She married him, and carried him off to Paris and set him up a salon in a large mansion. It was in their large Parisian mansion that Elgin first encountered Hahnemann. He embraced the Hahnemann system eagerly and set about making himself one of its promoters, as he had done with smallpox innoculation all those years ago in Constantinople. He spent his time 'doing what I can to open people's minds to the advantages and claims of homeopathy', urging important people in England to read the *Organon*. Jephson became an open enemy. But alas, Hahnemann was no more successful with Elgin than other doctors had been. Hahnemann himself died impoverished in 1843, being buried with a long plait of Melanie's hair wound about his neck.

The health of George, Lord Bruce, had been deteriorating badly. He became forty in April 1840. He was but a tortured shadow, lovingly cared for in Bath by his devoted servant, Burke. The family was harassed by gossip that Bruce had fathered an illegitimate child in Stirlingshire, but this proved utterly false. He was courageous in his illness, seeking to hide it from others, undergoing a dreadful but useless operation without complaint. Religion became his only solace; he spent his time compulsively reading his Bible and the sermons of Chalmers and others. In his last agony as imbecility closed in upon him he would call with piercing shrieks upon the name of Jesus. He died November 1840. His passing was a relief to the family, for poor Bruce had complicated their lives and unintentionally caused tensions among them although James had eased the stress between Bruce and Matty, being greatly liked by both. With Bruce went the last hope that the estates of his mother would be united with that of Broomhall; she lived another fifteen years. George's death meant that James became Lord Bruce and heir to his father.

In time the plight of James Bruce, languishing at Broomhall, did not go unnoticed. Sir Robert Preston, his father's old friend and steeplechase companion and a man of public spirit, was so impressed by his frustrated ability and high ideals, that he undertook to pay his election expenses in seeking a more hopeful seat. Thus assisted, James won Southampton in the general election of July 1841 at the age of 30. He sat as a Conservative, but of a liberal-paternalist kind. As was so often the case at that time, his defeated opponent raised a petition to the House of Commons to have the election declared invalid, but by judicious talking to the proper people, James succeeded in having it quashed. On 24 August the young Scottish aristocrat seconded the amendment to the Address, acquitting himself well. Much of his philosophies were expressed during the election and in his maiden, and only, speech to the Commons.

All this time James had been a bachelor. On 22 April 1841, three months before the

Southampton election, at the age of nearly thirty, he had married Elizabeth Mary, known as Elma. She was the only child of Charles Lennox Cumming Bruce of Dunphail and Roseisle in the Highlands and Kinnaird, near Falkirk, a distant kinsman and M.P. for the counties of Elgin and Nairn, and of Mary Elizabeth Bruce, granddaughter of James Bruce the distinguished traveller in Abyssinia. The old house at Kinnaird was full of Bruce's travel treasures together with his library. Born 13 April 1821, Elma was just twenty, a young woman of great beauty. As an an only child, she brought the prospect that the Cumming Bruce fortune might in due course come to the aid of the Elgin family. By mid January 1841 the courtship was well advanced, with 'Jam' showing her his poetry. She told her mother of 'many beautiful verses of J's (which he had forgotten all about).' For their honeymoon they went to Paris, where Elma visited the convent sisters who had taught her French. Back at Broomhall she looked out Greek books that the Countess, Elizabeth, wished sent to her in Paris. She entered into Broomhall's problems, sharing her husband's fears that the ships which filled Charlestown harbour at this peak season would not wait to load if coal stocks were not immediately available.

The connection between James Bruce's family and that of his young wife was a curious one. Down to the early fourteenth century the Highland clan of Comyn or Cumming had been of vast possessions and power. But the Chief of the Comyns, the Red Comyn, had been stabbed to death in a sudden passion by Robert the Bruce while alone at prayer at Greyfriars Church in Dumfries. When Bruce became King of Scotland the territories and influence of the Comyns were accordingly reduced, though the Cummings continued to be a wealthy and leading Highland family, assuming an uncompromising Tory allegiance. Elma's grandparents had had sixteen children. Charles and his wife had only Elma. Elizabeth Bruce was the first Bruce to marry a Cumming since Robert the Bruce's murder of the Red Comyn. The marriage of James Bruce and Elma was the second such union. James was to find his father-in-law a great support in his career and in the affairs of Broomhall.

Elgin, as one of his last acts, warmly welcomed his daughter-in-law Elizabeth Mary. By this time he was very disabled and had quarrelled with Hahnemann. On 14 November 1841 Elgin died in Paris, at the age of seventy-five. He continued to the end incurably optimistic about the estate, proud that he had so enlarged what he had inherited. Eliza was at his bedside comforting him, reading to him and retailing news of the family.

Eliza loved her husband to the last and beyond. His damaged nose, his tic, his convulsive jaw never repelled her: instead she thought of his dark blue eyes and deep black eyelashes. But the child-wife of 1810 had grown up along with her children, to become a powerful influence on their characters. She had born Elgin eight children (five sons and three daughters), as well as assuming responsibility for those of Mary. As she grew older she became more and more interested in questions of religion, personal purity and good conduct, as well as pursuing her Greek and mathematical studies. Two years after Elgin's death she pondered on her marriage, writing, 'I had not the slightest idea or thought of the difficulties connected with such a change. I little knew my own heart or the self denying nature of the duties that would devolve upon me. I think it was better so.' She had withdrawn to Paris, there at last to pursue a life of her own. Elgin's death left her and her children ill provided for. And yet his daughters had loved him, referring to him as 'our beloved Daddy'. The feelings of his sons are less clear.

The question of spiritual control by a parent is always difficult to interpret: certainly Elizabeth's boys did not sink into religiosity but were prepared to act positively, accepting responsibility in the real world. Deeply engrained within them was a sense of answerability, together with the need, resulting from their father's chronic impecuniosity, to seek public employment. James was driven by a belief that his job was to ameliorate, against all the odds, the pressures on those at the bottom rungs of the successive exotic societies into which the British government was to thrust him, while at the same time heading off the explosion that could so easily result.

James was now eighth Earl of Elgin and twelfth of Kincardine. Two sets of problems confronted him regarding both his career and the Broomhall estate. The status in parliament of a Scottish lord like Elgin was obscure, though the general belief was that he was disbarred like the English peers from the Commons. He might have contested this in the courts, but decided not to do so, not least perhaps because of the expense. There was also the curious punctilio that the Scottish peers might feel that their station would be slighted (like that of the Irish peerage) should they not be excluded from the Commons. And so James's parliamentary career came to an abrupt end after a few months. With politics at home ruled out, as his father had done, he looked to service abroad.

Broomhall was a most unwelcome inheritance, its finances were as unpromising as ever. Indeed the new Elgin sought legal advice as to how he might avoid assuming responsibility for the estate. He held long discussions with Frederick, now established as a lawyer in London, who had also studied Scots law. A career of service overseas would ease the home financial burden. In a sense the eighth Earl was being forced into exile by his father's business incompetence.

It had appeared about the time of James's accession that economic relief was at hand. Sir Robert Preston, the family friend and James's financial supporter at Southampton, owner of 3,000 acres with active minerals, at Culross, Saline and Spencerfield, had died leaving an odd and ill defined will. It laid down that his estates were to go first to four of his nieces and should they fail to have issue, to the second son of the Earl of Elgin. The will expressly forbade 'the Earl of Elgin' to inherit, no doubt because of Preston's fear of the the seventh Earl's financial extravagance. The four nieces duly died off without children. The question then arose, who was to be regarded as the second son of the Earl of Elgin? Charles Dashwood Preston Bruce was the second son of the second surviving son of the fifth Earl (Andrew who had gone to India), and so was a claimant. But the seventh Earl (son of the fifth), also had a second son, namely James Bruce. The Trustees were deadlocked in their deliberations. While they were pondering, Charles Dashwood was thrown from his horse and killed, leaving no children. The way thus seemed clear for James Bruce to inherit. But by the death of the seventh Earl, James Bruce became the eighth Earl: this made him ineligible because Preston's will decisively excluded all Earls of Elgin. The Trustees decided to delay any award until it should be seen whether the eighth Earl was to have a second son.

CHAPTER 11

James and the Jamaican Apprenticeship

Elgin, in spite of his ancient family, good connections, high ideals, Oxford success and promising beginning in the House of Commons, had to face the humiliation of seeking a place in either the colonial or the foreign service. His father's attempts to bring him to the attention of great men had availed little. Success depended a good deal on chance—on what government was in power, who of its members were responsible for diplomacy and the colonies, and which posts fell vacant at any particular time. By the time his father was James's age he had been in the heart of the politics of the Scottish peers as well as being known and liked by George III. Partly as a consequence of these connections the seventh Earl had been sent as a young man as ambassador to the courts of Europe and Constantinople to play his part in grand affairs. For his son the prospect was very different.

The Elgin connection with royalty had weakened after Martha's death. It now began to revive. After Elgin's death Eliza wrote from Paris to the Duchess of Kent, Queen Victoria's mother, asking if a place could be found for her daughter Augusta on the Duchess' staff. Augusta, aged eighteen, was accepted and took up residence at Frogmore House in Windsor Park where in addition to her service to the Duchess she was in frequent contact with the Queen. As Lady in Waiting to the Duchess and later the Queen she was to be at Court for some twenty years. Through Augusta the entire Elgin family was to come to Victoria's attention. When Augusta arrived the Duchess of Kent's ménage was a dull, almost morose affair. The freshness, vitality and sensitivity of the young girl revived the ageing and somewhat disconsolate Duchess. For this the Queen, having excluded her mother from public affairs, was grateful.

In April 1842, Elgin was appointed Governor of Jamaica by Lord Stanley (later the Earl of Derby), Secretary of State for the Colonies in Sir Robert Peel's administration. This was to be a humble apprenticeship. Jamaica was no longer the prize possession it had once been, being peripheral to the Empire. Whereas Elgin's father had enjoyed contact with the high culture of kings, their courts and palaces, he was going to have to make do with the company of planters, overseers and attorneys, without benefit of art, music or polished conversation. Life was to be set in a sea of black faces; a revolt in which 50,000 slaves had broken loose had happened only ten years ago. Out of a population of 377,500 there were but 16,000 whites, together with 68,500 coloureds (people of mixed race): and so the blacks outnumbered all others by twelve to one. Based on sugar, the island's economy was threatened by soil exhaustion. Lower-cost rivals like Cuba still worked their plantations with slaves. In Jamaica an ex-slave

addresses to which Elgin replied. On reaching Montreal the party went at once to Monklands, the Government House in the country some three miles from the town. The house set in a handsome eigthteen-century estate looked down on the city from the slopes of Mount Royal and the distant blue outline of the Adirondacks. The following day Elgin was accorded civic and governmental welcomes, with all the trades and societies turning out with their banners. Among the latter were the Orange Lodges, then the most powerful group organisation in Montreal and indeed in Canada.

Elgin was not deceived by the apparent warmth of his welcome. He soon acquainted himself with the reality of his position. As he wrote, 'Whereas under Constitutional Monarchies the Sovereign can do no wrong, under Constitutional Government as understood in British North America, the Governor can do no right'. By this he meant that 'Everybody who fails to obtain what he wants in the shape of employment or legislation falls to abuse of the Governor, while the Ministry get the credit for all that is liked by individuals or parties.'

Mary Louisa followed in May, also travelling via Boston. She was accompanied by

6 La Chine, 4 October 1847. One of Lady Elgin's watercolour sketches showing the wooden houses and sailing boats associated with a small riverine community in Canada at that time.

her sister Lady Alice Lambton, and by little Lady Elma, an endearing young child resembling her father. The tempestuous weather she too met with was very hard on her as her pregnancy advanced. But when she got there life in Canada was pleasant enough. There were receptions, drawing rooms, levees, at homes, fairs, cattle shows and meetings of agricultural societies. At most of these Lord Elgin continued to make speeches of great acceptance. His fluent use of French charmed the *Canadiens* but did not endear him to the touchy Anglo-Scots. Lord and Lady Elgin would sometimes dance a Scottish reel, with the Governor General excelling. They toured their realm, marvelling at Niagara ('this must be one of the most stupendous works of nature'). On the advice of Lord John Russell, the Queen awarded Elgin the status of Knight of the Thistle, Scotland's order of chivalry. Limited to sixteen members, Elgin took the place of the late Duke of Argyll. This he welcomed as it added to his standing in Canada, allowing him to appear in public in the green ribbon and resplendent star of the Order. Twice his father had tantalisingly failed to gain this honour. At a Grand Dejeuner he was admitted a member of Osgoode Hall, the Law Society of Upper Canada (Certificate number 682). Shingvaconse, or Little Pine, chief of the Chippeways, addressed him from the head of Lake Superior as 'the Great Father', appealing for protection against the mining companies who were driving away the game that was their principal livelihood. Elgin soon became expert on snowshoes, often making part of his way into Montreal on them.

Back at Broomhall Tobo was optimistic, writing 'We may be able to set the property in such a condition before you return that you will no longer be forced to absent yourself from your native land.' But in reality the railway negotiations dragged on. Coached by his mother, Tobo himself was expected to take high honours in mathematics at Cambridge, even becoming Senior Wrangler. But the strain was to prove too great; and poor Tobo broke down. Though he did in the end take a respectable degree, he was never, however, to be admitted to the inner circle of his older brothers, James, Robert and Frederick.

Lord Elgin inherited the government in power from both Lord Cathcart, his short-term predecessor, and more especially from Sir Charles Metcalfe, remembered for his courageous reading of the speech from the Throne through his painful mouth cancer. Metcalfe, poor man, had been a disaster, ageing and ill, with an autocratic outlook acquired in India and Jamaica. The government represented the oligarchy of business-based Anglo-Scottish Tories who had become accustomed to win dubious elections with the Governor's support. It had two principal foci, namely Montreal in Lower and Toronto in Upper Canada. Of these the Montreal element, so stongly of Scottish descent, was dominant. It had long enjoyed economic supremacy in the city and indeed in Lower Canada, especially in the Eastern townships. This power was, of course, exercised over the French Canadian majority. The Montreal Tories cherished a deep dislike, amounting in some to a hatred, of their French compatriots: this was fiercely reciprocated by French *Canadiens* like Louis Joseph Papineau and to some degree by many others. The Montreal Tories had powerful weapons: their press was their means of influencing the Anglo-Scottish population, while for consciousness-raising they used the Orange Lodges with their secret oaths as well as the St. Andrews Society. The Church of England clergy were also part of this ascendancy especially the High Church party among them. Then there was patronage—the place-hunters knew where to go and what was required of them in return.

In Toronto also the Tories showed their anti-French feeling, but with somewhat less virulence, though anti-Catholic animosity was strong. The Toronto Tories, too, like their Montreal brethren, were a business-based and professional oligarchy, expecting to rule as of right, and to enjoy the Governor-General's support in so doing. They too had their Orange Lodges (which Elgin described as exercising 'a great *in terrorem* influence), together with their High Church clergy, headed by the redoubtable Bishop Strachan. They favoured the empire tie, but they expected it to be used in their favour. Like the Anglo-Scots in Montreal they were quick to appeal to London should the Governor-General act in their eyes inappropriately.

Confronting these somewhat ill-assorted Tories were opposing parties that were also distinct. In Lower Canada the 'liberal' party, though it had an Anglo-Scottish element, was preponderantly French. It was for the *Canadien* the defender of the institutions inherited from their forebears, including religion, language, education and law. But it was monarchist and fundamentally conservative. It was harassed on the left flank by the Papineauists, who abhorred the British connection. In Upper Canada there was an Anglo-Scottish opposition of liberal-radicals who detested the Tory regime, many of them seeing it as a transplant to Canada of the Toryism of England and Scotland. Strong among them were Scottish immigré radical liberals like William Lyon Mackenzie and George Brown. As Elgin said of these acerbic fellow Scots, they 'want something freer than the institutions of their own land'. They too had generated their own vigorous and vituperative press. This was the highly complex and potentially explosive mixture which Elgin had to face.

Until 1846 the Canadian economy had been enjoying good times. Kingston, Toronto and Hamilton in the upper province, though so new on the European timescale, had produced many of the attributes of old settled places. Elgin discovered that there was a good deal to admire in the public buildings and wharfs of Montreal, the fortifications of Fort George in Kingston, the seats of learning and impressive residences of Toronto and its vicinity, the mercantile activity of Hamilton and other towns, together with the canals traversing the country and the new electric telegraph. The Great Western Railroad running through Upper Canada had at its eastern end made connection with the Albany and Buffalo Railroad and at its western with the Michigan Railroad linking with Chicago.

Meanwhile the balance between Lower and Upper Canada had been altering dramatically. Whereas in 1825 Lower Canada had contained 423,000 inhabitants as opposed to Upper Canada's mere 155,000, by the mid 1840's the numbers had become roughly 700,000 to 500,000. By 1849 there was near parity at 765,000 to 720,000. Of Lower Canada's population some 650,000 were of French descent, with about 100,000 Anglo-Scots, based mostly in Montreal and the Eastern townships. While the Anglo-Scots dominated Upper Canada the powerful minority in Lower Canada who had preempted so much of the trade and finance of Montreal, could hardly be ignored.

Elgin discovered that there were mounting economic difficulties. The general depression following the collapse of the railway boom in 1847 was having this effect. The grain business had been temporarily stimulated after 1843 by a British preference for Canadian wheat, reinforced by a similar preference for Canadian flour. Canadian and American wheat had thus been funnelled down the St. Lawrence, causing much investment around Montreal in milling, shipping and harbour facilities. All this ended in 1846 with the repeal by the British of the Corn Laws—a devastating blow to the Canadian economy. Thus British free trade policy, to which Elgin subscribed, had turned upon Canada, provoking bitter resentment.

Papineau, exiled for his part in the 1837-8 rebellion, returned to Montreal in 1845 and was working again arousing in French Canadians a sense of injustice. To this the Tory Ultras and Orange Lodges were all too ready to respond, generating a reciprocal extremism. The parliamentary opposition with its French component under Lafontaine was gaining in confidence and support. Before Elgin arose the prospect of having to transfer power to it in the face of intense and irresponsible Tory resistance.

A further blow now struck Canada. The Irish famine had caused a wave of poverty-stricken people to seek a future in the new country. In 1847 some 100,000 immigrants reached Canada. Of these 32,000 were from England, 3,750 from Scotland, 7,700 from Germany and no less than 54,329 from Ireland. Nearly 14,000 persons died at sea or in quarantine at Grosse Isle, Quebec and Montreal. In addition some 4,000 succumbed after arrival, from disease and 'decay of the system'. Thus about one in five of those who sought a better life found only death. Those who survived did so in a state of great poverty. 'The immigration from Ireland', wrote Elgin, 'is becoming a most serious evil. The suffering among the poor wretches is frightful and they are spreading disease among the inhabitants of the province. My members of Parliament are becoming so frightened that I think the session will be brought speedily to a close.'

The Elgins had family sorrows also. Early in August 1847 Mary Louisa, after seven months pregnancy, gave birth to a stillborn child. Her old friend Harriet Martineau wrote to her in sympathy. Elgin believed the rigours of her Atlantic journey to be responsible. The perennial problem of family finance continued. Elgin had been awarded from the Canadian Civil List an annual income of £7,777, together with £1,925 for secretarial aid. This proved none too much, as large-scale hospitality was expected and travel in Canada proved a good deal more expensive than anticipated. To Elgin's intense annoyance there was a movement among the Trustees of the British Museum to cancel the arrangement whereby he and his sucessors should remain one of their number. 'God knows,' he wrote, 'the Elgin Marbles have cost the family enough'. The move failed.

Elgin's trusted confidant in England was his first wife's father, Cumming-Bruce. To him Elgin recounted his hopes, fears and frustrations, contrasting strongly with the cool and controlled tone of his official despatches. Seeing both the public and the private man, Cumming-Bruce was highly supportive.

By this time Elgin had formed a view of Canadian politics and politicians. It was not a flattering one, and was perhaps a little premature. His Tory ministers seemed to him to be men without any sense of long-term policy, thinking and acting at the level of petty manoeuvre and party and personal gain. He found himself pestered with attempts to alter constituencies and to make unjustified appointments in the judiciary and elsewhere. He stuck to his decision not to take any action that could be interpreted as favouring either party, thus causing resentment. The Tories considered themselves

11   Watercolour by Mary Louisa, Countess of Elgin. Niagara Falls, 1847. The picture of Niagara Falls shows her sister Lady Alice Lambton. Mary Louisa was a skilled watercolourist. She had already done a volume of charming scenes when she visited Canada as a girl with her father Lord Durham. When she returned with Elgin she continued her hobby.

12 Wolfe's Cove, from Spencer's Wood, Canada 1852. Watercolour by Mary Louisa, Countess of Elgin.

entitled to his support as of right. This lack of vision among Canadian politicians, especially on the Tory side, seemed to Elgin to mean that any real thought concerning the needs and development of the country, and her relations with her vast neighbour (which also involved relations between Britain and the United States), lay with him, the Governor General. The governing Tory Party had no plans for national reconciliation; on the contrary they were deeply hostile to the French community, and resented Lord Durham's recommendation, embodied in the Canada Act of 1840, that they should unite with the French in one polity.

This pettiness of mind and action had two roots. One lay in the historical divisions of the country which resulted in the fact that any real attempt at policy for the newly united Canada at once encountered deadlock between the two principal parties with their respective radical outriders. Secondly, there was the character of government, whereby power resided with the Governor General; thus depriving the politicians of any real responsibility. This last aspect had been exacerbated by earlier Governors who had meddled in the elections to the Assembly, and by their practice of choosing the ministers and awarding them in effect indefinite tenures. The British parliament at Westminster, though not necessarily the Colonial Secretary, assumed that there should be a high degree of direct rule in Montreal as in Dublin, for that was the nature of colonies, lying open to free discussion in the Parliament at Westminster. With these two great barriers to constructive political life it was hardly surprising, Elgin thought, that the general level of political behaviour was so low.

Thus, a seemingly inescapable dilemma was inherent in the situation. On the one hand, Elgin believed, Canadian politicians would only be brought to act in a constructive, principled manner when they bore real responsibility for their actions and for the future of their country. But how could power be passed from the Governor General to the political parties when there was such bitter hostility between them? How could patronage be safely given to one or other party so that it might not be used to perpetuate its own power? Political enmity was deeply compounded by the fact that the seat of government was located in Montreal. It was a city in which the Anglo-Scots minority of Lower Canada was not only economically dominant, but its members deeply resented any concessions to the French Canadians who themselves reciprocally detested the wealth and power of men who were in their eyes *arrivistes*.

Moreover, as if Elgin's position was not difficult enough, he had to deal with the further complication of the role of the Colonial Secretary, his immediate master back in London. The latter was subject to other pressures. Firstly came the question of Britain's foreign policy, diplomacy and defence, especially as it related to the United States. This was seen by the British Parliament in imperial terms, Canada, with no separate identity, was at the disposal of the British government. Secondly, there was the question of general colonial policy for Britain. There was a strong element in Britain who saw Canada and other parts of the empire as a means of relieving population pressure in the mother country. But this required a theory of how emigration, settlement and land allocation should be carried out, and how the costs involved were to be shared—colonial reformers like Edward Gibbon Wakefield had gained the ear of Lord Grey the Colonial Secretary on the subject. Thirdly, there was the school of thought in Britain which, in the tradition of Adam Smith, regarded colonies as a liability, to be disposed of as soon as possible. To this group young Gladstone belonged; one of its chief spokesmen in the Commons was William Holdsworth. Finally there was the possibility that Canadian politicians who did not get their way could proceed to London and there lobby Members of Parliament, seeking to reverse verdicts arrived at in Canada. Elgin found it hard to deal with a situation in which his superior, the Colonial Secretary, without really understanding the complexities of the Canadian scene was subject to such pressures. It is not surprising that Elgin concluded that any real thinking about the future of Canada would have to come from himself, at least until Canadian politics could be made more constructive.

And yet there were men on the liberal radical side, led by Louis Hippolyte Lafontaine, (who incidentally modelled himself on Napoleon by wearing a curl on his brow and his hand tucked within his coat), Robert Baldwin and Francis Hincks, who had done some positive thinking. They had considered both reciprocity in primary products with the United States, and the building of railways to link the colonies with each other, east and west, as well as north and south with the United States. With both parts of this growth programme Elgin was in sympathy. The obstacles to reciprocity lay largely in American attitudes to Canada, a mixture of hard-headedness and indifference. The great difficulty with the railway programme was finance, with Canadian credit so low in London. Quite early Elgin exchanged ideas with Hincks, a connection that was to continue throughout his Governor Generalship. But Elgin was not entirely carried away by Hinck's schemes: he rejected the proposal that Britain should guarantee railway debts for Canada, (as had indeed been done for canal building), on the grounds that Britain would have no say in what was done with the funds raised, while powerful Canadian politicians would be deeply involved, giving rise to serious conflicts of interest.

In February 1848 Elgin, in State, opened the Canadian Parliament. He did so with some foreboding, and amid great political excitement, much of it focused on guesses as to what course Elgin would pursue. He announced that the Parliament at Westminster had placed the French and English language on a parity as official languages in Canada, and read his speech from the Throne in both. The formerly entrenched Tory government of Canada was in fact losing its grip on the Legislative Assembly. It was defeated in the March election. This was partly due to the fact that Elgin broke with the practice of his predecessors Sydenham and Metcalfe by refraining from interfering with the election by bribery or patronage, an abstinence which the defeated Tories regarded as tantamount to betrayal. He chose his new Executive Council from a new majority party headed by Lafontaine, Baldwin and Hincks, sending for the first two on March 7. And so in this way Canada achieved responsible government for the first time. The Governor General abdicated from the choice of ministers, accepting those who enjoyed the greatest degree of confidence in the Assembly.

This the defeated Tories under Sir Allan MacNab refused to accept. At once they launched an attack on Elgin and his new ministers. The faction fighting had already attracted a surprising range of newspapers, with those of Montreal and Toronto dominant, but with many small towns also raising their journalistic voices. In Montreal reports in the powerful Tory press made Elgin increasingly uneasy. He requested his staff to keep a complete set of relevant newspaper clippings. The new government was being presented as a band of dangerous radicals with Elgin their creature. As the *Hamilton Spectator*, the Tory organ in MacNab's constituency, put it:

> A puppet sits in an easy chair,
> While Hincks some prosy statement garbles
> There might as well be seated there
> One of the famous *Elgin Marbles*.

But Elgin was not passive. He held frequent meetings with Sir Benjamin D'Urban, Commander in North America, because of alarm, both at an intended meeting of French Canadians and Irish to express sympathy with the 1848 revolution that had just taken place in France, and with the rising in Ireland. But the French and Irish split among themselves, lacking real leadership. The more serious problem remained the Tories and Elgin tried hard to deflect them from abuse and violence. In later life he remarked 'I often used to say to my Scotch friends in Lower Canada, "You are playing my game."' By this he meant that simple justice toward the French Canadians in the matter of representative government would not be enough to overcome their touchiness and suspicion, but that denunciation and the threat of violence from the Tories would establish the Governor General and the British Parliament in the eyes of the French Canadians as entities to be trusted. Elgin did not want matters to be pushed to the brink, being by nature a man of peace and a reconciler, but he saw clearly that, provided he could forestall open conflict, some good might yet come out of the Tory abuse by way of strengthening the Imperial tie among the French Canadians.

Meanwhile Papineau the leader of the 1837 rebellion in Lower Canada was also attacking Elgin, by working against the reconciliation of the French. He sounded the grand notes of French Canadian national identity and of racial liberty. He sought to spread the spirit of 1848 from Europe to Canada, infusing French Canadians with revolutionary zeal for their ancestral country, summarised as it was in the slogans of liberty and equality, but muting the concept of fraternity, at least as between the races. Elgin remarked drily that there were among the urban French 'plenty of fools' who were taken in by 'the trash which they get from the democratic press of France', but that in Lower Canada he had 'more reliance on the French *habitants* than any other class.' But Papineau could also cut up rough on more immediate issues. He attacked Elgin's salary, and the general principle of a non-elected Governor General, urging that the Canadians should choose one of their own number at one-tenth of the cost.

Elgin was particularly incensed by reports from Britain of 'that fool Holdsworth (who) has made a speech in the House of Commons endorsing all Papineau's views.' The rebellion in Ireland, also had dangerous implications for Canada. In July 1848 Elgin expressed fears that the American Irish and disbanded soldiers now returned from the Mexican war would seek 'to revolutionise Canada by way of making a diversion in favour of Ireland ... There is a great deal of swagger at New York.' 'Politicians even of the most reckless class,' he wrote to Cumming-Bruce, 'see the danger of trifling with a colony which might be occupied by 40,000 Yankees in six weeks ... there is a real ignorance at home of what is going on here and of the real character of party contests.' Canada too had its annexationist movement, toward which the business community of Montreal had considerable inclination. Such feeling had been stimulated by the commercial crisis, together with the belief that Britain in her economic policies of free trade was indifferent to the fate of Canada. There was a further form of annexationism in Montreal and the Eastern Townships, based on the idea that if the French had gained the upper hand in the government of Canada, the only way forward was to join the United States.

Seeing the country as part of the larger pattern that had convulsed Europe in 1848, Elgin took pride, as he put it, in

> having carried Canada unscathed through a year of revolutions. If I had pursued any other policy than that which I have followed we should ... either have been expelled from Canada or be in a most uncomfortable position, perhaps at war with the States. It is something to have spared the Empire such a shock in 1848.

Moreover, with the Lafontaine-Baldwin government with a majority of 3 to 1 in the Assembly, he had persuaded it 'to act in a perfect harmony with the Imperial government.' But he remained greatly depressed over the attitude taken in Britain. 'I receive nothing', he wrote, 'but hints from all sides at home that the Colonies, and Canada more especially, are a bore and that everyone wishes they were at the bottom of the sea!' British ignorance of Canadian affairs, he believed, 'is extreme'. 'Bear in mind', he wrote, 'that I am presiding over one of the most democratic communities that ever existed—that our constitution is most popular in character, consisting virtually of one Assembly, elected by very extensive constituency.' Of the United States he said, 'I have alongside of me a powerful people who acknowledge none of the restraints which international law and the community of nations impose on other peoples ... Annexation and invasion are themes discussed daily ...'

Moreover he was aware that in spite of the majority enjoyed by the new government, his personal situation was as precarious as ever. On 29 March 1849 he recorded:

> The most unprincipled of our factions has been labouring for the past six weeks to get up a violent excitement in the colony in the hope firstly to frighten me to a *coup d'etat* (which would be the certain prelude to rebellion), and secondly, failing that, a feeling in England against me so as haply to lead to my recall.'

The Canadian Tory ultras took no account of Elgin's warnings. They were looking for a precipitating cause. The liberal-radical government led by Lafontaine, impelled by the logic of its own situation, provided it in the form of the most contentious of issues. This was the advent, in 1849 of the Rebellion Losses Bill. There was the curious irony, as so frequently happens, that the politics of one phase was dogged by left-overs from the previous one, in this case the risings of 1837-8. In Upper Canada those who were innocent of rebellion but who had suffered damage from it had already been compensated by the previous Tory government. But in Lower Canada, with its great preponderance of French Canadians, the situation was more explosive and unresolved. The Tory government had indeed earlier proposed a Bill, whereby Commissioners would decide on individual compensation taking care that no rebel benefitted, but it had been allowed to lapse. Now, early in 1849, the Baldwin-Lafontaine government brought in its own enactment, proposing that $90,000, should be allocated to those who could substantiate claims that their property had been damaged during the rebellion. The sum of money involved was small but the idea, of compensating people in those areas from which the rebellion had emanated, was explosive. The Bill was passed by a majority of fifty to twenty-two.

Elgin himself had serious reservations. 'I do not at all wonder', he wrote, 'that the Rebellion Losses Bill should be received with disfavour in England, for it has an ugly look, and prepossessed as people in England are with the notion that the party to which my present ministry belongs is a party of rebels, and their opponents one of loyalists, they must think it a great deal worse than it is.' 'But', he wrote, 'the measure itself is perfectly defensible to anyone who knows as I do all the circumstances'. Elgin insisted that the Baldwin-Lafontaine ministry was much more sympathetic in reality to the imperial tie than its predecessors had been: they were the truer 'loyalists' as well as being dedicated monarchists.

Confronted with the prospect of such a Bill and its implications, Elgin had a number of choices. He might from the outset, when the prospect was first discussed in his Council, have refused permission for it to be introduced. Retrospectively, the Duke of Wellington believed this would have been the correct course. But quite apart from the retrogression from responsible government this would have involved, there was always the danger that the French would become seriously disaffected. Moreover, as Elgin put it, 'I am confident that I should have opened the gates of the Province to 20,000 or 30,000 Irish Americans', who were very potent in American politics 'while Polk was in power and the jobbers of every party in the Union were toadying them for the sake of their votes.' Or he could, of his own motion, refuse to sign it, thus killing it. This would mean that he had abandoned his Ministry, doing so on the ground that the risk to the civil peace was too great: in short he would be capitulating to the threat of violence.

Such a course would be intolerable to this highly principled man, who saw himself as the heir of Durham, whose daughter was his beloved wife. Even on the grounds of expediency such a policy would not work. If he refused the Bill he would have to dissolve the Assembly. But the Tory opposition was in no position to form a government. 'The old set being now a fragment (their ablest man (Draper) having been placed on the bench)', Elgin reported, 'could not make a government which could last a month even if they were again to be allowed the same latitude in intriguing and jobbing which was permitted them under the late incumbency.' Even if some sort of Tory government could be patched together, there would in the face of such an affront be a strong possibility of rebellion on the part of the French Canadians. Thirdly, Elgin could refer the matter to the Imperial Parliament at Westminster. This would mean that he had lost his nerve, and in so doing reversed the trend toward Canadian self-government. Moreover it would involve entrusting the arbitrament of Canadian affairs to a fundamentally ill-informed and not greatly interested body of men in the British Parliament. On it the full lobbying power of Canadian Tory vested interests would be brought to bear, together with the factional party influences within Britain itself. Moreover the British Parliament would have no sense of the danger of a 'war of the races'. Finally, he could sign the Bill, making it law, and face the consequences. This he chose to do in full awareness of the danger. 'Disaffection exists in many other countries as well as here,' he told Cumming-Bruce, 'but this is the only country in the world where rebellion is the resource always present in the minds of place hunters, where to threaten this *ultima ratio* is not considered an imprudence even, far less a crime'.

As the storm-clouds gathered Elgin in an address to the young clerks and merchants of Montreal urged them to cultivate a moral sense in public affairs, and to reject superficial appeals, seeking an understanding of the general, long term principles that should govern human affairs, closing their ears to the demagogues.

The prospect of the Rebellion Losses Bill made it possible for the Tory Ultras, the Orange Lodges and the 'loyalists' newspapers to whip feeling in Montreal to a dangerous level. On 25 April 1849, on a bitterly cold day, Elgin rode in his coach from Monklands to the Parliament House to give the Royal Assent to the Customs Bill, urgently needed because the ice was breaking up on the St. Lawrence and new regulations had been agreed. The Lafontaine-Baldwin government had decided to end the uncertainty about the Rebellion Losses Bill and asked Elgin to sign it at the same time. This he did, thus performing the irrevocable act of his Canadian career.

As soon as word having got about, the galleries at Parliament House were packed with Tory supporters in a very hostile mood (there were no ladies, a sign that a strong protest was premeditated). As Elgin signed the Bill these well dressed and apparently respectable men set up a great groan, rushing from the galleries, stamping their feet and bawling their way down the stairs. On emerging from Parliament House Elgin was confronted with a growing crowd alternately cheering ironically and hooting. These soon turned to shouted insults. Some of the crowd, pelted Elgin's carriage with stones and rotten eggs. The postillions whipped up the horses and Elgin was carried clear.

Within an hour notices had been circulated calling for an open air meeting in the Champ de Mars for eight o'clock in the evening: this was accompanied by a highly inflammable *Extra* from the *Gazette*. The bells of the city were set ringing. By eight the crowd had become a mob of about 1,500 people, led, as the *New York Tribune* put, 'by brawny fellows of Scotch, English or Northern Irish descent'. Alfred Parry, the chief of the fire brigade, placed himself at their head shouting 'The time for speeches is past: follow me to Parliament House!' It was a massive stone building two stories high and some 200 feet long, containing the parliamentary library and the Canadian national archives reaching back to the earliest times. Its legislative chamber was fitted out in a style similar to that of the House of Commons at Westminster. The gas jets were burning as the Assembly debated, the chief of police was cracking jokes behind the Speaker's Chair. By nine o'clock, thousands of men surrounded the building, and a volley of stones came hurtling through the windows on both sides of the Assembly, smashing the gas globes. Then a dozen men pushed their way into the Chamber itself and prancing about Speaker Morin's chair, began to hack at it. One pronounced 'I dissolve this French House'. The mace was thrown through the window to the crowd where it was paraded through the street in a caleche. Soon the library was on fire and the flames, fed by escaping gas, reached the Chamber, igniting the velvet drapes. Morin sat in his place calmly waiting to conduct an orderly adjournment. The members gathered round him and as the Chamber went up in flames he led them to the main entrance and out into the street. Some of the enraged mob were busy cutting the firemen's hoses. Then from the burning building came Sir Allan MacNab, bearing the portrait of Queen Victoria in his arms. Little else was saved: within hours there remained only a blackened shell within which lay the ashes of the library, the historical records of Canada, and the current working papers of government.

The following day at 10 a.m. the government felt obliged to convene the Legislative Assembly, proposing a motion that it stand prorogued until the situation became clearer. There was still much disturbance in the streets. The Assembly met in the Bonsecours Market Hall. Its cold discomfort added to the gloom of the members. Security was provided by fifty soldiers of the 71st Highland Regiment who waited in an adjoining room. Bent and battered by the previous night's misadventures the mace was placed in position.

But Sir Allan MacNab and his Tory supporters, far from seeking conciliation, launched an attack on the government, blaming it for the riot and destruction. With the connivance of the Governor General, the government, said MacNab had tried to smuggle the Rebellion Losses Bill through, and it had made no preparations to contain the justified indignation of the citizenry at what it had done. Moreover the violence should be seen in the light of the Bill, 'consecrating', as MacNab put it, 'the highest crimes known to our laws, treason and rebellion backed by the recommendation of the Queen's Representative.' After bitter exchanges between the two sides at the resumed meeting two days later, Mr. H. Boulton, the member for Norfolk, proposed a Loyal Address to the Governor General.

The differences now became very explicit. MacNab and his followers would willingly do honour to the Queen, expressing their limitless loyalty, but rejected out of hand the words approving the conduct of Lord Elgin. From this position the 'loyalists' would not budge. Lafontaine was not in the House; Baldwin now had no choice but to persist in the Address with no hope of unanimity. All this was reported by letter by Hincks to Lord Elgin at Monklands. The opposition helped to keep the city of Montreal in a state of unrest. But Elgin, being the man he was, decided to enter the disturbed city to receive the Address. This made for great uneasiness at Monklands where Lady Elgin was in advanced pregnancy. There was certain to be a hostile demonstration, but no one knew how it would develop. Elgin remained very cool, though his Ministers were greatly alarmed.

Monday, 30 April was set for Elgin to receive the address from the Assembly. Whereas no precautions had been made on the day when Parliament was raised, there was now a strong military presence. At the Bonsecours Market where the Assembly met, and along the streets to the Chateau de Ramzay, the Governor General's town house where the address was to be presented, there were 1,500 soldiers.

With a population of some 50,000, Montreal had only some sixty police officers, a hopelessly inadequate force in the face of mass disturbance. The protection of the Governor General thus lay with the military, consisting of a battalion of the 71st Highlanders and the Toronto and Montreal militia cavalry. Of the loyalty of the latter there was some doubt. The plan was that if there was trouble the mayor would assess its seriousness: if he judged civil disturbance was imminent he would read the Riot Act ordering the crowd to disperse: if it did not do so, he would order the commanding officer to use the military. The latter was to judge whether to use the cavalry or to order the troops to fire.

There followed the most shocking scene in Canadian or indeed imperial political history, the only occasion on which the Sovereign's representative has ever been put in physical danger by the mob. Accompanied by his brother Robert, Elgin set off in his coach escorted by a troop of Dragoons, leaving Mary Louisa in deep anxiety at Monklands.

It was a parlous situation. At all costs the Dragoons in the midst of a howling mob must not be provoked into using their sabres which would have precipitated a blood bath. In the event the mob put the Queen's representative to flight hurling macadamized stones at the carriage. The Dragoons and Elgin, very pale and holding his ceremonial hat in front of his face for protection, rattled and clattered clear of the mob and made their way back to Monklands. The Montreal cavalry, the young bloods who were the sons of the Anglo-Scots business oligarchy, sat on their horses, laughing at the rout of the Governor General.

Elgin was now in a very difficult position. To return to Montreal would be to precipitate further violence. His enemies of course accused him of cowardice, skulking at Monklands. Even Lord Grey questioned his seclusion, though mildly. The death and funeral of poor General D'Urban in Montreal made for further embarrassment: Elgin sent a deputy. Gangs roamed about the city. Elgin could have used the soldiers to clear the streets: indeed as he put it, 'we were within an ace of martial law'. But the use of the soldiery was itself dangerous, for the Orange Lodges were organised, armed and reckless. Military action would not only increase the violence, it might create new and unpredictable situations that would make long-term reconciliation more difficult than ever.

Elgin therefore, in spite of pressure, decided that the largest British garrison in North America should not not be used to clear the streets. Nor could he expect the Ultras to call off the mob. 'I have no doubt that MacNab (who will swear in England that he

7   Two of the stones thrown at the Governor General, Lord Elgin, in Montreal, 30 April 1849. Lady Elgin wrote the notes and preserved the stones.

disapproved of the riots)', wrote Elgin, 'actually got them up.' Elgin seems to have feared that, once he was under attack and his government appeared to be breaking down, followers of Papineau would join in. He blamed 'Those miscreants, bankrupt traders, annexationists, place hunters and Papineauists' who had 'set their mobs to murder me.' Nor did the bourgeoisie of Montreal act as a restraint: 'Not a step has been taken,' wrote Elgin, 'by the respectable class to express regret at what has taken place.' There remained only the possibility of swearing in special constables to keep the peace. Under pressure from Elgin this was tried, with the result that most volunteers were French-Canadians, giving rise to the rumour that Elgin was arming 'disloyal' men. The whole British population of Montreal, Elgin believed, 'from the highest to the lowest have one idea, to crush the French.'

Elgin's Scottish compatriots, whom he had tried to pacify, were among his most bitter attackers. The St. Andrews Society of Montreal resolved: 'That the Earl of Elgin having so conducted himself as to insult and outrage the feelings of every British subject in Canada and to disgrace the Scottish name ... should be expelled from membership and from the office of patron.' The Thistle Curling Club followed suit. On the other hand in Upper Canada the St. Andrews Society of Toronto and the Highland Society of Hamilton drank Elgin's health with all the honours.

Meanwhile there were nervous times at Monklands, where Lord and Lady Elgin feared a surprise attack. A considerable guard was provided. Though showing no fear, Lady Elgin was bitter against her husband's assailants saying 'I am disgusted with such an ungrateful people.' Elgin wrote to Grey saying 'I confess I did not before know how thin is the crust of order which covers the anarchical elements that boil and toss beneath our feet.' Meanwhile his effigy was burned in Quebec, Toronto, Brockville, Belleville and other towns.

There was further disturbance on 15 May, when a delegation of liberals, greatly concerned about the violence inflicted on Elgin and his entourage, arrived from Toronto, with a view to conferring with the Lafontaine-Baldwin government. The party, which included the Speakers of both the Assembly and the Council, was dining in Tetu's hotel when the news got about. Immediately the hotel was surrounded by the mob and its windows were stoned—the troops arrived just in time to stop a battering ram from smashing down the barred door. With the tension thus maintained, MacNab sailed for England in June to beg the British parliament to disallow the Act and recall Elgin. He had some success in that Mr. Gladstone proposed a motion in the Commons that ratification should be suspended until there were assurances that no public money would go to the rebels. Sir Robert Peel took the opposite view: the motion was lost by 35 votes to 24.

MacNab and his friends were not the only ones laying siege to the British parliament. Hincks also made the journey to London, proving himself a very effective advocate with both the politicians and the press for the Lafontaine government and for Elgin. He had, in effect, a double mission, namely to present the actions of the Canadian government in a positive light and to reassure the City of London of Canada's credit-worthiness. He saw several financiers including Alexander Baring. Hincks was very conscious, as was Elgin, that the breakdown of civil order in Montreal had a lot to do with the depressed economy. It was recognised that renewed expansion of the railway system could create a new future for the colony, but for this it was necessary that the city of London, if it was to lend, should be confident that there was effective government in Canada, able to service its debts. It was a curious circumstance that both Hincks and MacNab were financially interested in the Great Western Railway.

On 16 May, 1849 Mary Louisa was delivered of a son. Queen Victoria signified her gracious desire to stand sponsor to the infant Lord Bruce, by requesting that he might be given her own two Christian names in their masculine form, Victor Alexander. She became a godmother and sent a christening cup—special marks of favour—in recognition of Lord Elgin's stand against the Montreal mob. The Broomhall tenantry held a dinner in honour of the new Lord Bruce. The child was christened at Monklands on 6 August, using Jordan water.

Some days later the magistrates of Montreal, decided that so monstrous an act as the destruction of the Parliament House could not go unpunished, attempted to arrest nine men on charges of incendiarism. This sparked off further mob action. Barricades were thrown up in Notre Dame Street and Lafontaine's house was surrounded. In fear of their lives, its defenders fired on the crowd, killing one man. Later there was an attempt to turn the funeral into a Tory demonstration.

But by this time the perpetrators were having difficulty in sustaining their violence. Described by Elgin as 'the rascally owners of property who have been countenancing riots and burnings', the ring leaders had at last begun to see how the suspension of civil government could be disastrous for business and property, and for Canadian credit especially in London. They took alarm, and withdrew what Elgin called their 'side wind of approval'. Moreover the reaction against such primitive behaviour was becoming more general, especially in Upper Canada. Even in Montreal there were increasing signs that the worst was over. A local composer dedicated *The Elgin Polka* for the pianoforte most respectfully to the Governor General: the *Monklands Polka* was humbly inscribed to Lady Alice Lambton, Lady Elgin's younger sister. 'We have had a dark night of it,' wrote Elgin, 'but the day is beginning to dawn.'

On 5 September 1849, five months after being attacked, Elgin left Monklands for a tour of Upper Canada. Although finding the accusations of cowardice made by his enemies harder to bear than the physical danger, he had waited out the violence. He now went seeking support for his actions, looking in Upper Canada for the renewal of Canadian political stability. In this he was successful, gathering a vast harvest of supportive addresses, with 164,000 signatures. While on this mission back home in London he was made a baron in the peerage of the United Kingdom, an honour his father had long sought in vain, and a further sign of royal and official approval. This also meant that he now had a permanent place in the British legislature, which might prove useful later.

Elgin's problem was to find grounds on which reasonable opinion in Upper and Lower Canada could be brought together. His recent actions, as he had expected, had secured him the support of the French Canadians. But Montreal Tories remained irreconcileable, and indeed continued their war against him, stirring up trouble in towns on his route and elsewhere. 'The Montrealers', Elgin reported, 'are moving heaven and earth to get as bad a name for the towns of Upper Canada as for their own.' Montreal, he wrote was 'rotten to the core'. He felt there was no choice but to deprive it of the status of capital. Elgin was convinced 'that it is impossible to conduct the government in this city which is occupied by a large and powerful organised body who recognise no law but its own will and which cannot be attacked even when its acts are most outrageous, without a war of races being risked.'

Elgin sought three types of support in Upper Canada; reconciliation first with the urban Tories largely based in Toronto, with the farmers of Upper Canada, and with 'a vast number of wavering reformers round the British connection.' For a start he confronted the urbanites head on, making an appearance as Chancellor of the University of Toronto, 'in the very hotbed of my bitterest opponents.' By so doing, said Elgin, 'I brought myself in immediate contact with a class of persons who have been most outrageous in their hostility. The result has been most satisfactory.' Elgin's success in Toronto was not unrelated to the fact that if Montreal ceased to be the capital, Toronto might succeed to the position. Elgin was able to play upon the fact that though Toronto was 'the most Tory' it was also 'the most British city in America'. Even more reassuring, he found that the farmers of Upper Canada were generally on his side, a reliable and stable 'yeoman' element. As to the liberal-radicals, the violence that had been used against Elgin and which had dominated the streets of Montreal for months had begun to have a chastening effect. The Toronto *Globe*, organ of the liberals wrote of 'that degraded city'.

Some sort of operation was required on the University of Toronto where the Tories, headed by the powerful Anglican Bishop Strachan, had a close grip on King's College, the principal component of the University. Strachan, an Aberdonian apostate from the Church of Scotland, had since 1837 steadily intrigued for an Anglican ecclesiastical establishment in Upper Canada. Little love was lost between Elgin and Strachan and no attempt at conciliation was made on either side. Indeed Elgin thought Strachan 'the most dangerous and spiteful man in Upper Canada'. Elgin delivered an eloquent address to the Congregation of King's College on the rightness of secularising the University, a brave act in view of his need for general support in Upper Canada. Strachan was not however, finished. He founded Trinity College, to perpetuate the Anglican presence in Toronto.

The decision was taken to have a peripatetic capital alternating between Toronto and Quebec. Elgin was a good deal attacked in England, causing him to say 'I sometimes feel inclined to throw up this office in disgust.' The Montreal Tories were furious. As the *Montreal Gazette* thundered: 'Our idea is to declare the supremacy of the Anglo-Saxon ... French laws, French tenures and French ideas must go to the wall.' *The Church* wrote of its Anglo-Scots readers; 'But for their superior intelligence and enterprise Lower Canada ... would be a wilderness.' The *Sherbrooke Gazette* was for a re-division of Canada: 'The combatants must be separated or the fearful scenes that are now devastating Europe, and of which we have recently had a foretaste in Montreal, will be re-enacted in Canada.'

An Annexation Manifesto was drawn up in October 1849, largely by a group of Montreal merchants, with 325 signatures. It demonstrated the cosmopolitan rather than the loyalist nature of large-scale capital by alleging that so long as Canada remained a colony they could not raise capital on the London money market, but as part of the United States they could. In support of this they pointed out that the

United States had several thousand miles of railway, whereas Canada had scarely a hundred.

Elgin's strategy was to isolate Montreal Toryism and its annexationists, and this he brought about by removing the capital. Also, by so doing its Tory press was at once reduced in stature; moreover the annexationist movement was thereby made a Montreal rather than a Canadian affair. In November 1849, the Elgins took up residence in Toronto, which was to share capital status with Quebec. In his mission to pacify Canada Elgin, exerting all his charm and energies, had been successful. He still however, had grounds for resentment over his treatment by the people of Canada. His salary was a subject that could crop up at any time. In July 1850 there was a move in parliament to cut it drastically by £2,777, with his secretarial provision proportionately reduced. Fortunately for Elgin the proposal failed.

In December 1851, the Elgins had a second son, Robert, born at Quebec. The trustees of the will of Sir Robert Preston now had the requisite second son of the Earl of Elgin to whom to pass the Preston estate. But the end of that story had not yet arrived; the trusteeship had to continue until Robert came of age. Elma and her papa danced the New Year in, she looking very nice in a white tablature frock and a red sash. A large passenger boat was launched named the Lady Elgin, (tragically only to be lost nine years later with three hundred drowned).

The key to railway development was capital. This had to be borrowed, much of it in the London money market where the status of Canada had fallen very low. Elgin's pacification of the country, did help to produce a notable improvement in the economy, aided by general economic recovery from 1850. This, together with prudently handled finance accompanied by buoyant revenues, brought a new credit-worthiness to Canada. By 1852 the Canadian debentures that had been so scorned in London in 1846 were selling at 119—higher, as Elgin noted with satisfaction, than those of the United States government: moreover Canada now had 2,000 miles of railway under construction.

Elgin believed that larger markets were essential for primary produce, especially grain, and that the United States was the obvious outlet. He came to the conclusion that a Reciprocity Treaty providing for the free exchange of a range of products, especially those of a primary kind, would in the long-run lead Canada to economic wellbeing. Though he was aware of the argument that such an arrangement might lead to Canada's economic and ultimately political, assimilation to the United States, he did not share this fear. He believed that like him Canadians believed that British political institutions were greatly preferable to those of United States. This was especially the case with the people of Upper Canada, now expanding rapidly through immigration, largely from the British Isles.

In the meantime, for reciprocity to succeed it was necessary to improve north-south railway communications. Elgin was enthusiastic about the Ogdensburgh-Boston Railway and attended its opening in 1851. But he was also well aware that Canada needed to strengthen her east-west axis. 'There are other lines', he told the American railroad promoters, 'some in progress and some in prospect, which are destined to connect Canada with the ocean, in which I feel an interest no less lively.' Meanwhile the railway negotiations at Broomhall had collapsed: it had proved impossible to arrange an advantageous sale. The debt continued its own stubborn existence.

(b)

(a)

8 The Eighth Earl of Elgin. (a) A daguerreotype by Doan of Nova Scotia, c. 1850, aetat 39. (b) A photograph by Senor Beato taken in Pekin in 1860, aetat 49. Although the determination of the man who ran the gauntlet in Montreal is evident in both pictures, the white hair in the Beato photograph gives the impression of a much older, sadder man.

The third great area of Canadian affairs in which Elgin became interested was that of landholding. In Lower Canada there was the vexed question of seigneurial rights, an aspect of the traditional pattern of land holding derived from French feudalism whereby the habitant owed his landlord certain services. These feudal services had no real justification, being a mere historical survival and so with Elgin's approval the Canadian parliament ended these archaic obligations. Then in Upper Canada there was the problem of the Clergy Reserves. This was a matter that fell under imperial jurisdiction for it was the British Parliament that in 1840 had set aside vast tracts of land in Upper Canada for the endowment of an established Anglican Church on the English model. Elgin recommended that the imperial parliament be asked to end its Act of 1840 and leave the future of the Reserves to the Canadian Parliament. Over this Bishop Strachan was one of Elgin's bitterest enemies. The Bishops in the House of Lords fought valiantly for the privileges of their Canadian brethren, but in 1854 the Reserves were finally ended.

Before Elgin could begin the final phase of his Canadian career he went through something of a personal crisis, just as he had done over Jamaica. By July 1853 he had been Governor General for six and a half years. He was 42. Against his deep affection for Canada and his involvement in its affairs, there was the question of his own future. Not surprisingly, so gifted a man who had been one of the great successes among the empire's governors, hoped for advancement. He applied for leave of absence and returned to Britain to seek promotion in the fall of 1853. He had two principal tasks ahead: one to haunt the corridors of power once more in the hope of new and larger appointment. The other was to try to find out what was really happening to the family estate at Broomhall.

Poor Elgin, a proud man, conscious of his achievements in Jamaica and Canada, had to submit himself again to the lottery of availability of colonial and diplomatic posts. His sponsor Lord Grey had left the Colonial Office in 1852, never to hold office again. After much waiting, Elgin was offered the Governorship of Madras. This he refused, for it was scarcely a promotion. But in the eyes of many this was a serious mistake on Elgin's part. Dalhousie the reigning Governor General and Elgin's old friend, believed that from Madras Elgin would have succeeded him, as ruler of British India. There was also some talk of Elgin being sent to Ireland. Dalhousie certainly regarded Elgin as an equal contender for the highest positions. 'I am poor, like Elgin' wrote Dalhousie, 'and however he may like reputation and honour, I like them too'.

Broomhall was of course added to the problem. Elgin, if he was to live on the estate without an offical appointment, would find himself very hard up. Moreover after his success in Canada he could not tolerate the reclusive life he had earlier lived at Broomhall. The long years spent by his father without an official appointment posed a discouraging prospect. He made every effort to discover the true position of the Broomhall estate, spending many hours inspecting the coal mines and the lime works and visiting the tenants. But the accounting system made this impossible. Throughout his time in Canada he had worried about Broomhall, pressing the trustees for real information. But the agent, Rolland, was a bit of a dawdler; not a man capable of handling complex affairs. Elgin had been told in 1849, when the estate had been placed in trusteeship, that a mere £30,000 had been paid off from a debt of £204,000. But he could not now ascertain whether this had lessened the terrible burden of interest payments. The family had drawn nothing from the estate over these years except for the jointure for the dowager Countess Elizabeth in Paris. The coal and lime businesses were threatened by the general spread of the railways, providing rival supplies. The estates' own little railways were still horse-drawn: they needed locomotives and that meant borrowing, which was done. Elgin considered selling a large part of the land in order to reduce the debt, but decided against it. Seeking to relate world and British economic conditions to the future of the estate, he reasoned that the Californian gold discoveries, might possibly raise the world's price level, thus bringing economic stimulus. This would alleviate the burden of the Poors Rate as well as providing better markets. Cobden's efforts to bring about retrenchment and a dimunition of the national debt might also ease the tax position. But these possibilities he had to conclude were remote and uncertain. Broomhall was to continue to be a worrying background to his life.

In May 1854 Elgin returned to Canada in some frustration to resume his Governor Generalship. His great objective was to seal his Canadian career by achieving a Reciprocity Treaty with America. He invited Laurence Oliphant, one of the most intriguing young men of his day, to accompany him as his private secretary. Oliphant's mother was a close friend of Elgin's sister, Lady Augusta. Oliphant had already travelled widely in Asia and the Crimea, and had made quite a name for himself as an author.

The Americans were not greatly interested in a Reciprocity Treaty with Canada. Elgin and his ministers offered a *quid pro quo* in the form of concessions to the Americans in Canada's fishing grounds, together with free navigation on the Canadian section of the St. Lawrence, but these proved not a very tempting bait. The real requirement, as Elgin soon discovered, was to find a political support base within American politics. The best hope lay in the Democratic Party, with its strength in the south. While the Southern democrats did not wish to have Canada added to the Union, thus strengthening the anti-slavery element, they could perhaps be persuaded that mutual trade advantages would be beneficial. Elgin and his entourage embarked on a round of Washington parties. The flood of champagne proved too much for Oliphant, but Elgin persevered. In spite of general American disappoval of lobbying by strangers, Elgin proved himself an immense success. The combination of his aristocratic titles and his charm and bonhomie worked wonders among the senators. The press was no less approving: one newspaper informed its readers that

> Lord Elgin is a short, stout gentleman on the shady side of forty, and is decidedly John Bullish in birth, talk and appearance and carriage. His face, although round and full, beams with intellect, good feeling and good humour. His manners are open, frank and amusing.

He used his expertise in public speaking badinage to the full, telling the Americans, who were inclined to think that they were the only free people:

> We, monarchists though we be, enjoy the advantages of self-government, of popular elections of deliberative assemblies, with the attendant blessings of caucuses, stump orators, lobbyings and log-rollings ... almost, if not altogether, in equal perfection with yourselves! (laughter).

Oliphant was much intrigued by Elgin's role playing. Oliphant was deeply involved in his own spiritual integrity and agonised to Elgin over what they were doing as lobbyists. Elgin too had been raised as a strong evangelical but did not allow this to inhibit him in the task in hand. In private he could and did fume away his frustrations but never allowed these feelings to show. In the event Elgin's visit to Washington was a great success. But there were further difficulties on his own side, leading to delay. He wanted all the British North American colonies to join, including the Maritimes where the fisheries lay. His office included the Governor Generalship of these colonies, but, consistent with his general principles, he believed it was necessary and right to gain their consent. Eventually the Treaty was signed on 5 June 1854, representing a *tour de force* on Elgin's part, a second climax to his Canadian Governor-Generalship. It was to last for ten years; the Americans ended it when its term expired. But Reciprocity was now established as a theme in Canadian politics. Meanwhile Toronto and other cites enjoyed a decade of prosperity enhanced by the Treaty.

Elgin's Canadian career ended with the adjournment of Parliament on 18 December 1854. He resigned the Governor-Generalship and returned to Britain with his future wholly unsettled. He had three achievements to his credit. He had instituted representative government in Canada in the face of violence (providing a model for later statesmanship in other parts of the Empire); he had healed the colony thereafter, making possible stable politics, and he had achieved the Reciprocity Treaty which encouraged a stable relationship with the United States.

CHAPTER 13

The Broomhall Interlude: the Challenge of the East

Elgin left Canada with a profound and sympathetic grasp of her affairs. He was deeply authoritative on them, having for over seven years been one of their major determiners. Back in Britain, he found himself worryingly uninformed. This was a difficult situation for such a man, believing as he did that he had a duty to participate in public matters, but only on the basis of knowledge of the facts and of the operative principles. There was too the chronic question of family finance. Moreover the political situation in Britain was still as fluid at it had been when he left for Canada in Peel's time. The commotion caused by Peel's repeal of the Corn Laws in 1846 had removed the landmarks of party which, as Elgin described them, 'if not a wholly sufficient guide, are yet some sort of direction to wanderers in the political wilderness.' He had accounted himself such a wanderer from his youth, and especially since his entry into politics in 1841, unable to adjust to an evolving political configuration. He was no partisan, and so could not rise within a party.

Lord Aberdeen's Ministry broke up in the spring of 1855. Lord Palmerston, the new Prime Minister, offered Elgin the Chancellorship of the Duchy of Lancaster, with a seat in the Cabinet—a flattering and appreciated offer, a tribute to his Canadian career, but Elgin declined it. He had decided that for at least a time he should remain independent of party. But he took his seat in the House of Lords, giving general support to the Palmerston government. He spoke twice there in 1855, strongly advising the government against sending to Canada many of the troops just returned from the Crimea. It was, he said, an action which ran counter to his own policy of promoting self-government in Canada by the reduction of the British military presence there, and might well have seemed to be provocative to the United States.

On the second occasion, in May, he opposed the Address to the Crown which Lord Ellenborough had moved condemning the conduct of the Crimean War. The realist in him caused him to say, 'Now we are in the war we must fight it out like men.' But *per contra* he rejected the exultation in which the war had been entered upon, speaking of 'desolation carried into thousands of happy homes—Europe in arms—Asia agitated and febrile—America sullenly expectant.' Perhaps Elgin was naive, for no government, exposed as was that of Britain to public opinion, could sustain a war without an initial exultation: the great question in such cases was whether the pro-war euphoria could be nursed along for a sufficient time to ensure victory, or at least stave off defeat. Elgin for his part put a premium on the patriotism and devotion to duty that had characterised 'the services of our soldiers in the field, and of the women of England at the sick-bed.' But he doubted the conviction of the country's public men, sombrely asking their Lordships if in 'those in whom fortune, or birth, or royal or popular favour has placed in the van, these qualities are wanting, who shall dare to blame the press and the people of England if they seek for them elsewhere?' All of this was typical Elgin: do not waver half-way in a course of action, do not be betrayed by false patriotism, and remember that the nation is at bottom sound, though its leaders must be constantly recalled to a sense of duty worthy of those they lead. Elgin's views also clashed with those of the government concerning American aspirations in Central America. 'In the nature of things,' he told Augusta, 'the people of the United States must spread themselves in that direction—we cannot keep them out by force.'

Mary Nisbet died in 1855. Both Ferguson and the 7th Earl of Elgin had preceded her in 1841. For nearly half a century she had lived a retired life, far from the limelight she had once adored. Her properties had become her principal concern, making her a considerable woman of business. Her eldest daughter Lady Mary Bruce inherited her great estate, the younger Mary becoming a classic *grande dame*, full of prejudices and conventionalities, living in great pomp and entertaining the *grand monde* of the day, a good deal laughed at by her half-sisters who like her had known a much more straitened regime. She married Robert Dundas, M.P., sometime Chancellor of the Duchy of Lancaster, who assumed, in deference to his wife's wealth, the name of Christopher Hamilton Nisbet.

The current Lord Elgin spent most of the two and a half years after his return to Britain at Broomhall, resuming his old struggle with its debts and management. He was back where he had been in his seven years between Oxford and Parliament, at the ancestral seat, trying to make it economically viable while at the same time continuing his ponderings on man, society and the proper course of public action. This was to be his longest period at home in the course of his diplomatic career, the time when he could get closest to his children—Victor Alexander being now five to six years old. But it was a worrying and perplexing period. Elgin had by now achieved such a status that there were relatively few imperial or diplomatic jobs available to him.

Then, quite suddenly, in the spring of 1857 he was called upon to represent Britain on the other side of the world, assuming the role of Britain's High Commissioner and Plenipotentiary, effectively without limitation of his powers. He was to play a primary part in prizing open the most ancient and populous of societies, that of China, together with Japan, as well as helping to save India from the mutineers.

The background was that on 8 October a *lorcha*, a Chinese-rigged river ship, called the *Arrow*, registered at Hong Kong, had been boarded by Canton officials, its British flag desecrated and the crew made prisoners, charged with piracy. The Chinese insisted that the *Arrow* crew were not British but Chinese, and had no claim to British rights under the Treaty of Nanking which since the 'Opium' War of 1842 regulated the relations between China and Britain. The representatives of the British government on the spot, John Bowring at Hong Kong and Harry Parkes at Canton had taken a characteristically aggressive line: demanding that the insult to the Union Jack be purged by a written apology and that the sailors be returned unharmed. The Chinese, equally characteristically, equivocated. Bowring, in spite of having been warned by the Foreign

Secretary, Lord Clarendon, against violence, requested Sir Michael Seymour, the British Admiral, to prepare the fleet to stand off Canton in readiness for action. Soon the British demands were extended to a full enforcement of the long-evaded Treaty 'obligations' of 1842, of which one of the most important was that all foreign representatives had free access to the city of Canton and its authorities. The Chinese response was to sit tight and offer a generous reward for the head of every Englishman.

The small British fleet was brought up river and ordered into action by Bowring, taking fort after fort and destroying suburb after suburb of the city. But it was too feeble for real action against Canton. The Chinese for their part burned the foreign settlement in December causing the British mercantile community to flee to Hong Kong. Something of a stalemate had thus ensued, not very flattering to British pretensions. The merchants, not unnaturally, wanted a decisive assertion of British power.

Palmerston and Clarendon, whatever their regrets, could not allow Britain to back down. They knew perfectly well that any concession would be seen by the Chinese as a British defeat. Indeed the ineffectual British action against Canton had already done damage to the British reputation and alarmed Palmerston, who determined to press for a new and more favourable general settlement with China.

The *Arrow* affair had something in common with the Rebellion Losses Bill that had led to Elgin's searing experience in Canada. Both were relatively minor incidents in themselves, but both served as detonators for powerful underlying tension, releasing pent-up forces. Just as the hostility of the Anglo-Scots and the French Canadians had to be discharged by a cathartic, so the mutual charges of bad faith between British and Chinese had to reach explosion point, bringing the Second China War.

A curiously assorted but powerful element in the House of Commons, led by Gladstone, Disraeli and Cobden, condemned the violence against the Chinese: they deplored Bowring's actions on the grounds of morality, legality and general wisdom. Early in 1857 Palmerston, seeking the approval of the Commons for his government's embroilment in China, was defeated on a motion moved by Cobden. Palmerston then dissolved Parliament and won a General Election. Thus encouraged, Palmerston decided to re-arrange his forces to ensure effective action in the much-extended military operation now intended. Bowring, a lesser man despite his bluster, was to his great chagrin, dropped. Who, then, was to undertake the extraordinary role of disciplining China and bringing her to sign and honour a new treaty? To this errand was added that of coming to terms also with Japan. After an anxious survey of the possibilities, Palmerston approached Elgin. He, after much soul-searching, accepted.

To be asked to undertake such a mission was indeed a high compliment. Elgin was to be entrusted with a large army and a formidable navy. It was to consist of the elements already on the scene off Canton, together with large reinforcements of ships and soldiers. These he was to use pretty well at his own discretion in bringing the world's largest nation to heel. As Elgin was later to remark, he would not know whether the government approved his actions until they had become a matter of history. At this stage Elgin did not realise that his power over his Admirals and Generals was limited.

China was a challenge antithetical to that of Canada, and on a vastly greater scale.

Instead of serving as a conciliator among men of his own European tradition as in Canada, Elgin was now to impose Britain's will upon an oriental empire of incredible complexity and great antiquity. He did not relish the job. How could he reconcile his task with his life-long search for the conditions necessary for free and autonomous societies?

Mary Louisa was, of course, greatly alarmed at the dangers ahead for her beloved husband embarking on a mission that would almost certainly involve him in running a war of greater or lesser ferocity in the Far East. Although she appreciated the strength of her husband's sense of duty, the events in Montreal had made their mark upon her. The children were growing and needed their father. But duty had indeed called and Elgin duly went, carrying in his heart the vision of his wife and children, including Bruce's 'large speaking eyes', inherited from Mary Louisa. He was always eager for her reactions, wondering in his letters 'what will your view of my proceedings be?' He left behind him, too, the chronic problem of Broomhall, still in need of close surveillance, but once more left to the factor and trustees.

Elgin had deep misgivings about Britain's role in the world, being particularly troubled by Britain's role in Egypt, India and China. Yet the presence of his countrymen living and working in these places was a reality that had to be faced. The summons from Palmerston was not to be denied. Yet, how could this highly sensitive man, striving always to live by conscience and principle, become party to the rape of an ancient empire and indeed accept the control of the forces attacking it?

Elgin judged the matter in his own way. He concluded that Palmerston was determined to send the mission and the force, setting in train unpredictable results. It was therefore necessary for someone of balanced and moral mind to accept the leadership so as to temper the ardour both of Palmerston in London and the British commanders and merchants in China. So it was in order to limit their destructiveness that Elgin agreed to be placed at the head of the British fire ships. But he did so with a heavy heart and with deep misgivings about the actions of merchants, whose capacity for irresponsibility he remembered from Montreal. Perhaps indeed, there was in this aristocrat of ancient lineage something of the contempt for the trader that many others, including the Chinese, felt.

Moreover he knew that the Chinese would be evasive and obfuscatory, would practise delay in a cloud of ambiguity, making it necessary not only to show force, but to use it with great firmness in order to minimise the bloodshed and disruption. Indeed these tactics of delay were the best means of defence for the Chinese, for only by embracing and exhausting an attacker, as the Russians had done with Napoleon, could they hope to emerge unscathed. It was an agony for Elgin thus to be obliged to temporise. He resolved to keep tight control of the expedition so as to be able, so far as possible, to stop cumulative and irreversible violence. He consoled himself with the thought that the outcome was in 'higher hands' than his own.

Throughout his Chinese and Japanese adventures Elgin was to struggle to come to terms with the role he was playing in Great Britain's thrusting overseas expansion. His difficulties were two-fold. He was painfully ignorant about China and Japan and had no generalised theory of the relationship between the West and the East. He sensed something of the sequence by which Britain had embarked upon her Eastern course.

At one level it was a curious mixture of inadvertence, absent-mindedness, lack of interest and accident, in a way reminiscent of Canada. At another it had the hallmark of historical inevitability, imposing a role on British governments to which they had no choice but to react. The primary impulse had come from the merchant community in their urge for market openings. Simplistic though the view of China as an almost unlimited outlet for Indian opium and British manufactures might be, it had taken a powerful hold. Many quick fortunes were indeed being made in the China trade. A powerful interest lobby had soon been built up, infused, especially at the China end, with a highly aggressive spirit. Hemmed in and pressed upon by hordes of Chinese, they needed total solidarity among themselves, requiring their government to maintain an invincible prestige, permitting no disparagement of Britain. The merchants having dragged Britain into China, needed diplomatic representatives on the spot, including Her Britannic Majesty's Minister and Superintendent of Trade, and the British consul at Canton. These, respectively John Bowring and Harry Parkes, were also by nature pugnacious men, their bellicosity reinforced by the buccaneering spirit of the merchants. (Bowring, borne up by his religion, was author of the hymn, 'In the Cross of Christ I glory'). At home the Cabinet and traditional diplomacy gave little thought to China itself (as to Canada), being much more interested in Britain's relations with the other European powers. Palmerston was clearly much more at home in Europe, the traditional theatre of real diplomacy. Moreover the Foreign Secretary had been obliged to rely for information largely on two blustering, fiery men who were his representatives in China. Finally, Britain had the most powerful naval force in the world, made possible by her industrial and trading success, giving her the power, at will, to intervene around the maritime perimeter of the continents. The British government thus found itself being inexorably dragged deeper and deeper into the vast and enigmatic mass of China.

Meanwhile China was also caught up in an inexorable chain of events. The Ch'ing dynasty of the Manchus had ruled China from the first half of the seventeenth century during which time there had been a long period of prosperity and expansion, presided over by coherent and effective government. But then the downward phase of the mighty cycle that had governed China's fate for so many generations manifested itself once more. Stable conditions had released the Malthusian devil: the population had more than doubled by the 1850's under the Manchus, from some 180 millions in 1751 to over 430 million in 1851. Though the area of cultivated land had also grown larger, it still fell far short of need. Agriculture underwent no technological or other change that could lift its output to a new plateau. No alternative employment in industry had been generated and there had been no territorial gain to which the surplus population could go. In consequence the land had undergone an intensification of cultivation together with a classic division and sub-division. But as numbers relentlessly rose these devices were reaching their limit: increasing poverty for the mass of peasants was the inevitable outcome, as in earlier Chinese cycles. Banditry and piracy grew correspondingly, placing a strain on government. Taxes on the peasantry were arbitrarily increased by local officials and by the landowning gentry. These latter, together with lesser men, often moneylenders, acquired more and more land, raising the rents. Respect for human life in terms of the peasantry did not exist. Government completed the syndrome, with gross decadence at court, compounded by concubines and eunuchs and the decay of a once–efficient government bureaucracy. There was mismanagement in the provinces, exacerbated by the sale of public jobs. The inevitable climax came with rebellion in 1851 of the Taipings with their pseudo–Christian fervour. By 1856 they had gained large areas of territory, especially in the south: indeed their movement could well be regarded as the first manifestation of China's modern revolution. This of course gave a further twist to the downward spiral.

This was the China into which Britain had intruded after the First Opium War. Before this, foreign trade had been confined to Canton, the southern port on the Pearl River; thereafter, following the Treaty of Nanking five treaty ports Canton, Foochow, Amoy, Ningpo and Shanghai, had been opened. This greatly diminished Cantonese trade, causing a hostility toward the British, the leading foreign devils. At the national level the Manchus were of course themselves foreigners, imposing themselves on the Chinese: as the abuses and failures of government grew, so did nationalism among the Chinese, adding to the sympathy for the Taipings, especially in the South. Partly because the Taipings embodied elements of Christianity in their syncretic religion, the British at first had been disposed to support them. But as the Taipings lost their inspiration and direction and as their leader, Hung Hsiu Chwan, subsided into decadence and indeed imbecility, they posed for the British a difficult dilemma, for the prospect faded of their being able or even disposed to form a government with which an effective treaty could be made.

So it was that the inadvertent dynamics of British and of Chinese history converged. The two countries went to war in a dense cloud of mutual ignorance, neither having any real sense of the power or intentions of the other. It was into this maelstrom of blind forces that Elgin was drawn.

CHAPTER 14

The Indian Mutiny, the Celestial Empire and Japan

Elgin began his eastern odyssey in the middle of April 1857. He passed through the Mediterranean with its memories of his father and the Greeks and the Turks, stopped briefly in Cairo, moved down the Red Sea and across the Indian Ocean to Ceylon. There he received the news through the electric telegraph that at Meerut near Delhi on 11 May an Indian regiment had mutinied and that an expeditionary force had left Bombay to put the rising down. This made Elgin more anxious than ever to finish the China business so that his forces could, with all possible speed, be made available in India. Elgin again chose Laurence Oliphant as his private secretary. Oliphant was later to provide an absorbing two-volume account of Elgin's mission. Frederick Bruce, Elgin's brother and close confidant, was also of the party.

Meanwhile Elgin had travelled accompanied only by his suite; the naval and military forces he was to use in China were to converge from different points. *HMS Caradoc* took him to Malta; thereafter he travelled in a succession of steamships. Britain had a linked chain of Governors commanding her imperial possessions who could not only entertain so great a dignitary as Elgin now was, but who were delighted to relieve their boredom by so doing. In spite of his apprehension about the China expedition, he was glad to be on the move, widening his experience and setting out his observations in a letter-journal to Mary Louisa. He tried to see through her eyes as well as his own, making a point of expanding on the things he saw which he thought would interest her. At Malta he attended the deathbed of a Fife neighbour, Lord Balgonie: 'There he lay; his arm absolutely fleshless, stretched out: his large eyes gleaming from his pale face.' He was delighted to find that the keeper of the inn at Malta 'was the son of an old servant at Broomhall, Hood by name, and that he had often played with me at cricket!'

At each place of call Elgin was received with great honour, especially in Egypt where he spent two days. He described for Mary Louisa the harem and the dress and deportment of the 'Mohamedan female'. He recounted that 'the persons who ascend to the top of the minarets to call to prayer at the appointed hours are blind men ... selected for this office lest they should be able to look down into the harems', a curious echo of Lusieri's difficulties at the Parthenon. The fertility of the Nile Valley deeply impressed him, 'teeming with production and life, animal and vegetable, as he remarked: 'What might not be made of this country if it were wisely guided!' The fault lay not altogether with the Egyptians: 'I suppose', he wrote, 'that France and

England by their mutual jealousies will be the means of perpetuating the abominations of a system under which that magnificent country is ruled.'

From Cairo he was conveyed part of the way to Suez by train, an exhilerating journey, travelling as he did for an hour and a half at 40 miles per hour across the desert, perched in a *coupe* in front of the engine. Passing down the Red Sea in the P & O steamer *Bentinck* he compared the physique of the Indian crewmen to that of the Chinese, to the great advantage of the latter. The Indians lived on the deck, each on his little patch, eating and doing his toilette. Elgin was intrigued by 'the composure with which the ladies [passengers] witness these proceedings. There is certainly', he pondered, 'great protection in a black skin.'

At Aden he was impressed with the immense water tanks constructed in remote antiquity in graded steps down the hillside, and only lately rediscovered—the Governor told him that only a few months earlier he had driven his gig over the largest tank, having no idea of its existence.

As Elgin travelled slowly across the Indian ocean he felt boredom, depression and foreboding descend upon him, together with a longing for Mary Louisa and the children. He was steadily making his way through the official prose of the blue-books and reports on China. The more he read, he told Mary Louisa, the stronger was his feeling 'that we have often acted towards the Chinese in a manner which it is difficult to justify.' On the other hand, 'their treachery and cruelty come out so strongly at times as to make almost anything seem justifiable.' He became increasingly anxious about Britain's role in China. How could he, as his mission required, justify its extension? The news from India deepened his gloom. The mutineers had murdered Europeans, seized the Fort and treasure of Delhi, and proclaimed the son of the Great Mogul as emperor. The effect of this news in China could only be that Britain's position there would be weakened. Would the view spread that Britain was finished in the East? In the phase of the journey from Ceylon the stink of 1,500 boxes of opium in the ship's hold pervaded the air.

At Penang Elgin met the Bishop of Lauan, northern Borneo, who recounted his dealings with the Chinese in Sarawak. For this insight Elgin was grateful, struggling as he was to form in his mind a picture of the Chinese, their character and culture, on desperately slender evidence. He concluded:

> I am about to do with a strange people; so much to admire in them, and yet with a perversity of disposition which makes it absolutely necessary, if you are to live with them at all, to treat them severely, almost cruelly. They have such an overweening esteem for themselves that they become unbearable unless they are constantly reminded that others are as good as they.

On arrival at Singapore he found an urgent message from the Governor General of India, Lord Canning, his old Oxford friend, now desperate in the face of the Mutiny, imploring Elgin to send him troops. Elgin as yet had not received a single man, and did not know when his forces would come. But he quickly made his decision, one that was to prove decisive in the history of India and the empire. The most pressing matter was to save India. Accordingly he sent orders far and wide that his troop transports should proceed to India. Augusta reported 'How grateful the Queen was to Elgin for his beautiful disinterested conduct.'

Elgin had now to wait at Singapore for the arrival of *HMS Shannon*, a magnificent ship-of-war carrying sixty 68 pounder guns, fitted with both sail and screw and scheduled to carry him to China. He visited an opium shop which, he ruefully remarked, 'We are supposed to do so much to encourage.' He was however appalled by what he saw:

> They are wretched places, with little lamps, in which the smokers light their pipes, glimmering on the shelves made of boards on which they recline and puff until they fall asleep. The opium looks like treacle, and the smokers are haggard and stupefied, except at the moment of their inhaling, when an unnatural brightness sparkles from their eyes.

Elgin's distaste was understandable. Opium was culturally acceptable as a symptom suppressant in Britain to about 1850; it was only seen as a social problem from about 1860, though Britain had never experienced its use on the Chinese scale. At Singapore Elgin was astonished that 'in this place where there are some 60,000 or 70,000 Chinese, and where the Europeans are always imagining they are plotting ... there is not a single European who can speak their language.' Misunderstandings were chronic, inflamed by the suggestibility of the Europeans. Some six months earlier, in a typical welter of confusion and suspicion, the rumour had spread that the Chinese were intending, out of sympathy for the Cantonese recently attacked by the British, to murder all the Europeans.

On 11 June the mighty *Shannon*, Captain Kepple commanding, arrived in Singapore, stirring in Elgin a deep strain of national pride, for she was indeed a splendid sight. The coming of the *Shannon* also renewed Elgin's awareness of the challenge ahead. But travel in her did not prove so uplifting. The ship had no poop, and the deck was closed in by high defensive bulwarks which shut out both the air and the view.

At last on 3 July Elgin reached Hong Kong. He had discovered that though supposedly splendid as an instrument of war, the *Shannon* was practically useless as a long distance steamer because she could only carry coal for five days. Also whereas a good merchant steamer could do ten direct miles per hour, the *Shannon* tacking under sail did only six. The 1,100 men almost stifled in her shut-in decks as the temperature soared.

He was soon made even more headachy and fagged, by a succession of interviews with the British Admiral and General and an array of bureaucrats, merchants and other civilians, each trying to impress Elgin with his own point of view. There was too a heap of despatches from London, out of date and hence perplexing. Moreover Elgin found almost at once that the course of moderation that he proposed was not to the liking of the belligerent British merchants. Elgin had hoped that his troops could be extricated from India in time for him to use them in China before the onset of winter, but a letter from Canning dis-abused him—no troops could be spared from India for many months. Moreover the French ambassador, Baron Gros, whose co-operation was crucial, would not reach China until the end of December; similarly no American representative had turned up. More letters came from Canning begging further help.

Elgin briskly decided that instead of wasting the next three months in Hong Kong, he would go to Calcutta, taking what troops he could collect, some 1,700 in all. He felt deeply the weight of such decision-taking and contrasted his position with that of a diplomat in Europe, 'where reference was made to headquarters by the new electric telegraph in every case of difficulty.' On 20 July, his birthday, Elgin was much depressed. As he wrote to his wife, 'Do not anniversaries stir this great fountain of sadness ... Is it not lawful to be sad?' The *Shannon* reached Calcutta on 8 August to the immense relief of Canning and the foreign population. There was a mighty exchange of salutes between the *Shannon* and the ships in the harbour and the shore batteries, as she proceeded up Garden Reach to Calcutta. Captain Peel and most of his men were formed into a Naval Brigade, Peel's 68 pounders were subsequently very useful. Canning, in the unhealthy climate of Calcutta, was literally working himself to death. According to Oliphant he had lost the confidence of the British community, being very reserved and unwilling to delegate to his subordinates.

Elgin was distressed by his first sight of the Indians and the attitude taken by the British toward them. 'It is a terrible business ...' he wrote to Mary Louisa, 'this living among inferior races. I have seldom from man or woman since I came to the East heard a sentence which was reconcilable with the hypothesis that Christianity had ever come into the world.' He found 'detestation, contempt, ferocity, vengeance, whether Chinamen or Indians be the object.' He noted how soon the feeling of awkwardness at being continually salaamed wore off: 'One moves among them with perfect indifference, treating them, not as dogs, because in that case one would whistle to them and pat them ... When the passions of fear and hatred are engrafted on this indifference, the result is frightful ...' Here Elgin was expressing his instinct about the root cause of the Mutiny. With a small detachment of soldiers and two hundred women and as many children, Lucknow was beleaguered by some 15,000 mutineers, facing a fearful fate.

On 3 September, having learned that a new body of troops was on its way to Hong Kong to replace those he had committed to India, Elgin headed once more eastward, arriving back at Hong Kong on the 20th. The vibration from the screw of this steamer, the *Avia*, was so great that it was almost impossible for him to write when she was at full speed. Elgin developed a fever, 'constantly falling off into dreamy dozes; kaleidoscopes, with the ugliest sides of everything perpetually twirling before my eyes.' With the portholes open to relieve the heat the sea crashed in, drenching him. Elgin joked to Mary Louisa ruefully that however ill he might be he never got credit for it, 'having a more florid appearance than most.' But the immediate sufferings of Elgin and his party were by no means at an end. The ships had to stand off Hong Kong for fear of typhoons. Elgin took this philosophically but poor Oliphant hated the enforced confinement.

There were further delays. Elgin's force was not complete until mid-November. He was determined that if negotiations failed he would overwhelm Canton by naval and military force, and so minimise massacre and bloodshed. As the ships and men assembled he was astonished at what supplies had been provided by the British government. These included 'oceans of porter, soda water, wine of all sorts, and delicacies I have never ever heard of for the hospitals ... This is the reaction after the economies practised in the Crimea, and will be persevered in, I suppose, till Parliament gets tired of paying, and then we shall have the counteraction the other way.' News came that the 5th and 90th Regiments together with the Naval Brigade that Elgin had sent to India were marching to the relief of Lucknow.

Elgin characteristically took the opportunity of his waiting time to explore the Portuguese city of Macao across the bay. Whereas Hong Kong had been a barren rock fifteen years earlier, Macao was some three hundred years old, and had its convents, churches and gardens. Yet in his view Protestant Hong Kong showed 'a wonderful superiority'. In Macao he stayed with the head of the agency house of Dent and Co. one of the princes of the opium trade. He wandered about the garden of the sixteenth century soldier-poet Camoëns, that disconsolate son of the Renaissance whose impassioned sonnets to his Beatrice, Caterina de Altaidan, had made him the most celebrated of Portuguese poets, together with his *Elegy of Exile*, a poem to which Elgin, for obvious reasons, could respond.

Around this time Elgin was deeply saddened by the news that his dear half-sister Matilda—'that good genius'—had died. He remembered how much she had meant to him as a boy and youth, and how she had worried about his future when he returned home from Jamaica and Canada. He remembered that it was Matty who had done so much to hold the family together, supporting her stepmother Eliza with such devotion and acting as a sympathetic listener to all the family. Distance bore heavily on him at such a time: 'Already', he wrote to Mary Louisa, 'when this letter reaches you, the green weeds will have begun to creep over the new-made grave, and the crust of habit to cover wounds which at first bled most freely.' His longing for Mary Louisa came over him as he waited for action. From Headquarters House in Hong Kong he wrote, 'I wish you could take wings and join me here, if it were even for a few hours.' He then described the walk they would take together through the garden as the sunset came on, looking over the harbour 'bright as a flower-bed with the flags of many nations', and lingering until 'tens of thousands of bright and silent stars were looking down calmly from heaven.'

By mid-November, with his force complete, Elgin could get down to serious work. Canton was his first concern where so much Chinese commerce was concentrated and which the British merchants regarded as one of their chief bases. The Cantonese, full of curiosity, had always delighted in the novelties which had come from the West. But it was here that Chinese obstructionism against the working of the Treaty of Nanking was at its most persistent and ingenious; it was not surprising that the *Arrow* incident had occurred at Canton. The resident British there demanded 'The total humiliation of Canton', but they also believed that Elgin should use his power directly against the capital Pekin, far away to the north. In the event Elgin's first step was to draw up a challenge to Yeh, the Lieutenant Governor of Canton and its province, doing so in conjunction with the French envoy Baron Gros, with whom by this time Elgin had established a cordial relationship. Yeh had made a reputation for himself for ruthlessness against the Taiping rebels. A man of truculent temper, often blinded by fury, he was a fanatical believer in himself and passionate in his hatred of the West. Elgin, the level headed liberal, honestly believed that the *Arrow* incident was 'a scandal to us, and is so considered, I have reason to know, by all except the few who are personally compromised', and so resolved that it should be no part of the British case instead he adopted two general principles. First as he conveyed to Yeh, he would use his great striking power to the limit if necessary. Secondly, he believed that the demands he made upon Yeh were moderate, of a kind that could be accepted without great loss of face. This temperateness, if accepted by Yeh, would, as Elgin well knew, bring upon his own head 'the imprecations both of the navy and army and of the civilians.'

His intention, as Elgin told Mary Louisa, was to 'stand towering above all, using calm and dignified language, moderate in our demands, but resolute in enforcing them.' Here on a much grander stage was the Elgin of Montreal speaking, seeking to combine firmness and reconciliation. He deeply regretted that this had not been the British attitude from the beginning. British policy in India and China provoked from him a little essay on how he regarded the outlook of 'men in power at present.' Their view was

> never to interfere to check an evil until it has attained such proportions that all the world see plainly the necessity of the case. You will then get any amount of moral and material support that you require; but if you interfere at an earlier period, you will get neither thanks nor assistance!

Thus did Elgin enunciate the law of necessary deterioration as it had operated in Britain's dealings with China.

Canton was remote from the capital, Pekin. Would Elgin, even if he could bring Governor Yeh to terms, arrive at an effective agreement with the Imperial Court? But it seemed right to begin at Canton, hoping that the affair would end there. Curiously, Governor Yeh was in a position somewhat similar to that of Elgin in the sense that both were remote from the final authority of their governments, each having to deal with a difficult situation on his own. The difference between them was that Elgin earnestly desired to be moderate and reasonable whereas Yeh was driven by an implacable hatred, refusing any sort of parley.

Elgin's ultimatum was delivered to Yeh on 12th December 1857. On the same day came the news that Lucknow had been relieved, largely by the troops that Elgin had provided. 'Tell Lord Elgin', wrote Sir William Peel the leader of the Naval Brigade, 'that it was the Chinese Expedition that relieved Lucknow, relieved Cawnpore, and fought the battle of 6th December.' It is interesting to reflect that India might well have been lost to the British in 1857 had it not been for the otherwise insignificant affair of the *Arrow* in Canton which allowed Elgin to deflect troops for China to India.

Yeh, of course, gave no real answer, but in the Chinese fashion indulged in what Elgin called 'twaddle'. For Elgin and Gros there was nothing for it but to pass matters over to the British and French admirals and generals. A few days before the bombardment of Canton Elgin made a reconnaissance in a gunboat and the full implications of what he was doing suddenly struck him. 'I never felt so ashamed of myself in my life', he wrote to Mary Louisa, 'There we were, accumulating the means of destruction under the very eyes, and within reach, of a population of about 1,000,000 people ... I feel that I am earning for myself a place in the Litany, immediately after "plague, pestilence and famine".' He tried to comfort himself with the thought that he could not do otherwise. But when he discovered from his Church of England prayerbook that the day chosen for the attack was that dedicated in the Church Calendar to the Massacre of the Innocents it was postponed. On Christmas Day Elgin recalled that of the previous year, spent in great happiness with Mary Louisa's family the Lambtons and Greys at Howick. Now he found himself a world away in *HMS Furious*, like St. Paul dropping an anchor from the stern, holding position some two miles from 'a great city, doomed, I fear to destruction, from the folly of its own rulers and the vanity and levity of ours.'

At 6 a.m. on 28 December 1857 Elgin's ships began to bombard Canton, an attack which continued for 27 hours. Later the troops went ashore and occupied the city. Almost at once Elgin's feelings of guilt were further fuelled by the looting of the French and British forces. He was fearful that the belligerent French Admiral would persuade his British colleague that a further bombardment was necessary. There was always the problem of controlling the professional bellicosity of his naval and military commanders: they, naturally enough, put a premium on the defeat of an enemy: moreover they needed to engage their men convincingly to maintain their morale. On going ashore Elgin found the people hiding in their single-storey houses in their narrow streets. The damage to the city, though serious, was less than he had expected.

Lieutenant Governor Yeh, the Terror of the Barbarians, had been taken prisoner by Parkes. Yeh turned out to be a man of immense and dirty proportions. Taken aboard *HMS Inflexible*, he inquired whether he was to be killed. A Bible was presented to him. Elgin was most anxious that Canton should be spared the humiliation and other evils of military occupation, but this could only be done if Yeh or some other mandarin would agree to govern the city and province under the Allies. 'You can imagine', he wrote to Mary Louisa, 'what it would mean to govern a province of more than 20,000,000 people when we have *in all* two or three people who understand the language.' Elgin planned to set up a provisional government of Three Commissioners, of whom Parkes was one. Pikwei, the native governor of the city, was also persuaded to resume his post. Brought from his prison cell, he coolly insisted on taking precedence over the British admiral and general, and Elgin, anxious for effective civil government, agreed.

After the capture Elgin wandered about the streets of Canton. He visited the prison looking for Europeans or Chinese who had been in the service of the British. In one cell he found prisoners in chains, covered with sores and plagued with rats, the dead lying unattended. All of this was against Chinese law, and was, Elgin thought, not so much the product of cruelty as of neglect and shortage. Though the Chinese gave little trouble, the looting still went on, much to Elgin's concern. 'No human power', he told Mary Louisa, 'shall induce me to play the office of oppressor of the feeble ... I send a leaf of a geranium, which I culled in the garden of the Tartar general.' To stop the looting he withdrew the allied forces, falling back on prepared lines. But this weakened the Allied position, and the Canton 'braves' began a sort of guerilla war against British and French.

It was now necessary to move northward to Shanghai to try to open negotiations from there with Pekin. Elgin, mindful of the savagery of Chinese internecine wars, and the present conflict with the Taipings and other rebel movements, comforted himself with regard to Canton that 'There never was a Chinese town which had suffered so little by the occupation of a hostile force.' He pondered on European ignorance of the East, noting 'the follies which people commit when they know nothing of the manners of those with whom they have to deal.'

After two months in Canton, which he hoped never to see again, spending much of his time 'checking, as I have best been able to do, the disposition to maltreat this unfortunate people', he began his northward journey. Meanwhile Palmerston's government had fallen, to be succeeded by that of the Earl of Derby, with Lord Malmesbury as Foreign Secretary. Malmesbury was anxious to follow a more conciliatory line in China. He issued a circular announcing Britain's peaceful intentions and repudiating any wish for territorial aggrandisement. No changes were made in Elgin's instructions. Indeed Malmesbury confessed to Elgin that he was submerged under 'such a mass of correspondence' that he could make no assessment of China on which to base a new brief for his Ambassador Extraordinary. Malmesbury was in the position not unlike that of Grenville in 1800 over the Convention of El Arish; Elgin's situation was like that of his father earlier, left to make British policy in China as he thought best.

The expedition called at the little island of Swatow, where the European settlement, in breach of the Treaty, consisted mainly of agents of 'the two great opium houses, Dent and Jardine, with their hangers on.' Elgin also discovered there a considerable business in the coolie trade, kidnapping men, as he put it and 'putting them on board ships where all the horrors of the slave trade are reproduced, and sending them on specious promises to such places as Cuba.' Amid the beauty of Foochow Elgin found confirmation that 'our trade is carried on on principles which are dishonest as regards the Chinese and demoralising to our own people.' He talked to European missionaries at various places, including Amoy, sadly doubting that even those tiny few Chinese who could be called converts 'accepted in any very earnest way the peculiar doctrines of Christianity', in particular that of the Atonement. He compared the exemplary devotion of the Catholic missionaries, with their abandonment of home and its culture, adopting the dress, food and housing of the Chinese, penetrating far into the hinterland, with the record of the Protestants who hardly left the ports, 'where they have excellent houses, wives and families.' Elgin became increasingly hopeful that there could be effective negotiation with the Imperial Court. An edict had been issued in which Yeh was downgraded, but moderate in tone toward the foreigners. Poor Yeh had been carried into exile to Calcutta where he shortly died.

Near Ningpo Elgin had his fortune told at a Buddhist temple by the traditional method of casting lots in the form of sticks: he was told that his was a No. 1 lot, the most fortunate of all. The temples, the principal buildings had a certain fascination for a religious man like Elgin, though he found them and their statuary primitive, the 'temples in tinsel and their bonzes (priests) in rags.' But he commended the Buddhist religion for its freedom from 'any bigoted antipathy to the professors of other creeds.' Considering that it had been severely battered by the Europeans in 1842, Ningpo showed 'the most friendly disposition to foreigners.' The resident British traders took this as confirmation of their view that the Chinese were best dealt with through violence and repression. In a despatch to the Foreign Secretary Elgin refuted this reasoning, arguing that the people of Ningpo and its region had always been 'the most inoffensive, perhaps, both by disposition and habit of any on the surface of the earth.'

Chusan he found a most charming island, marvelling that Hong Kong should have been preferred to it by the British. He came upon the graves of the British killed in the occupation of the island in 1842, and ordered that these derelict resting places be tended. He reflected with some bitterness that 'in the plundering expeditions which we Christians dignify with the name of war in these countries, idols are ripped up in the hope of finding treasure in them, temple ornaments seized, and in short no sort of consideration is shown for the religious feelings of the natives.' Elgin had developed a depressing sense of the precariousness of human discipline among men whose business was war. It was little consolation that the Taiping war bands and the imperial troops were much more ruthless.

At the mouth of the Yangtze Kiang river, Shanghai was the most northerly of the Treaty Ports, and the nearest to Pekin the capital. The foreign settlement there already gave the place a surprisingly European appearance, with European ships prominent in the harbour, ladies and gentlemen strolling along the quay and policemen dressed like Sir Robert Peel's London force keeping the peace. The organ in the Catholic cathedral, with its bamboo pipes, greatly intrigued Elgin. All this had been created within a few recent years.

Now began a long period of fencing with the Imperial Court. From Pekin Elgin was told to return to Canton and wait there. The Shanghai European merchants presented an Address to Elgin urging action: in his reply he made it plain that he had decided to proceed to Pekin, there to apply direct pressure on the Emperor. But he also 'endeavoured to give the British merchants a hint that they must exert themselves and not trust to cannon if they intend to get a market in China.' The 'manufacturing West', he told them, can achieve victories 'only by proving that physical knowledge and mechanical skill, applied to the arts of production, are more than a match for the most persevering efforts of unscientific industry.' More pointedly, in replying to an address from the Protestant missionaries of Shanghai seeking extended rights for themselves and protection for their converts, he pointed out that, unless he was greatly misinformed, 'many vile and reckless men, protected by the privileges to which I have referred, and still more by the terror which British prowess has inspired, are now infesting the coasts of China ... they bring discredit on the Christian name.' Moreover he feared that Chinamen adopting Christianity might be 'tempted to put on a hypocritical profession in order to secure thereby the advantages of abnormal protection.'

Elgin agreed with Baron Gros that they and their respective fleets should meet at the mouth of the Peiho (on a tributary of which Pekin stands), with the moral support of the Russian and American plenipotentiaries. But there were many weeks of delay while Elgin waited for light draught gunboats that could pass over the mud bar at the mouth of the river. He had asked Admiral Seymour, British naval commander in the Far East, to send him as many such gunboats as possible. But Seymour delayed. For five weeks Elgin waited eight miles off the mouth of the Peiho River in the Gulf of Pechili, under torrid skies, getting more and more desperate. He was humiliated by the delay, as well as having lost all hope of making a surprise attack. Finally on 15 April 1858 Seymour and the gunboats reached the mouth of the Peiho. The bar was crossed without real difficulty and about a week later the Taku Forts were taken. A reconnaissance force proceeded without hindrance up the river causing Elgin to express astonishment at Chinese vulnerability: was he reminded of Cortez when he wrote 'Twenty-four determined men, with revolvers and a sufficient number of cartridges, might walk through China from one end to another'? Elgin feared that the Emperor might flee to Tartary, creating more problems. He was concerned also about the possibility of a further change of government at home. On 19 May he had a despatch from Lord Malmesbury empowering him 'to do anything I choose if I will only finish the affair.' The Chinese neither resisted nor showed any sign of negotiating.

On 29 May Elgin and Gros proceeded with their main force up the Peiho River toward Tientsin and Pekin.

> There we went ceaselessly on', wrote Elgin, 'through the silvery silence, panting and breathing flame. Through the night-watches, when no Chinaman moves, when the junks cast anchor, we laboured on, cutting ruthlessly and recklessly through the waters of that glancing and startled river, which, until within the last few weeks, no stranger keel had ever furrowed! Whose work we are engaged in, when we burst thus with hideous violence and brutal energy into these darkest and most mysterious recesses of the traditions of the past?

On the other hand, however, Elgin had formed a low opinion of China:

> There is certainly not much to regret in the old civilisation which we are thus scattering to the winds ... a dense population, timorous and pauperised.

The ship's company watched from the deck as the inhabitants of each mud village ran to the bank and bowed to the strange craft which seemed to need no help from nature to propel them onward. At the point where the Great Canal joined the river, at Tientsin, fifty miles from Pekin, Elgin's forces gathered. The Chinese plenipotentiaries were there to meet them.

By this time Elgin had made up his mind, distasteful as it was, to play the part of the 'Uncontrollably Fierce Barbarian', as he was described in official Chinese reports. He presented a front of truculence that was otherwise quite out of character. He went ashore for the meeting with a guard of 150 marines and the band of *HMS Calcutta*, with his whole suite carried in chairs, *tambour battant*. After due pleasantries concerning the health of the Emperor, Elgin exhibited the documents setting out the fullness of his powers. He then affected to regard those of the Chinese as inadequate; rising he ordered his chairs and escort. He felt justified in using truculent tactics for he had learned how well the Chinese authorities could play the game of creating confusion by their prevarication and equivocation. 'We went on fighting and bullying and bullying', he wrote to Mary Louisa, until the terms of the Treaty were settled.

While he negotiated and waited, Elgin's doubts about the whole affair worked in his mind and conscience. He was disgusted with his fellow countrymen 'since I have found them in the East among populations too timid to resist and too ignorant to complain.' Even while he was putting relentless pressure on the Chinese plenipotentiaries he could write: 'I have an instinct within me which loves righteousness and hates iniquity, and all this keeps me in a perpetual boil.'

A last minute hitch arose. The Chinese Commissioners pleaded that two of Elgin's demands be withdrawn, namely that the British and French should have the right to send an ambassador to Pekin and that they should have permission to trade in the interior of China. Elgin believed these concessions to be essential although Baron Gros and the Russian and American Ministers were for conceding. But Elgin was adamant: he sent for Admiral Seymour, asking and receiving his backing. His brother, Frederick Bruce, was sent to tell the Imperial Commissioners that if there was any delay or retraction of what had been agreed, the force would move on Pekin, demanding a great deal more. The Chinese capitulated.

The Treaty of Tientsin was signed on 16 June 1858. Under it five additional Treaty Ports were to be opened, and the interior of China made accessible, as was the commerce of the Yangtze when the Taiping rebels had been put down. Costs of some £1,300,000 were imposed on the Chinese. The conditions of the tariff were left to be settled later at Shanghai, where the Imperial Commissioners agreed a rendezvous. Frederick was sent home to Britain with the Treaty. 'In sending Frederick away', wrote Elgin, 'I have cut off my right arm.' Elgin and his force then moved back to Shanghai to mark time until the Commissioners should reappear. This was the third tedious waiting period the expedition had suffered.

Elgin then decided that this barren interlude could be turned to profit. He had been instructed before leaving England to negotiate a Treaty with Japan also. Accordingly he left on 31 July in *HMS Furious* for Edo (now Tokyo), to the intense relief of Oliphant and the company, glad to escape from the hot and leaden skies of Shanghai. Accompanying the *Furious* were the *Retribution* and the gunboat *Lee*, together with the steam yacht *Emperor*, specially built for presentation to the Japanese ruler. It was a small and propitiatory force, intended by Elgin to convey to the Japanese that he was coming not as an aggressor but as a diplomat: in this he deliberately rejected the display of force that had been intended by Bowring. Elgin was aware that in one sense his negotiating position was weak: successive Foreign Secretaries including Clarendon and Malmesbury did not believe that Japan justified much risk, certainly not that of war.

Elgin had no idea of what he was to encounter in Japan. It was to his surprise that he learned that there was no way of communicating with any precision with the Japanese in any European language other than Dutch. He had to borrow from Townsend Harris, the American Consul, his man Henry Heusken. Whereas Britain had taken the lead in China, it was the Americans who had taken the initiative in Japan. Townsend Harris had succeeded, after much negotiation, in drawing up an American-Japanese Treaty that might serve Elgin as a model. Elgin believed that it was probable that his own firmness in China, especially in bombarding Canton, had contributed a good deal to Harris's success. The British had felt some annoyance that the Americans had stood by, letting them bear the brunt of opening by far the largest country in the East, only to step in and gain the same concessions: there was a strong opinion in England that it was the turn of the United States to take initiative in Japan.

Elgin looked in at Nagasaki with his little fleet. There the Dutch, confined to their tiny settlement at Deshima had maintained Japan's tenuous link with the West. The Governor tried to get Elgin to hand over the steam yacht *Emperor* to him; needless to say he declined. Elgin then moved on to meet the American envoy in Shimoda. Townsend Harris's Treaty had been signed at Kanagawa shortly before, on 29 July. Elgin examined it and decided that it would serve as the model for his own. It was loose on extraterritoriality, but neither Harris nor Elgin were lawyers. Harris was an astute and devious man, having urged on the Japanese Commissioners that if they did not accept his 'reasonable' Treaty, Elgin would start afresh, imposing harsher terms, but that if they signed his document he would seek to persuade Elgin to use it as his model.

Elgin then stood off Edo in the *Furious*, waiting for an overture by the Japanese: the *Furious* was the first Western ship to enter Edo Bay since Japan had been closed in the seventeenth century. In moving up channel to the capital Elgin had passed into forbidden waters, ignoring Japanese signals. A group of magnates, the Shogun's Commissioners, tagged behind in their archaic craft, eventually coming aboard. Their chief interpreter was Moriama Einosuke (the 'wooded mountain' as Elgin reported to Mary Louisa). Moriama had sharpened his wits, his Dutch and his English on the negotiations with Townsend Harris. He had learned quickly, becoming an accomplished negotiator. He sought discreetly to brief Elgin by telling a member of the British staff a little of the Japanese background. He disclosed that the Commissioners were 'Free Traders', favouring the signing of a Treaty, but that some of the hereditary princes or *daimyo* were hostile and threatening rebellion because of the concessions the government was making to the West. It was thus conveyed to Elgin in this informal way that the Japanese were divided in their attitude to Britain and the West, but that those seeking terms of accommodation were firmly in the ascendant. Elgin, of course, had no means of assessing such subtleties. Oliphant proved useful in making friends in his easy way with Iwasi Higo No Kami, one of the Commissioners, one of the principals behind the drafting of the Harris Treaty, and a strong convert to the idea of Western ways. He noted English words on the fans he carried in his bosom and hoped to be chosen as a Japanese ambassador to the West. Indeed much of the understanding between the British and Japanese was generated at a secondary level by Moriama, Oliphant and Heusken.

Elgin continued to act as in China, asserting his high dignity and power. One way of doing so was to object to the accommodation initially provided for him and his party as being insufficiently grand: this seems to have been a sound move, producing the desired effect of enhanced respect. Elgin appears to have had but the vaguest idea of the way in which the government of Japan was carried on through the Shogun, with the Emperor incommunicado in Kyoto, a problematic figure. He could not know that the Emperor could have no need for a yacht. But in essence Elgin's judgment was correct: 'The government', he remarked, 'seems to be a sort of oligarchy in the hands of the hereditary princes.' As in China, there was always the difficulty of discovering the true status and intentions of those with whom he was negotiating, together with the fear that what had been agreed would be repudiated at a higher level, or by a shift of power among the Japanese factions.

The British party landed on 17 August, Elgin in his barge, resplendent in full dress and the ribbon and star of a Knight of the Thistle, with 'Rule Britannia' rendered by the ship's band. Great crowds rushed out to see this strange sight, some of them dripping from the bath. Elgin settled in with his suite at the Tozenji Temple. There were of course no hotels or guest houses sufficient for the purpose in Edo. The use of one of the *yashikis* or great housing complexes of one of the *daimyo* lords was out of the question. So it was that Elgin found himself, like a Buddhist in retreat, living in guest quarters provided by the priests. The temple was an impressive place, with its gardens, ponds and pines, close to Shinagawa on the edge of Tokyo Bay, well removed from the Shogun's castle in the centre of Yedo. The Japanese provided European chairs, tables and beds, copies of Townsend Harris's furniture, which Elgin's party found touching. There was a lack of privacy, with the locals coming to peer, some of it official surveillance and some of it spontaneous. But the British, by removing partitions and making other adjustments, were comfortable enough, though the midsummer heat of Edo was very tiring.

Though Elgin now understood that a Treaty would not be acceptable to all the Japanese, he knew little of the depth and bitterness of division in Japan. Nor could he know that the issue of whether to accept or resist the barbarian and his technology had been divisive among the powerful men of Japan long before Commodore Perry's arrival in 1853, though it had reached a climax over Harris's Treaty. Elgin was unable, as with most westerners of the day, to make the elementary distinction between the Emperor and the Shogun, much less to grasp the complex loyalties and groupings surrounding each. He knew nothing of the surging conflict between those around the Shogun, who had mostly supported the idea of coming to terms with the West, and the Emperor who with his court had forbidden the treaties and indeed negotiations. Much less could Elgin know that the mighty earthquakes, fires and floods that Japan had recently suffered were pointed to by the exclusionists as signs of the wrath of the gods and that they believed that the Emperor and the nation were being betrayed.

The six Commissioners sent by the Shogunate to negotiate with Elgin were all men of note, chosen because they had had experience of dealing with the West, either with the British Admiral Stirling in 1854, or with Perry or Harris. Two at least were men who had risen from the lower echelons by reason of their ability. Elgin found them all businesslike and very shrewd. They were realists, well aware that Elgin, though appearing in Edo Bay with a small and unaggressive force, had at his command in China an army and a powerful fleet. The British, indeed, were more to be feared than the United States. Elgin responded to Higo no Kami and his jokes, so there was soon a genial and relaxed atmosphere.

The Commissioners, nominally the envoys of the Shogun, in reality represented the will of Ii Naosuke, the *Tairo*, or Regent Minister, for unknown to the westerners the old Shogun had died and had been replaced by Iyemochi, a minor and a figurehead. His Regent Minister, Ii Naosuke of Hikone, had temporarily silenced the opposing anti-foreign party using arbitrary and strong-arm methods. Elgin never met the Regent Minister, believing that it would detract from his status to confer with anyone less than the head of state. It might have been an interesting encounter, for both Elgin of Broomhall and Ii Naosuke of Hikone were younger sons who had inherited, having spent part of their early years in semi-retirement, seeking to build a philosophy of life and cherishing the family estate. Ii was to be assassinated within a year by those hostile to the treaties.

Elgin for his part had come with a predisposition in favour of the Japanese, then current in Britain. In 1852 the *Edinburgh Review*, one of the great opinion makers, had carried a thirty-five page article in which Japan had been much lauded. It stated in glowing terms how the chivalrous Japanese, 'midst the Asiatics ... stood supreme.' The British idealised image of the Japanese was as another island race, with a distinct and impressive culture. Elgin shared this inclination.

In the intervals of negotiation Elgin made his customary tours and excursions, trying to grasp at first hand the society around him. He was delighted with Japan, comparing its atmosphere to the lassitude and decay he had observed in China. He found the country and its people 'wonderfully clean after China'. He called the sacred mountain of Fujiyama, 'the matchless mountain' arising as it did from the plain. Elgin was greatly impressed with the Palace at Edo, the residence of the Shogun with its moats and walls. He found the samurai especially intriguing, acting as 'innumerable officials with their double swords.' It seems to be a matter of course, wrote Elgin 'that every man should fill the place and perform the function which custom and law prescribe, and that he should be denounced if he fails to do so.' Japanese temples did not contain 'the hideous figures' characteristic of the Chinese; Japanese homes with the family living in so ordered a fashion on the floor on their tatami mats also greatly attracted him, as did the bath houses where men and women bathed together.

Indeed Elgin's captivation by Japanese life inspired him to write of 'The absence of anything like want among the people; their joyous, though polite and respectful demeanour.' Moreover 'The social and moral condition of Japan has astonished me quite as much as its material beauty. Every man, from the Emperor ... to the humblest labourer, lives under a rigid rule, prescribed by law and custom combined, ... but insofar as one can judge, this system is not felt to be burdensome to any.'

Here was the living antithesis of the society he had dealt with in Canada. It is hardly surprising that this enlightened British aristocrat, who had striven so hard among British and French Canadians to reconcile the chaotic initiatives of a free people, endowed as they were with vast tracts of land and imbued with the market spirit, found Japan appealing. It was a relief to contemplate this idealised feudalism on the other side of the world: 'An inexhaustible fund of good temper,' he recorded, 'seems to prevail in the community.' Japan, indeed, seemed in 1858, after two centuries of withdrawal from the world, to have produced 'A perfectly paternal government; a perfectly filial people; a community entirely self-supporting; peace within and without; no want; no ill-will between classes.' Britain, Elgin reflected sadly, in spite of her immense economic and military power, had none of these characteristics. She was in the throes of revolutionary economic and social change, together with the incipient challenge of democracy.

Mixed up in all these observations there was a fair amount of preconception, stemming from ideology. Elgin, since his Oxford days, had been attracted by the ideal of an Aristotelian state in which men were connected by association, community, reciprocal duty and hierarchy, each regarded as the fundamental condition of happiness and order. He shared with his friend Gladstone the dilemma of sympathising with the liberal movements of the day, but having an innate conservatism that made him feel the need for order and authority. Unlike Gladstone, however, Elgin was an aristocrat with an aristocrat's instincts, and one who had been thrust, with enormous authority, into disordered situations in other lands. Perhaps it was the sheer relief at the apparent orderliness of Japan that charmed him. He was not to know that beyond his vision Japan was wracked with problems, with the Shogunate tottering to its fall. In the longer run, however, Elgin's apparently naive view of the Japanese was perhaps not wide of the mark: the elements of structure, order, hierarchy, discipline and loyalty which he saw and admired were to serve Japan well in her transition to the industrial age.

But his favourable reactions to Japan merely fed his profound misgivings about his own mission which were even deeper than in the Chinese case. Japan seemed to Elgin to exemplify many of the civic and social virtues. What right he asked had Britain to intervene in Japan where the rulers of that country were debating whether to abandon their isolationist policies. 'Twenty years hence', Elgin asked himself as he pondered what seemed to him the balanced and peaceful society of Japan, 'what will be the contrast?' The opening of China had been a matter of intruding into a society far gone in decay and civil war; Japan, in Elgin's elegaic mood, seemed to be a society greatly to be admired and envied.

And yet he was borne along inexorably by his commitment to his mission, caught up in the swirling forces released by the demon of western industrialisation which had flowed from Britain. Moreover, like Oliphant, Elgin was much impressed by the capacity of the Japanese to benefit from the knowledge and skills of the West: he agreed with Oliphant's views that the Japanese

> are competent to manage their own steam engines, and to navigate their own ships... They are extremely sensitive at being supposed incapable of acquiring any branch of knowledge which is possessed by others and have a high estimate of their powers in this respect.

The Japanese for their part had their difficulties in understanding Elgin. This barbarian *daimyo* from so far away who had subdued China with his fleet and army, was so different from the Yankee Harris. They were greatly puzzled at first whether he was one person or two, his titles designating him as both Earl of Elgin and Kincardine. In dealing with Townsend Harris they had been obliged to supply him and Heusken with Japanese women, doing so in the hope that Harris's troubled spirit would be soothed and so ease the negotiations. Elgin, with his strict morality, self control and genial though highly dignified relations with the Japanese, gave rise to no such problem. Indeed Heusken had been sharply rebuffed when he had attempted to bring his own geisha with him on the *Furious*.

The negotiation of the Japanese Treaty encountered no serious difficulty; it was signed on 26 August 1858, two months after the Treaty of Tientsin. Though Elgin's instructions were to base his Japanese Treaty on that with China, he had not done so, adopting instead Harris's milder form, already accommodated to Japanese views. Elgin's respect for the Japanese was confirmed by the realism they showed in accepting the Treaty: unlike the Chinese they did not involve their country in a pointless and hopeless war. Elgin could not know that Ii Naosuke was coping with domestic crisis throughout the discussions. Elgin's Treaty included the opening of five Treaty ports, recognition of the immunities of foreigners through extraterritoriality, three naval bases, the opening to British nationals of Japanese markets without the intervention of the Japanese authorities, and a foreign coinage clause that was to prove highly adverse to the Japanese. The Treaty, along with those with the United States, the Netherlands, Russia and France, was to take effect on 1 July 1859. Elgin was also responsible for introducing a Most Favoured Nation Clause into the Treaty, a provision omitted by Harris. It meant that a benefit gained by any one of the European Powers would be shared by all, thus creating a uniformity of treatment. This Clause was greatly to increase the subsequent difficulties of the Japanese when they sought a revision of the terms of the Unequal Treaties, for it meant that any concession to Japan had to be agreed by all the Western powers.

The ceremony of signing was immediately followed by the presentation of the steam yacht. As the Shogun never left his palace at Edo, and the Emperor was confined to his at Kyoto, Oliphant found the presentation of the yacht a comical affair, remarking 'One might as well request the Pope's acceptance of a wife.' Nevertheless the Japanese reciprocated with a torrent of gifts of lacquer, silk, china, ivory and gold, together with a special present from the Shogun to Elgin, a pair of splendid bronze cranes. To restore the balance the stores of the *Furious* were raided for flannel, soap and chocolate, with rifles as the most appreciated gifts. Affection was expressed from both sides. Complementary salutes of gunfire were exchanged and the fortifications of Yedo illuminated in honour of Elgin and his party.

Onerous though the Treaty was for the Japanese, it provided a resolution of the dilemma that confronted the modernising element among them. If they wished to open their country, drawing upon the knowledge and resources of the West, a workable basis for a trading nexus had to be made available in the legal terms that only a Treaty could provide. Moreover by confining the Westerners to the prescribed sites of the Treaty ports the Japanese were given a means of delimiting their activities and keeping them under surveillance. Elgin remained ignorant of the fact that for some years after the Treaty was signed there were strong moves to re-assert the power of the Emperor who, innured in Kyoto, still absolutely forbade all concession to the barbarians and demanded that his government prepare a force to expel them.

The day following the signing Elgin was at sea again, feeling that at last he had begun his journey home, with both his treaties made, and at a minimal cost in violence and bloodshed. But he still had deep misgivings writing of 'this abominable East,— abominable not so much in itself, as because it is strewed all over the records of our violence and fraud, and disregard of right.'

On the signing of the Chinese and Japanese Treaties the *Daily Telegraph* wrote: 'The Earldom of Elgin is just now a new and mighty wonder to the Eastern world. It passes like the Comet over islands, continents and seas and emperors and nations bow down ...' Back at Shanghai Elgin found, however, that he had not yet escaped from the

Chinese quagmire. Canton was disturbed again, and the Imperial Commissioners with whom he was to make final arrangements had not appeared. When they did eventually arrive Elgin resumed his high and peremptory tone. He demanded the abolition of the Committee of Braves, formed in and around Canton to enrol volunteers to resist the British. Hivang, the new Governor-General of Canton province, had sanctioned hostilities contrary to the Treaty; Elgin demanded his removal. He also conveyed to the Commissioners through a secret channel that he was prepared to appear again at Tientsin with his force, an eventuality that would have cost the Commissioners their heads and so they agreed to do what was demanded, as well as proclaiming the Treaty.

Elgin had other troubles. There was a violent reaction and general ill will in Hong Kong that China had been 'opened', creating a more competitive situation; at Shanghai too the British settlement 'who think it very hard if they are not rich enough to retire in five years', was deeply resentful. Both the Hong Kong and Shanghai contingents took the opportunity to denigrate Elgin in Britain, which made it all the more important to consolidate the Treaty position.

The unfinished business of the Chinese Treaty was mainly concerned with the tariff and with opium. By stipulating a tariff on the drug, trade in it was legalised for the first time. Elgin had concluded that, whatever the rights and wrongs of its introduction into China, it was now in compulsive demand and could not be stopped: any attempt to do so would simply result in wholesale smuggling. This, indeed, was also the view of the Chinese authorities. There remained only regulation and restriction, together with as high a duty as could be levied without stimulating the smugglers. This was Elgin's chosen course. Moreover, whereas British subjects were to have access to the Chinese interior for general trading purposes, opium could be carried by them only to the port of entry, with the interior trade confined to the Chinese, and therefore under the jurisdiction of the Chinese authorities.

Elgin seems to have warmed to the Commissioners Kweleang and Kwashena in their thankless task, as he had done to certain of the Japanese Commissioners, referring to them as 'my poor friends.' He had them photographed: they were greatly intrigued by their images. He told them of the marvel of the electric telegraph which their Emperor could install and use to unite his vast dominions.

As a final sealing of the bargain Elgin sought and obtained permission to make an expedition up the great river, the Yangtze Kiang, treating the journey as a demonstration of cordiality between the two countries. In spite of his yearning for home he took pleasure, now that he had obtained his Treaty, in travelling on waters which as far as was known, no Englishman had ever seen; indeed no European had navigated the river beyond Nanking. Also he wished to make observations of the interior of China for the Foreign Office and for the use of British traders. He left in November with four ships, the *Furious*, the *Retribution* and two light gunboats.

On this journey Elgin encountered the Taiping rebels. They were in possession of Nanking, the centre of the rebellion, where they had destroyed the marvellous Porcelain Pagoda. From its forts they fired upon Elgin and his little fleet, killing one member of his force and badly wounding two others. Elgin was standing on the paddle-box bridge when a shot passed close over his head: Captain Osborn advised him to go below. The *Furious* was struck seven times, one of the shots entering Elgin's cabin.

The British of course returned the fire. But Elgin soon desisted, not wanting to get involved to the point of taking the town and handing it over to the Imperialists who had it under siege on every side. The rebels then proposed to Elgin that he and his ships should join them against the Imperial forces: to Elgin's amusement his 'humble younger brother' (the rebel chief) prayed to him to join in annihilating the 'demons' (the Imperial forces). The town of Woo-hoo was also in rebel hands but under Imperial siege. Further on, the British flotilla witnessed several engagements between Imperial and rebel forces, but these seemed to be more like skirmishing, flag waving and gambolling than killing, causing Elgin to remark that 'The war, in short, seems to be carried on in a very soft manner, but it must do a great deal of mischief to the country.'

Elgin was much intrigued by their Chinese pilot, a Cantonese, he was the most vivacious Chinaman he had encountered, 'inquiring about everything, proposing to go to England, like a Japanese'. The pilot regaled Elgin with the legends of the river. Some days later however he had lost his esprit, having found no passage in the channel he had specially recommended. When asked what had gone wrong fatalistically he said, 'The ways of the waters are like those of men, one day here, one day there, who can tell?' It was this same pilot who explained to Elgin the psychology of the Rebels. 'At present', he said, 'the rich have a great advantage over the poor. They can afford to spend a good deal more on joss-sticks and other offerings', so that, of course, the gods favour them. The rebels, in order to destroy this unfair system, simply destroyed the temples. This destruction was, however, also part of a psuedo-Christian syncretism.

At Kewkiang Elgin walked about inside the five-mile circumference wall, finding only a single street in use, the rest a wilderness of ruin and weeds. The rebels had done this, a reminder that however inept their battles might be, they left behind them great devastation. Navigation became progressively more difficult as they proceeded, leadsmen sounding at the bow and stern, as well as at the two paddles. They became accustomed to the whole population of a town crowding the river bank to see the marvel of the barbarian fire ships. But part of Elgin's heart was at home: he found the hills rising from the water have 'a kind of Loch Katrine look'; a solitary rock standing out of the river like a sentinel he compared to the Bass Rock in the Firth of Forth not so far from Broomhall.

On 6 December they reached Hankow, having moved 600 miles in four weeks from the sea. Here was the heart of Chinese commerce with the town, despite its earlier destruction by the rebels showing strong signs of recovery. Elgin maintained the same remote and fierce attitude with the authorities that he had discovered worked so well, thus obtaining, and paying for, coal and other necessities. The Governor General of the province visited the four ships with all due pomp. Elgin's flotilla, dressed over all with the yards manned, welcomed his huge junk, built like a Roman trireme, pulled by six boats, surrounded by men in archaic uniforms, bearing ineffectual arms.

On 12 December they began their return journey to the sea. Its water level was now a good deal lower, adding greatly to the navigational hazards, there being real danger that they would become stuck on the sandbars. In the end they were forced to leave the warships behind for three months or so until the river rose again, and proceed in the gunboats. The expedition was not, however, downhearted. Lieutenant D, a distant relative of Mary Louisa's, composed and sang a song with the chorus:

13   Lord Elgin and the Japanese Commissioners, signing the Treaty of Edo (now Tokyo),
Japan, August 1858. Watercolour from a delightful Far East Album by Captain Bedwell.

14   Riding on Pekin. Lord Elgin and his entourage approach Pekin. Watercolour by
Colonel H.H. Crealock.

15　The official processional entry into Pekin. 'Lord Elgin in state', *Illustrated London News*, 1860.

16　Burying the bodies of the murdered emissaries. In this watercolour Colonel Crealock has caught much of the shock which the torture and death of their comrades, captured under a flag of truce, engendered in the British party.

> Come fill up the cup, come fill up the can,
> We've polished off Yeh and we've polished off Tan;
> Kweikang and Kwashena have set their ports free,
> And allowed us a trip up the glorious Yantze.

The penultimate verse ran

> There are hills beyond Pentland and lands beyond Forth,
> Oft we'll think of our Chief in his home in the North;
> Sunny memories with him connected will be,
> Of Canton, the Peiho, and the Gulf Pecheli.

Elgin reached Shanghai on New Year's Day, 1859. He composed a detailed despatch setting out what he had learned in China.

Two new challenges arose almost at once. There was the need to instruct the British merchants of Shanghai on their role in China and Japan, and there was, yet again, fighting between the Chinese and British at Canton. Elgin told the merchants 'We have ... incurred very weighty responsibilities. Uninvited, and by means not always the gentlest, we have broken down the barriers behind which these ancient nations sought to conceal from the world without the mysteries, perhaps also, in the case of China at least, the rags and rottenness of their waning civilisations.' Neither conscience nor the judgment of mankind would forgive them if it should be said that 'we have filled our pockets from among the ruins we have found or made.' As to the attacks being made on the British by the Canton Braves, Elgin conveyed to the Chinese authorities that he was once more ready to fight, and indeed to move on Pekin itself. Again Canton was pacified and the region overawed. On 3 March Elgin was at last on his way home, euphoric at leaving China behind.

At Aden Elgin encountered the two great African explorers Richard Burton and John Haining Speke, the latter a friend of Oliphant. He offered them both passage home on the *Furious*. Speke accepted, but Burton, still suffering from fever, declined. There was a rivalry between the two men as to their claims of discovery in central Africa, including that of the source of the Nile. Speke's early return to England allowed his friend Oliphant to present him in a highly favourable light to the Royal Geographical Society, the great sponsor of expeditions, and to its Council to which he was now elected. Elgin inadvertently helped to create the celebrated Speke-Burton controversy.

On 19 May 1859 two years and a month after leaving England, Elgin reported to the Foreign Office.

CHAPTER 15

The Chastising of China: the Burning of the Summer Palace

Back home, apart from his delight in returning home to Mary Louisa and the children, Elgin found himself a celebrity, widely acclaimed by both high and low. In the House of Lords Derby and Grey, leaders from opposite sides of the House, sang his praises. When Palmerston, in June 1859 formed a new administration he invited Elgin, along with other former Peelites, into the cabinet as Postmaster General. He was feted at the Mansion House and made a freeman of the City of London. At the University of Glasgow the students expressed their approval by electing him their Lord Rector although they hoped he would pay the expenses they had incurred in running his campaign. In the popular mind he had saved India and humbled China and Japan, carrying British power to the farthest corners of the world to confront ancient civilisations. Whereas his long and significant service in Canada had passed almost unnoticed except among a knowledgeable few, his mission to the East had made him famous. In China, however, some British merchants were not so euphoric. Canton was still a restless place. Some were seriously concerned that Elgin had not insisted on reaching Pekin, and threatening the Chinese more effectively.

In Canada he had always felt that his efforts and indeed his dangers had passed largely unnoticed in Britain. Now at last he had found recognition. For many he was a hero enabling Britain to fulfill her destiny. By making his country the leading power in the Far East, he had outshone France her traditional rival, (though acting in amity with her). Though the Americans had obtained the first treaty with Japan, their presence in the east could not rival that of Britain's, and, in any case, had not Elgin's bombardment of Canton made possible America's success in Japan? But in all this Elgin never forgot the darker side of Britain's role, both in terms of the military force used and the aggression of the mercantile community. On the question of both China and Japan he was still confused and equivocal; by contrast he looked back on his Canadian career as having been wholly constructive. Moreover he was well aware that his supposed triumphs in China and Japan would be a kind of seven days wonder, to be eclipsed in the public mind when the next great continental or imperial crisis arose.

In spite of his place in the Cabinet as Postmaster General, he again found that he could not enter into home politics with any enthusiasm. Gladstone in assessing the attitudes of his Cabinet colleagues on the issues of the day found Elgin silent and remote.

Meanwhile there was the continuing chronic problem of Broomhall. Once more

Elgin applied himself to the affairs of the family estate. This he had always seen as a trust, both for the family and those who were dependent upon it for incomes or jobs. There were the usual visits to the coal mines, limeworks, and farm tenants. This part of his life Elgin enjoyed, for among his own people he was their chief and mentor as a good Scottish landowner should be. Even when in China, Broomhall had never been far from his mind. When one of his ships had run aground in the Yangtze near Hankow he had gone ashore, only to find the Chinese quarrying and making lime. The Chinese limemasters were doing a good business: 'I wish', Elgin had written, 'I could do as well at Broomhall!'

Always fluent with his pen, Oliphant now wrote at great speed an account of Elgin's mission. He stayed at Broomhall discussing this with Elgin. The most controversial theme Oliphant had to cover was the conduct of Admiral Sir Michael Seymour who had kept Elgin waiting on the Peiho for the gunboats. Captain Osborne was fearful that Elgin would tone the incident down, saying 'Over finesse is the Earl's failing: he always flinches at a climax.' But he need not have worried: Elgin had felt deeply humiliated and let Oliphant have his head. By the time Oliphant's book was published Seymour back in England had become an MP; he and Elgin exchanged fire, the one from the Commons, the other from the Lords.

Elgin himself was not yet free from involvement with China. Whereas his Japanese treaty stuck, that with China did not. Applying the pragmatism that Elgin so admired, the dominant faction of the Japanese recognised for the time being at least, the reality of Western power. It is true that Japan was divided bitterly for some years yet over the admission of the foreigners, and that those in favour of the Treaty soon turned their minds with skill and subtlety to limiting its effects. But the Japanese government made no overt challenge. Perhaps part of Elgin's admiration for the Japanese lay in the fact that they accepted for all practical purposes the dominant position western weaponry and organisation imposed. Not so the Chinese. Incoherent and incompetent though the Imperial regime might be, the Chinese did not accept the terms imposed by the barbarians in the Treaty of Tientsin. A stiffening of will had resulted from the labyrinthine politics of the Chinese court, with the anti-foreign element once more dominant.

By this time Elgin's brother, Frederick who had been so useful on the China mission, had been placed as Minister to China in charge of arrangements for the ratification of the Treaty in June 1859. Accordingly he set sail with a small force towards Pekin in order to put this final seal on the arrangements but arriving at the mouth of the Peiho river, he discovered that the Taku Forts, taken by Elgin's force in April 1858, had now been restored and rearmed to pose a much more formidable obstacle. When the British men-of-war tried to break the boom and to remove the rafts with which the Chinese had blocked the river, they were fired upon from the Forts. The British flagship, *Plover*, was almost sunk, being caught like the other British ships under the guns of the forts. In desperation the Admiral, Sir James Hope, ordered a land assault on the forts. This ended in disaster. British marines and soldiers were unable to cross a vast quagmire of mud bristling with sharpened stakes. In this humiliating defeat, there were 89 dead and 345 wounded. The Chinese, of course, claimed a great victory over British arms. Frederick had no choice but to return to Shanghai, report home and await instructions. He carefully abstained from criticism of Sir James Hope's precipitous and unwise attack. The British remonstrated to the Chinese and then receiving no reply issued an ultimatum. Again there was no reply and Palmerston resolved to send a second force much larger than the first against the Chinese.

On the first of April 1860 the Dowager Countess Elizabeth, Elgin's mother, died. She had presided to the last over her salon in the Rue de Varennes in Paris. The quiet, plain, romantic minded girl whom Thomas had so purposefully swept off her feet in 1810, had established her own independent mode of life during her long widowhood. Among those who had visited her salon were Lamartine, Victor Hugo, Rémusat, Jenny Lind, Mérimée, de Tocqueville, Guizot, Thiers, Renan and Doré. She also welcomed young Mr. Worth who dressed the Empress Eugenie. Her eccentricities had made her increasingly formidable over the years, her mode of dismissing a bore was to confront the unfortunate with a series of prodigious yawns. Augusta was with her at the end, pondering on her extraordinary life: 'Oh', she wrote, 'When I ... trace the footsteps by which she has been led, I feel how precious her soul must have been in His sight...'

It was inevitable that Elgin should be asked to lead the expedition that was to chasten the Chinese. On 17 April 1860 he was officially asked to undertake this heavy responsibility, for there could be little doubt that if the Chinese continued in their recalcitrant ways it would be necessary to proceed with a powerful force to Pekin, threatening the Chinese Emperor himself.

Elgin was now forty-nine. He had only begun to re-settle into family life: in the eleven months since his return he had come to know his growing children better than ever before, a source of profound satisfaction. There was too, his deep love for Mary Louisa, together with his awareness of the responsibilities and burdens she had borne in the two years of his absence. His view of a husband he told her was that of 'One who ought to be your constant protector, and always at your side.' He was depressed at the prospect of another year or so of communicating only by letter, with his and hers out of phase, with long gaps when the post did not come through. So too, once more, did the morality of Britain's role in the east disturb him especially now that he was being asked, once and for all, to break the Chinese resistance. There were too, the discomforts and dangers that Elgin now knew awaited any leader of a second mission. As for Mary Louisa she was strongly opposed to her husband disappearing once more into the China Seas. She sat gloomily in her room, grieving over the prospect. Oliphant, for all his affection for Elgin, said he could not face China a second time.

As before, Elgin could not refuse to go. Frederick argued that in career terms he really had no choice, for Elgin was not really happy and could see no way of furthering his career in the Cabinet. But Frederick was not wholly consistent. 'China is a terrible place' he had written after the debacle of the Taku Forts, telling Malmesbury the Foreign Secretary 'that it is fatal to any reputation'. Meanwhile Frederick was waiting at Shanghai with the city under threat by Loyal Prince Lee, the Taiping general, at Nanking further up the Yangtze. Elgin tried hard to modify Palmerston's plans, urging that the best course would be a limited and inexpensive operation, retaking the Taku Forts and blockading the Peiho River and with it Pekin. But Palmerston was adamant: the Chinese must be punished, and the disaster at the mouth of the Peiho must be revenged. Elgin then argued for a modest force of some 5,000 men to move quickly

18 Lord Elgin, the senior British diplomat, warmly wrapped against the bleak cold winds which swept across the north China plain, did not relish his bullying role and longed for home.

17 Prince Kung, the Chinese leader, with whom Lord Elgin felt some affinity as Kung struggled to bring some realism into Chinese official thinking.

20 Constance Carnegie, Countess of Elgin, who bore her husband eleven live children.

19 Victor Alexander, 9th Earl of Elgin and 13th of Kincardine, born in Montreal in 16 May 1849 and given, as a compliment to his father's stand as Governor General in Canada, the male versions of her own names by Queen Victoria herself.

property, I daresay £50,000 will be realised. French soldiers were destroying in every way the most beautiful silks, breaking the jade ornaments and porcelain etc. War is a hateful business. The more one sees of it, the more one detests it.

A certain amount of money was found in the Treasury. All who had taken articles from the Palace were ordered to pass them to the prize agents: these were subsequently sold at auction, the proceeds being distributed to the army through the general fund. In this way looting on the grand scale, impossible to resist, was at least rationalised. Charles Gordon (later, after leading the Ever Victorious Army against the Taipings to be nicknamed 'Chinese Gordon') arrived just in time for the looting. 'We got upward of $48 apiece prize money', he recorded, 'One man bid 16 shillings for a string of pearls which he sold next day for $500. It was wretchedly demoralising work for an army. Everyone was wild for plunder.' Some of the loot reached Queen Victoria: among her share was a Pekinese dog, the first to appear in the West: Her Majesty called her new pet 'Looty'.

The worthless Emperor, a puppet of his Court, yet the embodiment of supreme authority, had by this time been carried, with his immediate entourage, to his hunting lodge in Jehol to the north, As the Allies were now surrounding the capital with their artillery batteries in position, the Chinese leaders, capitulated to avoid the storming of the city. On 13 October the great Am-ting Gate, the key to Pekin, was surrendered. In this way Elgin gained some kind of control, though as part of the bargain he had agreed not to invest the city. It was a typical Elgin arrangement.

Five days earlier the first of the surviving captives from the party held hostage had been released. Only Parkes, Loch and five soldiers survived. Their experience as Elgin learned, had been horrifying. Only Parkes and Loch seemed important enough to count as hostages with the Chinese Court: the rest of the party had been left to their terrible fate at the hands of lesser officials. At first Parkes and Loch had been no less harshly treated. On capture they were surrounded by Chinese soldiery who pressed their matchlocks eagerly into their bodies and awaited impatiently the order to fire. Then cast in the mud in front of Sang-Ko-lin-sin, they were all cuffed and beaten, their faces rubbed in the dirt. Later tightly bound, they were thrown into springless carts and bumped for some miles of excruciating pain, the whipcord on their wrists being wetted to tighten it further, and carried to the Board of Punishments in Pekin, the most notorious prison in China. Handcuffed, with iron collars and ankle chains, they were cast among the half-naked crowd of the lowest class of criminals. Semi-starved, they were left in this condition for days their only solace being the kindness shown to them by some of the miserable prisoners. Their greatest terror was of the maggots that infested the soil under the floor, ready at once to enter any broken skin and to colonise the body.

During their incarceration the power struggle continued in the inner circle of the Court between Prince Kung who wanted to negotiate with the barbarians, and Sang-Ko-lin-sin who demanded all-out resistance, and the execution of the prisoners. On September 29 Parkes and Loch were taken from prison and placed in comfortable quarters, in the care of Hang-Ki, a high mandarin of Prince Kung's party. It was thought that the two Englishmen could be used as a means of bargaining with Elgin

Europe and America, China seemed imprisoned by her circumstance. But although its culture had over the centuries produced 'a mass of abortions and rubbish', there was amid all this 'some sparks of a diviner fire, which the genius of my countrymen may gather and nurse into a flame.'

Elgin seemed to be implying that Britain (and perhaps the progressive parts of Europe and America) could help China escape from her containment, preparing the way for fundamental changes upon which a new, vigorous and sustained national life could be built. But he remained vague on the subject of what this would require. There would first have to be a shift away from the cultural and political values of Confucianism which respected not the activists in society, but the learned and the studious. In the eyes of Confucianism the technology of Europe, so far as it was known, was merely a set of minor contrivances, beneath the dignity of scholars, an attitude which made it impossible to develop experimental science, much less to integrate it as central to national life. Moreover the state bureaucracy would have to surrender its strangling grip on the economy. Finally and perhaps most difficult of all, the entire system of power, so corruptly centred on the Emperor, would have to be replaced. All these things he felt could only come about through a new release of energy provided by an entrepreneurial class, together with an injection of new technology, of which the railway would be a leading part. The presence of the European merchants in China could help to generate the necessary atmosphere.

At this point in his argument Elgin was in great difficulty. He had seen so much of the seamy side of European merchant behaviour, shored up as it was by the naval and the military. So it was that, at the Mansion House dinner, he appealed to the merchants and bankers of the City of London, in the presence of their Lord Mayor, to accept responsibility for Western business behaviour in the East. There had been honourable merchants and devout missionaries in plenty, but there also 'slip out from among us dishonest traders and ruffians who disgrace our name and set the feelings of the people against us.' In opposition to such the City must exert to the full its moral influence. 'Force and diplomacy ... (had) ... effected in China all that they could legitimately accomplish,' but the main work that had to be done in the Chinese Empire was still only beginning. The great task of bringing China, 'with its extensive territory, its fertile soil and its industrious population, as an active and useful member into the community of nations,' lay ahead. It was of course a forlorn hope, as Elgin suspected in his heart that the men of the City could not or would not persuade their colleagues in the East to adopt a self-denying moralism that could make China 'a fellow labourer with ourselves in diffusing over the world happiness and well-being.' The conditions of British trading there were such that there was no effective way of curbing commercial ruffianism, which of course Elgin knew in his troubled mind.

While in China Elgin had always made a point of learning so far as he could the condition of the Chinese peasant, the underdog. He saw how heavily the regime bore upon the peasant and his family, and wished that their condition could be relieved. As in Jamaica there seemed to be only one possible solution—modernisation. But even with this type of progress would not the peasantry once more be the ultimate victims? He knew also that the British government, having resolved the 'Chinese question', would not be interested in undertaking a really positive surveillance of the impact of the West, but would let China sink far into the background of the political, bureaucratic and public mind.

He returned home in sombre mood but rejoiced as he was re-united with his family. Within a month of his return, in April 1861, he was called to another even more demanding post, that of viceroy of post-Mutiny India. 'Poor Mary!' wrote Augusta, 'After her short time of perfect happiness it was an awful blow.'

CHAPTER 16

The Doomed Viceroy

Elgin had known that Palmerston's government would consider him as a strong candidate to succeed Canning as viceroy. Indeed the question had arisen before, when Canning followed Dalhousie in 1856—Elgin could well have found himself presiding over the crushing of the Mutiny. Now the call to such tremendous responsibilities was irresistible. This, the most magnificent Governorship in the Empire and indeed the world, would crown his career, and above all it would allow him to employ his positive energies as he had done so successfully in Canada.

But there was also a sombre side. Elgin felt forebodings. Would he ever return from India? In an address at Dunfermline he thanked his Fife neighbours for the warmth of the welcome they had always given him on his return from foreign duty: but this time 'the prospect of our again meeting is more remote and uncertain.' He had a melancholy instinct that the call upon his energies in the climate of India might just be too much. He knew that India was a young man's game, and that at fifty he was on the old side. Lord Ellenborough, a former Governor General of India said to him, 'You are not a very old man, but, depend upon it, you will find yourself by far the oldest man in India.' He also felt guilt at having been absent while his children were growing up and of having imposed upon Mary Louisa heavy responsibilities that should have been his. However he consoled himself with nine happy months in Britain, enjoying life in Scotland at Broomhall where his tenants dined him as their chief.

While Elgin had been away, in November 1858, his brother Robert like their sister Augusta, had joined the royal circle. The behaviour of the Prince of Wales, not yet seventeen, had become a cause of concern to Victoria and Prince Albert. His tutor retired and Major General Robert Bruce took his place, gazetted as the Prince's 'governor'. Robert was a conscientious, kindly, dapper man of forty-five. He reported frequently to the royal parents, receiving their copious instructions in return.

The affairs of Broomhall had once again reached crisis point. Once more there was, in 1861, the prospect of selling off at least part of the estate, including the railway. The debt stood at some £170,000. But once again Elgin had to leave the matter to others while he sailed away to distant duties. The day before he left he paid £23,000 to the Royal Bank toward the reduction of the estate debt, and £5,000 paying off personal debts on the estate. The family's sense of stringency was as great as ever.

Some months before leaving, early in January 1862, Elgin and Mary Louisa visited the Queen at Osborne. The royal household was in deep mourning. The Queen's mother, the Duchess of Kent, had died in March 1861 and in December the death of

Albert, the Prince Consort, had brought the grief of widowhood to the Queen. Augusta had been the main support to the Queen on both occasions, often the only person apart from her children who Victoria would see.

The Queen's distress, in spite of the efforts of Robert, had been compounded by the Prince of Wales. He had spent periods at both Oxford and Cambridge, Robert had been sorely tried, but had failed utterly to keep the prince in check. Before his father's death 'Bertie', the Prince of Wales had set his heart on serving with the Guards. General Bruce knew that in the Guards, wealthy officers kept as many women as they did horses. The Prince however persisted in his pleas so that the Prince Consort, in consultation with the governor, finally agreed that his son should go into training at the great military base at the Curragh in Ireland, on condition that the discipline was tight and continuous, and that the Prince remained under close surveillance. By this time Bertie was a deeply frustrated young man: all his life he was to be fascinated by women. His fellow officers obliged by supplying him with Nellie Clifden who aspired to be an actress, smuggling her past the governor. But having made so great a conquest, Nellie, not unnaturally, talked. The story reached a court gossip who told the Prince Consort who was horrified and heartbroken. He urged Bertie to confess all. This was done, and Bertie and his father reconciled. But the Prince Consort, while in his dying delirium, had babbled to the Queen. She was never able to forgive Bertie, holding him, in part at least, responsible for his father's death. 'Poor Robert,' wrote Augusta, 'He has had a tremendous burden laid upon him.' Baron Stockmar may have created in the Prince Consort an exemplary serious young man but Robert was no Stockmar, and indeed Bertie no Prince Albert. Robert Bruce could, however, on occasion assert his authority as when the Prince was in audience with the Pope, who sought to draw him out on the question of the restored Roman hierarchy in England. The audience was quickly terminated.

Despite her grief, Victoria made an effort to receive the first viceroy ever to be appointed by the sole act of the Crown. She felt much sympathy for the Elgins, having to be separated once more. Elgin sailed on 28 January 1862 and reached Calcutta on 11 March. Mary Louisa was once again pregnant; she remained behind to await her delivery and would follow Elgin later.

While passing down the Red Sea on what he suspected might be his last mission Elgin read over the manuscript books that contained his thoughts written as a young man during the interval between Oxford and Parliament. He was intrigued to look back on those years in which he was searching so earnestly for truth and right, while managing the baffling affairs of Broomhall. But he decided that the manuscripts would never again be read by himself or anyone else: and consigned them one by one to the Red Sea. It may be that he was embarrassed by the simple idealism they displayed, showing no awareness of the complications generated in the real world of Jamaica, Canada, China, Japan and now, most challenging of all, India.

On 12 March he was installed in Calcutta as Governor-General and viceroy, with Canning his predecessor in attendance. Elgin's appearance was commented upon: there being some surprise that the bearer of such an ancient name and the holder of so splendid an office should be on the short side, bald, with whitish whiskers framing a somewhat florid face, so different from the pale and pre-occupied Canning.

In the first, cool months he functioned well. But then came the heat and dust of June, July and August and a sequence of bad news. The news came that Mary Louisa had miscarried. In June news of his brother Robert's death arrived, stirring Elgin deeply and bringing memories of their boyhood together, and of Robert's support in Jamaica and Canada. Robert had escorted the wilful Prince of Wales in 1862 to the Holy Land and Egypt where Robert caught a disease that killed him. His widow Katherine, and perhaps his family, felt that the Prince had overstrained poor Robert, helping to cause his death. The compact between the brothers that had sustained them through their growing up and their careers, through prosperity and adversity, was ended by Robert's death. Elgin, indeed, had hoped that Robert would care for his family should he die in India. An impressive monument was erected in Dunfermline Abbey, depicting the General, as a reclining figure, and a pilgrim to the Holy Land. The Queen showed great interest in its design.

On 6 July there was a telegraphic message from England that Canning was dead, 'So Canning and his wife, as Dalhousie and his, have fallen victims to India!' mused Elgin. He then sought escape from Calcutta, going to the great military station at Barrackpore. But his official residence there was haunted by the memory of Lady Canning, for whom it had been a favourite retreat. The broad terrace walk in the garden terminated with her grave, which dominated the finest view point. Though it was not yet properly finished Canning himself, who had mourned so deeply over it, was now himself dead in England. Mindful of how quickly even famous names faded into the Indian past, Elgin wondered of Lady Canning's grave 'Who will attend it now?' The sadness of India and the transience of life it epitomised bore down upon him. He could not but question whether he was right in exposing Mary Louisa to the Calcutta climate. In a desperate attempt to find a breeze that would make the heat slightly more bearable, he climbed onto the roof of his house, to find himself in the company of vultures, hideous and filthy.

In his loneliness and depression Elgin reflected that Canning had been buried in Westminster Abbey, whereas Dalhousie who preceded him, had not: Canning's place in the nation's pantheon owed much to the fact that he had died immediately after his return 'On what accidents such things hinge!' he wrote. As to his own prospect of making a success of India, Elgin was pessimistic but reconciled. 'I do not in the least believe', he wrote, 'that any man can win a name here unless there be some great events, such as the Mutiny, Dalhousie's annexations, etc. to set his qualities on a pedestal.' But Elgin believed it was wrong to hope for conflict and aggression in order to climax his own career. 'We must content ourselves with maintaining peaceful measures of improvement and progress ...' He could not however suppress his impatience with the London politicians and bureaucrats to whom he had always been ultimately answerable, any ameliorative proposals he made having to be laid before 'the Secretary of State and his fifteen colleagues to pick at.'

Elgin enjoyed the ceremonial side of his duties. In spite of his unregal appearance, he knew, aristocrat that he was, and as his bearing in Canada, China and Japan had shown, how to be the centre of the many great occasions in India. Elgin appreciated the vast receptions at Government House, with eight or nine hundred people, where the costumes of the Indian potentates dazzled great and small. There were the public durbars to receive maharajahs, elaborate in their ceremonial. To these splendours were added that of riding on the Maidan (Calcutta's equivalent to Hyde Park) in his barouche with four horses and postillions and an escort of the splendid mounted body-guard. He continued Canning's practice of holding an Eton dinner, with some fifteen to twenty sons of his old school present.

On the 8 January 1863 his loneliness was ended by the arrival in Calcutta of Mary Louisa and their youngest daughter, Lady Louisa Bruce, aged eight. Little Louisa soon had her favourite elephant. But in June that year they were devastated by the news of the death of their third son Charles, at the age of ten: he had been a promising pupil at Trinity Glenalmond School.

As always Elgin sought to understand his vast domain and its peoples; there was so much that had to be learned, and quickly. He found it particularly useful to hold small dinners with a few well-informed persons, where in after dinner discussions he could form a judgment for himself. He prided himself on being accessible 'to those who have anything to say, whether they be civilians, soldiers or interlopers.' But a good deal of reading was thrust upon him: the pressure of the official boxes never ceased.

The office of viceroy was the supreme example of the English tradition of the amateur in government, thrusting aristocratic men from the shires into the world's most complex melange of societies without previous knowledge and with the most cursory of briefings. There they were to reign (for such was the expression) for five years. The balance of authority between the viceroy and London was never very clear; in the event of crisis and disagreement then London, with parliament the final arbiter, prevailed. Short of this the viceroy had to come to terms, on the trot, with the Secretary of State for India and his Council, full of old India hands, soldiers and administrators, often rendered opinionated by semi-retiral and a false confidence in their own local, often semi-obsolescent knowledge of their part of India. For though some things were slow to change, such as the pattern of peasant life, India was a mass of local peculiarities which precluded easy generalisation. There was too a volatile element in Indian life, with the politics of the princes difficult to interpret and the north-west frontier tribes prone to erupt on a wide variety of pretexts. There was also the need to adjust to post-Mutiny conditions; were the men of standing in Indian society to have a place in government?

It seemed almost impossible for one man to have all the characteristics needed by a good viceroy. The post called for diligence, steadiness, limitless patience, affability as required, sound judgment on inadequate information, a capacity to sense trouble without taking fright, an ability to get on with two Councils, (the viceroy's own in Calcutta and the Cabinet's in London), and the instinct to choose good subordinates and retain their confidence. Behind all this there had to be a commitment to India and its peoples. Perhaps the most important requirement of all was the need for sustained energy. Finally, the viceroy needed a supportive wife who could combine the facility to be merely decorative and ceremonial, along with the strength to sustain her husband not only in his quiet times but also with his public problems. In spite of the weariness and impatience which sometimes overcame them, Elgin and Mary Louisa met this formidable set of specifications as well as any viceroy and vicereine. He knew from earlier experience in Jamaica and Canada that it took a long time to assess even a single, fairly simple society of no great age. India was a collectivity of societies compounded many times in complexity and antiquity. He knew he was a beginner, and indeed, however assiduous he might be, would remain one to the end of his term.

Having pondered a good deal on the Chinese character, Elgin was not tempted to make superficial judgments of Indian magnates. Far from thinking as many British in India did that all Orientals were children, 'amused and gratified by external trappings, ceremonies and titles,' and being thus easily diverted from reality, Elgin believed that quite the reverse was true. He sensed that the high drama of ceremonial indicated a well-developed sense of symbolism. This culture gap he did he best to bridge, having himself an acute sense of the meaning of ceremony.

Elgin sought to bring to bear upon India both his philosophical and practical turn of mind, both still infused as they were with the evangelical urge to do good and to act rightly in the eyes of God. India was in a sense now dormant with post-Mutiny exhaustion. Elgin had worked out and held fast to three governing ideas. There was the belief that it was the 'jealousies of race' that had almost destroyed British India, and could do so still. One way of easing relationships between ethnic groups would, he believed, be to open posts of responsibility to 'that class of natives who consider they have a natural right to be leaders of men and to occupy the first places in India': in this way Moslems and Hindus might learn to work together. This, at the time, was a highly radical notion. Secondly, he felt that the deep stresses both between and within Hindu and Moslem societies exacerbated the difficulties between white rulers and the communities. It was an appalling challenge to the Raj to adjudicate these conflicts of the two major cultures. Elgin was unwilling that Britain should deliver up whole populations to arbitrary rule, rejecting appeals from those who were being abused. But many of the Indian princes and magnates had little concept of the claims of the individual as conceived of in the liberal West. This led to the third conviction concerning the most difficult group of all, that of the Indian peasant, the underdog, who provided the fundamental basis of society. Elgin believed that something should be done for him.

In order to make some progress Elgin believed that there were two general directions in which British rule should move. The first was towards reconciliation, by extending participation in government to some at least of native talent and aspiration. Secondly, while the Raj could not seek directly to remake the fabric of society (except perhaps in those areas where the land tenure system was so grossly exploitative or inefficient as to make this inescapable) it could extend its general interest in modernisation and development. If the infrastructure including railways, canals and roads were improved then, as market incentives operated, the social and political pattern would change. An emergent middle class would provide wage-earning opportunities that would help to lever up peasant incomes, and their impact would do the job of political renovation.

But as always there were immediate challenges to deal with. The Lieutenant-Governor of the North West Provinces was jumpy about attacks from Afghanistan, the talk in the bazaars was that a new Prophet might be declared. Elgin became very annoyed at what he called 'the military panic-makers of the North-West', who feared another rising of native troops, or conspiracies to assassinate Europeans, and who discussed freely such matters at mess-tables disregarding the native servants who might well be political or military agents. The English language newspapers seized such rumours eagerly, successfully spreading them throughout India. Moreover this loss of nerve was cumulative in its effect: as Elgin put it, 'The man who runs terror-stricken into his barracks tonight because he mistook the chirp of a cricket for the click of a pistol, indemnifies himself tomorrow by beating his bearer to within an inch of his life.' Elgin told the Lieutenant Governor of the North West that he must control his anxiety and make it clear to all concerned that any disturbance in any part of India would be put down with promptitude and severity. He added that the British would not 'be much decomposed even if the 12th Iman himself were to make an appearance.'

When these matters came to his attention, Elgin considered the whole question of the army. Why should the army in India be so vast? He was very conscious of the tax burden which could, he believed, become a source of grievance. Caught up in this was his idea of obtaining a balance between numbers of British and Indian troops. He also considered the matter of balance within the Indian component of the army itself. Whenever he asked his advisors or dinner companions about this he invariably received the same answer, namely, 'You can never tell what will happen in India. Heretofore you have held the Sikhs in subjection by the aid of the Sepoys, and the Sepoys by means of the Sikhs.' But recent conversions of Sikh soldiers to Hinduism suggested that the checks and balances that held the structure together might dissolve.

But on one point Elgin was quite clear. There must be equality before the law. Ex-Private Budd, who had murdered an Indian in the Punjab, was convicted and sentenced to death. An agitation was got up among the Europeans to commute his sentence. Elgin went carefully through the transcript of the trial and ruled that Budd must die. He was intensely conscious of 'the extreme difficulty of administering equal justice between natives and Europeans.'

In inter-race relations and in the general government of India the princes and chiefs were a critical factor. Elgin held out for them the promise of an attractive future, with irrigation and canal systems, railways, the electric telegraph and the new steam-powered technology of Britain, all of which would increase the value of their estates. As a good free trader he urged them to forego the transit and other duties on goods moving through their respective states, saying that in the end all would gain from such a ruling. He called upon them to participate actively in the process of modernisation, implying that much of the essential railway capital in particular should come from India herself, drawing upon the inert wealth of the princes. More pointedly, he appealed to them to share a reasonable proportion of the benefits to their peasantry—a suggestion which he knew would fall on stony ground. Elgin felt that these rich men were a terrible incubus on their peoples, having lost or never had any sense of the crushing burden they represented. Like his appeal to the City of London to exercise a moral surveillance over British merchants in China, to ask the Indian Princes to share simply ran contrary to all experience. Though Elgin paid the necessary ceremonial honour to the native rulers and magnates at durbars and on other public occasions, he had his reservations about their moral worth. As he wrote to Sir Charles Wood, the Secretary of State for India:

'When I consider what Oriental Society is, when I reflect on the frightful corruption, both of mind and body, to which the inheritors of wealth and station are exposed, the general absence of natives to call forth good instincts, or of restraints to keep bad in check ... I am overwhelmed with pessimism.

In India there was little place for the Burkean ideal of an enlightened and conscience-guided aristocracy. So it was that Elgin rejected Canning's policy of allowing almost unrestricted power to such men over their underlings and peasantry. He believed that Canning's concessions might have been necessary to stem the Mutiny, but had no place under conditions of peace. For Britain, could not, in Elgin's view, abdicate responsibility for these millions of underdogs.

On the other hand, he could not but urge the princes to assist in the modernisation of India and to share in its benefits. In the Punjab he praised the valour of the Sikh regiments in the taking of Pekin. But alongside this he extolled the arts of peace. As he told the Sirdars in Durbar:

'The waters which fall on your mountain heights and unite at their base to form mighty rivers, are a treasure which, duly distributed, will fertilise your plains and largely augment their productive powers. With electric telegraphs to facilitate communication, and railways and canals to render access to the seaports easy and expeditious, we shall be able to convey the surplus produce of this great country to others where it is required, and to receive from them their riches in return.

Elgin believed the railways to be great engines of progress. He hoped that their building and operation would in India make for fruitful collaboration between the British and the Indians and that the railways would have cultural as well as economic benefits. But, as in Canada, he was against the provision of a financial crutch in the form of government guarantees. It was private capital that was needed. On the other hand, government could not escape a supervisory role: it should insist on a uniform gauge throughout India. He urged that subsidiary railway lines should not all be built on *pucca* (perfectionist) lines, but to a *kutcha* (lesser) standard instead, costing three to four thousand pounds per mile rather than ten to fifteen. He greatly favoured irrigation schemes although he feared that private companies, unless regulated by law to supply water at reasonable rates, would keep water prices prohibitively high and so hold whole districts to ransom.

He believed that cheap unskilled labour was, as in Jamaica, a great evil. The fact that even private soldiers in the British army each had a *punka wallah* to pull a fanning device over him day and night was to him an indication both of the pitiful level of wages and living, and of the technical backwardness it perpetuated. A greater expenditure of capital, beginning with railway investment, would start a most necessary rise in wages, which in turn would stimulate innovations in production. If there were more skilled workers to work for example on the railways they would demand better education and thus would lead to cumulative gains. Thus to a new entrepreneurial class would be added a new artisan class, versed in the skill requirements of a new age. This was his Jamaica programme on a much grander scale. If these effects could become cumulative, linked with sound government and a good credit status in the London money market: 'showing a good balance sheet, an improving country, and a contented people, and leaving capitalists to draw their own inferences from these phenomena.'

Canning had urged Elgin to travel around India, to learn aspects of life in the different Indian areas and to revive his energies for his task. Elgin was keen to see more. He felt the need to visit the North-West and the Punjab. Accordingly a tour was planned. Elgin and his party including Mary Louisa and young Louisa, their daughter, were to travel by easy stages to Simla, spending the hot season in the hills. This was to be followed by an inspection of the Punjab. Elgin would summon his Council to him at some principal city in the North-West, thus improving their knowledge of India and breaking the closed and claustrophobic circle of Calcutta. Lahore was chosen for the Council rendez-vous. Along the way at Benares and Agra Elgin held Durbars. On each occasion he spoke to the princes and chiefs of his hopes and plans for India, asking them to assist in the process of modernisation. The journey was partly undertaken by the new marvel of the railway and partly by the traditional, more stately procession replete with bedecked elephants and armed retainers, emblazoned as they were with all the ancient accoutrements and splendour of an eastern monarch.

At Agra, with its Fort and the Taj Mahal, was held the most gorgeous Durbar India had ever seen. The viceroy's camp occupied a plain outside the city to which converged princes, maharajahs and chiefs, each with his retinue. The viceroy himself sat resplendent at the centre of an escort of ten thousand men. Concentric around him were ranked in order of arrival, camp after noisy camp, with miles upon miles of tents, containing, as Thurlow, Elgin's secretary described them, 'thousands upon thousands of ill-conditioned-looking men from Central India, and the wildest part of Rajpootana, the followers of such maharajahs as Jeypoor, who marched to meet the viceroy with an army of thirty thousand strong, found in horse and foot and guns, ready for the field.'

This Grand Durbar was held on the morning of 17 February. Although his personal tastes were so simple and unostentatious, Elgin daily took his place as Suzerain of this assembly of princes. He was surrounded by men bedecked in the most splendid costumes, covered in costly jewels and decorated with exquisite ornaments and weapons, the effect climaxing in elaborate and ostentatious head-dresses. Beneath this extraordinary millinery, which reflected so many cultures, there were dark faces, with bright, perceptive eyes, each of a man who had his own family history of ascent to power, together with his own calculation of gain. In their midst sat Elgin, the debt-ridden laird of Broomhall, on a massive golden throne with a crimson velvet cushion and two lions for armrests, his Scottish feet on a carpet of gold. From his position of eminence he gave ceremonial greetings to his regal vassals, observing all the necessary forms and honorifics. But when they were complete he gave them a lecture on their responsibility to modernise India, to build the railways, fund new roads and open better markets. There was also, he said, the need for the princes to educate their peoples, and to suppress 'barbarous usages and crimes, such as infanticide, suttee, thuggee and dacoitee.' He concluded on a warning note that any disturbances would be put down sternly by the army Her Majesty the Queen had put at his disposal. If, however, the princes' were loyal and created conditions of prosperity for their people they would establish 'the strongest claim on the favour and protection of the British government.'

In April Elgin and his party reached Simla where they stayed comfortably for five months. Amid a dry and cool climate Elgin resumed the mundane concerns of his viceroyalty, writing endlessly to the Secretary of State in London, to his Council members and to his subordinate Governors, planning the meeting scheduled for Lahore in the spring at which the programme for his reign would take shape. Among other considerations was whether to remove the capital of India from Calcutta to another place, (a curious echo of events in Canada). While he was at Simla there was an outburst of fanaticism at Sitana: Elgin at once ordered 'a sudden and vigorous blow to check this trouble on our frontier while it is in a nascent condition.'

On his way to Peshawar, the remotest station in the North-West frontier, the party,

16   Peterhoff was a modestly proportioned unpretentious house with corrugated iron roof, similar to many other hill station houses.

including Lady Elgin, made its way across rugged country, scaling the Rotung Pass, at about 13,000 feet. On 12 October they arrived at the gorge of the Chandra river. The only way to cross was by a twig bridge made of birch branches over which the natives and their animals passed. Many beasts fell through the meshes of the bridge and died. At the end of the summer season the bridge was dilapidated and was due to be replaced. Elgin accepted the challenge of the old bridge. But his health had been deteriorating and his struggle over the gorge was to precipitate heart failure from which he never recovered. Elgin continued the march on horseback, but on the 22nd came an attack that completely prostrated him. With great difficulty the viceroy was carried forward in slow stages.

On 4 November the striken viceroy reached Dhurmsala, a military station. Lady Elgin immediately sent for Dr. Macrae, his personal physician. Within two days Macrae knew that Elgin was dying. Knowing the man; he told him so at once. By this time increasing quantities of body fluid, were being retained making for a lingering and painful death. Elgin questioned Macrae closely about his condition, obtaining confirmation that there was no hope. Elgin suffered a phase of incredulity and sadness, grieving at leaving Mary Louisa and the children. But his faith remained strong, 'We shall all meet again', he told her. In his distress he knew the frustration of being struck down just when he was preparing for positive action to help the peoples of India. While he still had phases of energy and clear thought he found it impossible to believe that his life was forfeit. But these periods of optimism faded: as his condition deteriorated he fell back increasingly on the religion he had learned from his mother, as he listened to Mary Louisa reading from the Bible. From the verandah he would look out on the splendour of the Himalayas, while Mary Louisa read from the Book of Job of the marvels of nature as God had created them. Elgin's mind went back to his Oxford days, and the eloquence of Dr. Chalmers, fragments of whose writing he could still quote. His mind receded yet further back to his boyhood. The sight of a portrait of his dead son Charles, his 'angel boy', set him talking in a vein reminiscent of his ardent childhood prayer. Deep in the man who had braved the Montreal mob and who had forced his army into Pekin was still the child instilled by his mother with evangelical fervour and trust in God.

Mary Louisa remained constantly with him, struggling with her grief, cutting a lock of his hair to keep with the others she had taken at their engagement and at various times during their married life. She wrote an almost hourly record of his drawn-out sufferings. She journeyed down into the valley to choose a place for his grave, describing to him on her return its restful location and view of mountains, hills and plain. This she thought, gave him comfort.

Fleetingly, Elgin rallied and remembering that he was still viceroy, wondered whether he might yet reach Lahore and carry out his programme. But he died on 20 November 1863, a year and a half into his viceroyalty, and was buried the following day in the place Mary Louisa had chosen at Dhurmsala. And so the widow and her daughter set out for Broomhall, escorted by Thurlow, who had been charged by Elgin with their safekeeping. Victor Alexander, a fourteen year old Etonian, was now the ninth Earl of Elgin and the thirteenth of Kincardine. The government of India raised a tall Gothic monument over the lonely grave of his father.

(a)

(b)

17   (a) The Rohtung Pass and the Twig Bridge. (Lady Elgin's comments were written on the photographs.)

    (b)   Ralha-Gorge of the Beeas River. 'Resting place where we parted before the fatal expedition'.

(facing page)

    (c)   The twig bridge at Kohsur. 'I watched him from below as he rode up the pass'.

    (d)   The fatal bridge.

(c)

(d)

For twenty years the eighth Earl of Elgin had been perhaps the most successful of Britain's proconsuls. He lived exiled from the home he loved, made necessary by the debts inherited from his father. He was shipwrecked in both western and eastern hemispheres, as well as nearly being swept overboard into the winter Atlantic. He faced the Montreal mob at risk of his life, came under fire in China and risked a fearful fate if captured. As viceroy he did not refuse the challenge of the twig bridge, although his weakened constitution could not withstand this final strain.

There can be little doubt that he was an ambitious man, who, given his undoubted abilities could expect to reach the highest office. Once embarked on service overseas it proved impossible for him to re-embark on home politics. At times he felt his exile, aware that lasting fame was unlikely to come from service in remote societies on the perimeter of the British Empire. And yet he was unable, after his Jamaican and Canadian service, to build a new career at home.

He was one of the first of his station to recognise the humanity of the Chinese, Japanese and Indian masses, and to concern himself with their welfare. But he was obliged by his career to play the part, though briefly, of conqueror or ruler over all three. In each case he strove to minimise coercion and to maximise reconciliation. But he knew in his heart that his appeals to the European business community in the East, based as it was on opium, for moral and sensitive conduct, and to the Indian princes for a new humanity, were up against the dynamic force of mercantile greed and the self-satisfied weight of princely parasitism. Nor could he really have placed much hope for the alleviation of misery of the Asiatic masses in the new technologies including the railway and the electric telegraph. Hence his profound misgiving over Britain's role in the East, and the character of his own contribution to it. Only his part in Canadian affairs, where he had succeeded in creating a new political unity and a new political responsibility provided a genuine fulfilment, representing as it did the triumph of thought-out principle, steadfastly adhered to.

CHAPTER 17

Victor Alexander, his Sombre Upbringing and its Curious Outcome

The lives of Victor Alexander and his four siblings had always been punctuated by their father's absences and returns; this all ended in October 1863 with the news of the 8th Earl's death and the account of his burial in the Himalayas. Victor Alexander had been born at Monklands in 1849 at the time when the Montreal mob, intent on burning the Parliament House and stoning his father's carriage, were running riot in the streets. He had enjoyed his early childhood in Canada, which provided him with many memories which he liked to recall in later life. His first public appearance was in 1855 when at the age of six he attended the banquet in honour of his father given by the people of Dunfermline on his return from Canada. Victor was to keep a drawing of the occasion in his room at Broomhall for the rest of his life.

Victor and his brothers had all attended Trinity College, Glenalmond, an English-type public school set up in Perthshire in 1841 by a group of powerful Scottish episcopalian families, including the Gladstones. It was a rigorous and spartan place, fully up to the austerities of its older English counterparts, a severe setting demanding a good deal of boyhood fortitude. Victor left Glenalmond for Eton at the age of twelve having been taken there by his father before he set out for India. The death of his younger brother, Charles of meningitis at Glenalmond on 12 June 1863, aged ten, came as a devastating blow. Victor was left with two brothers, Robert and Frederick John and a sister Louisa, who, in India with her mother, had been present at her father's death.

Though she had remained in command throughout, Mary Louisa, in her grief at his passing had undergone a character change, making her even more involved with her husband in death than in life and bringing out a deep morbid strain that was to effect the lives of her children. To them their father had been an idealised but remote figure, held up by their mother as exemplary in all respects. In spite of the joy he took in them during his intervals at home, he remained a paragon in their eyes. Now, having died and been buried so far from home, he became almost a figure of apotheosis: a mixture of saint and man of intellect and of action, whose memory must ever be hallowed. In trying to hold on to him by her meticulous recording of his last days Mary Louisa had experienced a kind of *suttee*, her own life expiring with his. Queen Victoria, grieving herself, sympathised deeply, writing to Lady Elgin on her widely black-banded letter paper and giving Mary Louisa a gold and onyx bracelet at Christmas with the inscription 'From VRI, a broken-hearted widow like yourself'.

He was then urged to be worthy of the glories of his name:

> May this young Lord, now come of age,
> Adorn, like *Sires*, his country's page
> And hand unstained to latest age
> The illustrious name of Bruce.

In 1874, after leaving Oxford, we find Victor touring the continent with his brother Robert. At the British Embassy in Rome they presented Scenes of Shakespeare, to the admiration of the ambassador's wife, Lady Paget, drawing Roman society to their performances. For Elgin could play the extrovert very well as long as it was in a borrowed character.

Victor had inherited his father's modest stature, (some five foot seven inches), together with his snub-nose. Quite early, however, he allowed his lower face to disappear behind generous whiskers. There was no question of his entering upon a political career in the House of Commons, for he had of course succeeded to his father's British peerage. This meant that he was destined never to confront the political world of the hustings as a candidate. Like other aristocrats he abhorred and avoided the public platform, though he could perform with credit when duty called.

But he was not politically passive. The sense of public responsibility, inherited from his father and confirmed by his mother, obliged him both to take a political stance and to participate in politics. He may have lacked the diplomatic ambition of his grandfather, with its revelling in the world of intrigue whereby confidential memoranda could be sent to the Foreign Secretary in which grand views on the fate of Europe and confidential comments on personalities could be directed to the heart of government. But he was certainly intrigued by power and its manifestation, as evidenced by his love of Shakespeare's plays. He was not driven by the philosophical and moral search that had played so important a part in the young manhood of his father: Victor Alexander was not an intellectual, but an honest pragmatic, ruled, as his father had been, by a powerful code of right conduct.

He was clear on his political stance: it was that of a loyal Gladstonian Liberal. It had been in his formative years that the Conservative-Liberal party configuration, with its organisational structure, had emerged. His father had been a kind of Liberal, serving in Palmerston's cabinet, but the full Gladstonian perspective had not then evolved. Victor Alexander believed (consistent with the family tradition of financial stringency), in Gladstone's view that there should be minimal state spending and minimal taxation. He was, he said, 'an opponent of extravagance and an enemy of display.' He shared Gladstone's abhorrence of foreign or imperial adventures. The self-determination of peoples was another part of his creed: Victor was to support Gladstone on Irish Home Rule from the first attempt in 1886.

His other great concern was Broomhall. In spite of the disposal of the mines and railway, it remained a considerable responsibility. And so he in his turn became deeply involved in estate management. In 1872 his younger brother, Robert, had come of age, and in consequence entered upon the long delayed inheritance of the estate of Sir Robert Preston. Shortly afterward Robert and Victor Alexander successfully petitioned to have the entail of that estate broken so that Robert could determine his own heir without further complication. This was done. Robert named Victor Alexander his heir should he himself have no issue.

On 9 November 1876, Elgin married Lady Constance Carnegie, daughter of the ninth Earl of Southesk. The Queen sent a clock as a wedding present. The mutual attraction was very strong: in spite of Elgin's normally undemonstrative nature, they swept each other up. For the rest of her life she was to call him Bruce or Brucie. She was to bear him eleven children, six boys and five girls, all of whom adored her. There was almost a conspiracy between the family doctor, Dr. Dow, who seemed to have encouraged the increase in the family, and consequently the nursery staff. Her pregnancies were spread over a period of some twenty years although she became a semi-invalid latterly spending periods recuperating in the south of France.

Lady Augusta, Elgin's aunt, in spite of her duties as wife of the Dean of Westminster, and her active concern for the poor, had continued as confidante and support of the Queen. She had come to play an extraordinary role at Court, not merely sustaining and comforting Victoria in her widowhood and with her frustrations over the Prince of Wales, but also widening the Queen's knowledge of what was going on within her Kingdom, a task requiring great discretion. Augusta, for example, felt that Victoria should take some interest in Ireland, much neglected in favour of Scotland. The gatherings of the great and the humble at the Deanery had provided Augusta with much that could be communicated to the Queen. But by 1875 Augusta had worn herself out looking after the Dean and the Queen. A long trip to Moscow to the Court of the Tzar where Stanley performed the Church of England service at the wedding of the Duke and Duchess of Edinburgh, consumed her last reserves of vitality. On 1 March 1876 she died, to the great grief of the Queen, and was buried in Henry VII's Chapel in Westminster Abbey. So ended the long intimacy of the Elgins with the royal court. The Dean placed her bust on the centre of her writing table to simulate her presence.

In some ways Elgin was very different from the typical country gentlemen in that he was no good with horses and an indifferent rider (in contrast to his grandfather and his father). The fact that he did not ride may have had its roots in the old Elgin habit of economy, for riding or hunting horses were expensive. He detested massive bags of game though he could enjoy a shoot with Robert and a few friends. His carefully kept game books show a full season at grouse, partridge and pheasant. He was hostile at a social level to the smart set with its brittle chatter and its pseudo–intellectualism. He greatly enjoyed forestry and digging in preparation for road building at Broomhall. Felling trees was a particular pleasure, a diversion shared with his mentor Gladstone, using axe, cross–cut saw and ropes in all of which he became expert. The happy culmination of a day so spent would be the building of a bonfire surrounded by his children, and finally its triumphant ignition. He was moderate to good at cricket and curling: there were clubs for these sports at Broomhall. Archery he practised with the Royal Company in Edinburgh.

This Lord Elgin was greatly interested in his family's history, reading the papers associated with his father and grandfather which survived in profusion at Broomhall. By the early 1880s the divorce between the seventh Earl and Mary Hamilton Nisbet

20   The House Party at Haddo House, Aberdeenshire, seat of the Earl and Countess of Aberdeen, during the shooting season, 1884.

was nearly eighty years in the past. He maintained a connection between the Elgins and the Hamilton Nisbets through Mary's children and grandchildren. Indeed there were regular parties at Biel right up to 1921 when the last of Mary Nisbet's kin died. One of Mary's granddaughters, was seized with an urge to justify Mary (who had died in 1855), on the matter of the divorce. She wrote around her female relatives seeking recollections. Aged ladies were pressed to remember what they had heard about the affair, but nothing firm emerged from their ruminations except a general sympathy for Mary in her distress.

Queen Victoria's golden jubilee of 1887 was celebrated in style at Broomhall, with some 2,000 people thronging the grounds, including 304 Sabbath School children and 145 Volunteers and their officers. Those who made their way into the house were intrigued to see the portraits, especially the dashing one of the seventh Earl. Among the oddities were a crutch of the Empress of China and a picture and a fire screen from her room in the Summer Palace. The rain stayed off long enough for the local photographer to capture the occasion with the Dowager Countess acting as a kind of proxy for the Queen, sitting centrally in the gathering, surrounded by grandchildren and wearing the same kind of black mourning dress she had worn for the twenty-four years of her widowhood, only two years short of that of the Queen herself. The highlight of the occasion was when the Dowager opened the Queen's Hall, her celebratory gift to the people of Charlestown. She had paid for it out of her pension from the government of India, as she had for the replica memorial to her husband at Broomhall and the completion of the porch there.

A dramatic backdrop to life at Broomhall in the 1880s was the building of the Forth Bridge. Elgin had sold the land on the northern Fife shore to the North British Railway Company taking up shares in the special company floated to finance the bridge. There was a great gathering of engineers and workmen at Queensferry, followed by gunpowder explosions as deep cuttings were driven through the living rock; there were clangs and clatter as the immense steel tubes and girders were assembled at the site. Gradually there arose a great civil engineering structure, one of the wonders of the world. Elgin became friendly with some of the engineers working on the bridge, one of them, Fowler, designed a dining room table for Broomhall, constructed, like the bridge, on the cantilever principle, which could be cranked out to thirty-two places. Andrew Carnegie, who had now returned to Scotland as one of the world's richest men, was among the many who inspected the vast framework. Elgin was present in March 1890 when the bridge was opened by the Prince of Wales driving home a golden spike. He served conscientiously on the Board as a director of the North British.

The Fife Liberal Association had been formed by 1878 with Victor and Robert involved. In 1881 Elgin was one of the founding members of the Scottish Liberal Association—created by a merger between the East and North of Scotland Liberal Association and the West of Scotland Association—and served as a member of its first Council. The Westerners from the industrialised part of Scotland were more radical, wishing to commit the party to a specific programme; the Whiggish Easterners wished the Association to be an organisational one only, concerned with the registration of voters and the like: and this was also what Elgin wanted. In 1884 the franchise in

21 Louisa, Dowager Countess of Elgin, on the lawn in front of Broomhall with members of the Bruce family, including the Earl and Countess of Elgin with their children, and villagers from Charlestown and Limekilns, on the occasion of Queen Victoria's Jubilee, 1887.

Britain was greatly widened by the third Reform Act: in that year Elgin became chairman of the Council. He was challenged almost at once by a renewed attempt by the radicals to force the party to adopt official policies. By this was meant the disestablishment of the Church of Scotland, Temperance reform and land reform in the Highlands—proposals that Elgin designated as 'slogans'. A group of radicals did however break away forming the National Liberal Federation of Scotland. In 1886 came an even more challenging split with a good many Liberals, in protest against Gladstone's Irish Home Rule Bill, leaving the party to form the Unionists. It was in this situation that Elgin showed his powers of conciliation, helping to limit the damage of the double split. In addition he did much to encourage improvement in the party's organisation, choosing election candidates and improving the registration of Liberal voters. It was this activity that commended him to his friend and neighbour, Lord Rosebery, Gladstone's Crown Prince, and to Henry Campbell Bannerman, another Scot deeply concerned with the party's performance in Scotland. On Home Rule Elgin was and remained a staunch supporter of Gladstone. In all these matters Victor and his brother Robert were of the same mind. But because so many landed Whigs had left the party over Ireland, Elgin was left as one of the very few Scottish peers loyal to Gladstone.

Elgin was made Lord Lieutenant of Fife by Gladstone in 1886 (a post his grandfather had so deeply desired but so briefly held); he continued in this office until his death. To his directorship of the North British Railway was added that of the Royal Bank of Scotland. The Royal had been for years the principal creditor of the estate, but with Broomhall at last viable Elgin became a proper ornament of the board.

It was with Gladstone's third ministry, between February and July 1886, that Elgin received his first political appointment, as Treasurer of the Queen's Household. In spite of knowing him since boyhood, the Queen did not warm to him because of what she felt to be a taciturn style. He became active in the House of Lords as spokesman on Scottish matters, a field in which by this time he was very well informed. Indeed he hoped to be appointed to the headship of the Scottish Office, newly set up in 1885, largely under Rosebery's influence in response to a nascent Scottish nationalism. This was a task where Elgin could have discharged his hereditary public duty most effectively and congenially. But though the post had a number of short-term holders, Elgin was not to be one of them. As compensation Gladstone made Elgin First Commissioner of Works, a post he held from April to the fall of the ministry in August 1886. In this brief period Elgin supervised the installation of drains in the Houses of Parliament. In August the storm over Home Rule for Ireland, doomed to dominate British politics for many years, had broken. And so Elgin, with others, followed the Grand Old Man into the political wilderness.

Once more he centred his life on Broomhall, there to busy himself with the affairs of Fife and of Scotland for a further eight years. He made higher education within the distinctive and flourishing Scottish system a particular interest. As a member of the University Court of St. Andrews, he learned of the inner workings of a particular institution; as a member of the Committee of the Council of Education in Scotland he gained the wider perspective. He sought to solve the major educational problems arising from the new age of science and technology (in which certain of the four

Scottish universities had been engaged long before the ancient universities of England): namely, how were the benefits of the classical education in which he himself had been raised to be reconciled with the demands of the new practical age? What of the common man? Though Scottish education—with its parish schools since the days of John Knox—had produced the most literate population of Europe, and had taken large steps in modernisation under the Education Act of 1872, it was not enough. Elgin had become a member of the first School Board set up in Scotland under the Act. For him the education question was a moral as well as a practical one: the poor

CULTCHAH !

(" *A little knowledge is a dangerous thing* " *!*)

Tommy. "Wasn't it Phidias who made the Eljin Marbles, Aunt Hippolyta !"

Aunt Hippolyta. "Pheidias, dear, not Phidias ; and you must say Elgin, not Eljin. The Greek G, or Gamma, is always pronounced *hard*, you know."

22   Cartoon from *Punch*, 10 March 1888. 'Cultchah!'

23 The arrival of the Viceroy at Government House, Calcutta, January 1894. The Elgins as a family, and especially perhaps the Viceroy himself, found the presence of so many retainers at Government House oppressive. Here they are marshalled on the steps while the military are ranked on the driveway.

net stays and a white petticoat.' Her husband soon adopted the dress of his staff—a flannel shirt and drab coloured Assam silk washing suit. Elgin was however in good spirits, informing himself, as his father had done, through interviews with informed and articulate men. Characteristically he insisted on dressing himself without assistance from his servants who were forced to wait outside his room while inside he gaily sang Scottish songs. Nor were there any servants present while he breakfasted alone with Constance. One reason for his general good-humour was the warmth of the welcome he had received as being his father's son.

As the pre-monsoon heat tightened its grip on Calcutta the Viceregal party prepared for the move to a more comfortable climate in the mountains. They were all enchanted with Simla. Constance described it as 'this wonderful place'; she even went so far as to say that the air might be 'too good'. 'I feel stunned by it all', she wrote, 'the air is keen, clear and rare, the brightness almost painful at present'. She kept a close eye on Elgin's health with Dr. Franklin his medical man, carefully noting the effects of the medicaments prescribed for diarrhoea and his liver. Tennis now became Elgin's favourite outdoor sport, although indoor curling became a close second. The stones had been specially made in Scotland: the game they played on the polished ballroom floor at Simla.

Elgin was well-supported by his personal assistant. After careful watch Constance approved of Henry Babington Smith, Elgin's private secretary. She noted his mastery of business, together with his sense of confidentiality: for her husband to be so well served in this critical function was a great relief to her. Babington-Smith, she also observed with approval, was an excellent tennis player and a beautiful dancer. He gave dancing lessons to the girls and some of the staff. Scottish reels were soon a feature of the Viceregal Court.

Babington Smith was indeed to prove an ideal choice. He had been a King's Scholar at Eton and was a notable athlete. At Cambridge he had been a member of the exclusive club, the Apostles, and had taken a first in both parts of the classical tripos. In 1891 he had become the private secretary to George Goschen, the Chancellor of the Exchequer, and as such had been secretary to the British delegation to the Brussels Silver Conference in 1892. The British had been strongly in favour of the single gold standard and opposed to the dual standard of silver and gold which the bimetallists had hoped would be adopted. Babington Smith's experience was to prove valuable to Elgin who found bimetallism part of the argument over Indian currency difficulties.

One of Elgin's first challenges related to the cow, sacred to the Hindus but regarded as dirty and unclean by the Moslems. Some Moslems resumed a campaign of cow killing and abuse, which provoked their Hindu neighbours. In the same areas trees were smeared with a mixture of mud and other insulting matter. Indian journalists publicised the Muslim campaign with provocative and perhaps seditious articles which greatly inflamed local passions.

Elgin and the Raj could either prosecute or forbear. Elgin kept his nerve and resisted the call to take people to court, feeling that this would only make things worse. With 96 per cent of the population illiterate, he judged that the influence of an ill-disposed press was limited. He had learned very quickly how difficult it was to discover the truth in India and he judged it was best to allow the press its head. In this way he

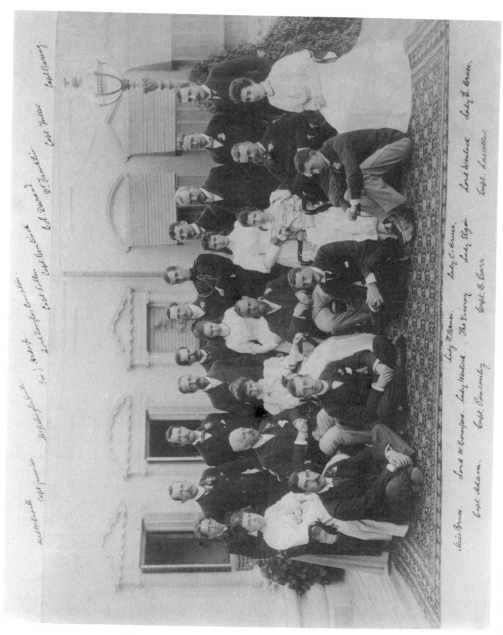

24 The Viceroy, Vicereine and Aides shortly after the arrival. The three eldest Bruce girls, Elizabeth, Christian and Veronica, are of the party.

would at least know what was being written. In following such a policy the liberal Elgin was wisely trying to keep the coercive power of government to a minimum. In time the policy worked: the Moslems desisted from their offensive behaviour. Elgin, against the advice of his staff, insisted upon receiving municipal addresses wherever he went, listening graciously to compliment and complaint. His patience was also useful giving him insight into matters which were of concern to his Indian subjects.

Indian finance presented a very different challenge: Indians, whether Hindu or Moslem, were united in feeling a sense of grievance. For some years Indian finances had been running at a deficit. Lansdowne's government in 1893 had proposed a revenue tariff, half of which would be raised by a tax on British cotton imports. Such a move would please Indian opinion, for it would be a sign that the interests of the Indian economy were not always to be subjected to those of the British. Indeed Indian industries, especially cotton, would be protected from British imports.

In London the Secretary of State, Lord Kimberley, rejected the proposal out of hand, reaffirming the principle of free trade and rejecting any suggestion that Indian finance was being manipulated to favour British manufacturers. The matter was highly emotive, being seen in Britain and India from diametrically opposite points of view. The powerful Lancashire cotton interest was already under serious threat. India was herself producing cotton manufactured cloth and Japan was rapidly capturing former Lancashire markets with her own cotton manufactured cloths in all Far Eastern markets. Lansdowne withdrew his revenue tariff and the financial deficit rose sharply. This was the financial situation which faced Elgin on arrival.

Sir Arthur Godley, the powerful Permanent Under-Secretary at the India Office in London, wrote to Elgin saying that while those in the India Office believed in the justice and appropriateness of an import duty that included cotton goods, the British government under Gladstone, was hostile. He suggested, however, that if such a proposal were strongly put by the viceroy and his Council, the British Cabinet would have to consider it.

Elgin's first reaction, himself a convinced free trader, was to resist the idea of a tariff altogether, rejecting in particular the taxing of British cottons. He understood very well the strength of opinion in Britain. But on the other hand there was the frightening rise in the Indian deficit. New to his job, Elgin found it very difficult to establish his position among the clamouring, conflicting interests. He wanted to encourage India's most important industry. He learned that in spite of India having been in the past wholly exposed to Lancashire imports, there had developed in Bombay (and elsewhere) large-scale competitive cotton enterprises run by Indians. The damage to the Indian village cotton industry of which nationalists complained, came not only from Lancashire but also from native Indian manufacturers.

In the end, Elgin decided that the adoption of a tariff was inescapable. The government in India decided to set it at 5 per cent with no exemptions. The British government was annoyed and so was the British community in India whose sympathies lay with British rather than Indian interests. The only people who approved were the activist Indians in the Congress party and elsewhere in India. But Elgin did not make a decisive stand which meant that Gladstone had no difficulty vetoing Elgin's proposal to levy a duty on cottons. Elgin then introduced legislation for a tariff which exempted cottons. He was disappointed with the outcome but did not feel he could make a serious fuss. The Gladstone cabinet felt on strong ground and so the tariff bill went through with cottons omitted.

But the issue was far from settled. In the winter of 1894–1895 it was suggested that British cottons should indeed be subject to the tariff—and so would those of India, to 'equalise' the conditions of competition between Indian and British producers. Elgin resisted the scheme, but without great vigour. In 1896 both the duty and the excise were reduced from 5 per cent to 3 per cent on all piece goods, and yarn of all counts was exempted from the tariff.

Elgin's indecisive behaviour over cotton was neither forgotten nor forgiven in India. The Indian press, Indian nationalists and Indian historians have always dismissed Elgin's viceroyalty because he failed to take a pro-Indian stand. In Britain too he came to be dismissed as ineffectual in India. At his old college, Balliol at Oxford, they did not invite him to pose for his portrait as they did later for Curzon. Elgin never subsequently sought publicly to justify himself on this issue. He believed, however, that the significance of the tariff was much over-rated both in India and in Britain, and that the cotton industries of neither India nor England were really affected by what he did in India. Moreover Elgin saw the issue as exemplifying the untenable relationship between his own Government of India and the British parliament. As the latter was constitutionally supreme those administering India had no option but to accept, ultimately, what London decided. Elgin's liberalism and constitutionalism prevented him from acting out of turn: for him the idea of the viceroy as autocrat simply did not occur.

Even more intransigent than the tariff was the problem of the rupee. Unlike the tariff, however, its very complexity shielded it to a considerable degree from political argument in India. The rupee had traditionally been based on silver, in common with the other currencies of the east. But the world price of silver relative to gold was highly unstable. In September 1890 the world silver price had reached a peak, being at its highest for over thirteen years: thereafter it fell dramatically so that by mid-1892 it had plunged to its lowest level ever. The Government of India, like those of other trading nations in the east, was greatly concerned at this switch-back effect, causing as it did the gold value of the rupee to fluctuate wildly. The relationship of gold to silver was supposed to be 1 to 15.5 but with silver prices rising and then plunging these proportions could not be maintained. After a long and complex debate world-wide, over the merits of keeping the double gold silver standard, or bimetallism, the British government had rejected the idea, reaffirming its faith in the gold standard. In the course of 1893 the Government in India acted to check the fall in the rupee with the intention of raising its value to 16 pence sterling. To this end it closed the Indian mints to the free coinage of silver. So it was that when Elgin arrived in India both the Indian budget and the rupee were in real trouble.

The issue of the rupee, like that of the tariff, was to rumble on throughout Elgin's viceroyalty. Here, in contrast to the tariff issue, he was perfectly clear and consistent. India must, he said like other countries, move onto the gold standard. In this his Liberalism shone through. The confusions of bimetallism he dismissed out of hand. It is likely that Babington-Smith, with his experience of the bemetallic question, had something to do with Elgin's attitude. Indian trade and the Indian economy needed above all a stable rupee: that there had to be a measure of deflation to bring this about, annoying exporters like the Bombay millowners, Elgin accepted as a necessary cost. By 1899 the Government of India had succeeded in raising the gold value of the rupee to its target of 16 pence at which figure it was successfully stabilised.

Visits to the princely states did not greatly appeal to Elgin for he was neither horseman nor hunter, two traditionally admired roles. But he had two sets of ceremonial duties: those performed at Government House in Calcutta, at the centre of power and of the British presence, and those involving autumn tours of various parts of India. These long journeys were planned to the hour over many days with precise instructions as to salutes, presentations, carriage occupancy, guards of honour, cavalry escorts and levees. The Elgins made their first tour in October 1894 with some sixty native servants in attendance. The climax came at the grave of his father at Dharmsala. As he stood before the Gothic memorial there were many memories including those of the day news of his father's death had reached him at Eton.

With a certain amount of groaning to his family, especially in the trying weather of the approaching monsoon, he disciplined himself to being watched, criticised and fussed over. To escape he became increasingly engrossed in his work, assisted by the quiet, reliable and never hurried Babington-Smith. Indeed with so many letters, despatches, reports and the like, his writing desk became the focus of his life. But there remained the great occasions which he sometimes found irksome. With a sense of living in a fantasy he would sit, enrobed, upon the Viceregal throne, dazzlingly gilded with its armrests of lions and its sunburst back surmounted by the imperial crown. Or he would lead off the first Quadrille with Constance at the great state balls, or bow from his carriage on arriving in state at the Calcutta racecourse for the viceroy's Cup. There was embarrassment when he declined to appear mounted at the military review. With their strong cavalry tradition, the officers had wanted his presence there on horseback amid the movement, the men, the dust and the bands. But he wisely demurred at taking such a risk of public catastrophe. At durbars, however, Elgin was to find himself. A particularly splendid one was held at the viceroy's camp at Kermal in 1894 on his first Viceregal progress. He did the honours in regal manner, addressing the princes on their relation to the Raj, just as his father had done, his voice as Constance said, 'carrying beautifully'.

Around this time he felt sympathy for a young Maharani who had been recently widowed. He wrote to his mother that he had alluded in a speech 'to my own knowledge of what a Mother's love can do', excusing himself on the ground that 'I do not often wear my heart upon my sleeve'. He wrote too of the new Maharajah, a boy of eleven, who performed his royal duties with great self possession, reminding Victor of his own nervousness when, as a boy, he had to face his new role as Earl.

Elgin's wife and daughters provided a secure home life for him. Bessie darned the socks he wore for his long walks just as he liked them. All three girls revelled in their social opportunities, riding out with young officers of their father's staff during the day and dancing them off their feet every Friday evening. Having reached the age of eighteen, Bessie was now 'out', with her hair up, dining downstairs with her parents and company, revelling in her gowns, to the considerable jealousy of her sisters. There

25 The Convocation at Lahore, November 1894.

26 The Viceroy's State (silver) Howdah, Lahore, November 1894.

were amateur theatricals, featuring 'Ticklish Times', in which Bessie played the wife of Babington-Smith to the amusement of her sisters. Christian had taken up photography: her sepia efforts were an attempt to catch the shapes and glamour of India, as well as family occasions. Although the girls were very fit Constance and Elgin took it in turns to worry about the others health.

Although Calcutta was their main base Simla was much preferred. There in the mountains the Elgins sought escape from the Viceregal Lodge. They rented a house, 'The Retreat', at Mashobra a few miles away, which despite being in bad repair became their favourite place. It was set among trees that enchanted Constance, covered with velvety moss out of which grew maidenhead fern, with white clematis and giant periwinkle.

The Elgins in India talked much of the family back home. Although Elgin and Constance were not to see four of their children for five years the two older boys, Edward and Robert, missed one half at Eton to spend time in India. They joined a Viceregal tour, greatly enjoying shooting buck and bringing back trophies.

Back in 1868 Elgin's half sister, Elma, heiress to the Cumming-Bruce fortune, had married their father's secretary, Lord Thurlow. In the 1890s Thurlow had become involved in unwise speculations which had eventually destroyed his wife's inheritance and left them pretty well penniless. Now while Elgin was in India he felt he must help the Thurlows by providing maintenance for Elma. He feared there would be much gossip and wrote anxiously to the Queen's private secretary, Sir Henry Ponsonby to inquire whether the matter had come to the Queen's notice. He was relieved to know that Victoria by now a very old lady, knew nothing of the matter.

Queen Victoria interested herself a good deal in Indian affairs, she asked Constance to place a wreath for her on dear Lady Canning's grave. Lady Elgin also found herself negotiating the complicated affair of moving the Dufferin Victoria hospital at Calcutta, a charitable institution, dealt with by each vicereine in her turn.

It was not long before Elgin encountered the Indian National Congress, created in 1885 by British liberals living in India and Indian nationals. It claimed to be willing to work with the Raj, not to be secessionist, and that its general objective was to gain entry for Indians into government service, both at a central and local level. Characteristically Elgin was not unwilling to make some contact with Congress although he was careful not to give any sort of encouragement which would permit any sort of claim for official recognition to be made.

The Congress agenda was soon established, it was that Indians be given a place on the viceroy's council, on the provincial councils, in the judicature, in the civil service and possibly as officers in the Indian Army. This meant in effect that Congress wanted a participatory government with Indians in the administration, especially in its middle and upper ranks. The problem for Elgin and the British generally was whether a system of shared responsibility and authority could ever make for a stable government. India was such a patchwork of states variously organised which the British had wielded, however precariously, into a whole, held together by strong central authority backed by an unquestioning army. In the event Elgin concluded that the British must reserve the army and the civil service to themselves. He was not convinced that, if the British wished to stay in India, the Indians could fill senior posts in the higher echelons of the

(a)

(b)

civil service although he recognised the frustration that would be caused to educated Indians by such a denial. Elgin simply accepted that there was a permanent dilemma and any serious power-sharing would merely herald the beginning of the end.

Claims were also being made that Indians should serve on the viceroy's council and the provincial legislative councils. The viceroy had the right to choose the members of his council. Similarly the members of the provincial councils were also nominated and their function was also limited to recommendations. At these two levels it seemed to Elgin that Indians could be brought into government without impairing British power. His view was that if allowed this degree of participation, Indians could learn the complexities of real affairs and so become responsible in their outlook: also their utterances and attitudes would, alongside those of the press, provide the British with much needed insight into the working of Indian minds. He therefore recommended councils for the Punjab and Burma.

The North West Frontier, always likely to erupt, threatened trouble in March 1895 when there were disturbances at Chitral in disputed Kashmir territory. In January the Mehtar (ruler) of Chitral had been assassinated; subsequently Robertson, the British agent, was besieged by rebellious chiefs in Chitral. Anxious to avoid trouble, and instinctively hostile to imperial adventures, the Liberal government in London thought that the right course was to abandon Chitral and hope that the Russians and the Amir of Afghanistan would cease their pressure and desist from further destabilisation. But Elgin in India took the opposite view, arguing that Chitral was strategically necessary. Moreover to abandon it would be a sign of weakness, likely to encourage the warlike Pathan tribesmen to rise and set the entire frontier ablaze.

Elgin, like his father, believed that in India any sign of weakness could be fatal, and that Britain must always be ready to demonstrate her power. Accordingly he urged that Chitral be made the focus of the British force, rather than Gilgit to the east. To this end the road to Chitral, guarded by levies over its entire course, would have to be kept open permanently, as in the Khyber.

Lord Rosebery, the Prime Minister, wrote to Elgin saying that, with the greatest reluctance, the government had decided that Chitral must be abandoned. Rosebery was more concerned with the threat to India from the French, intruding not from the west, but from the east through Indo-China. In the event the Rosebery administration fell in June 1895 before Chitral could be evacuated and the new Conservative government backed Elgin. As a result of strengthening Chitral that part of the frontier remained reasonably stable until the Raj itself ended in 1947. Certainly Elgin's decision over Chitral was influenced by his military advisers: but on this occasion Elgin's own instincts recognised the justice of the army's reasoning.

27   (a) Although the Viceregal Lodge on Observatory Hill, Simla, was very grand, built by Lord Dufferin as Viceroy, it was too large for the Elgins who whenever possible escaped from it.
(b)   The Retreat at Mashobra was rented by the Elgins and used as home whenever possible. There Lord Elgin could indulge his favourite pastime of walking, as it were incognito.

This did not however fully dispose of the problem of the frontier tribes and the slippery claims of the Amir of Afghanistan. The frontier between him and the tribes of Waziristan was particularly contentious. An agreement of November 1893 had seemed to settle the matter, but raids and outrages by Afghans and Waziristanis continued. As the Waziristani headmen were wholly unable to control their tribesmen there were constant disturbances. The government of India had tried to encourage quiescence by paying subsidies to the tribes. Elgin in July 1894 came to the conclusion that this arms-length policy had failed. He was very much against punitive expeditions, except as a desperate last resort, objecting to the blind brutalism of such incursions with their kills, burning of villages and destruction of crops, savaging the innocent, while the guilty probably escaped untouched. Instead he proposed a new boundary commission together with a permanent garrison with a British political officer who would explain what the British were doing to the tribes. The commission sat in 1895 and 1896 and made slight alterations to the frontiers which helped to calm the area.

28   The Viceregal train which was so much more a feature of life for the Bruce family
      in the 1890s than it had been for Elgin's father in the early 1860s.

29   The 'Xmas Tree' Viceregal Lodge, illuminated with electric lights. Children's Fancy
Dress Ball, September 1894.

But behind the boundary problem lay the waywardness of the tribes with their disorderly conditions and arbitrary chiefs. The challenge lay in preserving tribal autonomy (any breach of which might bring serious trouble), and in bringing stability and improvement in the conditions of life by promoting internal security through the civilising influence of better communications and trade. It was British policy with which Elgin agreed, not to exercise direct control, but to act through the laws and customs of the tribes, through the agency of chiefs and native authorities. If the British showed themselves to be strong enough then they could afford to offer generous terms of autonomy to the tribes who knew that the threat of further force, in the event of misbehaviour, was always there. In all this Elgin was a liberal optimist, believing that even the wildest of peoples would respond to the prospects of stability and cultural advance. In September 1898 he reaffirmed his stand, writing that 'I hold the view that the forces of civilisation are even now beginning to penetrate into the Hills', and that 'the gradual extension of our institutions will come, ... as an act of incorporation rather than annexation'.

And so it was that the perennial issues on the viceregal agenda hit Elgin within a few months of his arrival in India: communal passions, the budget and the tariff, the rupee, the claims made by Indians and their British liberal allies both in India and Britain for the opening up of the civil service and the army, Indian participation in the councils and the instability of the frontier. These were the standing items, none of which was capable of any easy solution.

There was, however, one direction in which Elgin's liberal optimism could be effective. This was the railway. The Eighth Earl of Elgin had hoped for much from the railway in Jamaica, Canada, China and India believing it to be the greatest single engine for civilising the underdeveloped world. Victor Alexander shared this view and moreover felt he knew and understood railways. By 1900 India was to have 25,000 miles of track; about one-fifth of which had been built or planned during Elgin's viceroyalty. Shortly after his arrival he turned to the railway department perhaps as a relief from other problems. There thoroughly at home, he endeavoured to improve the service. Where new lines were planned he was keen to encourage private enterprise, being always keen to increase the flow of private capital into Indian enterprises. Elgin believed that by stimulating railway planning and building he had made a serious contribution to the well-being of the Indian sub-continent.

But while Elgin placed much hope in economic development generated from above, he quickly learned that if Indian society was looked at from below, the problems seemed quite insoluble with rural poverty, the complexity of land tenure systems and peasant debt making a circle of deprivation from which few could break loose. The rural moneylender was everywhere in India, often an unrelenting village tyrant. Elgin collected a good deal of material on agricultural indebtedness, but, like so many others could see no remedy that would not disturb peasant India at its roots. This was probably the closest Elgin got to the basic problems of India.

CHAPTER 19

Mother India, Famine and Plague

By mid 1897 Elgin was half-way through his term. He and his family had adjusted to their Indian setting. Constance became pregnant again after an interval of nearly five years, and in March produced another son. It was a conscious decision to have a child in India. When the Queen was told of the forthcoming event she forebore to use her favourite phrase, 'how extraordinary!' At the registration of the birth the father's occupation was entered as 'viceroy', the father immediately preceding being described as 'sweeper'. (Bessie joked about this as 'democracy in action'.) The Queen expressed her wish that he be given her and his father's names, Victor Alexander. Though Constance made a good recovery from the birth, her semi-invalid status was now confirmed. On outdoor occasions she was transported in a carrying chair; on picnics she remained a central figure while her husband walked about the scene in an apparently indefatigable manner. Indeed the viceroy had become famous both in Calcutta and Simla for his pedestrianism, using his feet where other viceroys had used their horses or their carriages. Bessie had become a stand-in for her mother both domestically and ceremonially, doing small personal services for her father and being at his side on social occasions.

The question of viceregal finance had been resolved after Elgin had discovered that with an A.D.C. and a Steward who knew their work, expenses could be kept within the various official allowances. Although the household establishment numbered about 700 persons, and cost a great deal, with efficient management, the viceroy could break even.

In 1896 everything was set aside, for the monsoon rains failed over large areas, causing catastrophic famine followed immediately by the plague. Nature, always the great arbiter, had decreed a series of crises. In all some three quarters of a million were to die, in what was probably the worst famine of the century. Elgin's famine relief organisation did him credit, easing conditions more effectively than in similar circumstances in the past; charitable relief was also efficiently administered. But the main thrust of Elgin's programme was the provision of relief work, building roads and reservoirs and the like to give heads of families a money wage, with which to buy the basic foods which the railways were bringing into the famine areas. In all some four million people were relieved.

During the crisis there was an agitation that Elgin should by-pass the dealers, buying up grain and distributing it by public agency. But this he was unwilling to do for it would upset the grain markets and make the situation worse than before. Moreover such action would have meant creating a short-term distribution system with all the attendant difficulties. There was criticism at the time over this, but Elgin's policy was probably the right one. A more formidable charge, also made against him, was that he had sought to hide the fact that there was famine, delaying making public announcements to that effect. It is true that he sought as long as possible to hold off such pronouncements, fearing that they would create panic and cause hoarding, thus worsening the situation further. Accordingly he managed to launch his relief programme with vigour, but with the minimum of fuss. The matter was complicated by the fact that there were great regional variations in conditions, and that reliable information about the course of the rains over the country was not easy to come by. Dufferin, one of Elgin's predecessors, commended Elgin's response to the famine as 'one of the most remarkable achievements of British rule in India.' Some of the resentments against the

30   Picnic in Baghi Forest. Although Lady Elgin's carrying chair is not shown in this picture, she does look thin and drawn: note also the family pets, the two dogs 'Flink' and 'Tim'.

Raj were temporarily laid aside in an atmosphere of gratitude for what had been done. When the food crisis had passed, Elgin set up a Commission to study the relief operation and to set out its lessons for the future; it reported in 1898.

At the height of the famine communal problems temporarily receded, but the plague which followed revived ethnic resentments. Fiercely held customs among both Hindus and Moslems collided with the British attempt to enforce better sanitation and segregation. The plague centres were Bombay and Poona, though everyone in India including the British residents, felt themselves under threat. Lord Salisbury the Prime Minister, proposed that the annual Haj pilgrimage of Indian Moslems be suspended. Elgin warned London that this might cause unrest, but Salisbury insisted.

There was already in existence a set of Plague Rules drawn up in accordance with western medical practice. The question was should they be enforced? To do so, especially regarding Hindu and Moslem women was to raise a hornet's nest. The women, quite clearly the property of their men folk, were kept apart in purdah. If the interfering British persisted in administering the Plague Rules they could have whole communities up in arms. At Poona on 15 June 1897 two British officials, one being the man in charge of plague operations, were shot dead in their carriages. Frustrated by their failure to find the murderers, the Bombay government made three arrests of B.G. Tilak and the Natu brothers. Matters were complicated by the full confession from another man. In the midst of the confusion B.G. Tilak took the opportunity of launching himself as the first great nationalist leader. In 1897 war broke out once more along the frontier.

These disturbances in the Bombay presidency encouraged the authorities to examine the basis of British rule in India and its stability. There was a dilemma: if the ethnic communities were to unite, then one great cause of disturbance would be removed, but such a Hindu–Moslem reconciliation would soon threaten the Raj. Elgin found such problematic discussion time consuming and unhelpful. During the famine he had kept his nerve, reassuring the home government that the implications of the Poona murders had been exaggerated, that they were not part of a widespread movement, and that there was no question of the loyalty of the Indian army, the ultimate basis of the Raj. In all his travels in India Elgin never, except in Peshawar, felt himself among a hostile population. In October something of an Islamic revival, a recurrent phenomenon, brought the Hindu peasantry and their landlords closer to the British. Elgin's view was that the British should always be vigilant, but that there was no immediate danger. The Raj had simply to respond as best it could to developments in India, which, as Elgin put it, 'they can no more stop than Canute could restrain the waves ...'

Plague re-surfaced again in Bombay in March 1898 where the local government lost control, frightened as it was by the rioting provoked by its faltering attempts to enforce the Plague Rules. It was proposed that instead of the forcible segregation of plague victims in special hospitals, private dwelling houses should be licensed as hospitals. Elgin agreed to allow local authorities discretion in applying the Plague Rules. He was worried that if the plague, reached Calcutta, where relations between Europeans and Indians was as he put it, 'as inflammable as touchwood,' would, if the Plague Rules were actively enforced, erupt into general rioting. On the other hand if no steps were taken the viceroy would be blamed by everyone both in London and in India.

All the while Elgin had to keep a close eye on what was being said in the mother of parliaments on the wide range of Indian problems. To this end Babington Smith carefully kept a book of cuttings from *The Overland Mail*. There was at Westminster a smallish group of pro-Indian anti-imperialists who watched out for any Indian crisis. There were also the aspiring politicians,—with the Liberal, H.H. Asquith, among them—who sought ammunition for party purposes wherever it could be found. And so Elgin received many requests for data on a wide range of Indian subjects, from the number of famine and plague victims to the incidence of venereal disease among the British soldiery. This kind of information, with no permanent statistical service was very difficult to gather.

Venereal disease was indeed a chronic problem in the army: the British military

31   Lord Elgin at ease, with 'Flink' and 'Tim', May 1896.

cantonments were frequented by native women on a large scale. When the force was mobilised for the Chitral campaign, a disturbing number of men were found to be unfit. Some favoured a system of inspection and licensing, subjecting the prostitutes to regular checks but the purity party would have none of this, arguing that the men could be diverted from this basic urge by religion and the provision of reading and games rooms. The issue rumbled on throughout Elgin's time. In Britain the law permitting a system of prostitution inspection had been repealed in 1886 after a bitter campaign led by Josephine Butler.

Constance, from the early days in India, had been aware of the attractions of Henry Babington Smith. Bessie had found him charming and the relationship had indeed flourished so that a wedding was arranged, to take place at Simla in 1898, during the Elgin's last season there. The service was held in Christ Church, after which everyone went in a colourful procession up to the Viceregal Lodge. The viceroy, vicereine and the wedding party went first in carriages, with the Viceregal Bodyguard and the Punjab Light Horse glittering and clattering about them. Then came the carriages of the Commander in Chief and the Governor of the Punjab. Finally, due to the narrowness of the Simla roads limiting the number of carriages, the rest of the company struggled cheerfully up in rickshaws and on horseback. A truly gay occasion, featured a vast wedding cake nearly six feet high, on which the viceregal chef, Tancredi, had lovingly laboured over a period of several weeks. Henry turned out to be an ideal husband. He had a distinguished career ahead as a senior civil servant.

As Elgin's viceroyalty drew to its close he naturally wondered who his successor might be. He hoped for Lord Balfour of Burleigh, a fellow Scot, and like himself a man of care, judgment and steadiness. Instead it was George Nathaniel Curzon who was chosen to succeed. Curzon had been a great traveller, especially in Persia, India and the Far East, and an under-secretary at the Foreign Office, and had strong views on most things—Bessie referred to him in her diary as 'that rash man'. He was tall, slim and clean shaven and was to revel in the pageantry of India, antithetical to the short, bearded and sartorially rumpled Elgin. Moreover in his voluminous travel writings Curzon had developed a sense of global geopolitics in which India played a crucial part. Driven by his ideas, he was a compulsive worker, and had indeed reduced his health to a low ebb by the time of his appointment. Elgin could but wonder what the impact of such a man, replete with drive and insensitivity, might be on the delicate fabric of India. Elgin had an instinctive distrust of the busy moderniser let loose in the sub-continent. Curzon had, however, approved of Elgin's frontier policy and had assured Elgin that 'I shall find your courage and coolness of judgment the best of examples.' Elgin set about doing all he could to help Curzon make his preparations and settle in.

During the five years she had written her letter diary, Bessie had matured into a confident and now happily married woman. In spite of Viceregal remoteness from the peoples of India, she had absorbed something of the magic of the sub-continent in a way in which her father, with his many preoccupations had probably missed. She shared with her grandfather a sense of the mystery of transience that is so Indian. One evening while sitting under a banyan tree on the ramparts at Barrackpore exactly where her grandfather had been overwhelmed by sadness over the grave of Lady

Canning, she noted, 'it was curious to sit there and watch the carriages hurrying along the dusty red road and think that by next year we too shall be part of the past.' Elgin was not the kind of man to swallow the idea that the east held the secret of life. The practical preoccupations of his job had insulated him from this type of thinking. The general tenor of life for the British in India, of whom Elgin was one, was to look to Christianity for answers to the problems of humanity rather than to eastern cults and swamis

When Elgin left India the Raj, for all its troubles, had still plenty of strength, vitality and confidence. But he had sensed that within the incipient nationalism, there were powerful forces that ultimately could not be contained. India offered an irreduceable dilemma for if their people were educated, a policy which was necessary to staff the civil service, as well as being right in itself, then Indian aspirations, would eventually demand independence and the withdrawal of the British. But Elgin had not exacerbated these tensions, except perhaps in the matter of the cotton duties. He was against repressive press laws, punitive expeditions, sedition trials and the creation of nationalist martyrs. His father had pondered how a viceroy could make a great name for himself, and had concluded that this could be done only if his tenure coincided with some great storm such as the Mutiny: Victor Alexander was content simply to stabilise the system as far as he could, both in the face of ethnic and nationalist pressures and under the natural disasters which befell the country. Such modest aims merely caused those in Britain and in India to label the man who held them as mediocre.

But this image of Elgin was quite wrong. Elgin was a quiet unassuming man of good judgment. It was right of Elgin to choose the railway system as a focus for his renovative energies rather than, as with his sucessor, Curzon, to attempt to remake the entire civil service. Elgin was no less percipient about the army: its paramount need, he realised, was a better system of logistics and of transport. Chronic ethnic conflict and incipient nationalism were simply permanent parts of the Indian scene, to be met with a combination of moderation and firmness. Moderation was preferable to repression, but the message must be maintained that firmness, as embodied in the Indian army, would be used against serious breaches of order. As for the clamour for Indian participation, it was Elgin's hope that bringing Indians into a consultative role on provincial councils and elsewhere would not only strengthen such councils, but would meet, the immediate demand for a role in government. Elgin was never to provide the world with his own account of his viceregal stewardship, thus leaving an open field to his detractors. But in his heart of hearts he may well have felt that his Roman matron of a mother would not have been displeased.

Packing up was an enormous task. Like his father, Elgin was a keen collector, so that his baggage contained a host of mementos, including a large collection of Indian weapons and armour. The trappings of the retainers of Maharajahs and Nawabs, were redolent of the age of chivalry in Europe each identified by its tiny numbered disk of ivory. There were two immense elephant tusks mounted in silver, the gift of Rajah Bahadur, together with the embroidered Elgin coat of arms that had adorned the forehead of the viceregal elephant. There were solar topees and an elephant's foot umbrella stand, together with a host of illuminated presentation addresses. The faithful Babington Smith packed vast quantities of correspondence and other papers bearing

32 The Ninth Earl in full Ceremonial dress with Star as Knight Grand Commander of the Star of India, and Star of Knight Commander of the Indian Empire, with Queen Victoria's Jubilee medal in gold, in the robes of the Order of the Star of India and the Collar of the Order of the Star of India.

the legend: 'The Private Secretary of the viceroy.' Lady Christian had her photographs to augment the family's memories when its caravanserai had settled down once more at Broomhall in 1899. Elgin's beard was now fast greying, lending dignity to the photographic portrait taken on return and showing him resplendent in the robes of Grand Master of the Most Exalted Order of the Star of India.

Salmon, Boer War Logistics and the Wee Frees

Back home the family reunion was a joyful affair, with brothers and sisters together for the first time in five years. Constance brought their new son back from India, making eleven children in all. But, later perhaps regarding her duty as well done, she made frequent recuperative visits to the South of France leaving Elgin much to his own resources.

Elgin now discovered that he had emerged from India as an elder statesman. En route for home he had been offered and had accepted the vacancy in the Knighthood of the Garter. But in real terms he was high and dry. India had been a great challenge, a great exercise of power but now in effect he was back where he had been in 1893, unemployed. He felt the loss of his brother Robert, formerly his closest political ally and confidant. His party was out of government and was to remain so until the end of 1905. He was as adverse as ever to 'slogans' in the Liberal Party and had little sympathy with the incipient movement toward welfarism. He was held in high regard by Campbell-Bannerman, now the leader of the party, and other prominent Liberals, and he knew that Asquith was not his friend. His directorship of the Royal Bank of Scotland had lapsed and the Bank was unwilling to renew it, making him Deputy Governor instead, a post which carried no automatic entitlement to directors' fees. The Bank of Scotland tried to poach him but he remained true to his old allegiance. The Royal Bank's remuneration of its directors was curiously arranged: the guineas being slipped into tiny envelopes for each director. Only if someone were absent would Elgin, as Deputy Governor receive one, if not, not: the envelopes became part of the family papers at Broomhall.

For the next five years Elgin resumed his place at Broomhall, renewing his involvement with the affairs of Fife and of Scotland, and at a modest level, with the Scottish Liberal Party. He would sometimes amuse himself by comparing the miniscule affairs of Fife County Council with the ponderous deliberations of his viceroy's council. He concluded that despite the differences in scale and complexity, that there was no great difference either between the behaviour of the councillors in their respective contexts or the ways in which they required to be managed.

Meanwhile as Curzon settled into India he developed an easy way of patronising Elgin's viceroyalty, 'the apotheosis of bureaucracy' he said, and that Elgin had been the mere tool of his civil servants. It was Elgin's misfortune, to be succeeded by such a man as Curzon, with his flamboyance, categorical views, articulateness and attention-attracting policies and actions.

On the domestic front the affairs of Elma and Thurlow were still in confusion. Elma's estate of Dunphail was now heavily encumbered with debt, to the extent of some £130,000. Thurlow's creditors were numerous, and included tenants on the estate. Elgin knew Dunphail well, and indeed was very fond of it for it had the dual attraction of both mountains and river. He decided to act by clearing the Dunphail debts and thus becoming the estate's owner. In this way he took the financial pressure off Elma and Thurlow, as well as acquiring a most attractive property. Dunphail became an important part of Elgin family life. It also meant that by laying out so much money Elgin had reduced the assets of Broomhall, and brought back a measure of stringency to the family. It would seem that his annual income at this time was about £14,000, half coming from the Broomhall estate and half from investments. Sadly Elma's son Sigmund, a lieutenant in the Seaforth Highlanders, died in November 1899 and one month later another son, Fritz, was killed leading the 42nd Highlanders in the deadly charge at Magersfontein in South Africa.

With the liquidity of the estate reduced the affairs of Broomhall became once more

33 Dunfermline High Street. The welcome received by the Elgins on their return to Dunfermline from India. The crowds were said to be bigger than any seen before in the town.

a close preoccupation. Elgin kept the accounts with meticulous care in his own hand. After the Boer War, the government was considering sites for a new northern naval base. After much discussion the choice fell on Rosyth, a small village adjacent to Broomhall. This development was to complicate Elgin's life.

Between 1899 and 1905 Elgin was asked by the Conservative government to undertake three public inquiries. The first was to consider the damage being done to the salmon rivers of Britain by pollution from whatever cause, the second was to seek lessons from Britain's war effort against the Boers, in terms of organisation and logistics, and the third was to sort out a bitter quarrel over property which had arisen between the new United Free Church of Scotland and the 'Wee Frees', that element of the Free Presbyterian Church which had rejected union. In each case Elgin demonstrated his skill as a chairman, enabling notable reports to be produced.

Enquiries into the salmon problem took place between March 1900 and July 1902 when Elgin with his colleagues, (including the Duke of Bedford and the Earl of Moray), toured the salmon rivers. It was, in effect, one of the first environmental, ecological surveys to be undertaken in Britain. It proved a highly congenial task, researching a subject with which these gentlemen had been familiar all their lives, but which they now pursued in a wider sense. A special treat was that they travelled by steamer from the Firth of Forth to Aberdeen.

The current popular view was that the salmon catch had deteriorated seriously in recent years, due either to the abuse of their privileges by the net fishermen at the mouths of the rivers or to the continued encroachment of industrial pollution. The first task for Elgin and his commissioners was to establish whether the yield had indeed diminished and then, if so, to ascertain the reasons. Adequate data as to catches was lacking, for the net fishermen were remarkably coy about their takings. In the event the commissioners came to the conclusion that there had indeed been a fall in the catch, though not so dramatic as was feared. They were much struck by how little was really known about the salmon fishery but became convinced that there were rivers where netting was excessive. Pollution was becoming a serious threat from sewage and manufacturing, brewing and distilling effluents. Moreover salmon were hindered from entering many rivers because of the damming-back of water loaded with oxygen-destroying hydrogen sulphide and indeed toxic substances. Furthermore water was being drawn off from the river system by the great cities themselves greedy for water and showing as little ecological concern as the industrial pollutors. The commissioners recommended that a Central Authority for Great Britain should be set up in charge of all river fishery matters, and that there should be a Watersheds Board to control the general system. Neither recommendation was carried out. Before they returned to their estates the members of the commission presented Elgin with a silver cigarette box adorned with a 'Jock Scott' salmon fly set into the glass lid. It was a thoughtful gesture: although Elgin did not smoke.

The Royal Commission 'to inquire into the Military Preparations and other matters connected with the War in South Africa' bore more fruit. It was set up in some haste. It dealt with a touchy subject. It was common knowledge that the state of preparedness and the conduct of the campaign had left a good deal to be desired: this was accompanied by doubts whether the lessons so dearly bought had been learned. Elgin

34   The family re-united. Lady Elgin holds the youngest son, Victor, born in India.
Behind Elizabeth (Bessie) (front right) is her husband Henry Babington Smith.

approached the problem characteristically, determined to head off recriminations or any
'argumentative discussion or controversial questions, especially as between individual
officers'. The Commission sat in private taking evidence over fifty-five days examining
'the main system of the military system at home as well as in the field'. The Report,
together with the Evidence, is a key document in the history of the South African
War and the military developments that followed it.

The lack of preparedness was striking. There had been a terrible shortage of officers:
'It is impossible,' said the Report, 'not to condemn the system which could allow
Militia regiments to be sent to the front under officers who, in many cases, were
wholly untrained.' Ordnance had been insufficient for the forces it was intended to
support. The Army Medical Service had been seriously below standard. Little thought
had been given to the requirements of transport. On the matter of procurement, the
financial arrangements were such that commanders did not know what purchasing
authority they actually had. At the level of military philosophy, the commanders had
failed to appreciate what wide-open warfare entailed: at the beginning of the war, said
the Report, 'it was impossible to convince either officers or men of the necessity of
taking cover in the face of rifle fire until they had learned by sad experience in severe

losses.' Whereas the Boers fighting a guerrilla war quickly dug narrow deep trenches, 'our men had not much idea'.

These lessons had been learned in the field at great human cost during the fighting, but as the Report concluded, 'We are not satisfied that enough is being done to place matters on a better footing in the event of another emergency.' The most important recommendation of Elgin and his colleagues was that 'no military system will be satisfactory which does not contain powers of expansion outside the limit of the regular forces of the Crown, whatever that limit might be.' Here was the kernel of the idea of the Territorial Army, which Haldane was to form in 1907 and which did such fine service in the First World War.

Elgin's final inquiry emphasised that India was not the only place that could generate religious faction to the point of zealotry. In Scotland, that land of hard-headed realists, religious passions had long been endemic and now there was still an issue that could cause them to boil. In the late 1890s the Free Presbyterian Church and the United Presbyterian Church, in a major act of healing of Scottish religious fissures, had begun negotiations for union. But a small minority of the Free Presbyterian Church who believed such talks to be a betrayal, broke away in 1898, thus encouraging the irreverent to call them the 'Wee Frees'. In 1900 the union of the two churches went ahead forming the United Free Church. But with their principal strength in the Highlands the Wee Frees continued with their Calvinistic, fundamentalist, theocratic principles, unaffected by the liberal theological thinking of the day. Indeed they claimed that they were not only the inheritors of the true doctrines of the Free Church, but also the rightful heirs of its physical property, including churches, schools and other assets. This placed the new United Free Church, which had managed to come into being largely by avoiding possible theological conflict, in a weak position ideologically. There may have seemed something slightly ridiculous about the rump or the tail wagging the dog and the Court of Session ruled that the United Presbyterian Church was in the right whereupon the House of Lords reversed the verdict and awarded the whole church property to the Free Presbyterian Church.

Here was an intimately Scottish imbroglio, quite mystifying to the English, for the resolution of which Elgin was the ideal man. In December 1904 a Royal Commision, with Elgin as its chairman, was set up to receive evidence and to divide the property. It was a telling tribute to his integrity that after three years deliberation, neither side, as *The Times* noted, disputed Elgin's final adjudication. But it was a heavy task, demanding much patience, preventing any resumption of his political career. As a Scot, Campbell-Bannerman appreciated the difficulty of the task: he especially admired Lord Elgin's Royal Commission work.

The inquiry first met on 11 January 1905, in the splendid Hall of the Merchant Company of Edinburgh. Elgin presided over twelve sittings, hearing fifty-two witnesses, some at great length. Each day drew a crowded and attentive audience, the matter concerning as it did so many Scotsmen deeply concerned with church affairs. Beneath the profound courtesy of the exchanges there was, often an extreme bitterness scarcely hidden. The evidence harked all the way back to the Great Disruption of the Church of Scotland in 1843 out of which the Free Church had emerged. In the generation that followed the Free Church had, by great effort and devotion, and at great cost, constructed an entire new system of Churches, manses, colleges and the like, as well as being very active in setting up missions in Africa and India. Antique veterans of the Disruption and the years following duly bore their witness. The Wee Frees had in a sense a good case, namely their claim that they were the true heirs of the theology of Dr. Chalmers, Dr. Candlish and other leaders of the new Church of 1843. They felt bound in conscience to fight for the full inheritance, incongruous though this might seem to others. On the other hand in the sixty or so intervening years the United Presbyterians had made concessions to a more liberal theology as they tried to come to terms with evolutionary science, and had failed to press home on its members the full weight of Calvinist doctrine. A final factor was that the Wee Frees had only a couple of hundred, mostly Highland, congregations and so did not have a valid claim to be a national church, whereas the United Free Church had over a thousand. It was inconceivable to Elgin and his colleagues that so tiny a cadre could possibly fulfil the functions and obligations implied in the buildings and monies involved. Accordingly they recommended that a neutral Commission be set up to allocate each property separately doing so partly on the basis of moral claim, but mainly in terms of which church could make the most effective use of the respective assets.

It was a fine testimony to Elgin's chairmanship that he could maintain this inquiry at a civilised level; elicit the facts concerning very complicated finances and apply them to resolve the problem. He had managed to contain the ever-increasing acerbity between the two ill-matched churches, but suggested that the United Free Church might have given more consideration earlier to their Wee Free brethern. By Act of Parliament a body was set up to proceed along the lines which Elgin had recommended.

CHAPTER 21

The Colonial Office and the Young Winston

Elgin's success in chairing his Royal Commissions, together with his reputation for steadiness in India, strongly commended him to Campbell-Bannerman, the new Prime Minister when, at long last, the Conservative government under the indeterminate Balfour fell in December 1905, and the Liberals came once more into power. Elgin's chairmanship of the 'Boer War' enquiry had contributed something to the Liberal victory, for a section of the public had been impressed with his Committee's revelations as to the incompetence with which the Unionists had conducted the Boer War. Elgin was called to the cabinet as Colonial Secretary. Campbell-Bannerman's first intention had been to raise Elgin to the eminence of Foreign Secretary; but Asquith persuaded the Prime Minister that Edward Grey would be a better choice. Elgin, for his part, would have preferred something less exacting in the cabinet hierarchy, renewing his preference for the Scottish Office.

Throughout his tenure at the Colonial Office Elgin continued his long established habit of sharing his problems with Constance. He wrote to her at length when she was so often away in the South of France expressing his puzzlement and misgiving about policies in so many parts of the world, especially South Africa, where there were so few real solutions and so much to be settled.

Joseph Chamberlain had regarded the Colonial Office as a major ministry, perhaps the most important of all, hence his preferring it to any other in 1895. Chamberlain envisaged a Britain returned to protectionism and the empire integrated by preferential tariffs as well as sentiment. Now a decade later, Elgin and his Liberal Party had no such integrating vision and grand goal, but saw the empire in much looser terms. There was thus no obvious objective for Elgin to strive for, just as was the case in India in both his and his father's time.

The rift in outlook between Elgin and some of his Liberal colleagues had grown wider. Like Gladstone, he could not sympathise with wide-ranging ideas involving the state in social welfare of the kind favoured by the young radicals, Lloyd George and Winston Churchill: this he believed was 'slogans' and faddism gone mad. Nor could he enthuse over 'Liberal Imperialism', a philosophy held by Asquith, Grey and others. This regarded the empire as a great moral force on the side of progress, justice and co-operation between peoples capable of bringing amelioration to much of mankind both directly and by example, combating oppression and spreading enlightenment. Elgin could not really warm to this vision. For these reasons he was of the old guard, without any sort of alliance in the cabinet or the party. He had, however, a

35   Lord Elgin as Colonial Secretary, in Frock Coat, the waistcoat was made specially with an additional deep pocket behind for carrying speeches and notes. Elgin also used it to carry the Cullinan diamond (uncut), from the Colonial Office to Buckingham Palace, *c.* 1907.

supporter in Haldane, the new secretary for war, who admired his Boer War Report and indeed based his own thinking about army reorganisation on part of it.

Campbell-Bannerman, perhaps a little mischievously, gave Elgin Winston Churchill as his under-secretary. Churchill was then thirty-one years old; Elgin was fifty six. Churchill had just, scarcely a year earlier, abandoned his Conservative allegiance for the Liberals. In consequence there was much distrust of him on both sides of the House as a careerist turncoat. Yet he had made such a mark and shown such capabilities that it was not considered safe to keep him out of office. For his part Churchill, with Elgin safely removed in the Lords, no doubt felt that he could project himself in the lower chamber as the true voice of the Colonial Office, a usurpation he was indeed to attempt.

Elgin had met Churchill briefly in India when as a subaltern the young man had visited him at Barrackpore newly returned from service with the Malakand Field Force. Bessie commented in her letter diary: 'Mr. Churchill (in Captain Baring's Regiment) ... is short, with reddish hair and face, blue eyes and 'some of his father's characteristics,' I have been told.' Churchill was in so many ways the antithesis of Elgin, being a self-made celebrity, adept at achieving centre-stage. He had served in the Indian Army for three years. In his popular account of the Malakand expedition he had used inside information of friends in high places, to criticise 'Bobs', later Lord Roberts, then the Commander-in-Chief in India, and the Conservative Secretary of State for War. He had seen further fighting in Cuba, the Sudan and South Africa, firmly establishing himself as a man of action. But he was also a man of ideas having strong convictions on all the major topics of the day, he had rejected the Tory drift towards protectionism and instead embraced free trade and the Liberal party. As a born orator Churchill had no fear of audiences in parliament or elsewhere; Elgin on the other hand was very nervous about making speeches in the Lords or anywhere. Churchill was driven by an overpowering ambition for power, reinforced by his urge to achieve what he believed had been denied his father, Lord Randolph Churchill. That his father had treated him so badly and had died of general paralysis of the insane he passed over. In short, Elgin and his assistant were antithetical men. Curzon had already busied himself upstaging Elgin's performance in India, and Churchill was now poised to do the same as Elgin's under-secretary at the Colonial Office.

There Elgin presided over the affairs of a myriad of societies of all shapes and sizes, doing so sight unseen. In India, however remote he had been from the daily life of the peoples, he had visited much of the country and met and conversed with a good many of its important men. In the case of the colonies, his dealings were concluded largely on paper: there were endless memoranda, reports, letters, submissions. A daily flood of such documentation reached the office, to be reduced by Elgin's civil servants to a mass that was manageable enough for his desk. In each case the colony concerned had a history and a culture which it was highly dangerous to ignore, but with which Elgin's staff had only a passing acquaintance. In the most recent chapters of many such colonial histories the previous government of the Conservative Unionist Party had intervened, sometimes giving undertakings with which the successor Liberal government did not agree. Each colony had a Governor whose views and susceptibilities had to be considered. As governorships fell vacant there was the task of finding an appropriate new man. Occasionally replacement happened prematurely when a governor resigned because of scandal or died in office.

Africa, South, West and East, were to be the great preoccupation of Elgin and Churchill at the Colonial Office with South Africa presenting the most intransigent problem of all. It had been conquered in the expensive Boer War, between 1899-1902, bitterly divisive in Britain and arousing great criticism and hostility in other countries including France, Germany and even Tsarist Russia. In all these countries the Boers were regarded as a fine God-fearing people, innocently cultivating their fields when they were gratuitously attacked by the greatest of imperial powers. But in fact the Boers were proud and determined men, bitterly resenting defeat and colonial status under an alien power.

Before the Liberal government came to power the Unionists had already made concessions to the Boers in the Transvaal which the Liberal Government found very difficult to accept or implement. The most serious of these had been to rubber-stamp the import of indentured Chinese labour to the mines of the Rand. Indeed as a Liberal election cry the attack on the idea of Chinese labour had been second only to the cry of free trade itself. Sir Alfred Milner had been High Commissioner in South Africa since 1897, and was virtually its ruler. To the Liberals he was a dangerous man, who by insisting upon outright imperial control had precipitated the South African War. His policies might still, they feared, induce in South Africa a running conflict between Briton and Boer, all too reminiscent of Ireland. On the other hand the Unionists had issued letters patent promising to establish representative institutions. Would not this mean handing the colony back to the Boers? The war, had already cost Britain thousands of lives and much treasure as well as the loss of international esteem. Was the only reward to be a set of insoluble problems?

In West and East Africa the Liberals found themselves presiding over the British share of the divided continent which had been pencilled out by the Europeans some twenty years earlier. When Elgin entered the Colonial Office in 1906 Britain had assumed responsibility for Northern and Southern Nigeria, the Gold Coast, Nyasaland, Uganda, Kenya and Somaliland. Here was a great African empire, which unlike India, was newly forged, stretching in its miscellaneous forms across the vast tracts of the continent. Other European nations, the French and Belgians and the Germans, had seized their chance to intrude and the Portuguese had extended their long-held territories. Until now the Gladstonian Liberals had had little to do with these vast acquisitions, having regarded them as an unfortunate extension of British interests which would without doubt cause trouble and worry. But they now had to administer them. What was to be done with these new possessions with conditions almost as varied as India, stretching from the tropical rain forest of the west to the savanna grass lands of the east, with ancient and warlike tribal divisions, in some places overlaid with the religion of Islam?

Apart from South and Mid-Africa there were the white self-governing colonies including Canada, Newfoundland, Australia and New Zealand, together with a mixed group consisting of the West Indies, British Guiana, Gibraltar, Malta, Cyprus, Fiji, Ceylon and many minor states. The white colonies were not without difficulties, but at least their mode of self-government had been settled. Could other parts of the empire be led along this path? In his agonised search for a solution in Ireland, Gladstone had drawn upon the example of Canada, brought to responsible government by Lord Durham and the eighth Earl of Elgin. He had even described the Canadian solution as 'the greatest triumph of British statesmanship'. Indeed some sort of self government, on the Canadian plan had become the great objective of Liberal imperial thinking, at least where participation in government by colonial people seemed reasonable.

But self-government no longer inspired the same all-round approval: Elgin himself, once ardent for Home Rule in Ireland, now hoped that the Irish Question would be left dormant, at least for the time being. In the South African case, however, Elgin did have confidence in the Canadian example as a means of reconciling Briton and Boer and of providing stable government. As an interested party he had carefully read the published accounts as well as his father's personal papers. He wrote to Lord Selbourne the new High Commissioner in South Africa that in Canada 'The feeling between the British and French had been even more hostile than that between Briton and Boer'. Elgin presented a copy of his father's published letters to Churchill, advising him to read the portions dealing with the Canadian crisis into which Elgin himself had been born.

The Peace of Vereeniging, signed at Pretoria on 31 May 1902, brought to an end a war, damaging and divisive. In order to achieve a treaty quickly all sorts of problems had been shunted to one side. By the time Elgin was settled at the Colonial Office the problems were clear and intractable. Who was to govern? How was power to be divided between Boer and Briton? What about the Chinese coolie labour, referred to in the Liberal election campaign of 1905 as 'Chinese Slave Labour' and did anyone give a thought to the rights of the black majority population?

In a sense it was the constitutional question that raised once more the very issue over which the South African War had been fought. Though defeated, the Boer generals wanted the Transvaal to become a Boer republic, hoping to gain through the new constitution what they had lost in arms. Meanwhile the British in the colony were terrified of being handed over to their deadly foes. The Liberals were in a dilemma. Their philosophy did not allow them to play the part of victors and impose a settlement: in any case this would be a dangerous game considering the tensions already there. They had pinned their hopes on the idea of self government similar to that in the white dominions, but the Boers and the Britons were roughly equal in numbers in the Transvaal (though the British paid nine-tenths of the taxes), so that a system of one man one vote ran the risk of giving power to the Boers. This was particularly abhorrent in respect of the Rand mining lords, who with their right to import coolie labour, were looked upon by the Liberals with suspicion if not contempt. More than that, the Treaty had laid it down that the question of political rights for the natives should remain in abeyance until the introduction of self-government. If some sort of dominion status were conferred on the white population in South Africa, then all non-whites, including coolies, Indians and the black races, might be entrusted in effect, to the white Boer majority.

After much discussion it was agreed, with Elgin's approval, that there should be full white adult male suffrage; property qualifications as a means of limiting the suffrage were also discussed but eventually abandoned. As to the constituencies, the case was made for the principal of 'one vote one value'. Constituencies were drawn not in terms of population but of voters. This favoured the urbanised British section of the population, which contained an unusually large proportion of adult males, as compared with the rural Boer areas where men lived in nuclear families, with wives, children and dependants. It was a form of rigging to which Elgin could see no alternative. Under the new constitution the Transvaal government took office under Botha, on 21 March 1907, with a strong British presence in the assembly.

Representative government having been granted to the Transvaal it could hardly be denied to the Orange River Colony. Elgin worked on this every day through the Christmas recess of December 1906. The Colony had an overwhelming Boer majority which had a reputation for being disaffected. Selborne, the High Commissioner, horrified at the prospect of a Boer republic, urged on Elgin that the Colony should be ruled by a Governor, in the manner of a Crown Colony. This advice was rejected by Elgin who argued that here was the supreme test of trusting the Boers, and that a truly representative form of government would improve the chances of the colony eventually favouring a South African Federation. As a protection for the British urban minority, provision was made for separate representation for the towns.

How would the Transvaal and Orange River Colony assemblies deal with the two great questions, Chinese labour and native rights? Elgin thoroughly distrusted the Rand magnates and the other new breed, the South African capitalist and speculator. But a heavy and irreversible dependence on the mines as a vital and growing part of the economy, had already developed in the Transvaal. Labour problems involving blacks and Chinese were inevitable. Life was particularly grim in the Chinese mine compounds where, without any women, sodomy was practised. Mine managers also countenanced flogging which was illegal. The Liberal Prime Minister, Campbell-Bannerman had referred to employment of indentured Chinese labour as, 'a system indistinguishable in many of its features from slavery' and the Liberal government had to decide what to do about it. By the end of February 1906 a four part policy had been worked out. The government agreed to accept existing licences, and those in respect of Chinese who had signed contracts but not arrived in South Africa, they would try to insist that the Chinese were not physically abused, they would repatriate those who wished to go home and they would hand over the ultimate decision as to the continuance of Chinese coolie labour to the newly created Tranvaal government when it took power. This last provision, however, was not absolute. Elgin and Churchill agreed that if the new government of the Transvaal did decide to continue the coolie system, the British government would advise the King to operate his right of veto. In this way it became clear that the British government, under certain circumstances, would maintain its ultimate responsibility for what went on in a colony.

The Chinese problem was immediate: the native one had not really matured. The old tribal pattern, with its chiefs, its villages and its largely self supporting economy was still largely unaffected. Nevertheless the warlike tendencies of the tribes were still strong. In February and March 1906 there were disturbances among the Zulus in Natal, when two white policemen were killed. Twelve Africans were convicted of the murders and sentenced to death. When the Colonial Office sent a telegram requesting that the sentence be suspended for a time, the government of Natal, resigned en bloc. The matter was smoothed over, Elgin expressing concern that the Natal government should think that London wished to interfere. Nevertheless the incident demonstrated a conflict of views between those whites remote from reality in the Colonial Office in London and those whites who lived close to African peoples whom they regarded as savages not entitled to consideration. Elgin sadly noted that the temper of the colonists was 'getting very dangerous'. Indeed three thousand Africans were killed that summer, and 4,000 were taken and held prisoner in order to stamp out black resistance. In this climate and with these attitudes there could be no hope for any policy which advocated that black men as well as white men should have the vote.

Elgin deeply regretted that under the Treaty of Vereeniging the Unionists had pledged that 'The question of granting the franchise to natives will not be decided until the granting of self-government'. Drawing on his Indian experience where his Council had had native representation, he believed that a reasonable presence of natives could do only good. He sensed the future risk of generalised conflict between black and white. The dilemma was the same as with the Chinese coolies: how were the rights of non-whites to be protected by the imperial power once the state in question had been granted self-government? Elgin did what he could: he kept Swaziland apart and under the direct rule of the British High Commissioner. He considered setting up a department of native affairs, again under the High Commissioner, but recognised that this would be hard to reconcile with colonial self-government. Dimly, in the background in the event of direct confrontation between London and the local government in South Africa was the possibility that the British government might veto colonial legislation, but this was a remote safeguard indeed. The first draft of the Transvaal Constitution had provided for a native trust, a corporation to take hold and dispose of lands in the interest of the Africans but certain clauses in this had not pleased the Lord Chancellor and it had been withdrawn. In the end it was agreed that there must be imperial consent for legislation imposing differentials on account of race, and a permissive clause was included which would allow a native council to be set up. Elgin, too optimistically as it turned out, believed that the new governments would seek to implement these clauses and thus seek to come to terms with the African population. Perhaps his inclination to trust the Boers owed something to his knowledge of his father's success with the French in Canada. But in Canada there was no complicating third party of natives, greatly outnumbering the whites, whose interests could so easily be unrecognised.

Although in the case of the black African Elgin's heart was in the right place and his instincts were correct neither he nor the British Parliament had in the long term the power to safeguard their future. Short of repudiating a critical clause in the Treaty and risking a renewal of conflict, or at the least an intransigent Boer population, Elgin had no choice but to trust the Boers. He was in effect in their hands, he had to believe that they would be loyal to British interests, and that they would give fair treatment to the African majority. The gamble in a sense did pay off, for South Africa remained in the Commonwealth for another fifty-five years. In the short run the Liberal government in London gained much prestige, which tended to nullify the bad press which Britain had had over the war. Certainly in British school textbooks the granting of self government to white South Africans was presented as a triumph of magnanimity and justice.

Elgin continued to ponder the role of all the native peoples under any sort of colonial government. He knew that the peasantry of the Punjab suffered greatly from being in a permanent state of indebtedness. He recognesed that the South African black had in effect no protection from exploitation. He resolved at least to gather evidence on this difficult and controversial matter. In September 1907 Elgin directed that the Colonial Office should conduct 'a comprehensive and exhaustive consideration of the whole subject'. Elgin's directive read 'I should like the great subject of the native populations to be thoroughly discussed in this Office'. It was his intention, after due preparation, to bring the whole matter to the Cabinet. But Elgin was dropped from the government soon after, so that his plan for a comprehensive enquiry was never carried out. The status and condition of the blacks in South Africa or indeed any other colony could continue to deteriorate. Although individuals may have deplored the unprotected position of many native peoples, no one of power and influence, after Elgin's departure, considered taking up their cause.

It seemed to Elgin that the newly acquired British possessions in East and West Africa might offer a better chance of generating a really enlightened form of imperialism. Both areas were free of entrenched whites and while West Africa, with its equatorial conditions, would never sustain white settlement, East Africa with its high plateau and fine climate could prove attractive to whites. The Liberals had never approved the phase of imperial African expansionism. Elgin like many other Liberals deplored the imposition of political boundaries on tribal societies. As Elgin remarked about the carve up, 'so far as I can see on absolutely arbitrary lines ... there was never any pretence whatever of consulting the desires or wishes of the millions of inhabitants of that great continent. There was a risk in multiplying what we call white man's countries, where there are a very small number of whites in the midst of an overwhelming number of blacks.' Here again was an Elgin, like his father before him, the reluctant imperialist. However the 9th Earl conceded that there had been 'difficulties which required a remedy,' and which had led to British intervention. He also believed that, troublesome though it was to control primitive tribes, the people of Britain had a 'mission as pioneers of civilisation,' discharging this duty largely by bringing peace to warring tribes. The Colonial Office staff took a more mundane view, believing that tropical possessions were essential for the provision of necessary food and raw materials.

Having inherited so much of tropical Africa as part of the job, the great questions became for Elgin how should British rule be most effectively expressed? Should the administration of a country like Nigeria be rationalised and made self-supporting through the tax system. In Nigeria the Colonial Office resisted Lugard's attempts to open up the country quickly by military means, emphasising the need for 'peaceful penetration'. In December 1905, the only unsubdued tribe, the Munshi, burned one of the Niger Company's stations; in the following February there was a Mahdi rising in Sokoto. Once more, as in India, Elgin was confronted with demands for a punitive expedition. In March some two thousand unarmed natives of Satiru were killed. Elgin, and indeed his junior, Churchill, deplored the unnecessary violence, especially as such actions inevitably made for awkward and damaging confrontations in parliament. In the end Elgin continued to resist the demands for punitive expeditions, for which he was given much credit, although he agreed that occasionally a show of force could serve a useful purpose.

Elgin, though he regretted that 'We engaged in a game of grab in the African continent,' accepted that with a *fait accompli* 'we cannot escape the consequences.' Had the British remained passive, others including the French, the Germans and the Belgians would merely have extended their claims. Such inaction would have outraged the British merchants who with their associates were eager to plant huge rubber forests and make other claims on the environment.

The other parts of the straggling colonial system made their demands and posed their own individual problems. In Ceylon how should the terms on which the pearl fishery be let to a British syndicate be negotiated? In Newfoundland there was a long

36   That the ministerial team at the Colonial Office should consist of the Colonial Secretary, the quiet Elgin, and as Under Secretary, the ebullient Churchill, aroused public interest and intrigued the cartoonists. A condominium was being arranged with the French in the New Hebrides at this time. *Punch* cartoon (E.T. Reed), 27 March 1907. Winston Churchill had labelled the Colonial Office 'an exceedingly fashionable department'.

37 The Colonial Conference was held in London from 15 April to 14 May 1907. In the course of the proceedings, the chairman, Lord Elgin, said 'Yes, self-governing Dominions is what we call you here'. (Colonial Conference Minutes, p. 82).

1. The Hon. H. H. Asquith, MP — Chancellor of the Exchequer
2. The Hon. Sir J. G. Ward, KCMG — Prime Minister, New Zealand
3. The Hon. Sir Wilfred Laurier, GCMG — Prime Minister, Canada
4. The Rt. Hon. The Earl of Elgin, KG — Secretary of State for the Colonies
5. The Hon. Alfred Deakin — Prime Minister, Australia
6. The Hon. R. F. Moor — Prime Minister, Natal
7. The Rt. Hon. D. Lloyd-George, MP — President of the Board of Trade
8. Winston S. Churchill, MP — Under Secretary of State for the Colonies
9. Sir Francis Hopwood, KCB — Permanent Under Secretary of State for the Colonies
10. General The Hon. Louis Botha — Prime Minister, Transvaal
11. Sir J. L. Mackay — India Office
12. H. W. Just, CB — Joint Secretary, Colonial Office
13. The Hon. L. P. Brodeur — Minister, Marine and Fisheries, Canada
14. Rt. Hon. Sir R. Bond, KCMG — Prime Minister, Newfoundland
15. Sir W. A. Baillie Hamilton — Dominion Department, Colonial Office
16. J. W. Holderness —
17. G. W. Johnson, CMG — Joint Secretary, Colonial Office
18. Hon. Sir William Lyne, KCMG — Minister, Trade and Customs, Australia
19. W. A. Robinson — Assistant Secretary, Colonial Office
20. Hon. Dr. Smartt — Commissioner, Public Works, Cape Colony
21.
22. Hon. Sir F. W. Borden, KCMG — Minister, Militia and Defence, Canada

NOT PRESENT: Hon. L. S. Jameson — Prime Minister, Cape Colony standing quarrel with the United States over fishery rights to be resolved. In the New Hebrides in the South Pacific, there was a delicate convention with the French to be negotiated, bringing into being a condominium, which had also to satisfy the requirements of the touchy Australians. Over this there was something of a stand off between Elgin and Arthur Deakin, the voluble Prime Minister of Australia. The white Australia policy was an embarrassment to Elgin's Colonial Office because some of its pronouncements implied the inferiority of 'Asiatics'; Elgin and his men tried to get such affronts toned down, especially as they might relate to the Japanese, bound by treaty to Britian since 1902. The Governor-Generalship of Australia proved not an easy position to fill.

The Colonial Conference of April and May 1907 was a testing time for Elgin. His cabinet colleagues were only mildly interested, being more concerned with the Hague disarmament conference going on at the same time. And yet the Colonial Conference aired many problems and proved a useful forum for many more. Elgin had discerned shortly after taking up his appointment that the Colonial Office required reorganisation in order to meet new demands. Had Elgin had time to work out reforms for the Colonial Office he might have forestalled a good deal of criticism. Unlike the 8th Earl, the 9th Earl was not good at conviviality either with colonials or anyone else, but he was a paragon of patience especially in dealing with Prime Minister Deakin of Australia who brought with him all his irritation with what he judged to be the condescension on the part of the Colonial Office staff. The Conference was of course confined to the self-governing Colonies, with India and the 'dependent empire' excluded. Its principal preoccupation lay with the question, how should Britain and these new self-governing countries relate to one another in future and could they provide the world with an altogether new concept of empire? The idea of a Dominions department, 'self-contained but within the Colonial Office' whose Secretary would also act for the regular colonial conferences, was favourably received and approved after discussion by the British government.

On the question of who was entitled to attend the colonial conference, however, there arose a war of wills. Elgin wished to keep the conference small and manageable, Churchill embraced the claims of the state premiers of the various South African and Australian colonies, and a mixed bag of others, arguing the right of all such men to be heard. Though King Edward VII shared Churchill's view, Elgin stuck to his guns and won.

By and large Elgin emerged from the Conference with credit. He had upheld the Liberal view of empire, and indeed had assisted notably with its transition to Commonwealth. He had contained under his chairmanship a host of men with strongly held views, whose susceptibilities about Britain's colonial role were very tender. Arthur Deakin had remained a thorn in the side of the Colonial Secretary while Sir Wilfred Laurier, the Canadian Prime Minister spent his time diplomatically manoeuvring around everybody trying to keep the peace. The University of Cambridge recognised his achievement on 12 June by awarding him an honorary degree along with Campbell-Bannerman the Prime Minister, Haldane, Curzon and Milner. One of the medical professors took the opportunity of calling Elgin's attention to the need to develop tropical medicine within the empire.

It was bad luck that the self effacing Elgin should have been in harness at the Colonial Office with the expansive and aggressive Winston Churchill. The younger man had ambitions to be prime minister by his early forties: he had no time to lose, hence the aura of relentless ambition that surrounded him, reinforced by his insatiable work drive. He was deeply unpopular, made so by his arrogance and his capacity for making enemies along with his reputation as a turncoat. But his energy and cleverness were already widely recognised. Elgin became accustomed to his *volte face*, his excitability, his exuberance, his audacity. His ebullience in writing papers made unnecessary labour for others, for his purple passages could not always go unchallenged. Occasionally

PUNCH, OR THE LONDON CHARIVARI.—JULY 31, 1907.

"PARTING IS SUCH SWEET SORROW."

LORD ELGIN. "WELL, MY BOY, YOU SEE I'M HELPING TO GET YOU OFF, THOUGH I SHALL MISS YOU TERRIBLY. YOU MUST BE SURE TO HAVE A GOOD REST, *AND, WHATEVER YOU DO, DON'T HURRY BACK!*"

[The COLONIAL SECRETARY has expressed a desire that Mr. CHURCHILL should visit Uganda and British East Africa in the recess.]

38   *Punch* cartoon (Bernard Patridge), 31 July 1907.

when he realised from Elgin's comments that he had gone too far he would modify his language. There was a sense in which from his youth Churchill had been taken prisoner by his own rhetoric, perhaps even his views being affected by the possibility of a felicitous phrase. There were times, moreover, when Churchill verged on disloyalty: he informed the prime minister that with respect to the Colonial Office, 'Practically all the constructive action and all of the parliamentary exposition has been mine.' His direct and privileged access to other ministers, the prime minister and indeed on occasion, the King, meant that Elgin could never be quite sure what seeds Churchill had sown outside the Office. Within it Churchill would air his disagreements with his chief in circulated minutes read by all in the Office.

All this Elgin bore with extraordinary restraint and fortitude. He carefully prevented any of his differences from degenerating into a quarrel. He described his Churchill problem to Constance, but kept his own counsel otherwise, in spite of the amused gossip and cartoons in *Punch*. One anecdote recounted that at the end of a long memorandum Churchill had concluded with the words, 'These are my views', below which Elgin had written 'But not mine.' A few perceptive colleagues realised that Elgin had his young charge well in hand: Haldane wrote of Elgin, 'He is absolute master of the Colonial Office.' There can be no doubt, however, that Churchill damaged Elgin's reputation there and in the cabinet, just as Curzon had allowed himself to hint at criticism of his viceroyalty in India. Elgin's reward for restraint as regards Churchill was that his junior may thus have helped to end his career by promoting an image of him as ineffectual and finicky. For all this, however, Churchill was not consciously malicious in his feelings toward Elgin, merely insensitive. His ambition required that he find a cause, indeed a series of causes to punctuate his career. The affairs of the Colonial Office, in their complexity, did not provide the ringing battle cries for which Churchill yearned, causing him to live in an atmosphere of continuous frustration. This was apparent from his inability to judge the relative importance of the views he so ardently embraced. Elgin had the misfortune to be one of the first victims of the pent-up ambition of this buccaneering spirit.

Sir Henry Campbell-Bannerman died on 22 April 1908. He had been a good friend to Elgin, one of the few who saw into the merits of the man. With him died Elgin's political career. The new Prime Minister H.H. Asquith, held Elgin in no great regard and dropped him from his cabinet. The news was leaked in the *Daily Chronicle*. Later Elgin received the briefest note of dismissal. It was deeply hurtful. He offered to make Elgin a marquis, which Elgin declined. Elgin wrote only to Lord Tweedmouth of his humiliating experience, 'I feel that even a housemaid gets a better warning'. He could discover no reason for his dismissal. There was no prospect of another appointment.

The points of view of both Elgin and Asquith, though antithetical, are both understandable. Elgin enjoyed his work within the Colonial Office, but he detested the necessary speeches in the Lords, especially in support of general government bills which were being systematically wrecked by the Unionist peers. The Smallholders (Scotland) Bill, of which he disapproved, providing for the extension of the Crofter Acts to the whole of Scotland, threw him into something of a panic. As a Scotch Liberal peer he was required to support such government bills in the House of Lords a task which he particularly disliked.

He poured out his misgivings to Constance, wondering whether 'to throw up the sponge.' 'I hate this debating,' he wrote, 'and do it so badly.' The House of Lords had become for him a place of fear and torture. Also telling against Elgin was his lack of participation in the social side of politics; he was seldom seen in the salon. Then, too, he was a member of no particular group of cronies and so could bring little influence to bear on the new Prime Minister. Even so it was a great shock to be dismissed from the cabinet in such a summary fashion. In this way Elgin was forcibly retired in April 1908, aged 59.

CHAPTER 22

The Thane of Fife

Elgin had been Lord Lieutenant of the Kingdom of Fife since 1886; as such he had been the direct representative of Victoria and Edward in the ancient kingdom of Macduff. He was indeed the Thane of Fife. It was in this role that, at the age of 60, he now settled down, immersing himself once more of the affairs of his Kingdom, his parish and his estate. At the request of Lord Crewe, his successor at the Colonial Office, he wrote a long letter setting out his experience of the Office and his ideas concerning it: this was his last political act. Thereafter he closed his official past, stored his papers in five boxes and sealed them for fifty years. The House of Lords knew him no more. The actions of the Asquith ministry under the driving force of Lloyd George and Churchill were in general no concern of his although they were to threaten Broomhall itself. Andrew Carnegie who had left Dunfermline as a penniless boy, still regarded Elgin as his clan chief and persuaded him to become chairman of the Carnegie Trust for the Universities of Scotland. He was elected by the students of the University of Aberdeen as their Lord Rector, and in 1914 became Chancellor of the University.

Constance died in 1909. She had born Elgin eleven children and had sustained a number of miscarriages. She had accepted the challenge of India without demur, encouraged her husband where he hesitated, and been her husband's confidante over public affairs. Over the many issues that had confronted Elgin, Constance had been no cypher, but had held and frequently offered her own views. Her later illnesses, involving long periods of separation, had been a sorry trial both to her and to Elgin.

The estate of Broomhall resumed its habit of troubling its owner as it had done for four generations. But this time there was a difference. The threat came not from within the economy of the estate, but from local and national government outside. Elgin owned all the land between old Dunfermline and the Rosyth Naval Base. He knew that the growth of the naval base and the town would increase the demand for working class housing. Accordingly he began to make a long-term plan to develop the estate. He wished to avoid housing congestion, and indeed proposed to develop a garden city. By feuing land in this way the additional population inevitably drawn into the area by the growth of Rosyth would be accommodated in a proper manner.

Others had different plans. A Tramway Company was promoted in 1906 to link Dunfermline with Rosyth: whatever its route it must travel over Elgin's land. The Burgh of Dunfermline now made a move, applying in 1911 to the government for power to extend its boundaries and thereby embrace much Elgin land within Dunfermline. The leading spirit in this was ex-Provost Macbeth, who was to become Elgin's bête noire.

Elgin would have preferred that responsibility for his land between Dunfermline and Rosyth should be left to the County Council, with only a limited extension of the Burgh. Having already town-planned a considerable part of the area himself, he felt that a collaboration with the County would be much more congenial. But the Dunfermline Burgh Extension and Drainage Act of August 1911 signalled Elgin's defeat. He accepted the outcome stoically remarking that now his land was included within the Burgh, 'we should loyally meet the Burgh in their Town Planning schemes.'

But Elgin had an even more formidable enemy than the Burgh of Dunfermline, namely the Liberal government. Under the dynamic influence of Lloyd George, Elgin's own Party had, at last, mounted a legislative attack on 'landlordism'. The Finance Act of 1909-10 imposed an Increment Duty and an Undeveloped Land Duty. By a curious irony it was Elgin's lands that were first in Scotland (and early indeed on the English scale) to attract the attention of the new District Valuers. The long-running battle between Elgin and the Burgh of Dunfermline had made Elgin's lands a test case for the new legislation. The outcome was that the Broomhall lands were assessed annually at very high rates for Undeveloped Land Duty, as well as being billed for Dunfermline Municipal Taxes. Poor Elgin, who might have thought that Broomhall was relieved at last of its century-old burden of debt, now found the estate assailed by the policies of his own party. The interminable negotiations and vexations of all this cast a deep shadow over Elgin's autumnal years, fearing as he did that Broomhall and its inheritance was once more under threat.

Rosyth Dockyard went rapidly ahead, becoming a critical element in Britain's naval deployment, especially after the outbreak of war in 1914. During this period some 20,000 stokers were briefly released from their infernal conditions within the fighting ships to play football on Broomhall's fields. A cruiser squadron rode at anchor off Limekilns and Charlestown, waiting the call to confront the German grand fleet.

Elgin's troubles were greatly eased from an unexpected quarter when in 1913, aged sixty-four, he married again. Gertrude Lilian, widow of Captain Frederick Ogilvy, RN, was a contemporary of Elgin's older children, who were at first startled by their young stepmother but Gertrude soon won them over. The second Countess brought a new brightness to Broomhall.

In these last years the house at Broomhall wrapped Elgin round. It had become the repository of his family's history from the sword of King Robert the Bruce secretly stored at Broomhall to the portraits, dating from the seventeenth century onwards, of the Elgins and their web of aristocratic relations looking down from the walls of the library, the ballroom and the grand staircase. Among them was Thomas, seventh Earl, featured in his ensign's coat, looking youthful and optimistic, not yet overtaken by the Marbles, impossible debt and the infidelity of his wife. There were impressive portraits of Lord Durham and the eighth Elgin, much featured in Canadian history textbooks, and finally those strong minded spouses who had entered the family, and over long periods, had run it as dowagers. All were widowed relatively early and so had borne heavy burdens. There was Janet, Countess of Kincardine who had cleared her dead husband's debts for her son; Martha Whyte who had rescued Broomhall from its creditors a second time before passing the estate to her son Thomas with his extravagant ways; Elizabeth Oswald who had provided a near desperate Thomas with his second family and raised them in the evangelical faith; and Mary Louisa Lambton, who had so idealised her dead husband, James Bruce, instilling a profound sense of duty into Victor Alexander.

Thomas the 7th Earl had left at Broomhall certain fragments from the Acropolis and Asia Minor—all that remained to him of his collection. Some of these were now set in the walls of the hall; some, including a carved foot and a small lion's head, reposed on the mantelpiece. Close by was the Greek sarcophagus. In the library, splendidly bound in red leather, were the letters of the ever-faithful William Hamilton, of the harassed and harried Lusieri, and of Nelson. Elsewhere was stored the enormous collection of documents generated by Thomas—his projects, replete with his self-justifications. Around the hall hung the massive pictures bought at the time of the French Revolution. In the ballroom was the group painting of Thomas and Mary's children, with their Greek nursemaids, commissioned by the Hamilton Nisbets in anticipation of a happy reunion that was never to take place. In the lower corridor were the Calmuck's drawings in various stages of completeness, and Lusieri's water colour of the monument to Philopappos, all that remained of his resolution to compensate with his own art for the 'barbarisms' he had committed on Elgin's behalf.

The library also was full of the past. In one section stood the books of Bruce of Abyssinia, relics of one of the most notable of early wandering Scotsmen and part of the history of the Cumming Bruce family. In another were those of the dowager countess Elizabeth who had set up her salon in Paris after Thomas's death and had received in tribute from the illuminati of France copies of their books. On a desk in the centre of the room were the stones that had been hurled at her son James, the eighth Earl, by the Montreal mob. The arch between the library and the ballroom was draped with the robes of the Emperor of China, in blue, while the ballroom windows were hung with the golden robes of mandarins, taken from the Summer Palace outside Pekin before Elgin had it burned. Two sinuous storks stood by the doorway, presented to Elgin by his staff, purchased from the general auction of the booty from the Summer Palace. Another pair of elegant bronze storks, a souvenir of Japan, a gift from the Shogun, stood sentinel by another doorway. In the schoolroom, high on the wall, was the replica of the sombre memorial to the eighth Elgin placed in Calcutta Cathedral, a reminder of the lonely grave at Dharmsala that Mary Louisa had left behind and that Victor Alexander had visited as viceroy. To all of this Victor Alexander had added his contribution. It was chiefly in the form of archaic Indian weapons and armour, relics of the days before effective small arms. A panoply of these objects decorated the main stairwell. Scattered in various parts of the house were the estate papers, reminders of the early nineteenth century days when the horse-drawn coal wagons on their wooden rails had been part of the scene, a field's breadth from the windows of Broomhall. These ledgers and letters were all that remained of the succession of factors, agents, managers and lawyers who had struggled over the generations to redeem Broomhall's debts. There was no full portrait of Victor Alexander himself, as was consistent with his self-effacing nature.

When the Great War came in 1914, so much more terrible than that of South Africa, it assailed nineteenth century gentlemen like Elgin threatening to destroy their world just as the French Revolution and Napoleon had destroyed that of their grandfathers. He could reflect that the new territorial army's success in helping to sustain the first shock of the German conscript armies and in meeting the challenge of the trenches, owed something to his South African report. In this at least he had been a modern. But the Liberalism of Gladstone that had guided him throughout his career had now vanished down the gulf of time. The peacetime demands of welfarism followed by the insatiable needs of war were inflating the role of the state out of all recognition. Changes in India were also gaining momentum, although communal enmities remained, national feeling was gaining ground, preparing to challenge the Raj.

It had been a curious career, earning for Elgin a poor press in his lifetime and a bad one after his death. It seems there were two principal reasons why this conscientious man was so easily written off. On the one hand he had no sense of political mission, having from his early years in Fife and Scottish Liberalism rejected the idea of a party programme, regarding the head of the Party, for example, as its policy maker, subject only to advice and consultation. In a sense this was an aristocratic view of the political process, regarding the leader not as first among equals but head and shoulders above the rest. In a Gladstonian world, from which Elgin never escaped, there was moreover only a minimal role for government. Elgin, in short, could not appreciate that in a changing world, the Gladstonian philosophy had exhausted itself. Accordingly he took no part in the search for a new basis for the Liberal Party; much less was his name associated with any innovative proposals. He was a man whose formative phase lay, like that of his grandfather, at the end of an era, rendering him old fashioned and out of phase with the current demands required of those who looked for a role in public life.

Secondly, and closely related, was his own personality. It was not easy to be brought up in the memory of an apotheosised father. It may be that a sense of inadequacy was thus engendered alongside a compulsion to public duty, creating in Elgin his deeply engrained caution. His sense of personal and family economy made it difficult for him to accept the new atmosphere of government spending on welfare. His reclusiveness, his unwillingness to enter the social round of London and the country houses, both confirmed his attitudes and made him incapable of building any sort of political support base for himself. His unbending integrity may well have generated hostility. When Edward March, Churchill's private secretary described Elgin as 'a rugged old thane of antique virtue' he was epitomising a generally held view, especially among the young of the Party.

Elgin had two main sponsors and supporters, namely Rosebery and Campbell-Bannerman. But both, like Elgin, were part of the past It was Campbell-Bannerman's death in 1908 that ended Elgin's career. Elgin had his enemies, among whom Asquith was perhaps the most damaging, persistently making known his low opinion of Elgin. Even more serious were the slights on Elgin's reputation suggested by the men against whose brilliance he did not shine. It was a great misfortune to be succeeded in India by Curzon, to have striven for a South African settlement in the shadow of Milner's achievements, and to have to try to run the Colonial Office, in harness with the ebullient, ambitious and not excessively loyal Churchill.

All these circumstances made it all too easy to patronise and even to pillory Elgin.

He had seen India through troubled years with credit, zealously working to forestall crises stemming from chronic communal enmities and the rise of an Indian intellectual element with its radical press. He kept his nerve amid famine and plague, administering an effective relief programme. At the Colonial Office he had shown the same urge for conciliation and justice, finding himself presiding over a colonial system the existence of which his basic philosophy could hardly justify, but which, as with India, he accepted as a duty to be undertaken as undramatically as possible. It is sad that so good a man, with his record of service, should have been slighted by those who deliver facile verdicts.

On 18 January 1917 Elgin died. Bernard was born to his widow posthumously. There were tributes in the House of Lords. That which would have pleased him most came from Curzon:

> He made ... no effort anywhere to strike the public imagination, but he did his work, whether it was public or local, diligently and well: and he was one of those men who seem to be put into the world to maintain, instinctively and faithfully, the highest ideals of duty in public life.

It was a fair summary of the life of this modest but capable man.

Elgin was not buried in the family vault in Dunfermline Abbey near the body of King Robert the Bruce and among his other kin, for when viceroy, following complaints from the burghers of Dunfermline, he had ordered it sealed. There remained the tiny cemetery on the shore of the Forth at Limekilns that his grandfather had given to its people in 1811. And so in a small walled enclosure in the corner they buried him. There he lies, in total obscurity among the good folk of Limekilns: Victor Alexander Bruce, Ninth Earl of Elgin and Thirteenth Earl of Kincardine, a Baron in the peerage of England, Knight of the Garter, Lord Lieutenant of Fife, Knight Commander of the Star of India, Knight Grand Commander of the Order of the Indian Empire, sometime Viceroy of India and His Majesty's Secretary of State for the Colonies, Chancellor of the University of Aberdeen and devoted member of Fife County Council.

APPENDIX

The Lineage of Bruce

The evolution of the Bruce family was a good deal complicated by the existence from the seventeenth century of three elements: these may loosely be called the English, the Kincardine and the Broomhall branches, the latter two closely interlinked. They all stemmed from Edward Bruce, (b. 1505) of Blairhall second son of Sir David Bruce of Clackmannan, chief of the name of Bruce whose direct forebear Sir Robert Bruce had been given the Barony by King David II using the style 'dilectus consanguineus noster'. Edward Bruce held the lands of Broomhall.

Edward, his second son, made himself a man of note, both in Scotland and England. He became wealthy as a lawyer, building the great house known as Culross Abbey, close to the ruins of the Cistercian foundation. James VI sent him as ambassador to the court of Queen Elizabeth in 1594; he became a Lord of Session in 1597. On the death of Queen Elizabeth in 1603 he went south with James VI and I. He became a naturalised English subject, rising high in the English judiciary as Master of the Rolls, and adding greatly to his fortune. The manor of Whorlton and part of the possessions of Jervaulx Abbey were conferred on him by the King. His son and heir, Thomas, attended Charles I to Scotland in 1633 and was created first Earl of Elgin in the peerage of Scotland, and Lord Bruce of Kinloss. Robert, his son, the second Earl of Elgin, became Earl of Ailesbury and Viscount Bruce in the peerage of England. The third Earl of Ailesbury was a 'failed Jacobite' although his contemporary Thomas, seventh Earl of Kincardine, was staunch 'coming out' in 1715 for the Old Pretender and acting as one of his chief advisers. The third Earl of Elgin was banished in 1697 from the United Kingdom living out his life in Brussels. He had several sons and was succeeded by Charles, his second son who although married had no male heir so on the death of Charles the fourth Earl, the Ailesbury earldom lapsed and that of Elgin passed to his kinsman Charles (1732-71) ninth Earl of Kincardine. In this way Charles became head of the Bruce family.

The Kincardine branch had remained in Scotland. The title of Earl of Kincardine had been granted in 1647 to Edward, grandson of George Bruce of Carnock. His heir and brother Alexander was made, on 10 July 1667, one of the King's Commissioners for the Government of Scotland by Charles II after his restoration. Bishop Burnet described him as 'the wisest and worthiest man that belongs to his country, and fit for governing any affairs but his own.' There is a tradition that Charles II died in his arms. The Kincardine line, like that of Ailesbury, ended with females, doing so in 1705. It was at this point that the Broomhall Bruces, a collateral branch, succeeded to the title,

Sir Alexander Bruce of Broomhall becoming fourth Earl of Kincardine. The seventh Earl of Kincardine had, like the third of Ailesbury, been a Jacobite: there are letters between the Kinsmen containing references to messages sent by word of mouth of trusty messengers 'such as the post may not read.'

One member of the family had, however, pursued a path other than that of royal servant or landowner. Sir George Bruce, the younger brother of Edward Bruce of Blairhall, the rewarded servant of James VI and I, turned to industry. He dramatically exploited the coal resources around Culross and constructed works for the evaporation of salt from the waters of the Forth, using his coal to heat large iron pans. Much of this rather inferior output would be used for salting herring, often for export. George carried out in Bruce territory, a little to the west of Broomhall, a kind of local proto-industrial revolution in Scotland. There had long been a good deal of mining in this part of West Fife, but it had been on a small scale and technically backward; Sir George Bruce's colliery at Culross was widely famed by 1600, being probably the first mine in Britain to employ the Egyptian wheel for drainage. James VI who visited the mine admired George's achievement and knighted him for it, at the same time making Culross a royal burgh which meant that it, (more specifically perhaps Bruce), had the right to trade abroad. Sir George represented Culross in the Scottish parliament. He served as a member of the abortive committee of 1604 set up to recommend the terms of a union between Scotland and England. His grandson Edward was made first Earl of Kincardine in 1647.

The Bruce lines converged in Charles Bruce of Broomhall (1732–71), son of William, eighth Earl of Kincardine and Janet his wife. Charles as fifth Earl of Elgin and ninth of Kincardine was the heir to titles and status much higher on the scale of nobility than his modest estate of Broomhall warranted. It is hardly surprising that he sought to lift his patrimony to a higher level by the exploitation of Broomhall's limestone.

These seventeenth century Bruces were much involved in the management of their estates. This often, and indeed even typically, involved a complex welter of indebtedness, accompanied by a search for additional income, which often aggravated rather than relieved the problem. Insolvency hung darkly over a long succession of generations of the family. Alexander Bruce of Broomhall, fourth Earl of Kincardine, partly by ineptly acting as a Tacksman or Commissioner of Supply, partly by raising and maintaining armed men from his locality for service abroad, in spite of selling the Carnock estate, encumbered Broomhall with heavy debts. The sixth Earl of Kincardine also by mishandling his accounts as a Commissioner of Supply, in the early 1700s took refuge in the sanctuary at Holyrood and so avoided imprisonment. The seventh Earl Thomas was still in a morass of debt in 1723, owing some £12,652, and considering whether Broomhall should be sold. The eighth Earl seems to have helped things temporarily by marrying Janet Robertson, a daughter and heiress of James Robertson, a principal Clerk of Session; once again however heavy debts accrued, burdening Janet his widow. None of the Bruces of Broomhall, with their relatively modest estate, could find a secure and lasting path out of the thickets of debt; none enjoyed the kind of bonanza of royal favour that had earlier blessed the Earls of Ailesbury.

Key to the Family Trees

CB	Companion of the Bath	GCSI	(Knight) Grand Commander of the Star of India
CH	Companion of Honour	KC	King's Counsel
CIE	Companion of the Indian Empire	KCB	Knight Commander of the Bath
DCL	Doctor of Civil Laws	KG	Knight of the Garter
dsp	*decessit sine prole*, died without issue	KSI	Knight of the Star of India
dvp	*decessit vita patris*, died in lifetime of father	KT	Knight of the Thistle
GBE	(Knight) Grand Cross of the British Empire	MBE	Member of the Order of the British Empire
GCB	(Knight) Grand Cross of the Bath	PC	Privy Councillor
GCIE	(Knight) Grand Commander of the Indian Empire	TD	Territorial Decoration

Sources: Compiled from various sources including J. Balfour Paul, *The Scots Peerage*, 1906.

FAMILY TREE OF CHARLES BRUCE, 5th EARL OF ELGIN & 9th EARL OF KINCARDINE

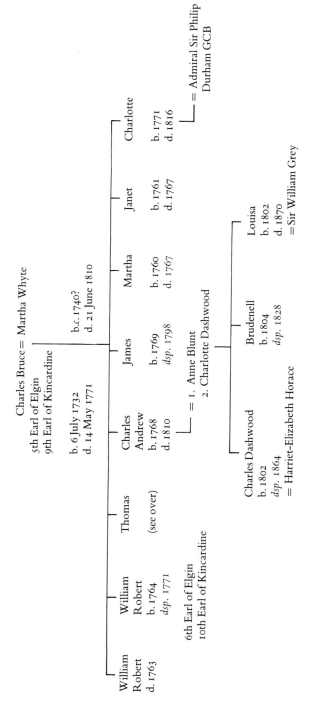

FAMILY TREE OF THOMAS BRUCE, 7th EARL OF ELGIN & 11th EARL OF KINCARDINE

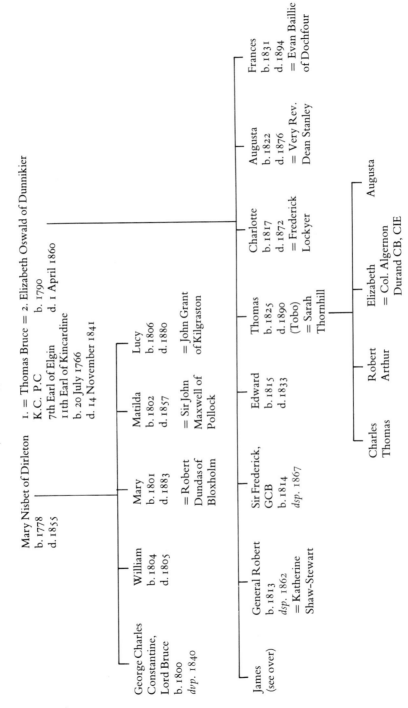

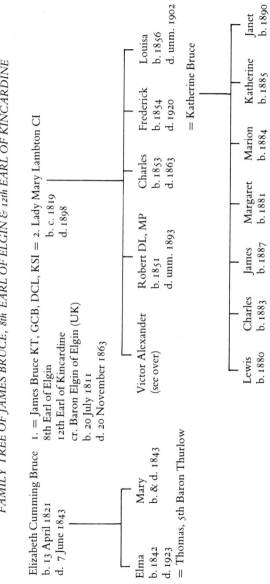

FAMILY TREE OF JAMES BRUCE, 8th EARL OF ELGIN & 12th EARL OF KINCARDINE

Elizabeth Cumming Bruce 1. = James Bruce KT, GCB, DCL, KSI = 2. Lady Mary Lambton CI
b. 13 April 1821   8th Earl of Elgin   b. c. 1819
d. 7 June 1843   12th Earl of Kincardine   d. 1898
                                      cr. Baron Elgin of Elgin (UK)
                                      b. 20 July 1811
                                      d. 20 November 1863

Elma   Mary
b. 1842   b. & d. 1843
d. 1923
= Thomas, 5th Baron Thurlow

Victor Alexander   Robert DL, MP   Charles   Frederick   Louisa
(see over)   b. 1851   b. 1853   b. 1854   b. 1856
                                  d. unm. 1893   d. 1863   d. 1920   d. unm. 1902
                                                                                    = Katherine Bruce

Lewis   Charles   James   Margaret   Marion   Katherine   Janet
b. 1880   b. 1883   b. 1887   b. 1881   b. 1884   b. 1885   b. 1890

FAMILY TREE OF VICTOR ALEXANDER BRUCE, 9th EARL OF ELGIN & 13th EARL OF KINCARDINE

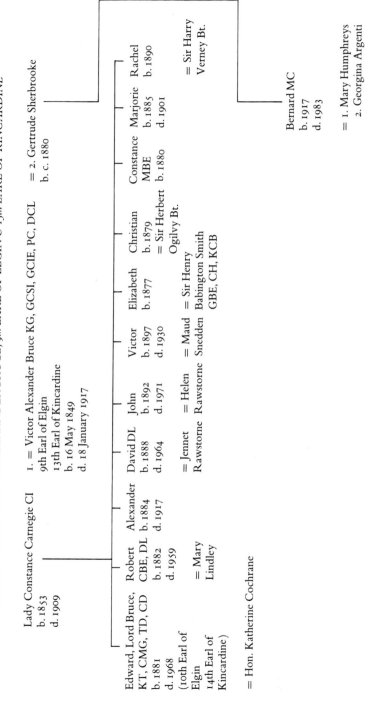

Select Bibliography

London is the place of publication unless otherwise stated

Abbot, C., Lord Colchester, *Diary and Correspondence*, 1861.

Akimoto, S., 'Lord Ii Naosuke and New Japan', translated and adapted by N. Nakamura, from *Ii Tairo to Kaiko*, Yokohama, 1909.

Alder, G.J., *British India's Northern Frontier, 1865-1895*, 1963.

Amery, L.S., *My Political Life*, Vols. 1 and 2, 1953.

Anon., *The New Statistical Account of Scotland*, Edinburgh, 1845.

——*Profiles of a Province. Studies in the history of Ontario*, Toronto, 1967.

Backhouse, F. and Bland, J.O.P., *Annals and Memoirs of the Court of Pekin*, 1914.

Baillie, A.V. (Dean of Windsor) and Bolitho, H.H., *A Victorian Dean, A Memoir of Arthur Stanley, Dean of Westminster*, 1930.

——eds., *Letters of Lady Augusta Stanley, a young lady at Court, 1849-1863*, 1927.

Baird, J.G.A., ed., *Private Letters of the Marquess of Dalhousie*, 1910.

Baldwin, R.M. and J., *The Baldwins and the Great Experiment*, Toronto, 1969.

Banno, M., *China and the West, 1858-61*, Cambridge, Mass., 1964.

Barrow, J., *Life and Correspondence of Admiral Sir William Sidney Smith GCB*, 1848.

Beasley, W.G., *Great Britain and the Opening of Japan, 1834-1858*, 1951.

Bell, H.H., *Glimpses of a governor's life*, 1946.

Bell, W.P., *From Strachan to Owen. How the Church of England planted and tended in British North America*, Toronto, 1938.

Bence-Jones, M., *Palaces of the Raj*, 1973.

——*The Viceroys of India*, Constable, 1982.

Bennett, G., *Kenya, a political history: the colonial period*, 1963.

Bernard,J.P., *Les Rouges: Liberalisme, Nationalisme et Anti-clericalisme an Milieu du XIXe Siecle*, Montreal, 1971.

Birkenhead, Earl of, *Halifax*, 1965.

Blakiston, T.W., *Five months on the Yang-Tsze*, 1862.

Blunt, W.S., *India under Ripon, a Private Diary*, 1909.

——*My Diaries*, part 2, 1920.

Bolitho, H.H., *A Century of British Monarchy*, 1951.

——*The Reign of Queen Victoria*, 1949.

Bonham Carter, V., *Winston Churchill as I knew him*, 1965.

Boustary, S., ed., *The Journals of Bonaparte in Egypt, 1798-1801*, Cairo, 1971.

Brash, J.I., ed., *Papers on Scottish Electoral Politics, 1832-1854*, Edinburgh, 1974.

Brett, M.V., ed., *Journals and Letters of Reginald Viscount Esher*, Vol. ii (1903-1910), 1934.

Brommer, F., *Die Giebel des Parthenon, eine Einfu 'hrung*, Mainz, 1959.

Brown, J.M., *Ghandi and Civil Disobedience*, Cambridge, 1977.

Bruce, Lady E., *Diary of Lady Elizabeth Bruce*, privately printed, 1898.

Bruce, M.E., *Family records of the Bruces and the Cumyns*, Edinburgh, 1870.

Bryce, J., *Impressions of South Africa*, 3rd edition, 1899.

——*Relations of the Advanced and the backward races of mankind*, Romanes lecture, 1902.

Buchan, J., *Lord Minto*, 1924.

Buck, E.J., *Simla, Past and Present*, Bombay, 1925.

Bullen, R., ed., *The Foreign Office*, University Publications of America, 1984.

Burne, Sir O., *Memories*, 1907. Burroughs, P., ed., *British Attitudes Towards Canada, 1822-1849*, Scarborough, Canada, 1971.

——*The Colonial Reformer and Canada, 1830-1849*, Toronto, 1969.

Bush, M.L., *The English Aristocracy: A comparative synthesis*, Manchester, 1985.

Bushnell, G.H., *Sir Henry Babington Smith, 1863-1923, Civil Servant and Financier*, 1942.

Bute, Marchioness of, ed., *The Private Journal of the Marquis of Hastings*, 1858.

Butler, I., *The Eldest Brother*, 1973.

——*The Viceroy's Wife*, 1969.

Byron, Lord, *English Bards and Scotch Reviewers*, 1809.

——*Childe Harold's Pilgrimage*, Cantos 1 and 11, 1812.

——*The Curse of Minerva*, 1812.

Cambridge History of the British Empire, Vol. iii, *The Empire-Commonwealth, 1870-1919*, Cambridge, 1959.

Cameron, N., *Barbarians and Mandarins. Thirteen Centuries of Western Travellers in China*, New York and Tokyo, 1970.

Campbell, G., *Modern India, A Sketch of the System of Civil Government*, 1852.

Campbell-Bannerman, H., *Speeches, 1899-1908*, selected and reprinted from 'The Times', 1908.

Campbell-Johnson, A., *Mission with Mountbatten*, New York, 1953.

Cannon, J., *Aristocratic Century: The peerage of eighteenth century England*, Cambridge, 1985.

Careless, J.M.S., *Brown of the Globe: The Voice of Upper Canada, 1818-1859*, Toronto, 1972.

——*The Union of the Canadas: The Growth of Canadian Institutions, 1841-1857*, Toronto, 1967.

——ed., *The Pre-Confederation Premiers: Ontario Government Leaders 1841-1867*, Toronto, 1980.

Cell, J.W., *British Colonial Administration in the Mid-Nineteenth Century: The Policy-making Process*, Yale, 1970.

Chamberlain, A., *Politics from inside: an epistolary chronicle 1906-1914*, 1936.

Chaudhary, R.B., *The British Agrarian Policy in Eastern India (Bengal and Bihar) 1859-60*, Patra, 1980.

Chaudhary, V.C.P., *Imperial Policy of British in India 1876-80, birth of Indian Nationalism*. Calcutta, 1968.

Chi, Tsui, *A Short History of Chinese Civilisation*, 1942.

Choiseul-Gouffier, Comte de, *Voyage Pittoresque de la Grece*, Paris, 1782.

Churchill, R.S., *Winston S. Churchill*, Vol. ii, *The Young Statesman, 1901-1914*, 1967.

Churchill, W.S., *For Free Trade: speeches ... during the fiscal controversy preceding the late general election*, 1906.

——*My African Journey*, 1908, reprinted 1962.

——*Liberalism and the social problem*, 1909.

Clarke, E.D., *The Tomb of Alexander*, 1805.

——*Greek Marbles*, 1809.

——*Travels in Various Countries of Europe, Asia and Africa*, 1810.

Clarke, M. and Penny, N., eds., *The Arrogant Connoisseur, Richard Payne Knight 1751-1824*, Manchester, 1982.

Coatman, J., *India, The Road to Self-Government*, 1941.

——*Years of Destiny*, 1932.

Cockerell, C.R., *Travels in Southern Europe and the Levant, 1810-1817*, 1903.

Cohen, P.A., *China and Christianity: the Missionary Movement and the Growth of Chinese Anti-foreignism, 1860-1870*, Cambridge, Mass., 1963.

Cohn, B.S., 'From Indian Status to British Contract', *Journal of Economic History*, Vol. XXI, New York, 1961.

The Committee on Orange History, *One Man's Loyalty*, Toronto, 1953.

Connolly, M.F., *Biographical Dictionary of the Eminent of Fife*, Cupar and Edinburgh, 1866.

Constantine, D., *Early Greek Travellers and the Hellenic ideal*, Cambridge, 1984.

Cook, B. F., *The Elgin Marbles*, British Museum, 1984.

Cook, T.M., *Samuel Hahnemann, the founder of homeopathic medicine*, Wellingborough, 1981.

Costin, W.C., *Great Britain and China, 1833-60*, Oxford, 1937.

Cotton, Sir H., *India and Home Memories*, 1911.

Craig, G., *Early Travellers in the Canadas, 1791-1867*, Toronto, 1955.

Crook, J.M., 'Broomhall, Fife: the home of the Earl and Countess of Elgin', *Country Life*, 29 January 1970.

——'A reluctant Goth: the architecture of Thomas Harrison,I', *Country Life*, 15 April 1971.

——'A most classical architect: the architecture of Thomas Harrison, II', *Country Life*, 22 April 1971.

——'A neo-classical visionary: the architecture of Thomas Harrison, III', *Country Life*, 6 May 1971.

——*The Greek Revival: Neo-classical Attitudes in British Architecture 1760-1870*, 1972.

Cross, M.S., *Free Trade, Annexation and Reciprocity, 1846-1854*, Toronto, 1971.

Cumming, C.F.G., *Memories*, Edinburgh and London, 1904.

Cumper, G.E., 'Labour Demand and Supply in the Jamaican Sugar Industry 1830-1950', *Social and Economic Studies*, Vol. 2, No. 4, 1954.

Cundall, F., *History of King's House, Spanish Town*, Kingston, Jamaica, 1929.

Cunningham, A.B., *Dragomania: the Dragomans of the British Embassy in Turkey*, St. Antony's Papers II, Oxford, 1961.

Cunningham, A.S., *Culross: past and present*, Leven, 1910.

Curzon, G., M.P., *Problems of the Far East—Japan, Korea, China*, 1896.

Curzon of Kedleston, Marquess, *British Government in India*, 2 vols., 1925.

Cust, L. and Colvin, S., *History of the Society of Dilettanti*, 1898.

De Mendelssohn, P., *The Age of Churchill, Vol. i, Heritage and Adventure, 1874-1911*, 1961.

A Description of the Collection of Ancient Marbles in the British Museum, 1812-1861.

Dictionary of National Biography, Lee, S., ed., 1898

——*Supplement, 1922-1930*, Weaver, J.R.H., ed., 1937.

Dilks, D., *Curzon in India*, 2 Vols. 1969-70.

Dodwell, E., *A Classical and Topographical Tour through Greece*, 1819.

Douglas, Hon. F.S.N., *An Essay on Certain Points of Resemblance between the Ancient and Modern Greeks*, 1813.

Douglas, R., 'Coal-Mining in Fife in the second half of the eighteenth century' in *The Scottish Tradition*, ed. G.W.S.Barrow, Edinburgh, 1974.

Dowson, R., ed., *The Legacy of China*, Oxford, 1964.

Dufferin and Ava, Marchioness of, *Our Viceregal Life in India*, 1890.

Durand, Sir M., *Alfred Lyall*, 1913.

Elgin, J., 8th Earl of, *Six essays on the best mode of establishing and conducting industrial schools, adapted to the wants of an agricultural population: written for a prize offered by the Earl of Elgin, Governor of Jamaica in November 1843*, Royal Agricultural Society of Jamaica, 1845.

——Extracts from the Letters of James, Earl of Elgin to Mary Louisa, Countess of Elgin, 1847-1862, Privately Printed, 1864.

Elgin, M., Countess of, *Letters of Mary Nisbet of Dirleton, Countess of Elgin*, 1926.

Elgin, T., 7th Earl of, *Memorandum on the Subject of the Earl of Elgin's Pursuits in Greece*, 1810.

——*Letter to the Editor of the Edinburgh Review on the subject of an article in that Journal on 'The Remains of John Tweddell'*, 1815.

——*Postscript to a Letter to the Editor of the Edinburgh Review*, 1815.

——*The Petition of the Earl of Elgin Respecting his Collection of Marbles*, p.828, Hansard ccci, 1815.

——*View of the present state of Pauperism in Scotland*, 1830.

The New Encyclopaedia Britannica, Goetz, Philip, W., ed. in chief, 15th Edition, 1974.

Farrington, J.R.A., *The Farrington Diary*, James Greig, ed., 8 vols., 3rd edition, New York, 1923.

Fergusson, Sir J., *The Sixteen Peers of Scotland*, Oxford, 1960.

The Trial of R. Fergusson, Esq., 1807.

The Trial of R.J. Fergusson, Esquire, 1807.

Fieldhouse, D.K., *Economics and Empire*, New York, 1973.

Finer, S.E., 'Patronage and the Public Service', *Public Administration*, 30, 1952.

Fischer, L.R. and Sagar, E.W., eds., *The Enterprising Canadians: Entrepreneurs and Economic Development in the Eastern Canada 1820-1914*, Toronto, 1981.

Fisher, H.A.L., *James Bryce*, Vol. i, 1927.

Fitzroy, Sir A.W., *Memoirs*, Vol. i, 1925.

Fleming, R.P., *The Siege at Peking*, 1959.

Forbin, Comte de, *Voyages dans le Levant*, 1819.

Fowler, E.H., *Life of H.H. Fowler, 1st Viscount Wolverhampton*, 1912.

Frank, A.G., *Crisis in the World Economy*, 1980.

Fuller, J., *Narrative of a Tour through some parts of the Turkish Empire*, 1830.

Galt, J., ed., *Letters from the Levant*, 1813.

——*Life and Studies of Benjamin West, Esq.*, 1816.

——*Life of Byron*, 1830.

——*Autobiography*, 1833.

Gann, L.H., *The birth of a plural society: Northern Rhodesia, 1894-1914*, Manchester, 1958.

Gardiner, A.G., *Prophets, priests and kings*, 1908.

Gardner, W.J., *A History of Jamaica*, 1971.

Gilbert, M., *Servant of India*, 1966.

Glendevon, J., *The Viceroy at Bay*, 1971.

Godsell, P., ed., *Letters and Diaries of Lady Durham*, Oberon, Ottawa, 1979.

Gollin, A.M., *Proconsul in politics: a study of Lord Milner in opposition and power*, 1964.

Gopal, R., *British Rule in India*, Delhi, 1963.

——*Indian Politics from Crown Rule to Independence, 1858-1947*, Aligarh, 1967.

Gopal, S., *The Viceroyalty of Lord Ripon, 1880-1884*, 1953.

——*The Viceroyalty of Lord Irwin, 1926-31*, Oxford, 1957.

——*British Policy in India 1858-1905*, Cambridge, 1965.

Gordon, W.E., 'Imperial Policy Decisions in the Economic History of Jamaica, 1664-1934', *Social and Economic Studies*, Vol. 6, No.1, 1957.

Grey, E., *Twenty-five years, 1892-1916*, Vol. i, 1925.

Gwynn, S. and Tuckwell, G.M., *Life of Sir Charles Dilke*, 2 vols., 1917.

Hailey, Lord, *An African Survey. Revised 1956*, 1957.

Hake, A.E., *The Story of Chinese Gordon*, 1884.

Hake, T.G., *Memoirs of Eighty Years*, 1892.

Halifax, Earl of, *Fulness of Days*, 1957.

Halfpenny, F.G., ed., *Dictionary of Canadian Biography*, Toronto, 1976.

Hamilton, W.R., *Letter (and Second Letter, Third Letter) to the Earl of Elgin on the Propriety of Adopting the Greek style of Architecture for the New Houses of Parliament*, 1836, 1837.

——*Memorandum on the Subject of the Earl of Elgin's Pursuits in Greece*, Edinburgh, 1810.

Hancock, W.K., *Survey of British Commonwealth Affairs*, 2 vols., 1937-42.

——*Smuts*, Vol. i, *The Sanguine Years*, Cambridge, 1962.

Hancock, W.K. and van der Poel, J., eds., *Selections from the Smuts Papers, ii, 1902-1920*, 1966.

Hardinge of Penshurst, Lord, *My Indian Years*, 1948.

Hardy, P., *The Muslims of British India*, Cambridge, 1972.

Hare, A., ed., *The Story of Two Noble Lives*, 1893.

Harlow, V. and Chilver, E.M., eds., *History of East Africa*, Vol. ii, 1965.

Harnetty, P., 'The Indian Cotton Duties Controversy', *English Historical Review*, 77, 1962.

Hassall, C., *Edward Marsh, a biography*, 1959.

Hay, M., 'The Chancellor of the University (Earl of Elgin)', *Aberdeen University Review*, Vol. 1, 1914.

Haydon, B.R., *Correspondence and Table Talk*, 1876.

——*Autobiography and Memoirs*, ed., Aldous Huxley, 1926.

——*The Diary of Benjamin Robert Haydon*, ed. W.B. Pope, 1960-1963.

Haynes, D.E.L., *An Historical Guide to the Sculptures of the Parthenon*, British Museum, 1962.

Headlam, C., ed., *The Milner Papers: South Africa 1897-1905*, 2vols., 1931-3.

Henderson, P.P., *Laurence Oliphant*, 1956.

Herald, J.C., *Bonaparte in Egypt*, 1963.

Hill, M.F., *Permanent way: story of Kenya and Uganda railway*, Nairobi, 2nd edition, 1961.

Hincks, Sir F., *Reminiscences of his Public Life*, Montreal, 1884.

Hinde, W., *George Canning*, 1973.

Historical Manuscripts Commission, 13th Report, *The Manuscripts of J.B. Fortescue, Esq., preserved at Dropmore*, 1892-1927.

Hobhouse, J.C., *A Journey through Albania and other provinces of Turkey in Europe and Asia to Constantinople*, 1813.

Hobhouse, L.T., *Liberalism*, 1911.

Hobhouse, R.W., *Life of Christian Samuel Hahnemann*, 1933.

Hodson, H.V., *The Great Divide Britain-India-Pakistan*, 1969.

Hodson, V.C.P., *Historical Records of the Governor General's Body Guard*, 1910.

Houston, C.C. and Smyth, W.J., *The Sash Canada wore: A Historical Geography of the Orange Order in Canada*, Toronto, 1980.

Hughes, Rev. T.S., *Travels in Sicily, Greece and Albania*, 1820.

Hunt, Rev. P., *A Narrative of What is Known Respecting the Literary Remains of the Late John Tweddell*, 1816.

Hunter, W.W., *Life of the Earl of Mayo*, 1875.

Hussey, C., *Life of Sir Edwin Lutyens*, 1950.

Hutchison, I.G.C., *Political History of Scotland, 1832-1924*, Edinburgh, 1985.

Hutter zum Stolzenberg, Baroness von, *The Elgin Marbles, a Novel*, 1937.

Huxley, E., *White Man's Country: Lord Delamere and the making of Kenya*, Vol. i, 1953.

Hyam, R., 'Partition of Africa: a review article', *Historical Journal*, Vol. vii, 1964, 154-169.

——'Smuts and the decision of the Liberal government to grant responsible government to the Transvaal, January and February, 1906', *Historical Journal*, Vol. viii, 1965, 380-398.

——Review of Le May, 'British supremacy in South Africa, 1899-1907', *Historical Journal*, Vol. ix, 1966, 149-151.

——*Elgin and Churchill at the Colonial Office, 1905-1908, the Watershed of the Empire-Commonwealth*, 1968.

'India under Lord Elgin', *Quarterly Review*, Vol. 189, 1899.

Ingham, K., *A history of East Africa*, 1962.

Irving, R.G., *Indian Summer, Lutyens, Baker and Imperial Delhi*, New Haven and London, 1981.

James, R. Rhodes, *Rosebery*, 1963.

Jebb, R., *The Imperial Conference*, Vol. ii, 1911.

Jenkins, R.H., *Asquith*, 1964.

Jones, E.P., 'Under Secretaries of State for foreign affairs—1782-1855', *English Historical Review*, Vol. 49, 1934.

Jones, R.A., *The British Diplomatic Service 1815-1914*, Gerrard's Cross, 1983.

Kaye, J.W., *A History of the Sepoy War in India, 1857-1858*, 1875-1876.

Kaye, J.W. and Malleson, G.B., *History of the Indian Mutiny*, 1889.

Keith, A.B., *Responsible Government in the dominions*, Oxford, 1928.

——ed., *Selected speeches and documents on British colonial policy, 1763-1917*, 1948.

Keith, Admiral Viscount, *The Keith Papers* selected from the letters and papers of Admiral Viscount Keith, Navy Records Society, 1927-1955.

Keen, M., *Chivalry*, Yale, 1984.

Kennedy, Vice Admiral Sir W.R., *Hurrah for the Life of a Sailor! Fifty Years in the Royal Navy*, 1910.

Kerr, Lord M., *Journals, 1847-1849: on the staff of the Earl of Elgin, Governor General, Canada*, privately printed, n.d.

Keynes, J.M., *Indian Currency and Finance*, 1913.

Kimble, D., *A political history of Ghana, Vol. i, Rise of Gold Coast nationalism, 1850-1928*, Oxford, 1963.

Kitto, H.D.F., *The Greeks*, Harmondsworth, 1951.

Knollys, H., *The Life of General Sir Hope Grant with Selections from his Correspondence*, 1894.

Kuper, H., *An African aristocracy: rank among the Swazi of Bechuanaland*, 1947.

La Ferreur, M., ed., *Dictionary of Canadian Biography, X: 1871-1880*, University of Toronto, 1972.

La Nauze, J.A., *Alfred Deakin, a biography*, Vol. ii, Melbourne, 1965.

Langstone, Rosa, W., *Responsible Government in Canada*, 1931.

Larrabee, S.A., *English Bards and Grecian Marbles*, 1943.

Le May, G.H.L., *British Supremacy in South Africa, 1899-1907*, Oxford, 1965.

Lee Warner, W., *The Life of the Marquis of Dalhousie*, 1904.

Legrand, Ph.E., 'Contribution a l'Histoire des Marbres du Parthenon', *Revue Archeologique*, 3rd series, XXV, 1894.

——'Encore les Marbres du Parthenon', *Revue Archeologique*, 3rd series, XXVI, 1895.

——'Biographies de Louis-Francois-Sebastien Fauvel', *Revue Archeologique*, 3rd series, XXX and XXXI, 1897.

Lemieux, L.J., *The Governors-General of Canada, 1608-1931*, n.p., n.d.

Lewis, I.M., *The Modern History of Somaliland*, 1965.

Lewis, M.A., *Napoleon and his British Captives*, 1962.

Loch, H.B., *Personal Narrative of occurrences during Lord Elgin's Second Embassy to China in 1860*, 1869.

Longley, R.S., *Sir Francis Hincks: A Study of Canadian Politics, Railways and Finance in the Nineteenth Century*, Toronto, 1943.

Low, D.A. and Pratt, R.C., *Buganda and British overrule 1900-1955*, 1960.

Lugard, F.J.D., *The Dual Mandate in British Tropical Africa*, 1929.

Lumby, E.W.R., 'Lord Elgin and the Burning of the Summer Palace', *History To-day*, Vol. 10 (7), 1960.

Lutyens, M., *Edwin Lutyens*, 1980.

——*The Lyttons in India*, 1980.

Lyall, Sir A., *Life of the Marquis of Dufferin and Ava*, 1905.

Lyttelton, E., *Alfred Lyttelton, an account of his life*, 1917.

Lytton, R., First Earl of, *Letters*, Balfour, Lady Betty, ed., 1906.

McCallum, R.B., *Asquith*, 1936.

MacCallum, S.A., *Winston Spencer Churchill*, 1905.

MacDonald, J.R., *Labour and the Empire*, 1907.

McGhee, R.L.J., *How we got to Peking: a Narrative of the Campaign in China of 1860*, 1862.

McGregor, R.W., *Kenya from within: a short political history*, 1927.

Mackenzie, J.M., *Propaganda and Empire. The manipulation of British public opinion, 1880–1960*, Manchester, 1984.

Mackesy, P., *War Without Victory: The downfall of Pitt*, Oxford, 1984.

——*The Strategy of Overthrow 1798–9*, 1974.

Maclagan, M., *Clemency Canning*, 1962.

Macmillan, W.M., *Road to Self-rule*, 1959.

McPhee, A., *The economic revolution in West Africa*, 1926.

Macrae, M., *MacNab of Dundurn*, Toronto, 1971.

Magnus, P., *King Edward the Seventh*, 1964.

Malhotra, P.L., *Administration of Lord Elgin in India, 1894–99*, New Delhi, 1979.

Mallett, B., *Thomas George, Earl of Northbrook*, 1908.

Malone, C.B., *History of the Summer Palaces under the Ch'ing Dynasty*, University of Illinois Press, 1934.

Mansergh, P.N.S., *South Africa, 1906–1961: the price of magnanimity*, 1962.

Marchand, L.A., *Byron, a Biography*, 1957.

Martin, C., *Empire and Commonwealth*: *Studies in Governance and Self-Government in Canada*, Oxford, 1929.

Martin, G., *The Durham Report and British Policy: A Critical Essay*, Cambridge, 1972.

——'The "Watershed" of the Empire-Commonwealth', *New Zealand Journal of History*, Vol. 8(2), 1974.

Martineau, H., *A British Friendship and Memoir of Lord Elgin*, 1866.

——'The Earl of Elgin & Kincardine' in *Biographical Sketches*, 4th edition, 1876.

Masterman, L., *C.F.G. Masterman, a biography*, 1939.

Matthew, H.C.G., *The Liberal Imperialists: The Ideas and Politics of a Post-Gladstonian Elite*, Oxford, 1973.

Maurice, F.B., *Haldane, Vol. i, 1856–1915*, 1937.

Mehta, V., *The New India*, Harmondsworth, 1971.

Menzies, Mrs. S., *Lord William Beresford, VC*, 1917.

Mersey, Viscount, *The Viceroys and Governors-General of India*, 1949.

Michaelis, A., *Ancient Marbles in Great Britain*, 1882.

——'Supplement on Marbles at Broomhall', *Journal of Hellenic Studies*, 1884.

——*Der Parthenon*, 1871.

Michie, A., *The Englishman in China*, Vol. I, 1930.

Michon, E., 'Les Fragments du Parthenon Conserves au Musée du Louvre', *Revue Archeologique*, 3rd series, XXIV, 1894.

Miller, C., *The Canadian Career of the Fourth Earl of Minto, the education of a Viceroy*, Waterloo, Canada, 1980.

Milne, A.T., *Correspondence of Jeremy Bentham*, Vol. 4, 1981.

Milner, A., Viscount Milner, *The nation and the empire: speeches and addresses*, 1913.

Minto, M., Countess of, *India, Minto and Morley*, 1934.

Mitford, A.B.F. (Lord Redesdale), *Memories*, 2 Vols., 1915.

Monet, J., *The Last Cannon Shot*, Toronto, 1964.

Montagu, E., *An Indian Diary*, 1930.

Moore, C.D. and Eldredge, D., eds., *India, yesterday and to-day*, the George School Readings, New York, 1970.

Moore, R.J., *The Crisis of Indian Unity*, Oxford, 1974.

Moore, T., *Letters and Journals of Lord Byron with Notices of his Life*, 1830.

Morel, E.D., *Nigeria: its peoples and problems*, 1912 edition.

Morier, J.P., *Memoir of a Campaign with the Ottoman Army in Egypt from February to July, 1800*, 1801.

Morison, J.L., *Eighth Earl of Elgin, a chapter in nineteenth century imperial history*, 1928.

——*Lawrence of Lucknow 1806–1857, being the life of Sir H.Lawrence re-told from his private and public papers*, 1934.

Morison, S.E., *John Paul Jones*, 1960.

Morley, Viscount J., *Indian speeches 1907-1909*, 1909.

——*Recollections*, Vol. ii, 1917.

Morrell, W.P., *Britain in the Pacific islands*, Oxford, 1960.

Morritt of Rokeby, J.B.S., *Letters descriptive of a Journey in Europe and Asia Minor in the years 1794-1796*, 1914.

Moser, C.A., 'The Measurement of Levels of Living—With special reference to Jamaica', *Colonial Research Studies*, No. 24, 1956.

Mungeam, G.H., *British rule in Kenya, 1895-1912*, Oxford, 1966.

Murray, J., ed., *Lord Byron's Correspondence chiefly with Lady Melbourne, the Hon. Douglas Kinnaird and P.B. Shelley*, 1922.

Nanda, B.R., *Gokale, The Indian moderates and the British Raj*, Oxford University Press, 1977.

Naramoto, T., ed., *Bakumatsu-Ishin Jinmei Jiken (Biography of the late Tokugawa and early Meiji)*, Tokyo, 1978.

New, C.W., *A Biography of John George Lambton, First Earl of Durham*, 1968 (reprint of 1929 edition).

Newton, Lord, *Lord Lansdowne*, 1929.

Nicolson, H., *Helen's Tower*, 1937.

Nikolaos, G., *Classical Greece. The Sculpture of the Parthenon—the Elgin Marbles, photographed by F.L. Kennett*, 1960.

North, M., *Journal of an English Officer in India*, 1858.

Okuma, S., ed., *Fifty Years of the New Japan*, 1910.

Oliphant, L., *Narrative of the Earl of Elgin's Mission to China and Japan in 1857, '58, '59*, Edinburgh, 1859.

Oliver, R. and Sanderson, G.N., eds., *The Cambridge History of Africa*, Vol. 6, *1870-1905*, Cambridge, 1985.

Olivier, S.H., Baron Olivier, *White capital and coloured labour*, 1929.

Orr, C.W.J., *The making of Northern Nigeria*, 2nd edition, 1965.

Osborn, S., *A Cruise in Japanese Waters*, Edinburgh, 1859.

Otter, W., *The Life and Remains of the Rev. Edward Daniel Clarke*, 1824.

Pakenham, V., *The Noonday Sun: Edwardians in the Tropics*, 1985.

Parkinson, C., *Colonial Office from within 1909-1945*, 1947.

Paul, Sir J.B., ed., *The Scots Peerage*, Edinburgh, 1906.

Pemble, J., *The Raj, the Indian Meeting and the Kingdom of Oudh, 1801-1859*, Harvester, 1977.

Perham, Dame M., *Lugard, Vol. ii, The years of authority*, 1960.

Philips, C.H. et al, *The Evolution of India and Pakistan 1848 to 1947. Select Documents*, Oxford, 1962.

Pollock, C., 'Lord Elgin and the Marbles', *Transactions of the Royal Society of Literature of the United Kingdom*, 1932.

Pope-Hennessy, J., *Lord Crewe, 1858-1945*, 1955.

Powis, J.K., *Artistocracy*, Oxford, 1985.

Proceedings under a Writ of Enquiry of Damages in an Action in the Court of Kings Bench in which the Right Honourable the Earl of Elgin was plaintiff and Robert Ferguson, Esq., defendant for Criminal Conversation with the plaintiff's wife, December 1807.

Pyrah, G.B., *Imperial Policy and South Africa 1902-1910*, Oxford, 1955.

Quennell, P., ed., *Byron, A Self-Portrait, Letters and Diaries*, 1952.

Reading, 2nd Marquess of, *Rufus Isaacs, 1st Marquess of Reading*, 2 Vols., 1943-5.

Reed, Sir S., *The India I knew*, 1952.

Rennie, D.F., M.D., *Peking and the Pekingese during the first year of the British Embassy at Peking*, 2 Vols., 1865.

Rivett-Carnac, J.H., *Many Memories*, Edinburgh and London, 1910.

Roberts, Field Marshal Lord, *Forty-one Years in India*, 2 Vols., 1897.

Robertson, Sir G., *Chitral*, 1899.

Robertson, J., *The Scottish Englightenment and the Militia Issue*, Edinburgh, 1985.

Robinson, K.E., *The dilemmas of trusteeship*, 1965.

Robinson, R.E. and Gallagher, J., *Africa and the Victorians*, 1961.

Roby, K., *The King, the Press and the People: A study of Edward VII*, 1975.

Ronaldsay, Earl of, *Life of Lord Curzon*, 3 Vols., 1928.

Rose, K., *Superior Person*, 1969.

Rothenberg, J., '*Descensus ad terram': the acquisition and reception of the Elgin Marbles*, New York, 1977.

Russell, G.W.E., *Collections and Recollections*, 1902.

Russell, J.R., M.D., *The History and Heroes of the Art of Medicine*, 1861.

Russell, W.H., *My Diary in India in the Year 1857-58*, 1860.

St. Clair, W., *Lord Elgin and the Marbles*, Oxford, 1967.

Samuel, H.L., Viscount Samuel, *Liberalism, its Principles and Proposals*, 1902.

——*Memoirs*, 1945.

Satow, E.M., ed., *Japan 1853-1864*, Tokyo, 1905.

Schreuder, D. M., *The Scramble for Africa, 1877-1895, the politics of partition re-appraised*. Cambridge, 1980.

Schull, J., *Rebellion: The Rising of French Canada, 1837*, Toronto, 1971.

Seaman, L.C.B., *Post-Victorian Britain, 1902-1951*, 1966.

Segal, R., *The Crisis of India*, Harmondsworth, 1965.

Senior, E., 'The Provincial Cavalry in Lower Canada, 1837-50', *Canadian Historical Review*, March 1976.

Senior, H., *Orangeism. The Canadian Phase*, Toronto, 1972.

Seymour, E.H., Admiral of the Fleet, *My Naval Career and Travels*, 1911.

Shirras, G.F., *Indian Finance and Banking*, 1919.

Sicilianos, D., *Old and New Athens*, translated by Robert Liddell, 1960.

Sinclair, Sir J., *The Statistical Account for Scotland*, Edinburgh, 1798.

Singh, H.L., *Problems and policies of the British in India, 1885-1898*, 1963.

Skidmore, P.G., 'Canadian Canals to 1848', *Dalhousie Review*, LXI, 1981, 718-34.

Smith, A.H., 'Lord Elgin and his Collection', *Journal of Hellenic Studies*, Vol. XXXVI, 1916.

——*The Sculptures of the Parthenon*, 1910.

——*Catalogue of Sculpture in the Department of Greek and Roman Antiquities, British Museum*, 1892.

Smith, R.B., *Life of Lord Lawrence*, 2 Vols., 1883.

Spear, P., *A History of India*, Vol. II, 1965.

Specimens of Ancient Sculpture, Dilettanti Society 1809 and 1835.

Spencer, T., *Fair Greece, Sad Relic*, 1954.

Spender, J.A., *Life of Rt. Hon. Sir Henry Campbell-Bannerman, Vol.ii*, 1923.

Spero, J.E., *The Politics of International Economic Relations*, 1978.

Stanley, Lady A., *Letters of Lady Augusta Stanley, 1849-1863*, 1927.

——*Later letters, 1864-1876*, 1929.

Stevens, G.P. et al, *The Erechtheum*, 1927.

Stokes, E., *The English Utilitarians and India*, Oxford, 1959.

Stuart, J., Capt., *A history of the Zulu rebellion of 1906*, 1913.

Stuart, J. and Revett, N. et al, *The Antiquities of Athens*, 1762.

Surtees, V., *Charlotte Canning*, 1975.

Taylor, A., *Laurence Oliphant*, 1982.

Temple, Sir R., *Men and Events of my Time in India*, 1882.

——*Progress of India, Japan and China in the Nineteenth Century*, 1902.

Templewood, Viscount, *Nine Troubled Years*, 1954.

Thompson, L.M., *The unification of South Africa, 1902-1910*, Oxford, 1960.

Todd, H.J., *Catalogue of the Archepiscopal Manuscripts in the Library at Lambeth Palace*, 1812.

——*An Account of the Greek Mss chiefly Biblical which had been in the possession of the late Professor Carlyle, the greater part of which are now deposited in the Archepiscopal Library at Lambeth Palace*, c. 1820.

Tulchinsky, G.J.J., *The River Barons, Montreal Businessmen and the Growth of Industry and Transportation 1837-53*, Toronto, 1977.

Tweddell, Rev. R., *The Remains of John Tweddell*, edns. 1815 and 1816.

Tyler, J.E., 'Campbell-Bannerman and the Liberal Imperialists, 1906-1908', *History*, Vol. xxiii, 1938, 254-262.

Vrettos, T., *A shadow of magnitude: the acquisition of the Elgin Marbles*, New York, 1974.

Waley, A., *The Opium War through Chinese Eyes*, 1958.

Walker, E.A., *W.P. Schreiner, a South African*, 1937.

——*History of Southern Africa*, 1957.

Walpole, Rev. R., *Memoirs relating to European and Asiatic Turkey*, 1817.

——*Travels in Various Countries of the East*, 1820.

Walrond, T., *Letters and Journals of James, Eighth Earl of Elgin*, 1872.

Walsh, Rev. R., *A Residence at Constantinople*, 1836.

Ward, J.M., *Colonial Self-Government: The British Experience 1759-1856*, Toronto, 1976.

Wavell, A. Lord, *The Viceroy's Journal*, 1973.

Webb, R.K., *Harriet Martineau. A Radical Victorian*, 1960.

Williams, H.W., *Travels in Italy, Greece and the Ionian Islands*, 1820.

Wilson, C.H., *History of Unilever*, Vol. i, 1954.

Wittman, W., *Travels in Turkey, Asia Minor and Syria*, 1803.

Wolf, L., *Life of Lord Ripon*, 1921.

Wood, A.C., 'The English Embassy at Constantinople 1660-1762', *English Historical Review*, Vol. 40, 1925.

Wood, J.C., *British Economists and the Empire*, 1983.

Wood, J.D., ed., *Perspectives on Landscape and Settlement in Nineteenth Century Ontario*, Toronto, 1975.

Woodruff, P. (Philip Mason), *The Men Who Ruled India*, Vol. I, *The Founders*, 1953; Vol. II, *The Guardians*, 1954.

British Parliamentary Papers

The petition of the Earl of Elgin respecting his Collection of Marbles, Hansard, ccc1, 1815, p.828

Report from the Select Committee of the House of Commons on the Earl of Elgin's Collection of Sculptured Marbles, 1816.

Correspondence relative to the Earl of Elgin's Special Mission to China and Japan, 1857-1859, 1859, Session 2, [2571], XXXIII, 1.

Report of the Commissioners on Salmon Fisheries, 1902, Cd 1188.

Report of His Majesty's Commissioners appointed to inquire into the Military preparations and other matters connected with the war in South Africa, 1903, Cd 1789, xl, i.

Interim Report of the Departmental Commission on Free and United Churches, Scotland, by Sir John Cheyne, 1905, Cd 2510, ci, 727.

Canadian Papers

The Elgin-Grey Papers, 1846-1852, Vols. 1-4, edited by A.G.Doughty, Ottawa, 1937.

Debates of the Legislative Assembly of United Canada, Vol. III, Part III, 1849, edited by A.G. Doughty, Ottawa, 1977.

Private Papers

The Bruce Family Papers, Broomhall, Dunfermline, Scotland.
Earl of Elgin, Correspondence with Persons in England on Famine, Plague and Frontier War, 1897, Broomhall.
——Letters from Persons in England, from January 1898, Broomhall.
——Letters to Persons in England, 1898, Broomhall.
Elgin, Colonial Secretary, 1905–8, Broomhall.

Unpublished Dissertations

Bell, K., The Constantinople Embassy of Sir H. Bulwer, London University Ph.D. dissertation, 1961.
Hyam, R., The African policy of the Liberal Government, 1905–1909, Cambridge University Ph.D. dissertation, 1963.
Porter, B., Radical and Labour attitudes to Empire, 1896–1914, Cambridge University Ph.D. dissertation, 1967.
Robinson, R.E., The Trust in British Central Africa Policy, Cambridge University Ph.D. dissertation, 1950.
Struthers, J.S., Broomhall, Fife, with particular reference to Thomas Harrison, Dissertation in Scott Sutherland School of Architecture, Robert Gordon's Institute of Technology, Aberdeen, 1974.

Index

Figures in bold type indicate whole chapters or sections. Figures in italics indicate illustrations. Alphabetical order: word by word, to first comma or colon. '*bis*' means twice; '*p*' means passim; '*q*' means quoted.

Abbot, Charles (*later* Lord Colchester), Speaker of the House of Commons, 83, 86

Abercromby, General Sir Ralph, 45*p*, 62, 65

Aberdeen, 89, 90, 241

Aberdeen, Lord, 4th Earl of (1784–1860), Prime Minister, 87, 89, 90, 139

Aberdeen University, 260

Aboo Talibkhan, *q*41

Aboukir Bay, 45*bis*

Abyssinia, 106, 216, 262

Académie des Inscriptions et Belles-Lettres (*f.* 1663), 11

Acre, Battle of (1799), 31

Acropolis, *see under* **Marbles, Elgin**

Adair, Lord, British Ambassador, Constantinople, 74

Aden, Yémen, 146, 163, *167*

Aegean, 55, 92, 214

Afghanistan, 193, 216, 228

Africa, 32; **248-53**;
> Boer War (1899–1902), 239, 241-3*p*, 245, 248, 249*bis*, 263;
> Chinese coolie labour, 250, 251;
> mining in Rand, 249;
> Orange River Colony, 250;
> Peace in Vereeniging, Pretoria (1902), 249, 251;
> Self government in Transvaal, 243-251

Agra, 195*bis*

Ailesbury, Lord, 2, 3, 6, 7, 8-10*p*, 11, 13, 14, 15-17*p*

Ailesbury, Dowager Lady, 7, 9

Ailesbury, Earldom of (*c.* 1603), *see under* **Bruce** *and also under* **Elgin**

Alabama, USN, 205

Albany and Buffalo Railroad, 121

Albert, Prince, Consort of Queen Victoria (1819–61), 188, 189

Alexandria, Battle of (1801), 45*bis*, 46, 48-50*p*

Alliance, Triple, Britain, Holland, Prussia, 21

Ambassador to France, British (Duke of Dorset), 12

America, United States of:
> American-Japanese Treaty, 164;
> fleet off Scottish coast, 8;
> reciprocity, 124, 126, 133, 134, 137, 138*bis*, 140

Amiens, Peace of (1802), 58

Amoy, 144, 152

Am-ting Gate, China, 179, 181, 182

Analytical Inquiry into the Principles of Taste, (Richard Payne-Knight), 82

Anglo-Scots, in Canada, *see under* Canada

Annesley, Mary, 270

Annexation Manifesto (1849), Canada, 133, 144

Anstruther, Colonel, 33

anti-Catholicism, *see under* Canada

anti-French, *see under* Canada

Antiquaries, Society of, 31

Apollo Belvidere, 35

Apostles Club, Cambridge, *see* Cambridge

Archerfield, East Lothian, 29, 65, 66*bis*, 71

Archery, Royal Company of, Edinburgh, 207

Argyll, Duke of, 13, 120, 213

Aristotle, *Politics*, 99

Armagh, N. Ireland, 25

Armstrong gun, 174

Army, Ever Victorious, 179, 182, 184

Army, Indian, 225, 234, 235, 236

Army Medical Service, 234

Army, Territorial (*f.* 1907), 243

Arnold, Matthew (1822-88), 203

Arrow, river ship (*lorcha*), 140, 141, 149
artefacts, 55, 56, 149, 150
Arthur's Seat, Edinburgh, 214
artists, 32, 42, *see also under* **Marbles, Elgin**
Asia, 32, *see also* China, India, Japan
Asia Minor, 47, 262
Asquith, Rt Hon H H (1852-1928), Prime Minister, 245, 258-9, 260, 263
Assembly, Legislative, Canada, *see under* Canada
Athena, Goddess of Wisdom, 42, 50
Athena Nike, temple of, 42, 43
Athenian Club, 47, 94
Athenian Games, 47
Athens, *see also under* **Marbles, Elgin**, 31, 35, 42-3, 47*bis*, 48-9*p*, 54, 55, 56, 58, 72, 73, 92-3*p*
Athens, Archbishop of, 47
Athos, Mount, Macedonia, 48
Australia, 248
Austria, 20-1*p*, 22*p*, 28
Austrian Netherlands, 20-1*p*, 22
Avia, 148

Babington Smith, Sir Henry, GBE, CH, KCB, 218*bis*, 221-222, 225, 234, 235, 236, *242*
Bahadur, Rajah, 236
Baillie, Evan, of Dochfour, 268
Bairan, feast of, 39
Baker Street, 20, 64
Baldwin, Robert, 124*bis*, 126, 127*bis*, 128, 129
Balfour, Rt Hon Arthur James, Earl (1848-1930), Prime Minister, 245
Balgonie, Lord, 145
Balestra, architectural draftsman, 42
Balliol College, *see* Oxford University
Bank of Scotland, 239
Banks, Sir Joseph, 64
Bannockburn, Battle of (1314), 1, 205
Baptist Herald, 112
Baptists, 110, 112*bis*, 113
Barèges, Hautes-Pyrénées, 59-65*p*
Baring, Alexander, 131, 247
Barrackpore, Military Station, 190, 235, 247
bath houses, Japanese, 157
Belleville, 131
Belloti, leader of chamber orchestra, 53
Benares, 195

Bentinck, P & O steamer, 146
Berlin, 25*bis*, 26
Beverley, Lady, 58, 66
Bey, Prince Isaac, 35-6
Bible, the, 6, 8, 71, 105, 151, 197
Biel, 64, 209
bimetallism, *see under* India
Bischoffswerder, Colonel, 21
Blue Mountains, Jamaica, 110
Board of Punishment, Pekin, 179
Boer War (1899-1902), 239, 241-3*p*, 245, 248, 249*bis*, 263
Bombay, 55, 145, 216*bis*, 220-3*p*, 233*p*
Bonaparte, Napoléon (1769-1821);
    abdication (1814), 88*bis*;
    acquisition of treasures, 52, 65, 82, 89, 92, 93*bis*;
    Egypt, xii, 27-8, 31-3*p*, 35, 38, 43, 45*bis*, 52;
    Emperor of France (1804), 62;
    imprisonment of British, 58, 59, 60*bis*, 262;
    Musée Napoléon, 89;
    Waterloo, Battle of (1815), 89
Bonnie Prince Charlie (Charles Edward Stuart) (1720-88), 1
Bonsecours Market Hall, 129*bis*
bonzes (Buddhist priests), 152
Boston, Massachusetts, 118, 119, 205
Boswell, James (1740-95), 9
Botha, Rt Hon Louis, General (1863-1919), 250
Bouchard, Madame, 11, 12, 14
Bouchard, Professor, 11-13*p*, 20
Boulton, H., MP, 129
Boustrophedon inscription, Sigaeum, *see also under* **Marbles, Elgin**, 36
Bouyouk, Dere, 47
Bowlby, Thomas William, 118, 169, 176, *178*
Bowring, John, 140-1*p*, 143, 155
Boyer, J-Pierre, French General (1776-1850), President of Haiti (1818), 60*bis*
Brabazon, Captain, 181
Brackel, troopship, 56
Braves, Committee of the, 161
Brigade, Naval, 149, 151
British Army, 45
British Guiana, 248
British Linen Bank, Dunfermline, 79

British Museum, London (*est.* 1743), 34, 46, 73, 81, 83*bis*, 88, 89, 91, 122

British policy in Indian and China, 150

Brockville, 131

Brooke, Francis (*Lady Julia Mandeville*), 14

Broomhall: xi*bis*, xiii-xiv*p*

  Arab horses, 56, 59, 77;

  Charlestown harbour, xii, 3*bis*, 17, 19, 23, 95, 101, 106, 188*bis*, 197, 203, 209, 260, 261;

  coal and colliers, 1, 17, 23*bis*, 24, 26, 34, 44, 71, 78, 95, 98*bis*, 101-2*p*, 203;

  communications: roads, 2, 17; rail and wagonways, 23, 26, 78, 95, 100-2, 118, 120, 134, 137, 188, 203; canal, 23;

  Cricket Club, 205;

  education, 23, 211-3;

  Estate management, 3, 10, 13, 17, 19, 22, 24, 78, 100-2, 106, 134, 140, 203, 206, 207;

  farming, 2, 17, 20, 22, 23-4, 34, 101, 203; brickworks, 95, 20;

  finances, 3, 7, 13, 23*bis*, 25, 32-3, 44, 61-2, 65-6, 71, 75-6, 77*bis*, 78, 79, 95, 98*bis*, 100-2, 107, 118, 134, 136-7, 140, 188*bis*, 203, 214, 240-1;

  government influence, 260-1;

  industrial enterprises;

  lime, 1, 2-3, 9, 17, 23*bis*, 24, 26, 34, 71, 78, 79, 95, 101*bis*, 136-7;

  memorabilia, 267;

  new house, 26, 29, 31, 34, 63, 209;

  rebuilding house, 24, 26, 31, 49*bis*

Broughton, Charles, 76, 78, 79*bis*, 91

Bruce: *see also under* **Elgin** and Lineage of Bruce, **265-270**

  Adam, xiv, 265-6

  Alexander (*d.* 1662), 6th Earl of Kincardine, 265

  Alexander, 2nd Earl of Kincardine, 265

  Alexander (1884–1917), 260

  Alexander, Sir, of Broomhall (*d.* 1704), 4th Earl of Kincardine, 265, 266

  Andrew Douglas Alexander Thomas (*b.* 1924) 11th and present Earl of Elgin and 15th Earl of Kincardine

  Anne, *formerly* Blunt, 267

  Augusta (1822-76), *later* Mrs Dean Stanley, 97, 147, *q*166, 187, 203, 207, 268

  Bernard (1917-83), 270

  Brudenell (*b.* 1804 *dsp* 1828), 267

  Charles (*b.* 1682), 4th Earl of Elgin and 3rd Earl of Ailesbury, 265

  Charles (1732-71) 5th Earl of Elgin and 9th Earl of Kincardine, 72, 78, 265, 267, *see also under* **Whyte**, **Martha**

  Charles (*b.* 1883), 201, 269

  Charles Andrew (1768-1810), 72, 267

  Charles Dashwood Preston (*b.* 1802 *dsp* 1864), 107, 267

  Charles Thomas, 268

  Charlotte, *formerly* Dashwood, 267

  Charlotte (1771-1816), *later* Lady Durham, 74, 75, 86, 26

  Charlotte (1817-72), *later* Lady Lockyer, 92, 111, *q*116, 268

  Christian (*b.* 1879), *later* Lady Ogilvy, 219, 225, 270

  Constance, **CI** (1853-1909), 9th Countess of Elgin and 13th Countess of Kincardine, *see* **Carnegie**, **Lady Constance**

  Constance, MBE (*b.* 1880), 270

  David, Sir DL (1888-1964), 265, 270

  Edward (*dsp* 1667), 1st Earl of Kincardine, 265, 267

  Edward, of Blairhall (*b.* 1505), 265

  Edward (1815-33), 268

  Elizabeth, *later* Durand, 268

  Elizabeth (*b.* 1877), 215, 270

  Elizabeth (*d.* 1860), 7th Countess of Elgin and 11th Countess of Kincardine, *see* **Oswald**, **Elizabeth**

  Elizabeth Mary (**Elma**) (1821-43), 8th Countess of Elgin and 12th Countess of Kincardine, *see* **Cumming Bruce**, **Elizabeth Mary (Elma)**

  Elma (1842-1923), *later* Baroness Thurlow, 269

  Frances (1831-94) *later* Lady Baillie of Dochfour, 97, 268

  Frederick, Sir, GCB (*b.* 1814 *dsp* 1867), 77, 97, 98*bis*, 100*bis*, 101, 104, 145, 155*bis*, 165-6, 174, 182, 184, 203, 205*bis*, 268

  Frederick (1854-1920), 201, 269

  George, Sir, 266

  George of Carnock, 265

George, Charles Constantine, Lord (*b.* 1800 *dsp* 1840), 64, 70, 77, 96, 97-90*p*, 101, 105, 268

Gertrude (*b. c.* 1800), 9th Countess of Elgin and 13th Countess of Kincardine, *see* **Sherbrooke**, **Gertrude**

James (*b.* 1769 *dsp* 1798), 166, 267

James, Lord, *later* Baron (1811-63), 8th Earl of Elgin and 12th Earl of Kincardine, *see under* **Elgin** *and also* **Lambton**, **Lady Mary**

James (*b.* 1887), 72, 269

Janet (1761-67), 267

Janet (*b.* 1890), 269

Janet (*d.* 1771), Countess of Kincardine, *later* Dowager

John (1892–1971), 270

Katherine Cochrane, 270

Katherine (*b.* 1885), 269

Lewis (*b.* 1880), 269

Louisa (1802-70), *later* Lady Grey, 267

Louisa (1856-1902), 269

Lucy (1806-80), *later* Grant, 268

Margaret (*b.* 1881), 269

Marion (1885-1901), 270

Martha (1740-1810), 5th Countess of Elgin and 9th Countess of Kincardine, *see* **Whyte**, **Martha**

Martha (1760-67), 267

Mary (1804-83), *later* Lady Dundas, 268

Mary (*b.* and *d.* 1843), 269

Mary (1778-1815), 7th Countess of Elgin and 11th Countess of Kincardine *see* **Nisbet**, **Mary Hamilton**

Mary (*b. c.* 1819 *d.* 1891), 8th Countess of Elgin and 12th Countess of Kincardine, *see* **Lambton**, **Lady Mary**

Matilda (1802-57), *later* Lady Maxwell, 141, 268

Rachel (*b.* 1890), *later* Lady Verney, 270

Robert, 2nd Earl of Elgin and 2nd Earl of Ailesbury, 265

Robert, Colonel, *later* General (1813-62), 77, 119, 130, 268

Robert, DL, MP (1851-93), 134, 201, 206-7*p*, 209, 211, 269

Robert, CBE, DL, 225, 270

Robert Arthur, 268

Robert the Bruce, Robert I, King of

Scotland (1274-1329) (*r.* 1306-29), 79, 106

Robert Preston, 214*bis*

Thomas, Lord, 1st Earl of Elgin and Lord Bruce of Kinloss (1559-1633), 265

Thomas, Lord, KG, PC (1766-1841), 7th Earl of Elgin and 11th Earl of Kincardine, *see under* **Elgin** *and also* **Nisbet**, **Mary Hamilton** *and* **Oswald**, **Elizabeth**

Thomas, Lord, of Tottenham, 1-6*p*

Thomas (*d.* 1740), 7th Earl of Kincardine, 265, 266

Thomas (Tobo) (1825-90), 118, 120, 268

Veronica, 216, *219*

Victor (1897-1930), 270

Victor Alexander, Lord (1849-1917), 9th Earl of Elgin and 13th Earl of Kincardine, *see under* **Elgin** *and also* **Carnegie**, **Lady Constance** *and* **Sherbrooke**, **Gertrude**

William (1726-40), 8th Earl of Kincardine

William (1804-05), 63*bis*, 268

William Robert (*d.* 1763), 267

William Robert (*b.* 1764, *dsp* 1771), 6th Earl of Elgin and 10th of Kincardine, 267

Brunswick, Charles, Duke of (1753-1806), 22, 25

Brussels, 1, 21, 22*p*, 24, 218, 265

Buccleuch, Duchess of, 14

Buccleuch, Duke of, 18

Buckingham House (*later* Palace), 62

Budd, ex-Private, 193

Buddhism, 152-3, 169

Burke, Edmund (1729-97), 194

Burlington House, 86, 88*bis*

Burnet, Bishop, Gilbert (1643-1715), 265

Burton, Richard Francis, KC, MG (1821-90)

Butler, Josephine (1828-1906), 235

Byron, George Gordon, 6th Lord, poet, (1788-1824), 77, 82, 83, 87-8*p*, 90*bis*

Byzantium, four horses of, *see under* **Marbles**, **Elgin**

Cabinet, British, 41, 252

Cadi, the (chief justice of Athens), 48, 73

Caimacan Pasha, 39, 48, 51, 74

Cairo, 46, 48, 145, 146

Calcutta, 148, 149, 152, 189*bis*, 190, 191*bis*, 195, 196, 202, 204, 216*bis*, *217*, 218, 222, 225*bis*, 231, 233, 262

Calmuck, Lord Elgin's (Theodor: Ivanovitch), 42, 56, 262

Calyninos, 62

Campbell Bannerman, Rt Hon Sir Henry (1836-1908), Prime Minister, 211, 213, 239, 243, 245, 247, 250, 256, 258, 263

Cambridge University, 32, 33, 120, 218, 256

Camöens, Louis de, soldier/poet (1525-80), *Elegy of Exile*, 149

Canada, **118-64**, 248-9
    American Irish, 125, 127;
    Anglo-Scots, 120*bis*, 121, 123, 125, 130, 133, 141;
    Canada Act, (1840), 123;
    Clergy Reserves, 136;
    constitutional crisis (1849), xi*bis*, 26;
    Customs Bill, 128*bis*;
    Democrats, 137, 201*p*, 202, 214;
    finances and economy, 118, 121*bis*, 122, 124;
    fishing grounds, 137;
    French Canadians, 125*bis*, 126, 132, 141, 158;
    immigration, 122, 127;
    liberal-radicals, 124, 126, 133;
    Lower, 132-6*p*; Annexation Manifesto (1849), 133, 134;
    Orange Lodges, 119, 120, 121, 122, 128, 130;
    Parliament, 124;
    politics, 120-1, 122-9*p*;
    railroads, 121, 124, 132, 134*bis*, 230;
    Rebellion (1837), 125;
    Rebellion Losses Bill, 126, 127-9*p*, 141;
    Reciprocity Treaty, (1854), 124, 134, 137, 138*bis*;
    Tory Ultras, 122, 126;
    Upper, 132-3, 134, 136;
    wheat, 101-2, 133;

Candlish, Dr Robert, 244

Canning, Charles, *later* Lord (1812-62), Governor-General of India (1855-62), 146, 147, 148, 188, 189, 190*bis*, 191, 194, 195

Canning, Lady, 190, 225

Canova, Antoine, Italian Sculptor (*d.* 1882), 58, 59

Canton, 140-1*p*, 144, 148, 149, 150-2*p*, 153*p*, 155, 161, 163*bis*, 168, 178, 184

Capucin Convent, 50, 59, 96

Carodoc, HMS, 145

Carlyle, Rev. Joseph Dacre, Professor of Oriental Languages, 32, 34, 44, 47-8*p*

Carlyle, Thomas, writer (1795-1881), 203

Carnegie, Andrew (1835-1919), US Steel Industry, 25, 100-1, 209, 260

Carnegie, **Lady Constance**, CI (1853-1909), 9th Countess of Elgin and 13th Countess of Kincardine, second, xii, 207, 214;
        Vicereine in India, 215, 216, 218*p*, *219*, 222*p*, 225*bis*, 231, 235;
        return from India, 239, 261, 270

Carnegie United Kingdom Trust (1913), 260

Carnock, Bruce of, *see under* **Bruce**

Caroline, Princess of Wales, *later* Queen (1768-1821), 25-6

Carrington, Lord, 213

Carrow, Dr de, 53, 55

Cart, Fauvel's, in Greece, 13-14, 51, 52, 62, 93

Caryatids, *see under* **Marbles**, **Elgin**

Catherine II, Empress of Russia (Catherine the Great) (1729-96), 20, 21*bis*

Catholicism, in France, 13-14

Cavendish, Lord George, 88

Central Authority for Great Britain, 241

Cerigo Bay, 56*bis*, 58, 59, 73

Ceremonies, Hall of, *183*

Ceylon, *now* Sri-Lanka, 145, 146, 169*bis*, 248, 253

Chalmers, Rev Dr Thomas (1780-1847), 96, 101, 103, 105, 197, 244

Chamber of Commerce, Bombay, 55, 145

Chamber Orchestra, 35, 53

Chamberlain, Rt Hon Joseph (1836-1914), 245

Champ de Mars, Montreal, 128

Chandra River, 197

Charles I, King of England (1600-49), 265

Charles II, King of England (1630-85), 265

Charles V (Robertson), 13

Charlestown, *see under* **Broomhall**

Charlotte Augusta, Princess, *later* Queen (1796-1817), 5, 6, 25-6, 59, 62

Chase, Mr, 96

Checkland, Sydney George, Professor (1916-86), xiii, xiv*bis*

Childe Harold, Pilgrimage of (Lord Byron), 81, 87*bis*

China, 119, **141-4**;
    Allied Army in, 174-8*p*;
    banditry and piracy, 143;
    Board of Punishment, 179;
    British Policy, 146, 150;
    Canton, 148, 149, 150*bis*, 151-2, 178;
    chastising of, **164-185**;
    Chinese policy, 176;
    Commissioners, 155, 156, 161, 171, 175;
    coolies, 152, 174;
    decadence at Court, 143-4;
    Dowager Empress Yi, 176, 184;
    Emperor, 176, *177*, 178, 179, 181, 182*p*, 184, 186, 262;
    Imperial Court, 181, 182, 184;
    Imperial Palace, 182;
    'Malabar', 170, 171, 172, 173;
    Manchus, 143, 144, 176, 181, 184;
    opium, 141, 143, 144, 146, 147*p*, 152;
    opium wars, 141, 144;
    peasants, 186;
    Pekin, 149-151*p*, 153*bis*, 154*bis*, 165, 166, 168, 174-5*p*, 176*bis*, 179*bis*, 181-4*p*, 213, 262;
    Plenipotentiaries, 153, 154, 155;
    policemen, 'Peelers', 153;
    Summer Palace, 178, 181, 184, 185, 209, 213, 262;
    Taku Forts, 154, 165, 166, 174, 175*bis*, 182;
    Taipings, 144, 149, 152, 153, 154, 161-2, 174, 176, 182, 184, 203;
    trade, 144, 147, 161, 163;
    Treaty of Nanking (1842), 144, 165;
    Treaty of Pekin, 182, *183*;
    Treaty of Tientsin (1858), 155, 159, 160, 160, 170, 182

'Chinese' Gordon (Major-General Gordon), 179, 184, 203

Chitral, 227*p*, 235

'choakings', 29

Choiseul-Gouffier, Etienne François, Comte de, (1719-85), 43-4, 50, 59, 66

Christ Church, Canon of, 99

Church of England, 12, 111-113, 120-121

Church Missionary Society, 174

Church of Scotland, 9, 101, 133, 211 *see also* religion

Churchill, Rt Hon Lord Randolph (Henry Spencer, PC) (1849-95), 247

Churchill, Rt Hon Sir Winston Spencer, KG (1874-1965), 245-247, 249, 252, *253*, 256, 257-8, 260, 263

Chusan, 153

Chwan, Hung Hsiu, 144

City of Dreadful Night (Rudyard Kipling), 215

Civil and Public Law, 12, 20-1

Clarendon, George William Frederick Villiers, (1800-70), 4th Earl of, Foreign Secretary, 141, 155

Clarke, Captain, 56

Clarke, Rev Edward, 48, 56, 90*p*, 94

Clergy Reserves, *see under* Canada

Clifden, Nellie, 189

climate, Indian, 190*bis*

coalmining & colliers, *see under* **Broomhall**

Cobden, Richard, MP (1804-65), 141

Cochrane, Hon Katherine Elizabeth, DBE, 10th Countess of Elgin and 14th Countess of Kincardine, 270

Colchester, Lord, *see* Abbot, Charles

Collingwood, Admiral Lord, RN (1750-1810), 73

Colonial Conference (1907), *254*, 256*bis*

Colonial office, 245-253*p*, 256, 260

Committee of Braves, 161

Commonwealth Act (1931) *formerly* Empire, 251

Commissary Court, Edinburgh, xiii

Commissioners, Chinese, 175, 176*bis*

communications, Indian, *see under* India

Comyn, Red, 106

Confucius (*c.* 551-479 BC), 185-6

Conservative-Liberal party, 206

Conservative-Unionist Party, 247

Constantine, George Charles (Lord Bruce), *see under* **Bruce**

Constantinople, 27, 28*bis*, 30-1, 32, 33, 35*bis*, 36, 37-8*p*, *40*, 44, 47*p*, 48, 49, 54-5*p*, 60, 73, 89

Convention of El Arish (1800), 39, 40, 46, 52

Conway, General, 7, 10

coolies, *see under* China

Corn Laws, Repeal of (1846), 103, 122, 139

Coromandel, The, 175

cotton, Indian, *see under* India

Countesses of Elgin, *see under* **Elgin** *and also* Carnegie, Lady Constance; Cumming Bruce, Elizabeth Mary (Elma); Lambton Lady Mary; Nisbet, Mary; Oswald, Elizabeth; Sherbrooke, Gertrude, Whyte, Martha

Count, Viceregal, India, *see under* India

Coutts, F. & Sons, Bankers (*est* 1724), 3, 74, 78, 86

Crawford, Quinton, 63

Crealock, Colonel H. H., *168, 178*, 180

Crescent, Turkish Order of (*c.* 1801), 49-50, 77

Crewe, Lord, KG (1858-1919), Colonial Secretary, 260

Crimean War (1854-55), 139, 149

Crofter Acts, Extension of, 258

Cruickshank, George, artist (1792-1878), 91

Cuba, 108, 152, 247

Culross Abbey, 107, 265, 266

Cumming Bruce, Charles Lennox, of Dunphail, 106*bis*, 116, 122, 262

Cumming Bruce, Elizabeth Mary (Elma) (1821-43), 8th Countess of Elgin and 12th Countess of Kincardine, xii, 106*p*, **109-110**, 262, 269

Cumming Bruce, Frederick (1889-1917), xi

Curragh, Irish Military Base, 189

Curzon, George Nathaniel, Lord (1859-1925), Foreign Secretary, 235, 239, 247, 258, 263, 264

Customs Bill, 128*bis*

da Empoli, artist, 63

Daily Chronicle, q258

Daily Telegraph, q160

daimyos (feudal lords), 157, 159

Dalhousie, James Ramsay, Lord, PC, KT (1812-60), Governor-General, India, 136, 188, 190

Dardanelles, 35, 36, 37, 73

Darwin, Charles Robert, FRS (1809-82), *The Origin of Species*, 175

Dartmouth, Duke of, 5, 14

Dashwood, Charles (*b.* 1802 *dsp* 1864), ●●

Dashwood, Charlotte, 267

David II, King of Scotland (1324-71) (*r.* 1330-70), 265

Deakin, Arthur, Prime Minister of Australia, 256

de Altaidan, Caterina, 149

Dean's Yard, London, 7

debentures, Canadian, *see under* Canada

debt, Elgin, *see* **Elgin** *under* finances

Delhi, 146

de Luc, Jean-André, physician, 35

Democratic Party, Canadian, *see under* Canada

de Norman, 181

Dent & Co., opium dealers, 149, 152

Derby, Earl, *formerly* Lord Stanley, 152, 164

Deshima, 156

Devonshire, Duke of, 76, 77

Dharmsala Military Station, 197*bis*, 222, 262

Diana, The, 58*bis*

Dijon, 15

Dilettanti Society, 31, 33, 82, 83, 86*bis*

Disdar, Military-Governor of the Acropolis, 43, 48, 50, 51, 55, 62, *see also under* **Marbles, Elgin**

Disraeli, Benjamin, Earl of Beaconsfield, KG, PC (1804-81), Prime Minister, 141

Disruption of the Church of Scotland (1843), 211, 243, *see also* religion in Scotland

District Valuers, *see under* **Broomhall**

divorce, of 7th Earl of Elgin, 70, 71

Dockyard, Rosyth, *see* **Broomhall** *under* Charlestown harbour

Donaldson, Hay, W. S., 65-6, 79

Doré, Gustave, artist (1833-83), 166

Dorset, Duke of, Ambassador to France, 12, 14

Dowager Empress of China, Yi, 176, 184

Downing Street, 16

Doyle, Sir Francis Hastings, poet, *The Private of the Buffs*, 184

Dragoman of the Porte, 49

Dragoon Guards, Royal Regiment of the, 130, 131

Dragoon Guards, Third, 29, 174, 176

drainage, Egyptian wheel, 266

Draper, Professor John William (1811-82), 127

Dresden, 15, 16

drivers, Chinese cart, 176

Drummond Fencibles, *later* Elgin Fencibles, 24

Drummond, Lady Rachel, 24

Drummond, Lord, 62

Dublin, 123

Duff, 34, 63

Dufferin and Ara, Lord (1826-1902), Governor-General of Canada, Viceroy of India, 216, 227, 232

Dumouriez, Charles François, French General (1739-1824), 22

Dundas, Henry, Lord, 18, 20, 21-2*p*, 24, 28, 32-3, 44, 140

Dundas, Robert, of Bloxham, 65

Dunfermline, 17, 23*bis*, 95, 100-2*p*, 188, *240*, 260-4*b*,

Dunfermline Abbey, 3, 8, 63, 79, 264;
    Burgh Extension and Drainage Act (1911), 261

Dunnikier, 74, 75*p*, 76

Durand, Colonel Algernon, CB, CIE, 268

D'Urban, General Sir Benjamin, 125, 130

Durbars, 195-6

Durham, Admiral Sir Philip, GCB, 75, 267

Durham, Lord, 116, 117, 123, 127, 214, 249, 261

Durham, Bishop of, 32, 47

Ecole de Droit, Paris, 11

ecology in Scotland, 241

Eden, Sir Frederick Morton (1706-1810), 22

Edinburgh, 13, 70, 86-7, 97, 214

Edinburgh, Duke and Duchess of, 207

Edinburgh Review, 90, *q*158

Edo (now Tokyo), 155, 156, 157, 157*bis*, 158, 160

Education Act, Scotland (1872), 212

Edward VII, King of Great Britain, *formerly* Prince of Wales (1841-1910), 7, 25, 189, 190

Egypt, 27-8, 31, 39-41*p*, 45, 49, 50, 54, 60, 142, 168-9, 205, 214

Einosuki, Moriama, 156

El Arish, Convention of (1800), 39, 40, 46

Elba, 88

Elections, General (1790-1807), 18*p*, 20

Elegy of Exile (Camöens), 149

Elgin:

    Earldoms of, (*c.* 1633) and Kincardine (*c.* 1647) *see also* Ailesbury, Earldom of, and Lineage of Bruce;

    Thomas Bruce, 1st Earl of Elgin and 3rd Lord Kinloss and Lord Bruce of Kinloss (1559-1633), 1, 265

    Robert Bruce, 2nd Earl of Elgin and 1st Earl of Ailesbury (*d.* 1685), 265

    Thomas Bruce, 3rd Earl of Elgin and 2nd Earl of Ailesbury (1682-1741), 1. 265

    Charles Bruce, 4th Earl of Elgin and 3rd Earl of Ailesbury (1682-1747), 265

    Charles Bruce, 5th Earl of Elgin and 9th Earl of Kincardine (1732-71), 1-3*p*, 72, 78, 265, 267, *see also under* **Whyte, Martha**

    William Robert Bruce, 6th Earl of Elgin and 10th Earl of Kincardine (*b.* 1764 *dsp* 1771);

    Thomas Bruce, General, PC (7th Earl of Elgin and 11th Earl of Kincardine (1766-1841), *see also under* **Marbles, Elgin** *and under* **Broomhall**

    Ambassador Extraordinary and Plenipotentiary to Turkey (1798-1803), **28-57**; *40*;

    diplomatic career, **20-6**;

    divorce (1808), 70, 71;

    Envoy Extraordinary, Brussels (1791), 21-2;

    Envoy Extraordinary, Vienna (1791), 21;

    finances, 24, 26, 32, 33, 59*bis*, 65-6, 72*bis*, 93;

    first marriage (1799), *see* **Nisbet, Mary Hamilton**

    Guards, 16*bis*, 18, 19;

    health, 4, 6, 11, 14, 25*bis*, 38, 41, 55, 104-5;

    patronage, 9-10;

    Plenipotentiary to Prussia (1795), 25;

    prisoner of Napoléon Bonaparte (1803-06), 58-65*p*;

Elgin—*continued*

religion, 11, 12;

second marriage (1801), 74-6, *see also* **Oswald**, **Elizabeth**

studies in France and Germany, 11, 12-13, 14, 15, 16, 24, 31;

upbringing and education, Harrow, **4-10**

James Bruce, KT, GCB, Lord Lieutenant of Fife, 8th Earl of Elgin and 12th Earl of Kincardine (1811-63), xi*bis*, xii, xiii*bis*, 26, 268, 269

created Baron (1849), 132;

economy, Canada, 118, 121-2*p*;

estate and finances, *see also under* Broomhall, 100-3*p*, 105, 107*bis*, 110, 111, 116, 118, 120, 122, 132, 134, 136-7*p*, 139, 140;

first marriage (1841), *see* **Cumming Bruce, Elizabeth Mary (Elma)**

Governor General, Canada (1846-54), *see also under* Canada, **43-54**, **118-134**, *130*, *135*, 136-8, 165;

Governor General, Jamaica (1842-46), *see also under* Jamaica, **108-113**, 116, 136*bis*;

High Commissioner and Plenipotentiary, China and Japan (1856-59), *see also under* China and Japan, **143-163**, **164-187**;

inherited Earldoms (1841), 105, 106, 107;

Monklands and social life, 120, 128, 129, 130*bis*, 132*bis*;

missionaries, 110-113*p*;

Orange Lodges, 119, 120-1, 122, 128;

Parliament House, 128-9, 132;

political career, 102, 104, 105-7*p*;

rebellions (1837-8), 118;

religion, 105, 106, 107;

second marriage (1847) *see* **Lambton, Lady Mary Louisa**

sugar, plantations, planters and slavery, 108*p*, 109, 110*p*, 111*p*, 112-114*p*;

tour of Upper Canada, 132-3*p*;

upbringing and education, Eton and Oxford, 96, 97-8*p*, 99-100*p*;

Viceroy and Governor-General, India

(1862-63), *see also under* India, **168-200**

Victor Alexander Bruce, KG, PC, GCSI, GCIE, Lord Lieutenant of Fife, Baron, 9th Earl of Elgin and 13th Earl of Kincardine (1849-1917), xi, xii*bis*, 132, **215-230**, **231-237**, *246*, 269, 270

Chitral, 227-8,

Communications, 230*bis*;

economy, *see also* India; *under* currency *and under* bimetallism, 216*p*, 220, 230*bis*, 231-2;

education concern, Fife, 211-3;

education, Glenalmond, Eton and Oxford, 201-3, 205-6*p*

estate and finances, *see also under* Broomhall, 203, 206-7, 209*bis*, *210*, 211

Forth Bridge and railways, 209, 211;

first marriage (1876), *see* **Carnegie, Lady Constance**

Government House and Viceregal Court, 216, *217*, 218, *219*, 222, 231;

governmental problems, 216;

Lahore, *223*, *224*;

Lord Lieutenant of Fife (1886), 211;

Mashobra, 226;

Monsoons, plague and plague rules, 231-3*p*;

Mutiny, 216;

National Congress, 225*bis*;

political career, 206*bis*, 206-7, 209*bis*, 210, 211

religious differences, 215, 218, 220, 230, 233*bis*;

Viceregal Lodge, Simla, 218, 225, *226*, *229*, 235;

Viceroy of India (1894-99), *see also under* India, 214, **215-230**, **231-237**;

Edward James Bruce, KT, CMG, TD, CD (1881-1968), 10th Earl of Elgin and 14th Earl of Kincardine

Andrew Douglas Alexander Thomas Bruce, Lord Bruce of Kinloss and Baron Elgin of Elgin, DL, JP (*b*. 1924), 11th Earl of Elgin and 15th Earl of Kincardine, xi, xiii*bis*, xiv

Elgin Fencibles, *formerly* Drummond Fencibles, 24, 26, 78, 79

Elgin Marbles, *see under* **Marbles, Elgin**

Ellenborough, Lord, Governor-General of India, 139, 188

Emma, Lady Hamilton, 34, 35

Emperor, steam yacht, 155, 156, 157

Empire, Chinese, *see under* China

Empire, Japanese, *see under* Japan

Empire, Turkish (Ottoman), 26-8, **37-41**, 43, 44, 50-1, 54

English Bards and Scotch Reviewers (Lord Byron), 82

Enlightenment, Scottish, 9, 31

Epicrates, Aelius, Sarcophagus of, *see under* **Marbles, Elgin**

Erechtheion, 1, 42, 50, *see also under* **Marbles, Elgin**

Erskine, Thomas 1st Lord, of Cardross (1750-1823), 33

Erskine, General, 45

Erskine-Wemyss, Captain, 104

Essay Club, *see* Oxford University

estate, paternalism, *see under* Broomhall

Eton, 97-8p, 99bis, 100, 201, 215, 218, 225

Eugénie, Empress (1826-1920), 166

Europe, Chancelleries, 27

evangelicanism, *see* Missionaries

'Ever Victorious Army', 179, 182, 184, 203, 205

Extra Gazette, 25

Faculty of Law, Paris, 11

famine in India, **231-234**;

famine in Ireland, 122, 125,

Fane, Horse Lancers of, 174, 176

Far East, 200, 235

farmers, Canadian *see under* Canada

farming, Fife, *see under* **Broomhall**

Farquhar, Sir Walter, physician, 65

Fauvel, Louis François Sébastian, 43-4, 51, 52, 62, 92, 93

Fencibles, Drummond, *later* Elgin, 24, 26, 78, 79

Ferchenbeck, Madame, 25

Ferguson the Elder, of Raith, 78

Ferguson, Mary Hamilton Nisbet (1778-1855), formerly 7th Countess of Elgin and 11th Countess of Kincardine, *see* **Nisbet, Mary Hamilton**

Ferguson, Robert the Younger, of Raith, 59, 61p, 63, 64bis, 66, **70-1**

Fergusson (*Institutes*), 9

Fife, 2, 8, 30, 76, 209, 211-2p, 260, 262

Fife, Lord Lieutenant of the Kingdom, 260

Fife, Thane of, 260, 262

Finance Act (1909-10)

finances, Elgin, *see under* **Broomhall**

firman, 48bis, 50-1, 55, 56, 62, 73

Fitzherbert, Alleyne, Lord St Helen's, 20

Flanders, Battle of, 45

Flaxman, John, RA, sculptor (1755-1826), 66, 82

flour, Canadian, *see under* Canada

Foochow, 144, 152

Forbes, Sir William, and Co., bankers, 66

Forbidden City, *see* Pekin

Foreign Office, British, 31, 33, 45, 65, 79

formatori, 35, 42, 43, 44, 47, *see also* **Marbles, Elgin**

Forth River, 209, 241, 264

Fouché, Joseph, French Minister of Police (1754-1820), 75

Fowler, Sir John, engineer (1817-98), 209

France: *see also* Bonaparte, Napoléon
army, 39-40;
French fleet, 27;
in Africa, 248
in China, 160, 176;
prisoners-of-war, 39, 60;
Revolution (1789-99), 262

Franklin, Benjamin (1706-90), 13

Frederick William III, King of Prussia (1770-1840), 20, 21bis, 25

Free Presbyterian Church, Scotland ('Wee Frees'), *see* religion, in Scotland

Free Trade, 103, 156, 220, *see also under* Canada, China, India, Jamaica, *and* Japan

frieze, *see under* **Marbles, Elgin**

Frogmone House, Windsor, 108

fruit shops, St. James's Street, 16

Furious, HMS, 151, 155, 156, 159, 160, 161bis, 163

Fuseli, Henry, 82

Gall, Dr Franz Joseph (1758-1828), 61

Galle, Ceylon, 169

Gazette-Extra, 25

General Elections (1790-1807), 18p, 20

George III, King of Great Britain (1738-1820), (r. 1760-1820), 2, 5, 6, 10, 17, 21, 22, 25, 26, 27, 28, 59, 72

George IV, King of Great Britain (1762-1830), (r. 1820–30),

Germany, 10, 11, 14, 16

Gibbon, Edward (1737-94), *Decline and Fall of the Roman Empire*, 13

Gibraltar, 34, 248

gifts, exchange of, 32, 36p, 38p, 41, 46, 53, 54, 65, 160

Gladstone, Rt Hon William Ewart (1809-98), Prime Minister, 97, 99-100p, 101-3p, 124, 131, 141, 159, 164, 207, 211bis, 213, 220p, 263

Glasgow University, 164

Glenalmond School, Perthshire, 191, 201

Glenorchy, Lady, 7

Globe, The, Toronto, q133

Gloucester, Duke of, 76, 78

Godley, Sir Arthur, Permanent Under-Secretary for India, 220

gold: discovered in California (1848)

Gold Coast, 248

gold and silver standards, *see* bimetallism

Golden Eagle, The, Yacht, 214

Gordon, Major-General Charles George (Chinese Gordon) (1833-85), 179, 184, 203

Gosling, maidservant, 64, 72

Government House, Calcutta, *see under* India

Graff, Anton, painter, 16

grain, *see under* Canada *and* India

Grand Seigneur, 38bis

Grand Vizier, 36, 38, 39, 40, 46, 48, 56

Grant, Sir James Hope, General (1808-75), 175

Grant, John, 17, 23

Great Canal, 154

Great Disruption of Church of Scotland (1843), 243

Great Panathenaea, *see under* **Marbles**, **Elgin**

Greece, 45, 55bis, 94, *see also under* **Marbles**, **Elgin**

Greek Sculpture and Architecture, *see under* **Marbles**, **Elgin**

Greenwood and Cox, military bankers, London, 25, 78

Gregson, prizefighter, 83

Grenville, Lord George (1712-70), Prime

Minister, 22, 25, 28, 30, 31, 33, 39bis, 40, 41, 44, 96, 152

Grey, Dowager Lady, 117

Grey, Viscount (1862-1935) Colonial Secretary, 21bis, 22bis, 114, 115, 116, 117, 123, 136, 164, 245bis

Grey, Sir William, 267

Greyfriars Church, Dumfries, 106

Gros, Antoine, Baron, French Ambassador, 147, 149, 150, 153, 154, 155, 168, 169, *170*, 174, 175, 176, 181

Grosse Isle, Canada, 122

Grotius, Huig van Groot (1583-1645), 9

Guards, 10bis, 18, 19

Guizot, 166

Gymnasiarch, Chair of, *see under* **Marbles**, **Elgin**

Hague, The, 20bis

Hahnemann, Samuel Christian Frederick, homeopath (1754-1843), xiii, 105, 106

Haiti, 112, 113

Haj, Moslem Pilgrimage, 233

Haldane, Viscount (1856-1928), Secretary for War, 243, 247

Halifax, Nova Scotia, 7, 118bis

Hall of Ceremonies, Pekin, 182, 183

Hamilton, Upper Canada, 121

Hamilton, Lady, Emma Lyon (1761-1815), 34, 35

Hamilton Nisbet, Christopher, *see* Dundas

Hamilton Nisbet, Mary, *see* **Nisbet, Mary Hamilton**

Hamilton Nisbet, Mr and Mrs, xiii, 28, 29bis, 33, 44, 47bis, 48, 58, 59, 62, 64bis, 66, 70, 78, 83, 90, 92, 94

Hamilton Spectator, q125

Hamilton, William Richard, philosopher (1788-1856), 33, 35, 42, 46, 56, 62, 64, 73bis, 76, 82-3p, 86, 88-9p, 91bis

Hamilton, Sir William, 34-5p

Hang-Ki, 179

Hankow, 162, 165

Hanover, 16

Hanum, 41, 53

harbour, Charlestown, 3bis, *see also under* **Broomhall**

Harris Treaty, *see* Townsend Harris

Harrison, Thomas, architect (1744-1829), 24, 26, 28

Harrow, 6-7, 33

Hawkesbury, Lord, *later* Lord Liverpool, Foreign Secretary, 60*bis*

Haydon, Benjamin Robert, painter, 82

Hayes, Edward, 73, 74

Heath, Benjamin, 6

Heavenly Peace, Gate of, 179, 181, 182

Heliopolis, Massacre of (1800), 39, 40, 41

Hellenism, 51

Herbert, Sydney, 99

Herschell, Lord, Lord Chancellor, 213

Hermes, *see under* **Marbles**, **Elgin**

Herodotus, Greek historian (484-425 BC), 62, 76

Hervilly, Marie Mélanie d', 105

Heuskens, Henry, 155, 156, 159

Hibernia, S.S., 118

hieroglyphics, Egyptian, 46

High Commissioner and Plenipotentiary, British, in Far East, *see* Elgin *under* Earldoms

Highland Regiment, 71st, 129*bis*

Highland Society, 113, 131

Hikone, 157, 201

Hill, George, Professor, 9*p*, 14, 17, 20

Himalayas, 197

Hincks, Francis, 124*bis*, 125, 131, 132

Hinduism, 192, 193, 215, 218, 220*bis*, 233

Hogarth, William, painter (1697-1764), 16

Holdsworth, William, 124

Holland, 20-1*p*

Holyrood House, Palace of, 18, 266

Home Rule Bill for Ireland (1886), 206, 211, 213, 216

Hong Kong, 140, 147, 148*bis*, 149, 153, 161, 174, 184, 205

Hope, Sir Archibald, 17

Hope, Admiral Sir James, RN, 165-6

Horace, Harriet-Elizabeth, 267

horses, Arab, 56, 59, 76, 77

Host, the, 13-14

Hoste, Captain, 56

House of Commons, 105, 107, 141, 206

House of Lords, 15-16, 18*bis*, 19, 21, 24, 29, 30, 78, 96, 260

Howdah, Viceroy's, *225*

Hugo, Victor Marie, French writer (1802-85), 166

Hung Hsiu Chwan, 144

Hunt, Rev Philip, 33, 34, 47-9*p*, 50-2*p*, 54, 55*bis*, 56, 62*bis*, 86, 90, 92*bis*

Hutchison, General, *q*45, 46, 50*bis*

Hutchison, Ian, xiv

Idylls of the King—(Tennyson), *q*169, 203

Ii Naosuke, 156-7, 160

Imperial Court, Pekin, 152, 153, 179, 181, 182, *see also under* China

India: **188-199**;
    Army, 225, 234, 236;
    British Policy, 216, 228, 230;
    Burkean ideal, 194;
    bimetallism, 218, 221-222*p*;
    Calcutta, 148, 149, 159, 189*bis*, 190-1*p*, 195, 196;
    Chandra River, 197;
    currency, 216, 218*bis*, 221-222, 230;
    cow, 218;
    Durbar, 195-6;
    economic development, 230;
    8th Earl of Elgin appointed (1856), 188;
    equality in law, 193;
    famine and plague, **231-234**;
    finance, 218, 220, 230;
    Government House, 190-1*p*, 216, 217, 218, 219, 221, 222, *228*, *229*;
    good Viceregal qualities, 191;
    India Office, 220;
    infrastructure, railways, canals, roads, 192, 194, 230, 231;
    irrigation, 194;
    magnates and princes, 192*bis*, 220-221, 236;
    Moslems & Hindus, 192, 193, 215, 218, 220*bis*, 233*bis*;
    Mutiny (1857), 146, 148, 169, 188, 190, 191, 194, 216, 236;
    National Congress, 220, 225*bis*, 227;
    North West Frontier Provinces, 192-3, 195;
    Raj, 192, 215, 218, 222, 225, 227, 233, 236;
    Ralha Gorge, *198*;
    Rohtung Pass, 197, *198*;
    Sepoys, 193;
    Sikhs, 193;
    Sirdars, 194;

India—*continued*
    Star of India, *237*, 238;
    tariffs, 220-221, 230;
    trade markets, 192, 216*bis*, 220-2, *223*,
        230, 233; 201, 202, 213, 214, **215-238**
    Viceregal Lodge, 225, *226*, 229, 235
Indian Ocean, 145, 169
Indo-China, 227
Inflexible, HMS, 151
Institutes, (Fergusson), 9,
Institutes, (Justinian), 12
Ireland, 25, 122, 125, 136, 206, 211, 214
Ireland, Home Rule (1886), 206, 211, 213, 214
Irish, 25, 122, 125
irrigation, in India, 194
Isaac Bey, Prince, 35-36
Italy, 31
Ivanovitch, Theodor, artist, 42
Iwasi Higo Nor Kami, 156, 157

Jacobites, 1, 2,
Jamaica, 26, **108-113**, 116, 149, 230, *see also*
    sugar plantations
James VI and I, King of Great Britain (1566-
    1625), 265, 266
Janissaries, Acropolis garrison, *see under*
    Marbles, **Elgin**
Japan, **155-163**, *see also* Pekin;
    Board of Punishment, 179;
    Emperor, 156, 160, 186;
    markets, 160;
    Shogunate, 156, 157-8, 160, 161*bis*, 220,
        262;
    State of, 159, 185;
    Treaty (1858), 155*bis*, 156, 157, 159-60,
        185;
    Treaty Ports, 144, 153, 155, 160*bis*
Jephson, Dr, 99, 104, 105
Jerusalem, Patriarch of, 90
Jervault Abbey, 265
Jews, 174, 203
Jeypoor, Maharaja of, *see under* India
Johnson, Dr Samuel, writer (1709-84), 9
Jones, John Paul (1747-92), 8
Joseph II, Emperor of Austria (1741-90), 20
Jowett, Dr, 205
Justinian, *Institutes*, 12

Keble, Rev John, poet (1792-1866), 100

Keio University, xiii
Keith, Sir Robert, 21
Keith, Lord, Admiral RN, 40, 50
Kent, Duchess of, 108, 188
Kenya, 248
Kewkiang, 162
Khosung, 199
Khyber Pass, 227
Kidnapped (Robert Louis Stevenson), 3
Kimberley, Lord, Secretary of State, 220
Kincardine, Earldom of (*c.* 1647) *see under*
    Bruce *and also under* **Elgin**
King's College, Toronto, 133*bis*
Kingston, Upper Canada, 121
Kinnaird, Lord, 18
Kinnaird, 106
Kipling, Rudyard (1865-1936), *City of Dread-*
    ful Night, 215
Kirkcaldy, 8, 61, 104
Kirkfarther, 101
Kléber, Jean-Baptiste, French General (1753-
    1800), 39-40*p*, 45
Knibbs, Reverend, 112
Knight, Richard Payne, *see* Payne Knight,
    Richard
Knights of the Thistle, 33
Koehler, General, 31, 37, 38, 39, 46, 47-8
Kohsur Bridge, *199bis*
Kung, Prince, 176, 179, 182*p*, 184
Kwashena, 161
Kweleang, 161
Kyoto, 160

labour, *see under* China, India, Jamaica
Lady Elgin, passenger boat (1851), 134
Lady Julia Mandeville (Frances Brooke), 14
Lafontaine, Louis Hippolyte, 124*bis*, 126*bis*,
    127*bis*, 128, 129, 131*bis*, 132
Lahore, 195, 197, *223*, 224
Lamantine, Alphonse de, French statesman
    and writer (1790-1869), 166
Lambton, Lady Alice, 120, 132
Lambton, Lady Mary, CI (*b. c.* 1819 *d.*
    1898), 8th Countess of Elgin and 12th of
    Kincardine, second, *later* Dowager, 116-7,
    119-20, 122, 131, 132, 134*bis*, 143;
        family reunited, 164, 166, 188-191*p*;
        letter journal, 145, 146, 148*bis*, 150, 168,
        169, 184*bis*;

Vicereine, in India, 191, 195, 197*p*, 201-2, *210*, 214, *219*, 262*bis*, 269

Lauan, Bishop of, 146

Lancashire, cotton, 220

land acquisition in Scotland, *see under* **Broomhall**

land reform in the Highlands, 213

Lansdowne, Lord Henry, 5th Marquis of (*b.* 1845), Secretary of State for War, 213, 220*bis*

Laocoon, The, 35

Laurier, Sir Wilfred (1811-1919), Prime Minister of Canada, 256

Lavater, Johann, philosopher and poet (1741-1801), 16

Laraux, 11, 12

Law Society, Upper Canada, *see under* Canada

Lawrence, Sir Thomas, portrait painter (1769-1830), 82-3

Le Brun, 35

Lee, HMS, 155

Lee, Loyal Prince, Taiping General, 166, 174

Leiger, Mademoiselle, 53

Leith Races, 5

Léopold II, Emperor of Austria (1747-92) (*r.* 1790-92), 20, 21*bis*

Levant, 27, 44, 45

Levant Company, 30-1, 38, 73

Levantines, 94

Liberal Association, Fife, 263

Liberal Association, Scotland, East and North, West, 209

Liberal Association, Scottish, 209, 211, 213

Liberal Federation of Scotland, National, 211

Liberals and Liberal-Radicals, *see under* Canada

Light Brigade, Charge of the, 184

Limekilns, xii, 3, 74, 264, *see also under* **Broomhall**

limestone quarrying, 2-3*p*, 9, 17, 23*bis*

Lincoln, Bishop of, 32, 47

Lincoln, Lord (Duke of Newcastle), 99

Lind, Jenny (1820-87), Swedish prima donna, 166

Lindley, Mary, 270

linen, spinning and weaving, *see* Dunfermline

Linlithgow, Lady, 7

Lisbon, 34

Liscar, 23

Liverpool, 25, 118

Liverpool, Lord (*formerly* Lord Malmesbury), 60*bis*

Lloyd George, Rt Hon David (1863-1945), Prime Minister, 245, 261

Lockyer, Frederick, 268

Loch, C. S. (1849-1923), 176, *178*, 179*bis*, 181

London, City of, 131, 185, 186

Long, Charles, Paymaster General, 89*bis*, 91

Longfellow, Henry Wadsworth, poet (1807-82), 205

Lothian, Lady, 7

Louis XIV, King of France (1633-1715) (*r.* 1643-1715), 13, 36, 63

Lourdes, fortress prison, 60*bis*, 61*bis*

Louvre, the, 35, 82, 93

Low Countries, 20

Loyal Address, Montreal, 129*p*

Lucknow, Relief of (1857), 148, 149, 150

Ludwig, Crown Prince of Bavaria, 89

Lugard, Lord Frederick (1858-1945), Colonial Administrator, 252

Lusieri, Giovanni Batista, Italian sculptor, xi, 35, 42, 44, 48*bis*, 49, 50*bis*, 52*p*, 54, 56, 58, 62-4*p*, 72-3*p*, 79, 88, 89, 91, 92*bis*, 93, 94, 96, 145, 262

Luxembourg, Palais de, 63

Lyons, 58

Lysicrates, monument of, 44, *see also under* **Marbles**, **Elgin**

Lytton, Lord Edward, novelist and dramatist (1803-73), 216

Macao, 149

Macduff, ex-Provost, 260

Mack, Charles, Baron, Austria (1752-1828), 22

McKean, John, accountant, 95, 98

Mackenzie, William Lyon (1791-1868), 21

McLean, Dr Hector, 32

MacNab, Sir Alan, 124, 125, 129*p*, 130-1*p*, 132

Macrae, Dr, 197

Madras, Governorship of, 136

Madras, immigration, 111

Magersfontein, 240

Maharajahs, 220-221, 236, *see also under* India

Mahdis, 252

Maidan, the, 191

Malabar, P & O steamer, 169, *170, 171, 172, 173,* 174

Malakand, 247

Malmesbury, Lord James Harris (1746-1820), Foreign Secretary, 22, 152, 154, 155, 166

Malta, 45, 54, 56, 58, 73, 74, 145

Maltass, Stephen, 73*bis*

Malthusianism, 143

Mameluke Beys, 27, 46, 50

Manchus, 143, 144, 176, 181, 184

Manila, 184

Manners, Lord Robert, 29

Mansion House, London, 185, 186

Marbles, **Elgin**, xi, xii, xiii, 24, 28, 31
 Acropolis, 42, 43, 44, 48*bis*, 54, 55, 262;
 approach to Government, 76-7*p*, **81-3**, *84, 85,* 86;
 Athenian Club, and Hamilton Nisbets, 47*bis*, 48, 58, 59, 62, 64*bis*, 66, 70, 78, 83, 90, 92, 94;
 Athens, 42-3, 47*bis*, 48, 55, 66, 72, 73, 92-3*p*;
 Bonaparte, 35, 38, 52, 54, 65, 82;
 British Museum, 34-5, 46, 73, 81, 83*bis*, *84, 85,* 86, 88, 89, 91, 122;
 Cadi, 48, 73;
 Commons Select Committee (1815), 89, 90-1;
 Comte de Choiseul-Gouffier, 43-4, 59, 66
 Erechtheion, 42, 50
 Fauvel (and his cart), 43-4, 51, 52, 62, 92, 93;
 firmans, 48*bis*, 50-1, 55, 56, 62, 73;
 first collection, 56, 59, 62;
 formatori, 35, 42, 43, 44, 47;
 Gymnasiarch's seat, 47, 92;
 Hermes, 50;
 Horses of Helios, 73;
 Hunt and Carlyle's involvement, **47-52**, 54, 55*bis*, 56, 59;
 hostility in Britain, 81, 82, 83, **81-90**;
 Lusieri's involvement, xi, 35, 42, 44, 48*bis*, 49, 50*bis*, 52*p*, 54, 56, 58, 62-4*p*, 72-3*p*, 79, 88, 89, 91, 92*bis*, 93, 94, 96, 145, 262;
 Minerva, 42, 43, 47, 50;

 Parthenon, 31, 33, 35, 42-3*p*, 47, 48, 50-2*p*, 54, 55, 92, 145;
 Pericles, 55, *see also* Pericles;
 Prévoyante, 62;
 Poseidon, 43, 50, 73;
 Rosetta Stone, 46; **47-56**;
 second collection, 72, 73-4*p*;
 sinking of *Mentor* in Cerigo Bay, 56;
 storage in London, 62, 63, 66*bis*, *67, 68, 69, 71,* 76, 77, 82, 83, 86, 87-8;
 Temple of Athena Nike, 42, 43;
 Voivode (Governor of Athens), 43, 48, 50-6*p*, 62, 64, 72-3*p*, 90;

March, Edward, 263

Marjoribanks, Edward, 213

Marlborough, John Churchill, Duke of (1650-1722), 5

Marmoris, 45*bis*

Martineau, Harriet, 116, 122

Marucelli, artist, 63

Mashobra, 225, *226*

Massachusetts, 118

Materia Medica (William Cullen), 105

Maxwell, Sir John, of Pollok, 116

Medical Services, Indian Army, 234

Mediterranean Sea, 54, 145

memorabilia, at Broomhall, xiii

Memorandum on the Subject of the Earl of Elgin's Pursuits in Greece, 86

Menou, Jacques-François, French General (1750-1810), 46

Mentor, 54, 55*bis*, 58, 62, 91

Merchant Company, Hall of the Edinburgh, 243

Mérimée, Prosper, writer (1803-70), 166

Merthyr Tydvil, 96

Merton College, *see* Oxford University

Metcalfe, Sir Charles, Governor of Jamaica, Canada, 109, 120, 124

metopes, 50, 51*bis*, 66-6, *see also under* **Marbles**, **Elgin**

Mexican War, 125

Michigan Railroad, Upper Canada, 121

Midbalbridge, 23

Military Asylum, London, 96

Millar, Ian, xiv

Millowners' Association, *see under* Bombay

Milner, Sir Alfred, Viscount (1854-1925), High Commissioner in South Africa, 248

Minerva, curse of, 81, 87
Minerva, Goddess of Wisdom, 42, 84, *see also under* **Marbles, Elgin**
mining, coal, *see under* **Broomhall**
missionaries; Baptist, 110; Catholic, 152, 174; Protestant, 152, 153
Mohammedans, *see under* India
monasteries, Turkish, 32, 48
Monklands, Mount Royal, Canada, 119, *see also under* Canada
Monkland Polka, 132
monsoons, Indian, 230, 231
Montagu, E. S., Duke of (*b.* 1870), Secretary of State for India, 4
Montague, Lady Mary Wortley, *Turkish Embassy Letters*, 3
Montego Bay, 113
Montreal, Lower Canada, *see also under* Canada, 118, 120, 122*bis*, 123*bis*, 124, 126, 128-133*p*
Montreal Gazette, q133
Moore, General Sir John (1761-1809), 45, 77
Moral Miscellany, 6
Moray, Earl of, 241
More, Hannah, 26
Morea (Peloponnesos), 49
Moriama Einosuke, 156
Morier, John Philip, Consul-General, Zante, 33, 39, 40*bis*, 73
Morin, Lord, Speaker, 128-9
Morlaix, 63
Morosini, General, 42-43
Morris, Captain, 36
Moscow, 207
Moslems, 192, 193, 215, 218, 220*bis*, 233*bis*
Mount Athos, 48
Mount Pentelicus, 42
Moyse, Private, 184-5
Mulgrave, Lord, First Lord of the Admiralty, 73*bis*
Munshis, 252
Musée Napoléon, Château de la Malmaison, 89
Musgrave, Lord, First Lord of the Admiralty, 73*bis*
musicians, 35, 42
Mutiny, Indian (1857), 146, 148, 216, 236, *see also under* India
Myalman, 111, 113

Myalism, 113

Nagasaki, 156
Nanking, Most Favoured Nation Clause, 144, 149, 160, 161*bis*, 165, 166, *see also under* China
Naples, King and Queen of, 34, 35
Napoléon, *see* Bonaparte, Napoléon
Natal, 250-1
National Gallery, Scotland, xi
nationalism, Indian *see under* India
Nawabs, 220-221, 236
Navigator, HMS, 74
Nelson, Horatio, Viscount, Admiral RN, KCB (1758-1805), 27, 31, 34, 35, 39, 45, 50, 59, 63, 262
Netherlands, 160
Netherlands, Austrian, 20*bis*, 21
netting of salmon, 241
Newcastle, Duke of (Lord Lincoln), 99
Newfoundland, 205, 248, 252
Newman, John Henry, Cardinal (1800-90), 100
Niagara Falls, 120
Nigeria, 248, 252
Nile, River, Battle of (1798), 27; source, 163
Nilsson, Christine, Swedish prima donna (1843-1921), 203
Ningpo, 144, 152-3
Nisbet, Mary Hamilton (1778-1855), 7th Countess of Elgin and 11th Countess of Kincardine, first *later m.* Robert Ferguson; **28-30**, 31;
    Barèges and Pau, 58*bis*, 59-60*p*, 61, 62, 63; and Robert Ferguson, 61*bis*, 63-4, 65, 66-7;
    divorce, 70-1, 72, 81, 141, 207, 268;
    health, 30, 34, 41, 55*bis*, 56, 63;
    Maltese slaves, 54-5;
    promotion of vaccination, 52-3;
    tours in Greece, 55;
    Valida Sultan, 53;
Nisbet Hamiltons *see* Hamilton Nisbet
Nollekins, J, RA, sculptor (1737-1823), 83
Norman, de, 181
Norman, Rt Hon Sir Henry, Bart (*b.* 1858), 213
North British Railway, see under Railways
North West Frontier, *see under* India

Notre-Dame, Cathedral of, 14
Nova Scotia, 117, 118
Nyasaland, 248

Oak Farm Ironworks, 102
Obeah, 111
Ogdensburg–Boston Railway (1851), 134, *see
  also under* Canada
Ogilvy, Captain Frederick, RN, 261
Ogilvy, Gertrude Lilian, *see* **Sherwood,
  Gertrude**
'Old Pretender', 265
Oliphant, Laurence, writer (1829–88), 137*bis*,
  138, 145, 148*bis*, 155, 156*bis*, 159, 160, 163,
  165
opium trade, 141, 143, 144, 146, 147*p*, 152
'Opium Wars' (1842), 141, 144
Orange Lodges, Canadian, *see under* Canada
Orange River Colony, South Africa, 250
orders, Doric and Ionic, *see under* **Marbles,
  Elgin**
Organon (William Cullen), 105
Origin of Species, The (Sir Charles Darwin),
  175
Orléans, Duchess of, 14
Osborne, Captain, 161, 165
Osborne, Isle of Wight, 188
Osgoode Hall, 120
Oswald, Lord of Dunnikier, 8, 33, 62, 74–5*p*,
  80
Oswald, Elizabeth (1790–1860), 7th Count-
  ess of Elgin and 11th Countess of Kincar-
  dine, second, *later* Dowager:
    courtship and marriage, **74–6**, 77, 86;
    in France, 95, 97*p*, 98*bis*, 106–7*p*, 108,
      166, 261, 268
Ottawa, xi
Ottoman Empire (The Porte), 20, 27–8*p*, 49
Overland Mail, The, 234
Owenism, 103
Oxford Movement (19th century), 1900, 113
Oxford: University, 19, 33, 99, 100*bis*, 101*bis*,
  197, 203, 205, 206, 221

Paget, Lady, 206
Pallas Athena (Minerva), 41, *see also under*
  Marbles, Elgin

Palmerston, Lord Henry John Temple, 3rd
  Viscount (1784–1865), Prime Minister,
  139, 141*bis*, 142, 152, 164, 166, 168, 206
Palermo, 34, 35
panopticon principle, 24
Papineau, Louis Joseph (1786–1871), 120, 121,
  122, 125*bis*, 131
paramanas, 57, 58, 60, 64, 71, 262
Paris, 11–13*p*, 30, 60, 61*bis*, 63, 6, 106–8*p*, 137,
  184
Parishes, Jamaican, *see under* Jamaica
Park Lane Museum, *see under* **Marbles, Elgin**
Parkes, Sir Harry (1828–85), 140, 143, 151,
  176, *178*, 179*bis*, *180*, 181, 182
Parliament, British, 111, 123, 131–2*p*
Parliament House, Montreal, *see under*
  Canada
Parry, Alfred, 128
Parthenon (built 447–432 BC) *see also under*
  Marbles, Elgin; 31–3, 35, 42–3*p*, 47, 48,
  50–2*p*, 54, 55, 92, 145
Pasha, the Captain, 35–6, 37, *40*, 41, 48, 50,
  53, 54, 90
patronage system, 9–10
Pau, 59, 62*p*
Paul Jones, John, 8
Paul, Tzar of Russia (1754–1801), 45
Payne Knight, Richard (*Analytical Enquiry
  into the Principles of Taste*), 82, 86, 88, 89,
  90
pearl fishing, 252
Pearl River, 144
Pechili, Gulf of, 153, 163
Pectoral of Water Parsnips, 9
Peel, Sir Robert (1788–1850), 131, 153
Peel, Sir William, 2nd Bt. (*b.* 1867), Secretary
  of State, India, 139, 150
peers, Scottish, election of (1790), 18
Pehtang, 174
Peiho, River, 153–4, 163, 165, 166, 174*bis*, 175
Peloponnesos, 49
Pekin, 149, 150, 151–153*p*, 154*bis*, 165, 166,
  168, 174–5*p*, 176*bis*, 178–81*p*, 182*bis*, *183*,
  184*bis*, 197, *see also under* China
Penang, 15, 146
Peploe, 76
Pepys, Sir Lucas, 30
Perceval, Spencer (1762–1812), Prime Minis-
  ter, 86*bis*

Pericles, 31, 33, 42, 48, 55, 92, 94, *see also* under **Marbles**, **Elgin**

Perigeaux, M., 59

Perry, Commodore, RN, 157*bis*

Persia, 55, 235

Peshawar, 196, 233

Peterhoff, *196*

Phaeton, 33-6*p*, 38

Phideas, 50, 51, 64, 72

Pitferrane coal workings, 32

Pitliver, *see* Wellwood

Pitt, William (1759-1806), Prime Minister, 10, 18, 21, 28, 231-234*p*

plague, 27, 32, 55, 56

Plague Rules, Indian, *see under* India

Planta, Joseph, Principal Librarian of the British Museum, 83*bis*

plantations, sugar, *see under* Jamaica

Plato (429-347 BC)

Plover, HMS, British flagship, 165

Plutarch, Greek biographer and philosopher (*c.* 46-120), 62

Poland, Alliance with Prussia, 20

Politics (Aristotle), 99

Pollok, Sir John Maxwell of, 116

pollution, 241

Ponsonby, Sir Henry, 225

Poona, 233*bis*

Poor Law (Scotland) Act (1845), 96

Poors Rate, 137

Porcelain Pagoda, Nanking, 161

Porte, The (Ottoman Government), 27-8, **37-41**, 43, 44, 50-1, 54

Portland, Duchess of, 62, 66

Portman Square, 6, 63

Portsmouth, 98

Poseidon, 50

Preaux, French painter, 44

Presbyterianism, Scottish, *see* religion, in Scotland

Preston, Sir Robert, of Kirkfarther, 101, 105, 107, 134, 206

Pretoria, 249

Prévoyante, 62

Prince of Wales (1841-1910) *later* Edward VII, King, 7, 25, 189, 190

Princes, Indian, *see under* India

Prison of the Seven Towers, Turkey, 27, 44, 56

Private of the Buffs, The, poem (Sir Francis Hastings Doyle), 184

Probyn, Horse Lancers of, 174, 176

Propylaea, 42*bis*, *see also under* **Marbles**, **Elgin**

prostitution, in India, 235

Protestant Missionaries in India, 152, 153

Prussia, 21, 25

Prussia, Frederick William III, King of (1770-1840), 20, 21*bis*, 25

Puffendorf, Baron, German historian (1632-94), 9

Punch, *177, 212, 253, 257*

Punishments Board, Pekin, *see under* China

Punjab, 193, 195, 235, 252

Punjab Light Horse, 235

punka wallahs, 194

Pusey, Edward Bouverie (1800-82), 100

Pyramids, Battle of (1798), 27, 168

Pyrénées, 59

quarantine, in Turkey, 27

Quarterly (Tory Review), 90

Quebec, 122, 131, 133, 134*bis*

Queensferry, 209

Queensland, 213

Queen's Hall, *see* Broomhall *under* Charlestown

Radicals

railroads and railways, *see also under* Broomhall, Canada *and* India;
    Albany and Buffalo Railroad;
    Dunfermline and Charlestown;
    Edinburgh and Northern, 118, 120;
    Great Western, Canada, 132;
    Liverpool-Manchester (1830), 99
    North British;
    Ogdensburg-Boston (1851);

Raith, 61

Raj, the, *see under* India

Rajpootana, 195

Ralha Gorge, *198*

Ramsay, General, 83

Ramsay, James (*later* Lord Dalhousie), 136

Ramzay, Château de, 129

Raschid Aga, 49

Rawstorne, Helen, 270

Rawstorne, Jennet, 270

realpolitik of Europe, 21

Rebellion Losses Bill (1849), 126, 127-129*p*, 141

Rebellion in Lower Canada (1837), 125

rebels, Taiping, *see* China *under* Taipings

Reciprocity Treaty (1854), 124, 134, 137, 138*bis*

Red Sea, 146, 189

reels, Scottish, 37, 41

Reform Acts (1832 & 1867), 104, 211

Reform Bill (1831), 100, 104

religion, in Scotland, 239, 243-244

Remains of John Tweddell, The (Robert Tweddle), 89-90

Rémusat, Claire Elisabeth Gravier de Vergennes, Comtesse de, writer (1780-1821), 166

Renan, 166

Rennie, John, engineer (1761-1821), 77

Retribution, HMS, 155, 161

Revolution, American (1776), 27

Revolution, French (1848), 125

Richmond, Duke of, 66

ringworm, 6

Riot Act, 130

Ripon, Lord, Viceroy of India, 216

Robertson, Sir Charles Grant, CVO (1869-1948), 255

Robertson, James, 266

Robertson, Dr William (*Charles V*), 13

Rockefeller Foundation's Study Centre, Bellagio, xiii

Rolland, agent at Broomhall, 136

Roman Catholicism in France, 13-14

Rome, 35, 58*bis*, 206

Rosebank, 23

Rosebery, Lord, 211, 213-214*p*, 227

Rosetta, Stone of, 46, *see also under* **Marbles, Elgin**

Roseisle, 106

Rosyth, Fife *see* **Broomhall** *under* Charlestown Harbour

Rotung Pass, 197, 198

Royal Academy, 82

Royal Bank of Scotland, 100, 111, 239

Royal Commission, Church property in Scotland (1904), 243-44

Royal Commission, Report on Military Preparations in South Africa, 241-245*p*

Roxburgh, Duke of, 14

Royal Company of Archers, Edinburgh, 207

Royal Engineers, 48

Royal Geographical Society, 163

Rundel and Bridges, court jewellers, 50

rupee, Indian, *see* India *under* currency

Russell, Sir John (1792-1878), Prime Minister, 120, 169

Russia, 20, 28, 73, 160

Russian Plenipotentiary to China, 153, 155

Rutland, Duke of, 5, 29

Rymen, Master Henry, 2

St Andrews Society; Montreal, 131; Toronto, 131

St Andrews University, 2, 8, 9*bis*, 211

St Helen's, Lord (Alleyne Fitzherbert), 20

St Sophia Mosque, 47

St Lawrence River, 137

salmon rivers, pollution of Scottish, 241

saltworks, Culross, 1

samurai, 158

San-Ko-Lu, *178*

Sandford, Bishop, 30

Sang-Ko-lin-sin, Prince, 176, 179*bis*

Sarawak, 146

Savernake Forest, 1, 5

Saxony, 16

Scotland, National Monument, Calton Hill, 96-7

Scott, Dr, 53

Scottish Enlightenment, 9, 13

Scottish Reform Acts (1832 and 1884), 100, 104, 211

Scrope, Henry, xiii

Seaforth Highlanders, 46

Seasons (Thomson), 74

Sébastiani, comte Horace (1772-1851), French Marshal, 59

Second China War, 141

Selborne, Lord, *formerly* Rowndell Palmer (*b.* 1859), High Commissioner of South Africa, 250

Selkirk, Earl of, 18, 29, 78

Selim, Sultan, 35-6

Seraglio Library, 47

Seraglios, 32

Seven Towers, Prison of the, Turkey, 27, 44, 56

Seymour, Rt Hon Sir Michael Edward Hobart (*b.* 1840), Admiral of the Fleet, 141, 153, 154, 155, 165

Shan-Tsia-Wan, *178*

Shanghai, 144, 151, 153, 155, 160, 163*bis*, 165, 174*bis*

Shannon, HMS, 147*bis*, 148

Shaw-Stewart, Katherine, 268

Sherbrooke Gazette, *q*133

Sherwood, Gertrude later Ogilvy (*b. c.* 1880) 9th Countess of Elgin and 13th Countess of Kincardine, second, xii, 261, 270

Shimoda, 154

shinagawa, 157

Shingvaconse, Chief of the Chippeways, 120

Shogunate, 156-8*p*, 160, 161*bis*, 220, 262

Siddons, Mrs Sarah, actress (1755-1831), 83

Sigaeum, 36, *see also under* **Marbles**, **Elgin**

Sikhs, 181, 184, 193

Simla, 195, 196, 219, 225, *226*, 227, 231, 235

Singapore, 146, 147*bis*

Sinho, 176

Sirdars, 194

Sitana, 196

skin infections, 6

slaves, Jamaican, 108-9; Maltese, 54-5

Smallholders (Scotland) Acts (1892, 1907 *and* 1908), 258

smallpox in Turkey, 27, 32, 53*p*, *see also* vaccination

Smirke, James, architect, 77

Smith, Adam (1723-90), 123

Smith, Admiral Sir Sidney, RN (1764-1840), 31, 34, 39-41*p*, 46

Smith, Spencer, 31, 37, 38, 39, 44*bis*

Smyrna, 33

Snedden, Maud, 270

South African War, Royal Commission, Report, 241-5*p*, 263

Southampton, 105-6, 107

Southesk, 9th Earl of, 207

Spanish Town, Jamaica, Cathedral, 110

Specimens of Antient Sculpture, see Dilettanti Society

Speke, Captain John Haining, explorer (1827-64), 163

Spencer, Lord, 5th Earl (1834-1910), First Lord of the Admiralty, 213

Spencerfield, 107

Sphinx, 168-9

sponge divers, Calyninos and Cynie, 62

Stanley, Lord (*later* Earl of Derby) (1826-93), Colonial Secretary, 116-7

Stanley, Very Rev. Dean, Arthur Penryn (1815-81), Dean of Westminster, 203, 207, 268

Stanley, Mrs Dean, *formerly* Augusta Bruce, *see under* **Bruce**

Star of India, Most Exalted Order of the, *237*, 238

Stark, William, architect, 77-9

Statuary, *see under* **Marbles**, **Elgin**

Stevenson, Robert Louis (1850-94), *Kidnapped*, *q*3

Stirling, Admiral, RN, 157

Strachan, Bishop (C of S), 121, 133

Stratton, Alexander, 44

Stuart, Charles Edward (Bonnie Prince Charlie, The Young Pretender) (1720-88), 1

Stuart, James, 65

Stuart Mill, John, 203

Sugar plantations, Jamaican, 108*p*, 109, 110*p*, 111*p*, 112-114*p*

Sultan of Turkey ('The Monster'), 21, 28, 36, 37, 38*p*, 47, 49, 53, 184

Sultan Selim, 35-6

Summer Palace of Emperor, *see under* China

Swatow, 152

Swaziland, 251

Sydenham, George, Baron (*b.* 1848), Governor-General of Canada, 124

syphilis, 70, 82

Syria, 36, 38, 39, 54

tackle, lifting, *see under* **Marbles**, **Elgin**

Tacksman, Commissioner of Supply, 266

Taipings, *see also* China, 144, 149, 152, 153, 155, 161, 174, 176, 184

Taku Forts, 154, 165, 166, 174, 175*bis*, 182

Talleyrand-Périgold, Charles Maurice de, prins de Bénévent, French Diplomat (1754-1838), 60, 64

Tang-chao, 175, 176*bis*

tariffs, *see under* China, India, Japan

temperance reform, 211

Tennyson, Lord (1809-92), *Idylls of the King*, q169, 203

Territorial Army (*f.* 1907), 243

Tetu's Hôtel, 131

Theseum, 44

Thiers, 166

Thistle Curling Club, Montreal, 131

Thistle, Knights of the Order of, 120, 157

Thomson, *Seasons*, 74

Thornhill, Sarah, 268

Thurlow, Lord, Thomas, 5th Baron, xiv, 225

Tientsin, Treaty of (1858), 154, 155, 159, 160, 175, 182

Tigre, 39

Tilak, B C, 233

Times, The, q169, 176, 181, 182, 243

Tokyo, *formerly* Edo, Bay, 157 *see also* Japan

Toquevillé, Alexis, comte de (1805-59), 106

Tory Ultras, Canadian, *see under* Canada

Toronto, 121-1, 131*p*, 133*p*, 134, 138

Toronto Globe, q133

Toronto University, 133*bis*

Torquay, 97-8

Tottenham, Lord Bruce of, 1-6*p*

Tottenham Park, 1, 5-6*p*

Townley, Charles, 91

Townsend Harris, American Consul, 155, 156, 159-60

Townships, Eastern *see under* Canada

Tozenji Temple, 157

Trade, British, 21, 30, 157

Trafalgar, Battle of (1805), 50

Tramway Company, Fife, 260

Transvaal, Annexed to Britain (1877), *see under* Africa

Treaties, Unequal, 160

Treaty Ports, 144, 153, 155, 160*bis*

Trinity College, *see* Toronto University

Triple Alliance of Britain, Holland and Prussia, 21

Turkey, 20, 21, 22, 27*bis*, 35-6

Turkey, Sultan of, 28*bis*, 37-8

Turkey, Treaty of (1774), 1, 31*bis*

Turkey, War with Britain and Russia, 73, 94

Turkish Embassy Letters (Lady Wortley Montague), 30

Turks Island, 109

Turner, J M W, RA (1775-1851), 32, 83, *84, 85*

Tweddell, John, writer (*d.* 1799), 44, 89-90

Tweddell, Rev Robert, 44, 89-90*p*

Tweedsmouth, Lord Edward Marjoribanks, 2nd Baron (1875-1940), 258

Tzar, Court of the, 207

Underdeveloped Land Duty, Scotland, 261

United Free Church of Scotland, *see* religion, in Scotland

United Presbyterian Church of Scotland, *see* religion, in Scotland

United States of America, *see under* America

Universities, Scottish and Carnegie Trust, 260

Upper Ossery, Earl of, 33

Usher, Victoria Mary, 11th Countess of Elgin and 15th Countess of Kincardine, xv

vaccination, 53*p*

Calida Sultanas, 48, 53

Van Dyke, Sir Anthony (1599-1641)

Vansittart, Nicolas, Chancellor of the Exchequer, 89

venereal disease in Indian army, 234-5

Venice, 43-4

Venus, 87

Venus de Medici, 35

Vereeniging, Peace of (1902), 249, 251

Verney, Sir Harry, Bt., 270

Versailles, 13

Viceregal train, in India, *228*

Victoria, Queen (1819-1901) (*r.* 1837-1901), 132, 184, 195, 201, 203, 207*bis*, 209, 211, 213, 214, 225, 237

Vienna, 21*bis*, 22*bis*

Visconti, Ennio Quinino (1751-1818), Director of the Louvre, 88, 89

Viceroyalty of India *see under* India

Voivode, the, Governor of Athens, 43, 50-1*p*, 56, 62, 64, 72-3*p*, 90

wagonways, *see* **Broomhall** *under* Communications

Wakefield, Edward Gibbon, 123

Wales, Prince and Princess of, 7, 25, 189

Wallsend coal mine (1839), 102, 111

Walrond, Theodore, 202

Wandsworth School, 6*bis*

War, South African (1899–1902), *see* Boer War

Warre, Dr, 205

Washington, DC, 137, 205

Waterloo, Battle of (1815), 89

Watersheds Board, 241

waziristanis, 228

weaving, linen, *see* Dunfermline

Wedgwood, Josiah, FRS, potter (1730–95), 35

'Wee Frees' (Free Presbyterian Church of Scotland), *see* religion, in Scotland

Wellesley, Lord, Richard Culley, KG (1760–1842), 73

Wellington, General Arthur Wellesley, 1st Duke of (The Iron Duke) (1769–1852), Prime Minister, 45, 99, 104

Wellwood, of Pitliver, 18, 23, 77–8*p*

West, Sir Benjamin (1738–1820), President of the Royal Academy, 32, 59, *68*, *69*, 82

West Indies, 60, 248

Westminster Abbey, 190, 203, 207; Hospital, 203; School, 8*bis*

'Whigs, dishing the' (1784), 10, 209

whist, 41, 62

Whyte, Martha (b. *c*. 1740, d. 1810), 5th Countess of Elgin and 9th Countess of Kincardine, *later* Dowager, xii
   upbringing and education of Thomas, **3–10**, 11*bis*, 12–17*p*, 25;

Governess to Princess Charlotte Augusta (1796), 26, 27, 59

Broomhall debt, 62; *see also under* **Broomhall**;

Thomas's divorce, 72;

Marbles, 81; 261, 267

Whitworth, Lord, British Ambassador, Paris, 58

Wood, Sir Charles, Secretary of State, India, 193

World Wars; I (1914–18), 243, 262; II (1939–45), xiv

Worth, Charles Frédérick, couturier (1825–95), 166

Yangtze Kiang, River, 153, 155, 161, 163, 165, 184

Yashikis, 157

Yedo, *now* Tokyo, 155, 156, 157*bis*, 158, 160

Yeh, Lieutenant-Governor of Canton (The Terror of the Barbarians), 149, 150*bis*, 151, 152, 155, 156, 157, 163, 184

yeoman element, *see under* Canada

Yi, Empress of China (*later* Dowager), 176, 184

Yuen–ming–yuen, Summer Palace, *see under* China

Zulu War (1879), 250